William Cowper.

WILLIAM COWPER'S
POETICAL WORKS
WITH
A Sketch of his Life,
AND
Illustrations.

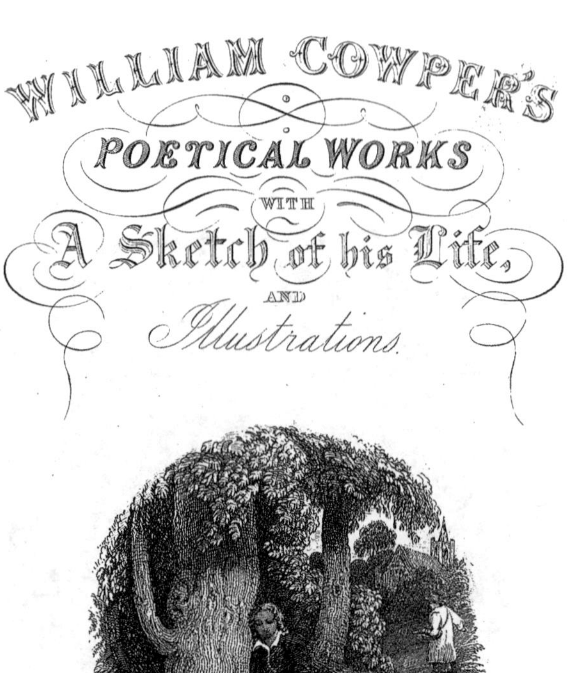

My soul should yield thee willing thanks and praise.

NEW YORK
J. C. DERBY.

THE

POETICAL WORKS

OF

WILLIAM COWPER ESQ.

AND

MEMOIR OF THE AUTHOR.

ILLUSTRATED WITH A PORTRAIT

AND

WENTY OTHER SPLENDID ENGRAVINGS ON STEEL.

BY G. STANDFAST.

NEW YORK:
J. C. DERBY, 119 NASSAU STREET
BOSTON: PHILLIPS, SAMPSON & CO.
CINCINNATI: H. W. DERBY.

1856.

MEMOIR

OF

WIILLIAM COWPER.

The subject of this brief Memoir was the descendant of an ancient and honorable family. His father was the second son of Spencer Cowper (a younger brother of the lord chancellor Cowper) who was appointed chief justice of Chester in 1717, and afterwards a judge in the court of Common Pleas. The poet's father was rector of Great Berkhampstead, in Hertfordshire, at which place William was born, Nov. 26, 1731; and from his infancy he appears to have been of a very delicate habit both of mind and body. In 1737, the year of his mother's death, he was sent to a school at Market-street, in Hertfordshire, under the conduct of Dr. Pitman, but was removed from it a few years afterwards, on account of a complaint in his eyes, for which he was consigned to the care of a female oculist for the space of two years.

Shortly after this he was sent to Westminster school, where he is reported to have suffered much from the wanton tyranny of his schoolfellows, who, with the usual unthinking cruelty o' youth, triumphed over the gentleness and timidity of his spirit, so that in his advanced years he retained none but painful recollections of what men in general remember with more pleasure than any other period of their lives, and these recollections, no doubt, animated his pen with more than his usual severity in exposing the abuses of public schools.

When he was eighteen years of age he left Westminster-school, and was articled for three years to Mr. Chapman, an attorney; in whose house he succeeded in gaining the esteem of all around him, by the gentleness of his manners, and the amiability of his temper, but suffering deeply from that incipient melancholy which had taken possession of his mind, and with an utter dislike to the study of the legal profession.

When he had fulfilled the terms of his engagement with Mr. Chapman, he entered the Temple for the purpose of finishing his studies as a barrister; but, like many other men of genius, he neglected the law, and gratified the bent of his mind in the cultivation of poetry. Indeed he appears to have aimed at the character of a literary man, in the general sense of the term; for he is known to have assisted various cotem porary publications with prose essays as well as with compositions in verse, and what considering his meekness, diffidence, and purity of conduct, is certainly remarkable—he cultivated the acquaintance of Churchill, Thornton, Lloyd, and Colman, who had been his schoolfellows at Westminster. It is, undoubtedly, to Churchill and Lloyd that he alludes in a letter to Lady Hesketh, dated September 4, 1765. "Two of my friends have been cut off during my illness, in the midst of such a life as it is frightful to look upon; and here am I in better health and spirits than I can almost remember to have enjoyed before, after having spent months in the apprehension of instant death. How mysterious are the ways of Providence! Why did I receive grace and mercy? Why was I preserved, afflicted for my good, received, as I trust into favour, and blessed with the greatest happiness I can ever know, or hope for, in this life, while these were overtaken by the great arrest, unawakened, unrepenting, and every way unprepared for it?"

He furnished Colman with some papers for the "Connoisseur," and contributed to various other periodicals; but so little was known of him in the literary world, that, on the appearance of his first volume of poems, when he had reached his fiftieth year, he was looked upon as a new writer. But his general occupations will best appear in an extract from one of his letters to Mr. Park, in 1792. "From the age of twenty to thirty-three (when he left the Temple), I was occupied, or ought to have been, in the study of the law; from thirty-three to sixty, I have spent my time in the country, where my reading has only been an apology for idleness, and where, when I had not either a magazine or a review, I was sometimes a carpenter, at others a bird-cage maker, or a gardener, or a drawer of landscapes. At fifty years of age I commenced author;—it is a whim that has served me longest and best, and will probably be my last." His first poetical effort was a translation of an elegy of Tibullus, made at the age of fourteen; after which he occasionally displayed his poetical talents in the composition of trifling pieces; but as little of his juvenile poetry has been preserved, all the steps of his progress to that perfection which produced "The Task," cannot now be traced.

In 1773 he sunk into such severe paroxysms of religious despondency, that he required an attendant of the most gentle, vigilant, and inflexible spirit. Such an attendant he found in that faithful guardian (Mrs. Unwin), whom he had professed to love as a mother, and who watched over him during his malady, which extended through several years, with that perfect mixture of tenderness and fortitude, which constitutes the inestimable influence of maternal protection.

His recovery was slow; and he knew enough of his malady,

to abstain from literary employment, while his mind was in any degree unsettled. The first amusement which engaged his humane affections, was the taming of three hares; a circumstance that would scarcely have deserved notice, unless among the memoranda of natural history, if he had not given to it an extraordinary interest, by the animated account he wrote of this singular family. While he thus amused himself, his friends were indefatigable in their endeavours to promote his recovery; and, in the summer of 1778, they had the gratification of seeing their attentions rewarded by his restoration to health.

Our author continued to amuse himself with reading such new books as his friends could procure, with writing short pieces of poetry, tending his tame hares and birds, and drawing landscapes, a talent which he discovered in himself very late in life, and in which he displayed considerable skill. In all this, perhaps, there was not much labour, but it was not idleness. A short passage in one of his letters to the Rev. William Unwin, dated May, 1780, will serve to mark the distinction. "Excellence is providentially placed beyond the reach of indolence, that success may be the reward of industry, and that idleness may be punished with obscurity, and disgrace. So long as I am pleased with an employment, I am capable of unwearied application, because my feelings are all of the intense kind. I never received a *little* pleasure from anything in my life: if I am delighted, it is in the extreme. The unhappy consequence of this temperament is, that my attachment to any occupation seldom outlives the novelty of it."

Urged by his amiable friend and companion, Mrs. Unwin, he employed the winter of 1780-1, in preparing his first volume of poems for the press, consisting of "The Table Talk," "Hope," "The Progress of Error," "Charity," &c. But such was his diffidence in their success, that he appears to have been in doubt whether any bookseller would be willing to print them on his own account. He was fortunate enough, however, to find in Mr. Johnson (his friend Mr. Newton's publisher), one whose spirit and liberality immediately set his mind at rest. The volume was accordingly published in 1782, but its success was by no means equal to its merit; for, as Mr. Hayley has observed, "it exhibits such a diversity of poetical powers as have been given very rarely indeed to any individual of the modern or of the ancient world."

Among other small pieces which he composed at the suggestion of Lady Austen was the celebrated ballad of "John Gilpin," the origin of which Mr. Hayley thus relates:—"It happened one afternoon that Lady Austen observed him sinking into increasing dejection; it was her custom, on these occasions to try all the resources of her sprightly powers for his immediate relief. She told him the story of John Gilpin (which had been treasured in her memory from her childhood) to dissipate the gloom of the passing hour. Its effect on the fancy of Cowper had the air of enchantment: he informed her the next morning, that convulsions of laughter, brought on by the recollection of her story, had kept him awake during the greater part of the night, and that he had turned it into a ballad."

The public was soon laid under a far higher obligation to Lady Austen for having suggested our author's principal poem, "The Task,"—"a poem," says Mr. Hayley, "of such infinite variety, that it seems to include every subject, and every style, without any dissonance or disorder; and to have flowed without effort from inspired philanthrôpy, eager to impress upon the hearts of all readers whatever may lead them most happily to the full enjoyment of human life, and to the final attainment of Heaven." This admirable poem appears to have been written in 1783 and 1784, but underwent many careful revisions.

In November, 1784, "The Task," was sent to press; and he began the "Tirocinium," the purport of which, in his own words, was to censure the want of discipline, and the scandalous inattention to morals, that obtain in public schools, especially in the largest, and to recommend private tuition as a mode of education preferable on all accounts; to call upon fathers to become tutors of their own sons, where that is practicable, to take home a domestic tutor, where it is not, and if neither can be done, to place them under the care of some rural clergyman, whose attention is limited to a few. In 1785 this work was published with other pieces, which composed his second volume, and which soon engaged the attention and admiration of the public, in a way that left him no regret for the cool reception and slow progress of his first. Its success also obtained for him another female friend and associate, Lady Hesketh, his cousin, who had long been separated from him. Their intercourse was first revived by a correspondence, of which many interesting specimens are given in Hayley's Life of Cowper, and of which it is there said, with great truth, that "Cowper's letters are rivals to his poems in the rare excellence of representing life and nature with graceful and endearing fidelity." In explaining the nature of his situation to Lady Hesketh, who came to reside at Olney in the month of June, 1786, he informs her, that he had lived twenty years with Mrs. Unwin, to whose affectionate care it was owing that he lived at all; but that for thirteen of those years he had been in a state of mind which made all her care and attention necessary. He tells her, at the same time, that dejection of spirits, which may have prevented many a man from becoming an author, had made him one. He found employment necessary, and therefore he took care to be constantly employed. Manual occupations, as he well knew by experience, do not engage the mind sufficiently; but composition, especially of verse, absorbs it wholly. It was his practice, therefore, to write generally three hours in the morning, and in the evening he transcribed. He read also, but less than he wrote, for bodily exercise was necessary, and he never passed a day without it. All this shows that Cowper understood his own case most exactly, and that he was not one of those melancholics who give themselves up to the indulgence of hopeless despair.

At length, after innumerable interruptions, the translation of Homer was sent to press, and published in two volumes quarto, in 1791; yet, notwithstanding it was nearly out of print in six months, it fell short of the expectations formed by the public and of the perfection which he hoped he had attained; so that instead of printing a second edition, he began, at no long distance of time, what may be termed a new translation. To himself, however, his first attempt had been of great advantage, nor were any of his years spent in more general tranquillity, than the five which he had dedicated to Homer. One of the greatest benefits he derived from his attention to this translation, was the renewed conviction that labor of this kind was, with occasional remissions, absolutely necessary to his health and happiness. This conviction led him very soon to accede to a proposal made by his bookseller, to undertake a magnificent edition of Milton's works, the beauties of which had engaged his wonder at a very early period of life. These he was now to illustrate by notes, original and selected, and to translate the Latin and Italian poems, while Mr. Fuseli was to paint a series of pictures to be engraved by the first artists. To this scheme, when yet in its infancy, the public is indebted for the friendship which Mr. Hayley contracted with Cowper, and which eventually produced that excellent specimen of biography from which our present notice is mainly derived.

It was about this period that Messrs. Boydell published a splendid edition of Milton, for which Mr. Hayley had written "a Life;" and being represented in a newspaper as the rival of Cowper, he immediately wrote to him on the subject. Cowper answered him in such a manner as drew on a closer correspondence, which soon terminated in mutual esteem and cordial friendship. Personal interviews followed, and Mr. Hayley has gratified his readers with a very interesting account of his first visit to Weston, and of the return by Cowper and Mrs. Unwin at his seat at Eastham in Sussex, in a style peculiarly affectionate. On Cowper's journey to Eastham he passed through London, but without stopping, the only time he had seen it for thirty years.

In the year 1794 his mind began rapidly to sink into a most melancholy state of despondency. The health of his watchful friend, Mrs. Unwin, had also undergone an alarming change, and the united weight of time and sickness had brought her to the last stage of helpless and imbecile old age. Mr. Hayley and his other affectionate acquaintances continued to visit him and use every means to restore his health, but their solicitude was vain, and he continued sunk in a melancholy which could neither be removed nor alleviated. It was at length determined to try the experiment of a change of air, and his amiable relative, the Rev. Dr. Johnson, took upon himself the charge of conducting him into Norfolk. While residing at Dunham Lodge, and afterwards at Mundsley, his spirits, with slight exceptions, continued in the same state; and though an occasional glimpse of hope now and then encouraged his desponding friends, they at length saw the gradual and certain approaches of decay under the most distressing circumstances in which death can visit an intellectual and reasoning being. Cowper had continued to compose several minor pieces of poetry, and to employ himself occasionally in reading during some time past; but in January, 1800, his strength began rapidly to decline, and on the 25th of April, of the same year, he yielded up his gentle and suffering spirit.

In summing up the character of Cowper, a cotemporary biographer thus writes: "Among the few, the very few, who have possessed the gift of a spirit full of the sweetness and the music of poetry, with its pure morality of purpose, is Cowper. The mind of its admirable writer was marked with the genuine traits which distinguish a poetical from other minds. He is, it is true, not to be compared with the great masters of the art, whose lofty and creative imaginations place them in a sphere of their own, but he had a power of collecting the scenes and harmonies of nature into the focus of his own heart, and of embuing them there with light and grace. He had an intensity and delicacy of feeling which made him perceive what is most beautiful in the complicated character of humanity, and he had that intuitive sense of the mind's action, which enabled him to present to others the objects and sentiments which influence with the greatest strength. By these qualities of his intellect, by the tenderness of his heart, and the extreme susceptibility of his nature, he was possessed of all the qualities, with the exception of a powerful imagination, which form the character of a poet; and in being denied the stronger excitements of fancy, he seems to have been formed by Providence to produce the works he composed. He was endowed with all the powers which a poet could want who was to be the moralist of the world—the reprover, but not the satirist of men—the teacher of simple truths, which were to be rendered gracious without endangering their simplicity."

To add much to this sketch respecting the merit of Cowper

as a poet, would be superfluous. After passing through the many trials which criticism has instituted, he remains, by universal acknowledgment, one of the first poets of the eighteenth century. Even without awaiting the issue of such trials, he attained a degree of popularity which is almost without a precedent, while the species of popularity which he has acquired is yet more honorable than the extent of it. No man's works ever appeared with less of artificial preparation; no venal heralds proclaimed the approach of a new poet, nor told the world what it was to admire. He emerged from obscurity, the object of no patronage, and the adherent of no party. His fame, great and extensive as it is, arose from gradual conviction, and gratitude for pleasure received. The genius, the scholar, the critic, the devout man, and the man of the world, each found in the works of Cowper something to excite their admiration, something congenial with their habits and feelings, something which taste readily selected, and judgment decidedly confirmed.

CONTENTS.

TRANSLATIONS FROM VINCENT BOURNE.

THE TASK, in six Books:

CONTENTS.

TRANSLATIONS OF THE LATIN AND ITALIAN POEMS OF MILTON.

TRANSLATIONS FROM THE FRENCH OF MADAME DE LA MOTHE GUION.

CONTENTS.

MINOR POEMS.

COWPER'S POEMS.

TABLE TALK.

Si te fortè meæ gravis uret sarcina chartæ,
Abjicito. *Hor.* Lib. i. Epist. 13.

A. You told me, I remember, glory, built
On selfish principles, is shame and guilt;
The deeds, that men admire as half-divine,
Stark naught, because corrupt in their design.
Strange doctrine this! that without scruple tears
The laurel, that the very lightning spares;
Brings down the warrior's trophy to the dust,
And eats into his bloody sword like rust.
B. I grant that, men continuing what they are,
Fierce, avaricious, proud, there must be war:
And never meant the rule should be applied
To him, that fights with justice on his side.
Let laurels, drench'd in pure Parnassian dews,
Reward his mem'ry, dear to ev'ry muse,
Who, with a courage of unshaken root,
In honour's field advancing his firm foot,
Plants it upon the line that Justice draws,
And will prevail or perish in her cause.
'Tis to the virtues of such men, man owes
His portion in the good that Heav'n bestows.
And when recording History displays
Feats of renown, though wrought in ancient days;
Tells of a few stout hearts, that fought and died,
Where duty plac'd them, at their country's side;
The man, that is not mov'd with what he reads,
That takes not fire at their heroic deeds,
Unworthy of the blessings of the brave,
Is base in kind, and born to be a slave.
But let eternal infamy pursue
The wretch, to nought but his ambition true
Who, for the sake of filling with one blast
The post-horns of all Europe, lays her waste.
Think yourself station'd on a tow'ring rock,

To see a people scatter'd like a flock,
Some royal mastiff panting at their heels,
With all the savage thirst a tiger feels;
Then view him self-proclaim'd in a gazette,
Chief monster that has plagued the nations yet.
The globe and sceptre in such hands misplac'd,
Those ensigns of dominion, how disgrac'd!
The glass, that bids man mark the fleeting hour,
And Death's own scythe would better speak his pow'r;
Then grace the bony phantom in their stead,
With the king's shoulder knot and gay cockade;
Clothe the twin brethren in each other's dress,
The same their occupation and success.
A. 'Tis your belief the world was made for man;
Kings do but reason on the self-same plan:
Maintaining yours, you cannot theirs condemn,
Who think, or seem to think, man made for them.
B. Seldom, alas! the pow'r of logic reigns
With much sufficiency in royal brains;
Such reas'ning falls like an inverted cone,
Wanting its proper base to stand upon.
Man made for king's! those optics are but dim,
That tell you so—say, rather, they for him.
That were indeed a king-ennobling thought,
Could they, or would they, reason as they ought.
The diadem, with mighty projects lin'd,
To catch renown by ruining mankind,
Is worth, with all its gold and glittering store,
Just what the toy will sell for, and no more.
Oh! bright occasions of dispensing good,
How seldom used, how little understood!
To pour in Virtue's lap her just reward;
Keep Vice restrain'd behind a double guard;
To quell the faction, that affronts the throne,
By silent magnanimity alone;
To nurse with tender care the thriving arts;
Watch every beam Philosophy imparts;
To give Religion her unbridled scope,
Nor judge by statute a believer's hope;
With close fidelity and love unfeign'd,
To keep the matrimonial bond unstain'd;
Covetous only of a virtuous praise;
His life a lesson to the land he sways;
To touch the sword with conscientious awe,
Nor draw it but when duty bids him draw;
To sheathe it in the peace-restoring close,
With joy beyond what victory bestows;—
Blest country, where these kingly glories shine!
Blest England, if this happiness be thine!

A. Guard what you say; the patriotic tribe
Will sneer, and charge you with a bribe. *B.* A bribe?
The worth of his three kingdoms I defy,
To lure me to the baseness of a lie:
And, of all lies (be that one poet's boast),
The lie that flatters I abhor the most.
Those arts be theirs, who hate his gentle reign;
But he that loves him has no need to feign.
A. Your smooth eulogium to one crown addrest,
Seems to imply a censure on the rest.
B. Quevedo, as he tells his sober tale,
Ask'd when in hell, to see the royal jail;
Approv'd their method in all other things;
But where, good sir, do you confine your kings?
There—said his guide—the group is full in view.
Indeed?—replied the don—there are but few.
His black interpreter the charge disdain'd—
Few, fellow?—there are all that ever reign'd.[1]
Wit, undistinguishing, is apt to strike
The guilty and not guilty both alike:
I grant the sarcasm is too severe,
And we can readily refute it here;
While Alfred's name, the father of his age,
And the Sixth Edward's grace th' historic page.
A. Kings then, at last, have but the lot of all:
By their own conduct they must stand or fall.
B. True. While they live, the courtly laureate pays
His quitrent ode, his peppercorn of praise;
And many a dunce, whose fingers itch to write,
Adds, as he can, his tributary mite.
A subject's faults a subject may proclaim,
A monarch's errors are forbidden game!
Thus, free from censure, overaw'd by fear,
And prais'd for virtues, that they scorn to wear,
The fleeting forms of majesty engage
Respect, while stalking o'er life's narrow stage;
Then leave their crimes for history to scan,
And ask, with busy scorn, Was this the man?
I pity kings, whom Worship waits upon
Obsequious from the cradle to the throne;
Before whose infant eyes the flatt'rer bows,
And binds a wreath about their baby brows;
Whom Education stiffens into state,
And Death awakens from that dream too late.
Oh! if Servility, with supple knees,
Whose trade it is to smile, to crouch, to please
If smooth Dissimulation, skill'd to grace
A devil's purpose with an angel's face;
If smiling peeresses, and simp'ring peers,

Encompassing his throne a few short years;
If the gilt carriage and the pamper'd steed,
That wants no driving, and disdains the lead;
If guards, mechanically form'd in ranks,
Playing, at beat of drum, their martial pranks,
Should'ring and standing as if struck to stone,
While condescending majesty looks on!—
If monarchy consists in such base things,
Sighing, I say again, I pity kings!
 To be suspected, thwarted, and withstood,
E'en when he labours for his country's good;
To see a band, call'd patriot for no cause,
But that they catch at popular applause,
Careless of all th' anxiety he feels,
Hook disappointment on the public wheels;
With all their flippant fluency of tongue,
Most confident, when palpably most wrong;—
If this be kingly, then farewell for me
All kingship; and may I be poor and free!
 To be the Table Talk of clubs up-stairs,
To which th' unwash'd artificer repairs,
T' indulge his genius after long fatigue,
By diving into cabinet intrigue
(For what kings deem a toil, as well they may,
To him is relaxation and mere play);
To win no praise when well-wrought plans prevail,
But to be rudely censur'd when they fail;
To doubt the love his fav'rites may pretend,
And in reality to find no friend;
If he indulge a cultivated taste,
His gall'ries with the works of art well grac'd,
To hear it call'd extravagance and waste;
If these attendants, and if such as these,
Must follow royalty, then welcome ease;
However humble and confin'd the sphere,
Happy the state, that has not these to fear.
 A. Thus men, whose thoughts contemplative have dwelt
On situations, that they never felt,
Start up sagacious, cover'd with the dust
Of dreaming study and pedantic rust,
And prate and preach about what others prove,
As if the world and they were hand and glove.
Leave kingly backs to cope with kingly cares;
They have their weight to carry, subjects theirs;
Poets, of all men, ever least regret
Increasing taxes and the nation's debt.
Could you contrive the payment, and rehearse
The mighty plan, oracular, in verse,
No bard, howe'er majestic, old or new,

Should claim my fix'd attention more than you.
B. Not Brindley nor Bridgewater would essay
To turn the course of Helicon that way;
Nor would the Nine consent the sacred tide
Should purl amidst the traffic of Cheapside,
Or tinkle in 'Change Alley, to amuse
The leathern ears of stockjobbers and Jews.
A. Vouchsafe, at least, to pitch the key of rhyme
To themes more pertinent, if less sublime.
When ministers and ministerial arts;
Patriots, who love good places at their hearts;
When admirals. extoll'd for standing still,
Or doing nothing with a deal of skill:
Gen'rals, who will not conquer when they may,
Firm friends to peace, to pleasure, and good pay;
When Freedom, wounded almost to despair,
Though Discontent alone can find out where;
When themes like these employ the poet's tongue,
I hear as mute as if a syren sung.
Or tell me, if you can, what pow'r maintains
A Briton's scorn of arbitrary chains:
That were a theme might animate the dead,
And move the lips of poets cast in lead.
B. The cause, tho' worth the search, may yet elude
Conjecture and remark, however shrewd.
They take perhaps a well-directed aim,
Who seek it in his climate and his frame.
Lib'ral in all things else, yet Nature here
With stern severity deals out the year.
Winter invades the spring, and often pours
A chilling flood on summer's drooping flow'rs
Unwelcome vapours quench autumnal beams,
Ungenial blasts attending curl the streams:
The peasants urge their harvest, ply the fork
With double toil, and shiver at their work;
Thus with a rigour, for his good design'd,
She rears her fav'rite man of all mankind.
His form robust and of elastic tone,
Proportion'd well, half muscle and half bone,
Supplies with warm activity and force
A mind well-lodg'd, and masculine of course.
Hence Liberty, sweet Liberty inspires
And keeps alive his fierce but noble fires.
Patient of constitutional control,
He bears it with meek manliness of soul;
But, if Authority grow wanton, woe
To him that treads upon his free-born toe
One step beyond the bound'ry of the laws
Fires him at once in Freedom's glorious cause,

Thus proud Prerogative, not much rever'd,
Is seldom felt, though sometimes seen and heard;
And in his cage, like parrot fine and gay,
Is kept to strut, look big, and talk away.
Born in a climate softer far than ours,
Not form'd, like us, with such Herculean pow'rs,
The Frenchman, easy, debonair, and brisk,
Give him his lass, his fiddle, and his frisk,
Is always happy, reign whoever may,
And laughs the sense of mis'ry far away.
He drinks his simple bev'rage with a gust;
And, feasting on an onion and a crust,
We never feel th' alacrity and joy
With which he shouts and carols *Vive le Roy*,
Fill'd with as much true merriment and glee,
As if he heard his king say—Slave, be free.
Thus happiness depends, as Nature shows,
Less on exterior things than most suppose.
Vigilant over all that he has made,
Kind Providence attends with gracious aid;
Bids equity throughout his works prevail,
And weighs the nations in an even scale;
He can encourage Slav'ry to a smile,
And fill with discontent a British isle.
A. Freemen and slave then, if the case be such,
Stand on a level; and you prove too much:
If all men indiscriminately share
His fost'ring pow'r, and tutelary care,
As well be yok'd by Despotism's hand,
As dwell at large in Britain's charter'd land.
B. No. Freedom has a thousand charms to show
That slaves, howe'er contented, never know.
The mind attains, beneath her happy reign,
The growth, that Nature meant she should attain;
The varied fields of science, ever new,
Op'ning and wider op'ning on her view,
She ventures onward with a prosp'rous force,
While no base fear impedes her in her course.
Religion, richest favour of the skies,
Stands most reveal'd before the freeman's eyes;
No shades of superstition blot the day,
Liberty chases all that gloom away;
The soul emancipated, unopprest,
Free to prove all things, and hold fast the best,
Learns much; and to a thousand list'ning minds
Communicates with joy the good she finds:
Courage in arms, and ever prompt to show
His manly forehead to the fiercest foe;
Glorious in war, but for the sake of peace,

His spirits rising as his toils increase,
Guards well what arts and industry have won,
And Freedom claims him for her first-born son,
Slaves fight for what were better cast away—
The chain that binds them, and a tyrant's sway;
But they, that fight for freedom, undertake
The noblest cause mankind can have at stake:—
Religion, virtue, truth, whate'er we call
A blessing—freedom is the pledge of all.
O Liberty! the pris'ner's pleasing dream,
The poet's muse, his passion, and his theme;
Genius is thine, and thou art Fancy's nurse;
Lost without thee th' ennobling pow'rs of verse;
Heroic song from thy free touch acquires
Its clearest tone, the rapture it inspires:
Place me where Winter breathes his keenest air,
And I will sing, if Liberty be there;
And I will sing at Liberty's dear feet,
In Afric's torrid clime, or India's fiercest heat.
A. Sing where you please; in such a cause I grant
An English poet's privilege to rant;
But is not Freedom—at least is not ours
Too apt to play the wanton with her pow'rs,
Grow freakish, and, o'erleaping ev'ry mound,
Spread anarchy and terror all around?
B. Agreed. But would you sell or slay your horse
For bounding and curvetting in his course?
Or if, when ridden with a careless rein,
He break away, and seek the distant plain?
No. His high mettle, under good control,
Gives him Olympic speed, and shoots him to the goal.
Let Discipline employ her wholesome arts;
Let magistrates alert perform their parts;
Not sculk or put on a prudential mask,
As if their duty were a desp'rate task;
Let active Laws apply the needful curb,
To guard the Peace, that Riot would disturb;
And Liberty, preserv'd from wild excess,
Shall raise no feuds for armies to suppress.
When Tumult lately burst his prison-door,
And set plebeian thousands in a roar;
When he usurp'd Authority's just place,
And dar'd to look his master in the face;
When the rude rabble's watchword was—Destroy
And blazing London seem'd a second Troy;
Liberty blush'd, and hung her drooping head,
Beheld their progress with the deepest dread;
Blush'd, that effects like these she should produce,
Worse than the deeds of galley-slaves broke loose.

She loses in such storms her very name,
And fierce Licentiousness should bear the blame.
Incomparable gem! thy worth untold;
Cheap though blood-bought, and thrown away when sold:
May no foes ravish thee, and no false friend
Betray thee, while professing to defend!
Prize it, ye ministers; ye monarch's spare;
Ye patriots guard it with a miser's care.
A. Patriots, alas! the few that have been found,
Where most they flourish, upon English ground,
The country's need have scantily supplied,
And the last left the scene, when Chatham died.
B. Not so—the virtue still adorns our age.
Though the chief actor died upon the stage.
In him Demosthenes was heard again;
Liberty taught him her Athenian strain;
She cloth'd him with authority and awe,
Spoke from his lips, and in his looks gave law.
His speech, his form, his action, full of grace,
And all his country beaming in his face,
He stood, as some inimitable hand
Would strive to make a Paul or Tully stand.
No Sycophant or slave, that dar'd oppose
Her sacred cause, but trembled when he rose;
And ev'ry venal stickler for the yoke
Felt himself crush'd at the first word he spoke.
Such men are rais'd to station and command,
When Providence means mercy to a land.
He speaks, and they appear; to him they owe
Skill to direct, and strength to strike the blow;
To manage with address, to seize with pow'r,
The crisis of a dark decisive hour:
So Gideon earned a vict'ry not his own;
Subserviency his praise, and that alone.
Poor England! thou art a devoted deer,
Beset with ev'ry ill but that of fear.
The nations hunt; all mark thee for a prey;
They swarm around thee, and thou stand'st at bay,
Undaunted still, though wearied and perplex'd;
Once Chatham sav'd thee; but who saves thee next?
Alas! the tide of pleasure sweeps along
All, that should be the boast of British song.
'Tis not the wreath, that once adorn'd thy brow,
The prize of happier times, will serve thee now.
Our ancestry, a gallant Christian race,
Patterns of ev'ry virtue, ev'ry grace,
Confess'd a God; they kneel'd before they fought,
And prais'd him in the victories he wrought.
Now from the dust of ancient days bring forth

Their sober zeal, integrity, and worth;
Courage, ungrac'd by these, affronts the skies,
Is but the fire without the sacrifice.
The stream, that feeds the well-spring of the heart,
Not more invigorates life's noblest part,
Than Virtue quickens, with a warmth divine,
The pow'rs, that Sin has brought to a decline.
A. Th' inestimable Estimate of Brown
Rose like a paper-kite, and charm'd the town;
But measures, plann'd and executed well,
Shifted the wind that rais'd it, and it fell.
He trod the very self-same ground you tread,
And Victory refuted all he said.
B. And yet his judgment was not fram'd amiss:
Its error, if it err'd, was merely this—
He thought the dying hour already come,
And a complete recovery struck him dumb.
But that effeminacy, folly, lust,
Enervate and enfeeble, and needs must;
And that a nation shamefully debas'd,
Will be despis'd and trampled on at last,
Unless sweet Penitence her pow'rs renew;
Is truth, if history itself be true.
There is a time, and Justice marks the date,
For long-forbearing Clemency to wait;
That hour elaps'd, th' incurable revolt
Is punish'd, and down comes the thunderbolt.
If Mercy *then* put by the threat'ning blow,
Must she perform the same kind office *now*?
May she! and, if offended Heav'n be still
Accessible, and pray'r prevail she will.
'Tis not, however, insolence and noise,
The tempest of tumultuary joys,
Nor is it yet despondence and dismay
Will win her visits, or engage her stay;
Pray'r only, and the penitential tear,
Can call her smiling down, and fix her here.
But when a country (one that I could name)
In prostitution sinks the sense of shame;
When infamous Venality, grown bold,
Writes on his bosom *to be let or sold;*
When Perjury, that Heav'n-defying vice,
Sells oaths by tale, and at the lowest price;
Stamps God's own name upon a lie just made,
To turn a penny in the way of trade;
When Av'rice starves (and never hides his face)
Two or three millions of the human race,
And not a tongue inquires, how, where, or when,
Though conscience will have twinges now and then;

When profanation of the sacred cause
In all its parts, times, ministry, and laws,
Bespeaks a land, once Christian, fall'n and lost,
In all, that wars against that title most;
What follows next let cities of great name,
And regions long since desolate proclaim.
Nineveh, Babylon, and ancient Rome,
Speak to the present times, and times to come;
They cry aloud in ev'ry careless ear,
Stop, while ye may; suspend your mad career;
O learn from our example and our fate,
Learn wisdom and repentance, ere too late.
  Not only vice disposes and prepares
The Mind, that slumbers sweetly in her snares,
To stoop to Tyranny's usurp'd command,
And bend her polish'd neck beneath his hand,
(A dire effect, by one of Nature's laws,
Unchangeably connected with its cause);
But Providence himself will intervene,
To throw his dark displeasure o'er the scene.
All are his instruments; each form of war,
What burns at home, or threatens from afar,
Nature in arms, her elements at strife,
The storms, that overset the joys of life,
Are but his rods to scourge a guilty land,
And waste it at the bidding of his hand.
He gives the word, and Mutiny soon roars
In all her gates, and shakes her distant shores;
The standards of all nations are unfurl'd;
She has one foe, and that one foe the world:
And, if he doom that people with a frown,
And mark them with a seal of wrath press'd down,
Obduracy takes place; callous and tough,
The reprobated race grows judgment-proof:
Earth shakes beneath them, and Heav'n roars above;
But nothing scares them from the course they love.
To the lascivious pipe and wanton song,
That charm down fear, they frolic it along,
With mad rapidity and unconcern,
Down to the gulf, from which is no return.
They trust in navies, and their navies fail—
God's curse can cast away ten thousand sail!
They trust in armies, and their courage dies;
In wisdom, wealth, in fortune, and in lies;
But all they trust in withers, as it must,
When He commands, in whom they place no trust.
Vengeance at last pours down upon their coast
A long dispis'd, but now victorious, host:
Tyranny sends the chain, that must abridge

The noble sweep of all their privilege;
Gives Liberty the last, the mortal shock;
Slips the slave's collar on, and snaps the lock.
A. Such lofty strains embellish what you teach:
Mean you to prophesy, or but to preach?
B. I know the mind, that feels indeed the fire
The muse imparts, and can command the lyre,
Acts with a force, and kindles with a zeal,
Whate'er the theme, that others never feel.
If human woes her soft attention claim,
A tender sympathy pervades the frame;
She pours a sensibility divine
Along the nerve of ev'ry feeling line.
But if a deed, not tamely to be borne,
Fire indignation and a sense of scorn,
The strings are swept with such a pow'r, so loud,
The storm of music shakes th' astonished crowd.
So, when remote futurity is brought
Before the keen inquiry of her thought,
A terrible sagacity informs
The poet's heart; he looks to distant storms;
He hears the thunder ere the tempest low'rs;
And, arm'd with strength surpassing human pow'rs,
Seizes events ss yet unknown to man,
And darts his soul into the dawning plan.
Hence, in a Roman mouth, the graceful name
Of prophet and of poet was the same;
Hence British poets too the priesthood shar'd,
And ev'ry hallow'd druid was a bard.
But no prophetic fires to me belong:
I play with syllables, and sport in song.
A. At Westminster, where little poets strive
To set a distich upon six and five,
Where Discipline, helps op'ning buds of sense,
And makes his pupils proud with silver pence,
I was a poet too; but modern taste
Is so refin'd, and delicate, and chaste,
That verse, whatever fire the fancy warms,
Without a creamy smoothness has no charms.
Thus, all success depending on an ear,
And thinking I might purchase it too dear,
If sentiment were sacrific'd to sound,
Aud truth cut short to make a period round,
I judged a man of sense could scarce do worse,
Than caper in the morris-dance of verse.
B. Thus reputation is a spur to wit,
And some wits flag through fear of losing it.
Give me the line that ploughs its stately course
Like a proud swan, conqu'ring the stream by force;

That like some cottage beauty, strikes the heart,
Quite unindebted to the tricks of art.
When Labour and when Dulness, club in hand,
Like the two figures at St. Dunstan's, stand,
Beating alternately, in measur'd time,
The clock-work tintinnabulum of rhyme,
Exact and regular the sounds will be;
But such mere quarter-strokes are not for me.
From him, who rears a poem lank and long,
To him who strains his all into a song;
Perhaps some bonny Caledonian air,
All birks and braes, though he was never there;
Or, having whelp'd a prologue with great pains,
Feels himself spent, and fumbles for his brains;
A prologue interdash'd with many a stroke—
An art contrived to advertise a joke,
So that the jest is clearly to be seen
Not in the words—but in the gap between:
Manner is all in all, whate'er is writ,
The substitute for genius, sense, and wit.
To dally much with subjects mean and low,
Proves that the mind is weak, or makes it so.
Neglected talents rust into decay,
And ev'ry effort ends in push-pin play.
The man, that means success, should soar above
A soldier's feather, or a lady's glove;
Else, summoning the muse to such a theme,
The fruit of all her labour is whipp'd cream.
As if an eagle flew aloft, and then—
Stoop'd from its highest pitch to pounce a wren.
As if the poet, purposing to wed,
Should carve himself a wife in gingerbread.
Ages elaps'd ere Homer's lamp appear'd,
And ages ere the Mantuan swan was heard.
To carry Nature lengths unknown before,
To give a Milton birth, ask'd ages more.
Thus Genius rose and set at order'd times,
And shot a dayspring into distant climes,
Ennobling ev'ry region that he chose;
He sunk in Greece, in Italy he rose:
And, tedious years of Gothic darkness past,
Emerg'd all splendour, in our isle at last.
Thus lovely halcyons dive into the main,
Then show far off their shining plumes again.
A. Is genius only found in epic lays?
Prove this, and forfeit all pretence to praise.
Make their heroic pow'rs your own at once,
Or candidly confess yourself a dunce.
B. These were the chief: each interval of night
Was grac'd with many an undulating light.

In less illustrious bards his beauty shone
A meteor, or a star; in these the sun.
The nightingale may claim the topmast bough,
While the poor grasshopper must chirp below.
Like him unnotic'd, I, and such as I,
Spread little wings, and rather skip than fly;
Perch'd on the meagre produce of the land,
An ell or two of prospect we command;
But never peep beyond the thorny bound,
Or oaken fence that hems the paddock round.
In Eden, ere yet innocence of heart
Had faded, poetry was not an art:
Language, above all teaching, or, if taught,
Only by gratitude and glowing thought,
Elegant as simplicity, and warm
As ecstasy, unmanacled by form;
Not prompted, as in our degen'rate days,
By low ambition and the thirst of praise;
Was natural as is the flowing stream,
And yet magnificent—A God the theme!
That theme on Earth exhausted, though above
'Tis found as everlasting as his love.
Man lavish'd all his thoughts on human things—
The feats of heroes, and the wrath of kings;
But still, while Virtue kindled his delight,
The song was moral, and so far was right.
'Twas thus, till Luxury seduc'd the mind
To joys less innocent, as less refin'd:
Then Genius danc'd a bacchanal; he crown'd
The brimming goblet, seiz'd the thyrsus, bound
His brows with ivy, rush'd into the field
Of wild imagination, and there reel'd,
The victim of his own lascivious fires,
And, dizzy with delight, profan'd the sacred wires.
Anacreon, Horace, play'd in Greece and Rome
This bedlam part; and others nearer home.
When Cromwell fought for pow'r, and while he reign'd
The proud protector of the power he gained,
Religion, harsh, intolerant, austere,
Parent of manners like herself severe,
Drew a rough copy of the Christian face,
Without the smile, the sweetness, or the grace:
The dark and sullen humour of the time
Judg'd ev'ry effort of the muse a crime;
Verse, in the finest mould of fancy cast,
Was lumber in an age so void of taste;
But when the Second Charles assum'd the sway,
And arts reviv'd beneath a softer day,
Then, like a bow long forc'd into a curve,

The mind, releas'd from too constrain'd a nerve,
Flew to its first position with a spring,
That made the vaulted roofs of Pleasure ring.
His court, the dissolute and hateful school
Of Wantonness, where vice was taught by rule,
Swarm'd with a scribbling herd, as deep inlaid
With brutal lust, as ever Circe made.
From these a long succession, in the rage
Of rank obscenity, debauch'd their age;
Nor ceas'd, till, ever anxious to redress
Th' abuses of her sacred charge, the press,
The muse instructed a well-nurtur'd train
Of abler votaries to cleanse the stain,
And claim the palm for purity of song,
That Lewdness had usurp'd and worn so long.
Then decent Pleasantry and sterling Sense,
That neither gave nor would endure offence,
Whipp'd out of sight, with satire just and keen,
The puppy pack, that had defiled the scene.
  In front of these came Addison. In him
Humour in holiday and sightly trim,
Sublimity and Attic taste combin'd,
To polish, furnish, and delight the mind.
Then Pope, as harmony itself exact,
In verse well disciplin'd, complete, compact,
Gave virtue and morality a grace,
That, quite eclipsing Pleasure's painted face,
Levied a tax of wonder and applause,
E'en on the fools that trampled on their laws.
But he (his musical finesse was such,
So nice his ear, so delicate his touch)
Made poetry a mere mechanic art;
And ev'ry warbler has his tune by heart.
Nature imparting her satiric gift,
Her serious mirth, to Arbuthnot and Swift,
With droll sobriety they rais'd a smile
At Folly's cast, themselves unmov'd the while.
That constellation set, the world in vain
Must hope to look upon their like again.
  A. Are we then left—*B.* Not wholly in the dark
Wit now and then, struck smartly, shows a spark,
Sufficient to redeem the modern race
From total night and absolute disgrace.
While servile trick and imitative knack
Confine the million in the beaten track,
Perhaps some courser, who disdains the road,
Snuffs up the wind, and flings himself abroad.
  Contemporaries all surpass'd, see one,
Short his career, indeed, but ably run;
Churchill, himself unconscious of his pow'rs,

In penury consum'd his idle hours;
And, like a scatter'd seed at random sown,
Was left to spring by vigour of his own.
Lifted at length, by dignity of thought
And dint of genius, to an affluent lot,
He laid his head in Luxury's soft lap,
And took, too often, there his easy nap.
If brighter beams than all he threw not forth,
'Twas negligence in him, not want of worth.
Surly, and slovenly, and bold, and coarse,
Too proud for art, and trusting in mere force,
Spendthrift alike of money and of wit,
Always at speed, and never drawing bit,
He struck the lyre, in such a careless mood,
And so disdain'd the rules he understood;
The laurel seem'd to wait on his command,
He snatch'd it rudely from the Muses' hand.
Nature, exerting an unwearied pow'r,
Forms, opens, and gives scent to ev'ry flow'r;
Spreads the fresh verdure of the field, and leads
The dancing Naiads through the dewy meads;
She fills profuse ten thousand little throats
With music, modulating all their notes;
And charms the woodland scenes, and wilds unknown,
With artless airs and concerts of her own:
But seldom (as if fearful of expense)
Vouchsafes to man a poet's just pretence—
Fervency, freedom, fluency of thought,
Harmony, strength, words exquisitely sought;
Fancy, that from the bow that spans the sky,
Brings colours, dipp'd in Heav'n, that never die;
A soul exalted above Earth, a mind
Skill'd in the characters that form mankind;
And, as the Sun in rising beauty drest,
Looks to the westward from the dappled east,
And marks, whatever clouds may interpose,
Ere yet his race begins, its glorious close:
An eye like his to catch the distant goal;
Or, ere the wheels of verse begin to roll,
Like his to shed illuminating rays
On ev'ry scene and subject it surveys:
Thus grac'd, the man asserts a poet's name,
And the world cheerfully admits the claim.
Pity Religion has so seldom found
A skilful guide into poetic ground!
The flow'rs would spring where'er she deign'd to stray,
And ev'ry muse attend her in her way.
Virtue indeed meets many a rhyming friend,
And many a compliment politely penn'd;
But, unattir'd in that becoming vest

Religion weaves for her, and half undrest,
Stands in the desert, shiv'ring and forlorn,
A wintry figure, like a wither'd thorn.
The shelves are full, all other themes are sped;
Hackney'd, and worn to the last flimsy thread,
Satire has long since done his best; and curst
And loathsome Ribaldry has done its worst:
Fancy has sported all her pow'rs away
In tales, in trifles, and in children's play;
And 'tis the sad complaint, and almost true,
Whate'er we write, we bring forth nothing new.
'Twere new, indeed, to see a bard all fire,
Touch'd with a coal from Heav'n, assume the lyre
And tell the world, still kindling as he sung,
With more than mortal music on his tongue,
That He, who died below, and reigns above,
Inspires the song, and that his name is Love.
For, after all, if merely to beguile,
By flowing numbers and a flow'ry style,
The tædium that the lazy rich endure,
Which now and then sweet poetry may cure;
Or, if to see the name of idle self,
Stamp'd on the well-bound quarto, grace the shelf;
To float a bubble on the breath of Fame,
Prompt his endeavour and engage his aim,
Debas'd to servile purposes of pride,
How are the pow'rs of genius misapplied!
The gift, whose office is the Giver's praise,
To trace him in his word, his works, his ways!
Then spread the rich discov'ry, and invite
Mankind to share in the divine delight;
Distorted from its use and just design,
To make the pitiful possessor shine,
To purchase, at the fool-frequented fair
Of vanity, a wreath for self to wear,
Is profanation of the basest kind—
Proof of a trifling and a worthless mind.
A. Hail Sternhold, then; and Hopkins, hail!—
B. Amen.
If flatt'ry, folly, lust, employ the pen;
If acrimony, slander, and abuse,
Give it a charge to blacken and traduce;
Though Butler's wit, Pope's numbers, Prior's ease,
With all that fancy can invent to please,
Adorn the polish'd periods as they fall,
One madrigal of theirs is worth them all.
A. 'Twould thin the ranks of the poetic tribe,
To dash the pen through all that you proscribe.
B. No matter—we could shift when they were not;
And should, no doubt, if they were all forgot.

THE PROGRESS OF ERROR.

Si quid loquar audiendum. *Hor.* Lib. iv. Od. 2.

Sing, muse (if such a theme, so dark, so long,
May find a muse to grace it with a song,)
By what unseen and unsuspected arts
The serpent Error twines round human hearts;
Tell where she lurks, beneath what flow'ry shades,
That not a glimpse of genuine light pervades,
The pois'nous, black, insinuating worm
Successfully conceals her loathsome form.
Take, if ye can, ye careless and supine,
Counsel and caution from a voice like mine!
Truths, that the theorist could never reach,
And observation taught me, I would teach.
Not all, whose eloquence the fancy fills,
Musical as the chime of tinkling rills,
Weak to perform, though mighty to pretend,
Can trace her mazy windings to their end;
Discern the fraud beneath the specious lure,
Prevent the danger, or prescribe the cure.
The clear harangue, and cold as it is clear,
Falls soporific on the listless ear;
Like quicksilver, the rhet'ric they display,
Shines as it runs, but grasp'd at, slips away.
Plac'd for his trial on this bustling stage,
From thoughtless youth to ruminating age,
Free in his will to choose or to refuse,
Man may improve the crisis, or abuse;
Else, on the fatalist's unrighteous plan,
Say to what bar amenable were man?
With nought in charge, he could betray no trust;
And, if he fell, would fall because he must;
If Love reward him, or if Vengeance strike,
His recompense in both unjust alike.
Divine authority within his breast
Brings ev'ry thought, word, action, to the test;
Warns him or prompts, approves him or restrains,
As Reason, or as Passion, takes the reins.

Heav'n from above, and Conscience from within,
Cries in his startled ear—Abstain from sin!
The world around solicits his desire,
And kindles in his soul a treach'rous fire;
While, all his purposes and steps to guard,
Peace follows Virtue as its sure reward;
And Pleasure brings us surely in her train
Remorse, and Sorrow, and vindictive Pain.
Man, thus endu'd with an elective voice,
Must be supplied with objects of his choice;
Where'er he turns, enjoyment and delight,
Or present, or in prospect, meet his sight;
Those open on the spot their honey'd store;
These call him loudly to pursuit of more.
His unexhausted mine the sordid vice
Avarice shows, and virtue is the price.
Her various motives his ambition raise—
Pow'r, pomp, and splendour, and the thirst of praise;
There beauty wooes him with expanded arms;
E'en Bacchanalian madness has its charms.
Nor these alone, whose pleasures less refin'd
Might well alarm the most ungnarded mind,
Seek to supplant his inexperienc'd youth,
Or lead him devious from the path of truth;
Hourly allurements on his passions press,
Safe in themselves, but dang'rous in th' excess.
Hark! how it floats upon the dewy air!
O what a dying, dying close was there!
'Tis harmony from you sequester'd bow'r,
Sweet harmony, that soothes the midnight hour!
Long ere the charioteer of day had run
His morning course, th' enchantment was begun;
And he shall gild you mountain's height again,
Ere yet the pleasing toil becomes a pain.
Is this the rugged path, the steep ascent,
That Virtue points to? Can a life thus spent
Lead to the bliss she promises the wise,
Detach the soul from Earth, and speed her to the skies?
Ye devotees to your ador'd employ,
Enthusiasts, drunk with an unreal joy,
Love makes the music of the blest above,
Heaven's harmony is universal love;
And earthly sounds, tho' sweet and well combin'd,
And lenient as soft opiates to the mind,
Leave Vice and Folly unsubdu'd behind.
Gray dawn appears; the sportsman and his train
Speckle the bosom of the distant plain;
'Tis he, the Nimrod of the neighb'ring lairs;
Save that his scent is less acute than theirs,

For persevering chase, and headlong leaps,
True beagle as the staunchest hound he keeps.
Charg'd with the folly of his life's mad scene,
He takes offence, and wonders what you mean;
The joy the danger and the toil o'erpays—
'Tis exercise, and health, and length of days.
Again impetuous to the field he flies;
Leaps ev'ry fence but one, there falls and dies;
Like a slain deer, the tumbrel brings him home,
Unmiss'd but by his dogs and by his groom.
Ye clergy, while your orbit is your place,
Lights of the world, and stars of human race;
But if eccentric ye forsake your sphere
Prodigies ominous, and view'd with fear;
The comet's baneful influence is a dream;
Yours, real and pernicious in th' extreme.
What then!—are appetites and lusts laid down,
With the same ease that man puts on his gown?
Will Av'rice and Concupiscence give place,
Charm'd by the sounds—Your Rev'rence, or Your Grace?
No. But his own engagement binds him fast;
Or, if it does not, brands him to the last,
What atheists call him—a designing knave,
A mere church juggler, hypocrite, and slave.
Oh, laugh or mourn with me the rueful jest,
A cassock'd huntsman, and a fiddling priest!
He from Italian songsters takes his cue:
Set Paul to music, he shall quote him too.
He takes the field, the master of the pack
Cries—Well done, saint! and claps him on the back.
Is this the path of sanctity? Is this
To stand a waymark in the road to bliss?
Himself a wand'rer from the narrow way,
His silly sheep, what wonder if they stray?
Go, cast your orders at your bishop's feet,
Send your dishonour'd gown to Monmouth-street!
The sacred function in your hands is made—
Sad sacrilege! no function, but a trade!
Occiduus is a pastor of renown,
When he has pray'd and preach'd the sabbath down,
With wire and catgut he concludes the day,
Quav'ring and semiquav'ring care away.
The full concerto swells upon your ear;
All elbows shake. Look in, and you would swear
The Babylonian tyrant with a nod
Had summon'd them to serve his golden god.
So well that thought th' employment seems to suit,
Psalt'ry and sackbut, dulcimer and flute.
O fie! 'tis evangelical and pure:

Observe each face, how sober and demure!
Ecstasy sets her stamp on ev'ry mien;
Chins fall'n, and not an eye-ball to be seen.
Still I insist, though music heretofore
Has charm'd me much, (not e'en Occiduus more,)
Love, joy, and peace, make harmony more meet
For sabbath ev'nings, and perhaps as sweet.
  Will not the sickliest sheep of ev'ry flock
Resort to this example as a rock;
There stand, and justify the foul abuse
Of sabbath-hours with plausible excuse?
If apostolic gravity be free
To play the fool on Sundays, why not we?
If he the tinkling harpsichord regards
As inoffensive, what offence in cards?
Strike up the fiddles, let us all be gay,
Laymen have leave to dance, if parsons play.
  Oh Italy!—Thy sabbaths will be soon
Our sabbaths, clos'd with mumm'ry and buffoon.
Preaching and pranks will share the motley scene,
Ours parcell'd out, as thine have ever been,
God's worship and the mountebank between.
What says the Prophet? Let that day be blest
With holiness and consecrated rest.
Pastime and business both it should exclude,
And bar the door the moment they intrude:
Nobly distinguish'd above all the six
By deeds, in which the world must never mix.
Hear him again. He calls it a delight,
A day of luxury observ'd aright,
When the glad soul is made Heav'n's welcome guest,
Sits banqueting, and God provides the feast.
But triflers are engag'd and cannot come;
Their answer to the call is—*Not at home.*
  Oh the dear pleasures of the velvet plain,
The painted tablets, dealt and dealt again!
Cards with what rapture, and the polish'd die,
The yawning chasm of indolence supply!
Then to the dance, and make the sober moon
Witness of joys that shun the sight of noon.
Blame, cynic, if you can, quadrille or ball,
The snug close party, or the splendid hall,
Where Night, down-stooping from her ebon throne,
Views constellations brighter than her own.
'Tis innocent, and harmless, and refin'd,
The balm of care, Elysium of the mind.
Innocent! Oh if venerable Time
Slain at the foot of Pleasure be no crime,
Then, with his silver beard and magic wand,

Let Comus rise archbishop of the land;
Let him your rubric and your feasts prescribe,
Grand metropolitan of all the tribe.
  Of manners rough, and coarse athletic cast,
The rank debauch suits Clodio's filthy taste.
Rufillus, exquisitely form'd by rule,
Not of the moral but the dancing school,
Wonder's at Clodio's follies, in a tone
As tragical, as others at his own.
He cannot drink five bottles, bilk the score,
Then kill a constable, and drink five more;
But he can draw a pattern, make a tart,
And has the ladies' etiquette by heart.
Go, fool; and, arm in arm with Clodio, plead
Your cause before a bar you little dread;
But know, the law, that bids the drunkard die,
Is far too just to pass the trifler by.
Both baby-featur'd, and of infant size,
View'd from a distance, and with heedless eyes,
Folly and Innocence are so alike,
The diff'rence, though essential, fails to strike
Yet Folly ever has a vacant stare,
A simp'ring count'nance, and a trifling air;
But Innocence, sedate, serene, erect,
Delights us, by engaging our respect.
Man, Nature's guest by invitation sweet,
Receives from her both appetite and treat;
But, if he play the glutton and exceed,
His benefactress blushes at the deed;
For Nature, nice, as lib'ral to dispense,
Made nothing but a brute the slave of sense.
Daniel ate pulse by choice—example rare!
Heav'n bless'd the youth, and made him fresh and fair.
Gorgonius sits, abdominous and wan,
Like a fat squab upon a Chinese fan:
He snuffs far off th' anticipated joy;
Turtle and ven'son all his thoughts employ;
Prepares for meals as jockeys take a sweat,
Oh, nauseous!—an emetic for a whet!
Will Providence o'erlook the wasted good?
Temperance were no virtue if he could.
  That pleasures, therefore, or what such we call,
Are hurtful, is a truth confess'd by all;
And some, that seem to threaten virtue less,
Still hurtful in th' abuse, or by th' excess.
  Is man then only for his torment plac'd
The centre of delights he may not taste?
Like fabled Tantalus, condemn'd to hear
The precious stream still purling in his ear,

Lip-deep in what he longs for, and yet curst
With prohibition, and perpetual thirst?
No, wrangler—destitute of shame and sense,
The precept, that enjoins him abstinence,
Forbids him none but the licentious joy,
Whose fruit, though fair, tempts only to destroy.
Remorse, the fatal egg by Pleasure laid
In ev'ry bosom where her nest is made,
Hatch'd by the beams of Truth, denies him rest,
And proves a raging scorpion in his breast.
No pleasure? Are domestic comforts dead?
Are all the nameless sweets of friendship fled?
Has time worn out, or fashion put to shame,
Good sense, good health, good conscience, and good fame?
All these belong to virtue, and all prove,
That virtue has a title to your love.
Have you no touch of pity, that the poor
Stand starv'd at your inhospitable door?
Or if yourself too scantily supplied
Need help, let honest industry provide.
Earn, if you want; if you abound, impart:
These both are pleasures to the feeling heart.
No pleasure? Has some sickly eastern waste
Sent us a wind to parch us at a blast?
Can British Paradise no scenes afford
To please her sated and indiff'rent lord?
Are sweet philosophy's enjoyments run
Quite to the lees? And has religion none?
Brutes capable would tell you 'tis a lie,
And judge you from the kennel and the sty.
Delights like these, ye sensual and profane,
Ye are bid, begg'd, besought to entertain;
Call'd to these crystal streams, do ye turn off
Obscene to swill and swallow at a trough?
Envy the beast then, on whom Heav'n bestows
Your pleasures, with no curses in the close.
  Pleasure admitted in undue degree
Enslaves the will, nor leaves the judgment free.
'Tis not alone the grape's enticing juice
Unnerves the moral pow'rs, and mars their use;
Ambition, av'rice, and the lust of fame,
And woman, lovely woman, does the same.
The heart, surrender'd to the ruling pow'r
Of some ungovern'd passion ev'ry hour,
Finds by degrees the truths, that once bore sway,
And all their deep impressions, wear away;
So coin grows smooth, in traffic current pass'd,
Till Cæsar's image is effac'd at last.
  The breach, tho' small at first, soon op'ning wide,

In rushes folly with a full-moon tide,
Then welcome errors of whatever size,
To justify it by a thousand lies.
As creeping ivy clings to wood or stone,
And hides the ruin that it feeds upon;
So sophistry cleaves close to and protects
Sin's rotten trunk, concealing its defects.
Mortals, whose pleasures are their only care,
First wish to be impos'd on, and then are.
And, lest the fulsome artifice should fail,
Themselves will hide its coarseness with a veil.
Not more industrious are the just and true,
To give to Virtue what is Virtue's due—
The praise of wisdom, comeliness, and worth,
And call her charms to public notice forth—
Than Vice's mean and disingenuous race,
To hide the shocking features of her face.
Her form with dress and lotion they repair;
They kiss their idol, and pronounce her fair.
The sacred implement I now employ
Might prove a mischief, or at best a toy;
A trifle, if it move but to amuse;
But, if to wrong the judgment and abuse,
Worse than a poinard in the basest hand,
It stabs at once the morals of a land.
Ye writers of what none with safety reads,
Footing it in the dance that Fancy leads;
Ye novelists, who mar what ye would mend,
Sniv'lling and driv'lling folly without end;
Whose corresponding misses fill the ream
With sentimental frippery and dream,
Caught in a delicate soft silken net
By some lewd earl, or rakehell baronet:
Ye pimps, who, under virtue's fair pretence,
Steal to the closet of young innocence,
And teach her, unexperienc'd yet and green,
To scribble as you scribbled at fifteen;
Who, kindling a combustion of desire,
With some cold moral think to quench the fire;
Though all your engineering proves in vain,
The dribbling stream ne'er puts it out again:
O that a verse had pow'r, and could command
Far, far away these flesh-flies of the land;
Who fasten without mercy on the fair,
And suck, and leave a craving maggot there!
Howe'er disguis'd th' inflammatory tale,
And cover'd with a fine-spun specious veil;
Such writers, and such readers, owe the gust
And relish of their pleasure all to lust.

But the muse, eagle pinion'd, has in view
A quarry more important still than you;
Down, down the wind she swims, and sails away,
Now stoops upon it, and now grasps the prey.
Petronius! all the muses weep for thee;
But ev'ry tear shall scald thy memory:
The graces too, while Virtue at their shrine
Lay bleeding under that soft hand of thine,
Felt each a mortal stab in her own breast,
Abhorr'd the sacrifice, and curs'd the priest.
Thou polish'd and high-finish'd foe to truth,
Graybeard corrupter of our list'ning youth,
To purge and skim away the filth of vice,
That so refin'd it might the more entice,
Then pour it on the morals of thy son;
To taint *his* heart, was worthy of *thine own!*
Now, while the poison all high life pervades,
Write, if thou canst, one letter from the shades;
One, and one only, charg'd with deep regret,
That thy worse part, thy principles, live yet:
One sad epistle thence may cure mankind
Of the plague spread by bundles left behind.
'Tis granted, and no plainer truth appears,
Our most important are our earliest years;
The Mind, impressible and soft, with ease
Imbibes and copies what she hears and sees,
And through life's labyrinth holds fast the clew
That Education gives her, false or true.
Plants rais'd with tenderness are seldom strong;
Man's coltish disposition asks the thong;
And without discipline, the fav'rite child,
Like a neglected forester, runs wild.
But we, as if good qualities would grow
Spontaneous, take but little pains to sow;
We give some Latin, and a smatch of Greek;
Teach him to fence and figure twice a-week;
And having done, we think, the best we can,
Praise his proficiency, and dub him man.
From school to Cam or Isis, and thence home;
And thence with all convenient speed to Rome,
With rev'rend tutor clad in habit lay,
To tease for cash, and quarrel with all day;
With memorandum book for ev'ry town,
And ev'ry post, and where the chaise broke down;
His stock, a few French phrases got by heart,
With much to learn, but nothing to impart;
The youth, obedient to his sire's commands,
Sets off a wand'rer into foreign lands.
Surpris'd at all they meet, the gosling pair,

With awkward gait, stretch'd neck, and silly stare,
Discover huge cathedrals built with stone,
And steeples tow'ring high, much like our own;
But show peculiar light by many a grin,
At popish practices observ'd within.
Ere long some bowing, smirking, smart abbé
Remarks two loit'rers, that have lost their way;
And being always prim'd with *politesse*
For men of their appearance and address,
With much compassion undertakes the task,
To tell them more than they have wit to ask:
Points to inscriptions wheresoe'er they tread,
Such as, when legible, were never read,
But, being canker'd now and half worn out,
Craze antiquarian brains with endless doubt;
Some headless hero, or some Cæsar shows—
Defective only in his Roman nose;
Exhibits elevations, drawings, plans,
Models of Herculanean pots and pans;
And sells them medals, which, if neither rare
Nor ancient, will be so, preserv'd with care.
Strange the recital! from whatever cause
His great improvement and new light he draws,
The squire, once bashful, is shamefac'd no more,
But teems with pow'rs he never felt before:
Whether increas'd momentum, and the force,
With which from clime to clime he sped his course,
(As axles sometimes kindle as they go)
Chaf'd him, and brought dull nature to a glow;
Or whether clearer skies and softer air,
That make Italian flow'rs so sweet and fair,
Fresh'ning his lazy spirits as he ran,
Unfolded genially and spread the man;
Returning he proclaims by many a grace,
By shrugs and strange contortions of his face,
How much a dunce, that has been sent to roam,
Excels a dunce, that has been kept at home.
Accomplishments have taken virtue's place,
And wisdom falls before exterior grace:
We slight the precious kernel of the stone,
And toil to polish its rough coat alone.
A just deportment, manners grac'd with ease,
Elegant phrase, and figure form'd to please,
Are qualities, that seem to comprehend
Whatever parents, guardians, schools intend;
Hence an unfurnish'd and a listless mind,
Though busy, trifling; empty, though refin'd;
Hence all that interferes, and dares to clash
With indolence and luxury, is trash;

While learning, once the man's exclusive pride,
Seems verging fast towards the female side.
Learning itself, receiv'd into a mind
By nature weak, or viciously inclin'd,
Serves but to lead philosphers astray,
Where children would with ease discern the way
And of all arts sagacious dupes invent,
To cheat themselves and gain the world's assent,
The worst is—Scripture warp'd from its intent.
The carriage bowls along, and all are pleas'd
If Tom be sober, and the wheels well greas'd;
But if the rogue have gone a cup too far,
Left out his linchpin, or forgot his tar,
It suffers interruption and delay,
And meets with hindrance in the smoothest way.
When some hypothesis, absurb and vain,
Has fill'd with all its fumes a critic's brain,
The text, that sorts not with his darling whim,
Though plain to others, is obscure to him.
The will made subject to a lawless force,
All is irregular and out of course;
And Judgment drunk, and brib'd to lose his way,
Winks hard, and talks of darkness at noonday.
A critic on the sacred book should be
Candid and learn'd, dispassionate and free!
Free from the wayward bias bigots feel,
From fancy's influence, and intemp'rate zeal:
But, above all, (or let the wretch refrain,
Nor touch the page he cannot but profane,)
Free from the domineering pow'r of lust;
A lewd interpreter is never just.
How shall I speak thee, or thy pow'r address,
Thou god of our idolatry, the Press?
By thee religion, liberty, and laws,
Exert their influence, and advance their cause;
By thee worse plagues than Pharaoh's land befel,
Difus'd, make Earth the vestibule of Hell;
Thou fountain, at which drink the good and wise;
Thou ever-bubbling spring of endless lies;
Like Eden's dread probationary tree,
Knowledge of good and evil is from thee.
No wild enthusiast ever yet could rest,
Till half mankind were like himself possess'd.
Philosophers, who darken and put out
Eternal truth by everlasting doubt;
Church quacks, with passions under no command,
Who fill the world with doctrines contraband,
Discov'rers of they know not what, confin'd
Within no bounds—the blind that lead the blind;

To streams of popular opinion drawn,
Deposit in those shallows all their spawn.
The wriggling fry soon fill the creeks around,
Pois'ning the waters where their swarms abound.
Scorn'd by the nobler tenants of the flood,
Minnows and gudgeons gorge th' unwholesome food.
The propagated myriads spread so fast,
E'en Lewenhoeck himself would stand aghast,
Employ'd to calculate th' enormous sum,
And own his crab-computing pow'rs o'ercome.
Is this hyperbole? The world well known,
Your sober thoughts will hardly find it one.
Fresh confidence the speculatist takes
From ev'ry hair-brain'd proselyte he makes;
And therefore prints. Himself but half deceiv'd,
Till others have the soothing tale believ'd.
Hence comment after comment, spun as fine
As bloated spiders draw the flimsy line:
Hence the same word, that bids our lusts obey,
Is misapplied to sanctify their sway.
If stubborn Greek refuse to be his friend,
Hebrew or Syriac shall be forc'd to bend:
If languages and copies all cry, No—
Somebody prov'd it centuries ago.
Like trout pursued, the critic in despair
Darts to the mud, and finds his safety there.
Woman, whom custom has forbid to fly
The scholar's pitch (the scholar best knows why),
With all the simple and unletter'd poor,
Admire his learning, and almost adore.
Whoever errs, the priest can ne'er be wrong,
With such fine words familiar to his tongue.
Ye ladies! (for indiff'rent in your cause,
I should deserve to forfeit all applause,)
Whatever shocks or gives the least offence
To virtue, delicacy, truth, or sense,
(Try the criterion, 'tis a faithful guide,)
Nor has, nor can have, Scripture on its side.
None but an author knows an authors cares,
Or Fancy's fondness for the child she bears.
Committed once into the public arms,
The baby seems to smile with added charms.
Like something precious ventur'd far from shore,
'Tis valued for the danger's sake the more.
He views it with complacency supreme,
Solicits kind attention to his dream;
And daily more enamour'd of the cheat,
Kneels, and asks Heav'n to bless the dear deceit.
So one, whose story serves at least to show

Men lov'd their own productions long ago,
Woo'd an unfeeling statue for his wife,
Nor rested till the gods had giv'n it life.
If some mere driv'ller suck the sugar'd fib,
One that still needs his leading-string and bib,
And praise his genius, he is soon repaid
In praise applied to the same part—his head:
For 'tis a rule, that holds for ever true,
Grant me discernment, and I grant it you.
 Patient of contradiction as a child,
Affable, humble, diffident, and mild;
Such was Sir Isaac, and such Boyle and Locke:
Your blund'rer is as sturdy as a rock.
The creature is so sure to kick and bite,
A muleteer's the man to set him right.
First Appetite enlists him truth's sworn foe,
Then obstinate Self-will confirms him so.
Tell him he wanders; that his error leads
To fatal ills; that, though the path he treads
Be flow'ry, and he see no cause of fear,
Death and the pains of Hell attend him there:
In vain; the slave of arrogance and pride,
He has no hearing on the prudent side.
His still refuted quirks he still repeats;
New rais'd objections with new quibbles meets;
Till, sinking in the quicksand he defends,
He dies disputing, and the contest ends—
But not the mischiefs; they, still left behind,
Like thistle-seeds, are sown by ev'ry wind.
 Thus men go wrong with an ingenious skill;
Bend the straight rule to their own crooked will;
And with a clear and shining lamp supplied,
First put it out, then take it for a guide.
Halting on crutches of unequal size,
One leg by truth supported, one by lies;
They sidle to the goal with awkward pace,
Secure of nothing—but to lose the race.
 Faults in the life breed errors in the brain,
And these reciprocally those again.
The mind and conduct mutually imprint
And stamp their image in each other's mint;
Each, sire and dam, of an infernal race,
Begetting and conceiving all that's base.
 None sends his arrow to the mark in view,
Whose hand is feeble, or his aim untrue.
For though, ere yet the shaft is on the wing,
Or when it first forsakes th' elastic string,
It err but little from th' intended line,
It falls at last far wide of his design:

So he, who seeks a mansion in the sky,
Must watch his purpose with a stedfast eye;
That prize belongs to none but the sincere:
The least obliquity is fatal here.
 With caution taste the sweet Circean cup;
He that sips often, at last drinks it up.
Habits are soon assum'd; but when we strive
To strip them off, 'tis being flay'd alive.
Call'd to the temple of impure delight,
He that abstains, and he alone, does right.
If a wish wander that way, call it home;
He cannot long be safe whose wishes roam.
But, if you pass the threshold, you are caught;
Die then, if pow'r Almighty save you not.
There hard'ning by degrees, till double steel'd,
Take leave of natures God, and God reveal'd;
Then laugh at all you trembled at before;
And, joining the free-thinkers' brutal roar,
Swallow the two grand nostrums they dispense—
That Scripture lies, and blasphemy is sense:
If clemency revolted by abuse
Be damnable, then damn'd without excuse.
 Some dream that they can silence, when they will,
The storm of passion, and say, *Peace, be still*;
But "*Thus far and no farther,*" when addres'd
To the wild wave, or wilder human breast,
Implies authority that never can,
That never ought to be the lot of man.
 But muse forbear; long flights forbode a fall;
Strike on the deep-ton'd chord the sum of all.
 Hear the just law—the judgment of the skies!
He that hates truth shall be the dupe of lies:
And he that *will* be cheated to the last,
Delusions strong as Hell shall bind him fast.
But if the wand'rer his mistake discern,
Judge his own ways, and sigh for a return,
Bewilder'd once, must he bewail his loss
For ever and for ever? No—the cross!
There and there only (though the deist rave,
And atheist, if Earth bear so base a slave);
There and there only is the pow'r to save.
There no delusive hope invites despair;
No mock'ry meets you, no deception there.
The spells and charms, that blinded you before,
All vanish there, and fascinate no more.
 I am no preacher, let this hint suffice—
The cross once seen is death to ev'ry vice:
Else he that hung there suffer'd all his pain,
Bled, groan'd, and agoniz'd, and died, in vain.

TRUTH.

"Pensantur trutinâ." *Hor.* Lib. ii. Epist. i.

Man, on the dubious waves of error toss'd,
His ship half-founder'd, and his compass lost,
Sees, far as human optics may command,
A sleeping fog, and fancies it dry land:
Spreads all his canvass, every sinew plies;
Pants for't, aims at it, enters it, and dies!
Then farewell all self-satisfying schemes,
His well-built systems, philosophic dreams;
Deceitful views of future bliss farewell!—
He reads his sentence at the flames of Hell.
Hard lot of man—to toil for the reward
Of virtue, and yet lose it! Wherefore hard?—
He that would win the race, must guide his horse
Obedient to the customs of the course;
Else, though unequall'd to the goal he flies,
A meaner than himself shall gain the prize.
Grace leads the right way: if you choose the wrong,
Take it and perish; but restrain your tongue;
Charge not, with light sufficient, and left free,
Your wilful suicide on God's decree.
O how unlike the complex works of man,
Heaven's easy, artless, unencumber'd plan!
No meretricious graces to beguile,
No clust'ring ornaments to clog the pile;
From ostentation as from weakness free,
It stands like the cerulean arch we see,
Majestic in its own simplicity.
Inscrib'd above the portal, from afar
Conspicuous, as the brightness of a star,
Legible only by the light they give,
Stand the soul-quick'ning words—*Believe and live.*
Too many, shock'd at what should charm them most,
Despise the plain direction, and are lost.
Heav'n on such terms! (they cry with proud disdain),
Incredible, impossible, and vain!—
Rebel, because 'tis easy to obey;

And scorn, for its own sake, the gracious way.
These are the sober, in whose cooler brains
Some thought of immortality remains;
The rest too busy, or too gay to wait
On the sad theme, their everlasting stat
Sport for a day, and perish in a night,
The foam upon the waters not so light.
Who judg'd the Pharisee? What odious cause
Expos'd him to the vengeance of the laws?
Had he seduc'd a virgin, wrong'd a friend,
Or stabb'd a man to serve some private end?
Was blasphemy his sin? Or did he stray
From the strict duties of the sacred day?
Sit long and late at the carousing board?
(Such were the sins with which he charg'd his Lord.)
No—the man's morals were exact, what then?
'Twas his ambition to be seen of men;
His virtues were his pride; and that one vice
Made all his virtues gew-gaws of no price;
He wore them as fine trappings for a show,
A praying, synagogue-frequenting beau.
The self-applauding bird, the peacock, see—
Mark what a sumptuous Pharisee is he!
Meridian sun-beams tempt him to unfold
His radiant glories, azure, green, and gold:
He treads as if, some solemn music near,
His measur'd step were govern'd by his ear:
And seems to say—Ye meaner fowl, give place,
I am all splendour, dignity, and grace!
Not so the pheasant on his charms presumes,
Though he too has a glory in his plumes.
He, Christian-like, retreats with modest mien
To the close copse, or far-sequester'd green,
And shines without desiring to be seen.
The plea of works, as arrogant and vain,
Heav'n turns from with abhorrence and disdain;
Not more affronted by avow'd neglect,
Than by the mere dissembler's feign'd respect.
What is all righteousness that men devise?
What—but a sordid bargain for the skies?
But Christ as soon would abdicate his own,
As stoop from Heav'n to sell the proud a throne.
His dwelling a recess in some rude rock,
Book, beads, and maple dish, his meagre stock;
In shirt of hair and weeds of canvass dress'd,
Girt with a bell-rope that the pope has bless'd;
Adust with stripes, told out for ev'ry crime,
And sore tormented long before his time;
His pray'r preferr'd to saints that cannot aid;

His praise postpon'd, and never to be paid;
See the sage hermit, by mankind admir'd,
With all that bigotry adopts inspir'd,
Wearing out life in his religious whim,
Till his religious whimsey wears out him.
His works, his abstinence, his zeal allow'd,
You think him humble—God accounts him proud;
High in demand, though lowly in pretence,
Of all his conduct this the genuine sense—
My penitential stripes, my streaming blood,
Have purchas'd Heav'n, and prove my title good.
  Turn eastward now, and Fancy shall apply
To your weak sight her telescopic eye.
The Bramin kindles on his own bare head
The sacred fire, self-torturing his trade,
His voluntary pains, severe and long,
Would give a barb'rous air to British song;
No grand inquisitor could worse invent,
Than he contrives to suffer, well content.
  Which is the saintlier worthy of the two?
Past all dispute, yon anchorite, say you.
Your sentence and mine differ. What's a name?
I say the Bramin has the fairer claim.
If suff'rings, Scripture no where recommends,
Devis'd by self to answer selfish ends,
Give saintship, then all Europe must agree
Ten starv'ling hermits suffer less than he.
  The truth is (if the truth may suit your ear,
And prejudice have left a passage clear),
Pride has attain'd its most luxuriant growth,
And poison'd ev'ry virtue in them both.
Pride may be pamper'd while the flesh grows lean
Humility may clothe an English dean;
That grace was Cowper's—his, confess'd by all—
Though plac'd in golden Durham's second stall.
Not all the plenty of a bishop's board,
His palace, and his lacqueys, and "My Lord,"
More nourish pride, that condescending vice,
Than abstinence, and beggary, and lice;
It thrive's in mis'ry, and abundant grows:
In mis'ry fools upon themselves impose.
  But why before us protestants produce
An Indian mystic, or a French recluse?
Their sin is plain; but what have we to fear,
Reform'd and well instructed? You shall hear.
  Yon ancient prude, whose wither'd features show
She might be young some forty years ago,
Her elbows pinion'd close upon her hips,
Her head erect, her fan upon her lips,

Her eye-brows arch'd, her eyes both gone astray
To watch yon am'rous couple in their play,
With bony and unkerchief'd neck defies
The rude inclemency of wintry skies,
And sails with lappet-head and mincing airs
Duly at chink of bell to morning pray'rs.
To thrift and parsimony much inclin'd,
She yet allows herself that boy behind;
The shiv'ring urchin, bending as he goes,
With slipshod heels, and dewdrop at his nose;
His predecessor's coat advanc'd to wear,
Which future pages yet are doom'd to share,
Carries her Bible tuck'd beneath his arm,
And hides his hands to keep his fingers warm.
She, half an angel in her own account,
Doubts not hereafter with the saints to mount,
Though not a grace appears on strictest search,
But that she fasts, and *item*, goes to church.
Conscious of age, she recollects her youth,
And tells, not always with an eye to truth,
Who spann'd her waist, and who, where'er he came,
Scrawl'd upon glass Miss Bridget's lovely name;
Who stole her slipper, fill'd it with tokay,
And drank the little bumper ev'ry day.
Of temper as envenom'd as an asp,
Censorious, and her ev'ry word a wasp;
In faithful mem'ry she records the crimes,
Or real or fictitious, of the times;
Laughs at the reputations she has torn,
And holds them dangling at arm's length in scorn.
Such are the fruits of sanctimonious pride,
Of malice fed while flesh is mortified:
Take, Madam, the reward of all your pray'rs,
Where hermits and where Bramins meet with theirs;
Your portion is with them.—Nay, never frown,
But, if you please, some fathoms lower down.
Artist attend—your brushes and your paint—
Produce them—take a chair—now draw a saint.
Oh sorrowful and sad! the streaming tears
Channel her cheeks—a Niobe appears!
Is this a saint? Throw tints and all away—
True Piety is cheerful as the day,
Will weep indeed and heave a pitying groan
For others' woes, but smiles upon her own.
What purpose has the King of saints in view?
Why falls the Gospel like a gracious dew?
To call up plenty from the teeming earth,
Or curse the desert with a ten-fold dearth?
Is it that Adam's offspring may be sav'd

From servile fear, or be the more enslav'd?
To loose the links that gall'd mankind before,
Or bind them faster on, and add still more?
The freeborn Christian has no chains to prove,
Or, if a chain, the golden one of love:
No fear attends to quench his glowing fires,
What fear he feels, his gratitude inspires.
Shall he, for such deliv'rance freely wrought,
Recompense ill? He trembles at the thought.
His Master's int'rest and his own combin'd
Prompt ev'ry movement of his heart and mind:
Thought, word, and deed his liberty evince,
His freedom is the freedom of a prince.
  Man's obligations infinite, of course
His life should prove that he perceives their force;
His utmost he can render is but small—
The principle and motive all in all.
You have two servants—Tom, an arch, sly rogue,
From top to toe the Geta now in vogue,
Genteel in figure, easy in address,
Moves without noise, and swift as an express,
Reports a message with a pleasing grace,
Expert in all the duties of his place;
Say, on what hinge does his obedience move?
Has he a world of gratitude and love?
No, not a spark—'tis all mere sharper's play;
He likes your house, your housemaid, and you pay;
Reduce his wages, or get rid of her,
Tom quits you, with—Your most obedient, Sir.
  The dinner serv'd, Charles takes his usual stand,
Watches your eye, anticipates command;
Sighs if perhaps your appetite should fail;
And if he but suspects a frown, turns pale;
Consults all day your int'rest and your ease,
Richly rewarded if he can but please;
And, proud to make his firm attachment known,
To save your life would nobly risk his own.
  Now which stands highest in your serious thought?
Charles, without doubt, say you—and so he ought;
One act, that from a thankful heart proceeds,
Excels ten thousand mercenary deeds.
  Thus Heav'n approves, as honest and sincere,
The work of gen'rous love and filial fear;
But with averted eyes th' omniscient Judge
Scorns the base hireling, and the slavish drudge.
Where dwell these matchless saints?—old Curio cries.
E'en at your side, Sir, and before your eyes,
The favour'd few—th' enthusiasts you despise.
And pleas'd at heart, because on holy ground

Sometimes a canting hypocrite is found,
Reproach a people with his single fall,
And cast his filthy raiment at them all,
Attend!—an apt similitude shall show
Whence springs the conduct that offends you so.
See where it smokes along the sounding plain,
Blown all aslant, a driving dashing rain,
Peal upon peal redoubling all around,
Shakes it again and faster to the ground;
Now flashing wide, now glancing as in play,
Swift beyond thought the lightnings dart away.
Ere yet it came the trav'ller urg'd his steed,
And hurried, but with unsuccessful speed;
Now drench'd throughout, and hopeless of his case,
He drops the rein, and leaves him to his pace.
Suppose, unlook'd-for in a scene so rude,
Long hid by interposing hill or wood,
Some mansion, neat and elegantly dress'd,
By some kind hospitable heart possess'd,
Offer him warmth, security, and rest;
Think with what pleasure, safe, and at his ease,
He hears the tempest howling in the trees;
What glowing thanks his lips and heart employ,
While danger past is turn'd to present joy,
So fares it with the sinner, when he feels
A growing dread of vengeance at his heels:
His conscience, like a glassy lake before,
Lash'd into foaming waves, begins to roar;
The law grown clamorous, though silent long,
Arraigns him—charges him with ev'ry wrong—
Asserts the rights of his offended Lord,
And death or restitution is the word:
The last impossible, he fears the first,
And, having well deserv'd, expects the worst.
Then welcome refuge, and a peaceful home;
Oh for a shelter from the wrath to come!
Crush me, ye rocks! ye falling mountains hide,
Or bury me in ocean's angry tide.—
The scrutiny of those all-seeing eyes
I dare not—And you need not, God replies;
The remedy you want I freely give:
The Book shall teach you—read, believe, and live!
'Tis done—the raging storm is heard no more,
Mercy receives him on her peaceful shore:
And Justice, guardian of the dread command,
Drops the red vengeance from his willing hand.
A soul redeem'd demands a life of praise;
Hence the complexion of his future days,
Hence a demeanour holy and unspeck'd,

And the world's hatred, as its sure effect.
  Some lead a life unblameable and just,
Their own dear virtue their unshaken trust:
They never sin—or if (as all offend)
Some trivial slips their daily walk attend,
The poor are near at hand, the charge is small,
A slight gratuity atones for all.
For though the pope has lost his int'rest here,
And pardons are not sold as once they were,
No papist more desirous to compound,
Than some grave sinners upon English ground.
That plea refuted, other quirks they seek—
Mercy is infinite, and man is weak;
The future shall obliterate the past,
And Heav'n no doubt shall be their home at last.
  Come then—a still, small whisper in your ear—
He has no hope who never had a fear;
And he that never doubted of his state,
He may perhaps—perhaps he may—too late.
  The path to bliss abounds with many a snare;
Learning is one, and wit, however rare.
The Frenchman, first in literary fame,
(Mention him if you please. Voltaire?—The same,)
With spirit, genius, eloquence, supplied,
Liv'd long, wrote much, laugh'd heartily, and died.
The Scripture was his jest-book, whence he drew
Bon mots to gall the Christian and the Jew;
An infidel in health, but what when sick?
Oh—then a text would touch him to the quick:
View him at Paris in his last career,
Surrounding throngs the demigod revere;
Exalted on his pedestal of pride,
And fum'd with frankincense on ev'ry side,
He begs their flatt'ry with his latest breath,
And smother'd in't at last, is prais'd to death.
  Yon cottager, who weaves at her own door,
Pillow and bobbins all her little store;
Content though mean, and cheerful if not gay,
Shuffling her threads about the livelong day,
Just earns a scanty pittance, and at night
Lies down secure, her heart and pocket light;
She, for her humble sphere by nature fit;
Has little understanding, and no wit,
Receives no praise; but, though her lot be such,
(Toilsome and indigent) she renders much;
Just knows, and knows no more, her Bible true—
A truth the brilliant Frenchman never knew;
And in that charter reads with sparkling eyes
Her title to a treasure in the skies.

O happy peasant! Oh unhappy bard!
His the mere tinsel, hers the rich reward;
He prais'd perhaps for ages yet to come,
She never heard of half a mile from home:
He lost in errors his vain heart prefers,
She safe in the simplicity of hers.
Not many wise, rich, noble, or profound
In science, win one inch of heav'nly ground.
And is it not a mortifying thought
The poor should gain it, and the rich should not?
No—the voluptuaries, who ne'er forget
One pleasure lost, lose Heav'n without regret;
Regret would rouse them, and give birth to pray'r;
Pray'r would add faith, and faith would fix them there.
Not that the Former of us all, in this,
Or aught he does, is govern'd by caprice;
The supposition is replete with sin,
And bears the brand of blasphemy burnt in.
Not so—the silver trumpet's heav'nly call
Sounds for the poor, but sounds alike for all:
Kings are invited, and would kings obey,
No slaves on earth more welcome were than they:
But royalty, nobility, and state,
Are such a dead preponderating weight,
That endless bliss (how strange soe'er it seem)
In counterpoise, flies up and kicks the beam.
'Tis open, and ye cannot enter—why?
Because ye will not, Conyers would reply—
And he says much that many may dispute,
And cavil at with ease, but none refute.
O bless'd effect of penury and want;
The seed sown there, how vigorous is the plant!
No soil like poverty for growth divine,
As leanest land supplies the richest wine.
Earth gives too little, giving only bread,
To nourish pride, or turn the weakest head;
To them the sounding jargon of the schools
Seems what it is—a cap and bell for fools:
The light they walk by, kindled from above,
Shows them the shortest way to life and love:
They, strangers to the controversial field,
Where deists, always foil'd, yet scorn to yield,
And never check'd by what impedes the wise,
Believe, rush forward, and possess the prize.
Envy, ye great, the dull unletter'd small:
Ye have much cause for envy—but not all.
We boast some rich ones whom the Gospel sways,
And one who wears a coronet and prays;
Like gleanings of an olive-tree they show,

Here and there one upon the topmost bough.
How readily upon the Gospel plan,
That question has its answer—What is man?
Sinful and weak, in ev'ry sense a wretch;
An instrument, whose chords upon the stretch,
And strain'd to the last screw that he can bear,
Yield only discord in his Maker's ear:
Once the blest residence of truth divine,
Glorious as Solyma's interior shrine,
Where, in his own oracular abode,
Dwelt visibly the light-creating God;
But made long since, like Babylon of old,
A den of mischiefs never to be told:
And she, once mistress of the realms around,
Now scatter'd wide, and no where to be found,
As soon shall rise and reascend the throne,
By native pow'r and energy her own,
As Nature, at her own peculiar cost,
Restore to man the glories he has lost.
Go—bid the winter cease to chill the year,
Replace the wand'ring comet in his sphere,
Then boast (but wait for that unhop'd-for hour)
The self-restoring arm of human power.
But what is man in his own proud esteem?
Hear him—himself the poet and the theme:
A monarch cloth'd with majesty and awe,
His mind his kingdom, and his will his law,
Grace in his mien, and glory in his eyes,
Supreme on earth, and worthy of the skies,
Strength in his heart, dominion in his nod,
And, thunderbolts excepted, quite a God!
So sings he, charm'd with his own mind and form,
The song magnificent—the theme a worm!
Himself so much the source of his delight,
His Maker has no beauty in his sight.
See where he sits, contemplative and fix'd,
Pleasure and wonder in his features mix'd,
His passions tam'd and all at his control,
How perfect the composure of his soul!
Complacency has breath'd a gentle gale
O'er all his thoughts, and swell'd his easy sail:
His books well trimm'd and in the gayest style,
Like regimental coxcombs, rank and file,
Adorn his intellects as well as shelves,
And teach him notions splendid as themselves
The Bible only stands neglected there,
Though that of all most worthy of his care;
And, like an infant troublesome awake,
Is left to sleep for peace and quiet's sake.

What shall the man deserve of human kind,
Whose happy skill and industry combin'd
Shall prove (what argument could never yet)
The Bible an imposture and a cheat?
The praises of the libertine professed,
The worst of men, and curses of the best.
Where should the living, weeping o'er his woes;
The dying, trembling at the awful close;
Where the betray'd, forsaken, and oppress'd,
The thousands whom the world forbids to rest;
Where should they find (those comforts at an end
The Scripture yields,) or hope to find, a friend?
Sorrow might muse herself to madness then,
And, seeking exile from the sight of men,
Bury herself in solitude profound,
Grow frantic with her pangs, and bite the ground.
Thus often Unbelief, grown sick of life,
Flies to the tempting pool, or felon knife.
The jury meet, the coroner is short,
And lunacy the verdict of the court;
Reverse the sentence, let the truth be known,
Such lunacy is ignorance alone;
They knew not, what some bishops may not know,
That Scripture is the only cure of woe;
That field of promise, how it flings abroad
Its odour o'er the Christian's thorny road!
The soul, reposing on assur'd relief,
Feels herself happy amidst all her grief,
Forgets her labour as she toils along,
Weeps tears of joy, and bursts into a song.
But the same word, that, like the polish'd share,
Ploughs up the roots of a believer's care,
Kills too the flow'ry weeds, where'er they grow,
That bind the sinner's Bacchanalian brow.
Oh that unwelcome voice of heavenly love,
Sad messenger of mercy from above!
How does it grate upon his thankless ear,
Crippling his pleasures with the cramp of fear!
His will and judgment at continual strife,
That civil war embitters all his life:
In vain he points his pow'rs against the skies,
In vain he closes or averts his eyes,
Truth will intrude—she bids him yet beware;
And shakes the sceptic in the scorner's chair.
Though various foes against the Truth combine,
Pride above all opposes her design;
Pride, of a growth superior to the rest,
The subtlest serpent with the loftiest crest,
Swells at the thought, and, kindling into rage,

Would hiss the cherub Mercy from the stage.
  And is the soul indeed so lost?—she cries,
Fall'n from her glory, and too weak to rise?
Torpid and dull beneath a frozen zone,
Has she no spark that may be deem'd her own?
Grant her indebted to what zealots call
Grace undeserv'd, yet surely not for all—
Some beams of rectitude she yet displays,
Some love of virtue, and some pow'r to praise;—
Can lift herself above coporeal things,
And, soaring on her own unborrow'd wings,
Possess herself of all that's good or true,
Assert the skies, and vindicate her due.
Past indiscretion is a venial crime,
And if the youth, unmellow'd yet by time,
Bore on his branch, luxuriant then and rude,
Fruits of a blighted size, austere and crude,
Maturer years shall happier stores produce,
And meliorate the well-concocted juice.
Then, conscious of her meritorious zeal,
To justice she may make her bold appeal,
And leave to mercy, with a tranquil mind,
The worthless and unfruitful of mankind.
Hear then how Mercy, slighted and defied,
Retorts th'affront against the crown of Pride
  Perish the virtue, as it ought, abhorr'd,
And the fool with it, who insults his Lord.
Th'atonement, a Redeemer's love has wrought,
Is not for you—the righteous need it not.
Seest thou yon harlot, wooing all she meets,
The worn-out nuisance of the public streets,
Herself from morn to night, from night to morn,
Her own abhorrence, and as much your scorn
The gracious show'r, unlimited and free,
Shall fall on her, when Heav'n denies it thee.
Of all that wisdom dictates, this the drift,
That man is dead in sin, and life a gift.
  Is virtue, then, unless of Christian growth,
Mere fallacy, or foolishness, or both?
Ten thousand sages lost in endless woe,
For ignorance of what they could not know?
That speech betrays at once a bigot's tongue,
Charge not a God with such outrageous wrong.
Truly not I—the partial light men have,
My creed persuades me, well-employ'd, may save;
While he that scorns the noonday beam, perverse,
Shall find the blessing unimprov'd a curse.
Let heathen worthies, whose exalted mind
Left sensuality and dross behind,

Possess for me the undisputed lot,
And take unenvied the reward they sought:
But still in virtue of a Saviour's plea,
Not blind by choice, but destin'd not to see.
Their fortitude and wisdom were a flame
Celestial, though they knew not whence it came,
Deriv'd from the same source of light and grace,
That guides the Christian in his swifter race;
Their judge was conscience, and her rule their law,
That rule, pursued with reverence and with awe,
Led them, however falt'ring, faint, and slow,
From what they knew, to what they wish'd to know.
But let not him, that shares a brighter day,
Traduce the splendour of a noontide ray,
Prefer the twilight of a darker time,
And deem his base stupidity no crime:
The wretch, who slights the bounty of the skies,
And sinks, while favour'd with the means to rise,
Shall find them rated at their full amount;
The good he scorn'd all carried to account.
  Marshalling all his terrors as he came,
Thunder, and earthquake, and devouring flame,
From Sinai's top Jehovah gave the law,
Life for obedience, death for ev'ry flaw.
When the great Sovereign would his will express,
He gives a perfect rule; what can he less?
And guards it with a sanction as severe
As vengeance can inflict, or sinners fear:
Else his own glorious rights he would disclaim,
And man might safely trifle with his name.
He bids him glow with unremitting love
To all on earth, and to himself above;
Condemns th'injurious deed, the sland'rous tongue,
The thought that meditates a brother's wrong
Brings not alone the more conspicuous part,
His conduct, to the test, but tries his heart.
  Hark! universal nature shook and groan'd,
'Twas the last trumpet—see the Judge enthron'd:
Rouse all your courage at your utmost need,
Now summon ev'ry virtue, stand and plead.
What! silent? Is your boasting heard no more?
That self-renouncing wisdom, learn'd before,
Had shed immortal glories on your brow,
That all your virtues cannot purchase now.
  All joy to the believer! He can speak—
Trembling yet happy, confident yet meek.
  Since the dear hour, that brought me to thy foot,
And cut up all my follies by the root,
I never trusted in an arm but thine,

Nor hop'd, but in thy righteousness divine :
My pray'rs and alms, imperfect and defil'd,
Were but the feeble efforts of a child:
Howe'er perform'd, it was their brightest part,
That they proceeded from a grateful heart ;
Cleans'd in thine own all purifying blood,
Forgive their evil, and accept their good ;
I cast them at thy feet—my only plea
Is what it was, dependence upon thee,
While struggling in the vale of tears below,
That never fail'd, nor shall it fail me now.
Angelic gratulations rend the skies,
Pride falls unpitied, never more to rise,
Humility is crown'd, and faith receives the prize.

EXPOSTULATION.

'Tantane, tam patiens, nullo certamine tolli
Dona sines?' *Virg.*

Why weeps the muse for England? What appears
In England's case, to move the muse to tears?
From side to side of her delighful isle
Is she not cloth'd with a perpetual smile?
Can Nature add a charm, or Art confer
A new-found luxury not seen in her?
Where under heav'n is pleasure more pursued,
Or where does cold reflection less intrude?
Her fields a rich expanse of wavy corn,
Pour'd out from Plenty's overflowing horn;
Ambrosial gardens, in which Art supplies
The fervour and the force of Indian skies;
Her peaceful shores, where busy Commerce waits
To pour his golden tide through all her gates;
Whom fiery suns, that scorch the russet spice
Of eastern groves, and oceans floor'd with ice,
Forbid in vain to push his daring way
To darker climes, or climes of brighter day;
Whom the winds waft where'er the billows roll,
From the world's girdle to the frozen pole;
The chariots bounding in her wheel-worn streets,
Her vaults below, where ev'ry vintage meets;
Her theatres, her revels, and her sports;
The scenes to which not youth alone resorts,
But age, in spite of weakness and of pain,
Still haunts, in hope to dream of youth again;
All speak her happy: let the muse look round
From East to West, no sorrow can be found;
Or only what, in cottages confin'd,
Sighs unregarded to the passing wind.
Then wherefore weep for England? What appears
In England's case, to move the muse to tears?

EXPOSTULATION

The prophet wept for Israel; wish'd his eyes
Were fountains fed with infinite supplies:
For Israel dealt in robbery and wrong;
There were the scorner's and the sland'rer's tongue;
Oaths, us'd as playthings or convenient tools,
As int'rest biass'd knaves, or fashion fools;
Adult'ry, neighing at his neighbour's door;
Oppression, lab'ring hard to grind the poor;
The partial balance, and deceitful weight;
The treach'rous smile, a mask for secret hate;
Hypocrisy, formality in pray'r,
And the dull service of the lip were there.
Her women, insolent and self-caress'd,
By Vanity's unwearied finger dress'd,
Forgot the blush, that virgin fears impart
To modest cheeks, and borrow'd one from art;
Were just such trifles, without worth or use,
As silly pride and idleness produce;
Curl'd, scented, furbelow'd, and flounc'd around,
With feet too delicate to touch the ground,
They stretch'd the neck, and roll'd the wanton eye,
And sigh'd for every fool that flutter'd by.
He saw his people slaves to every lust,
Lew'd, avaricious, arrogant, unjust;
He heard the wheels of an avenging God
Groan heavily along the distant road;
Saw Babylon set wide her two-leav'd brass
To let the military deluge pass;
Jerusalem a prey, her glory soil'd,
Her princes captive, and her treasures spoil'd;
Wept till all Israel heard his bitter cry,
Stamp'd with his foot, and smote upon his thigh:
But wept, and stamp'd, and smote his thigh in vain;
Pleasure is deaf when told of future pain,
And sounds prophetic are too rough to suit
Ears long accustom'd to the pleasing lute:
They scorn'd his inspiration and his theme,
Pronounc'd him frantic, and his fears a dream;
With self-indulgence wing'd the fleeting hours,
Till the foe found them, and down fell the tow'rs.
Long time Assyria bound them in her chain,
Till penitence had purg'd the public stain,
And Cyrus, with relenting pity mov'd,
Return'd them happy to the land they lov'd;
There, proof against prosperity, a while
They stood the test of her ensnaring smile,
And had the grace in scenes of peace to show
The virtue they had learn'd in scenes of woe.
But man is frail, and can but ill sustain

A long immunity from grief and pain;
And after all the joys that Plenty leads,
With tiptoe step Vice silently succeeds.
When he that rul'd them with a shepherd's rod,
In form a man, in dignity a God,
Came, not expected in that humble guise,
To sift and search them with unerring eyes,
He found, conceal'd beneath a fair outside,
The filth of rottenness, and worm of pride;
Their piety a system of deceit,
Scripture employ'd to sanctify the cheat;
The Pharisee the dupe of his own art,
Self-idoliz'd, and yet a knave at heart.
When nations are to perish in their sins,
'Tis in the church the leprosy begins;
The priest, whose office is with zeal sincere
To watch the fountain, and preserve it clear,
Carelessly nods and sleeps upon the the brink,
While others poison what the flock must drink;
Or, waking at the call of lust alone,
Infuses lies and errors of his own;
His unsuspecting sheep believe it pure;
And, tainted by the very means of cure,
Catch from each other a contagious spot,
The foul forerunner of a gen'ral rot.
Then Truth is hush'd, that Heresy may preach;
And all is trash, that Reason cannot reach;
Then God's own image on the soul impress'd
Becomes a mockery, and a standing jest;
And faith, the root whence only can arise
The graces of a life that wins the skies,
Loses at once all value and esteem,
Pronounc'd by graybeards a pernicious dream:
Then Ceremony leads her bigots forth,
Prepar'd to fight for shadows of no worth;
While truths, on which eternal things depend,
Find not, or hardly find, a single friend:
As soldiers watch the signal of command,
They learn to bow, to kneel, to sit, to stand;
Happy to fill religion's vacant place
With hollow form, and gesture, and grimace.
Such, when the Teacher of his church was there,
People and priest, the sons of Irsael were;
Stiff in the letter, lax in the design
And import, of their oracles divine;
Their learning legendary, false, absurd,
And yet exalted above God's own word;
They drew a curse from an intended good,
Puff'd up with gifts they never understood.

He judg'd them with as terrible a frown,
As if not love, but wrath, had brought him down:
Yet he was gentle as soft summer airs,
Had grace for others' sins, but not for theirs;
Through all he spoke a noble plainness ran—
Rhet'ric is artifice, the work of man;
And tricks and turns, that fancy may devise,
Are far too mean for Him that rules the skies.
Th'astonish'd vulgar trembled when he tore
The mask from faces never seen before;
He stripp'd th'impostors in the noonday sun,
Show'd that they follow'd all they seem'd to shun;
Their pray'rs made public, their excesses kept
As private as the chambers where they slept;
The temple and its holy rites profan'd
By mumm'ries, he that dwelt in it disdain'd;
Uplifted hands, that at convenient times
Could act extortion and the worst of crimes,
Wash'd with a neatness scrupulously nice,
And free from ev'ry taint but that of vice.
Judgment, however tardy, mends her pace
When Obstinacy once has conquer'd Grace.
They saw distemper heal'd, and life restor'd,
In answer to the fiat of his word;
Confess'd the wonder, and with daring tongue
Blasphem'd th'authority from which it sprung.
They knew by sure prognostics seen on high,
The future tone and temper of the sky;
But, grave dissemblers! could not understand
That Sin let loose speaks Punishment at hand.
    Ask now of history's authentic page,
And call up evidence from ev'ry age;
Display with busy and laborious hand
The blessings of the most indebted land;
What nation will you find, whose annals prove
So rich an int'rest in almighty love?
Where dwell they now, where dwelt in ancient day
A people planted, water'd, blest as they?
Let Egypt's plagues and Canaan's woes proclaim
The favours pour'd upon the Jewish name;
Their freedom purchas'd for them at the cost
Of all their hard oppressors valued most;
Their title to a country not their own
Made sure by prodigies till then unknown;
For them the states they left, made waste and void;
For them the states to which they went, destroy'd;
A cloud to measure out their march by day,
By night a fire to cheer the gloomy way;
That moving signal summoning, when best,

Their host to move, and when it stay'd to rest.
For them the rocks dissolv'd into a flood,
The dews condens'd into angelic food,
Their very garments sacred, old yet new,
And time forbid to touch them as he flew;
Streams, swell'd above the bank, enjoin'd to stand,
While they pass'd through to their appointed land;
Their leader arm'd with meekness, zeal, and love,
And grac'd with clear credentials from above;
Themselves secur'd beneath th'Almighty wing!
Their God their captain, lawgiver, and king;
Crown'd with a thousand vict'ries, and at last
Lords of the conquer'd soil, there rooted fast,
In peace possessing what they won by war,
Their name far publish'd and rever'd as far;
Where will you find a race like theirs, endow'd
With all that man e'er wish'd, or Heav'n bestow'd?
  They, and they only, amongst all mankind,
Receiv'd the transcript of th'eternal mind;
Were trusted with his own engraven laws,
And constituted guardians of his cause;
Theirs were the prophets, theirs the priestly call,
And theirs by birth the Saviour of us all.
In vain the nations, that had seen them rise
With fierce and envious yet admiring eyes,
Had sought to crush them, guarded as they were
By pow'r divine, and skill that could not err.
Had they maintain'd allegiance firm and sure,
And kept the faith immaculate and pure,
Then the proud eagles of all-conqu'ring Rome
Had found one city not to be o'ercome;
And the twelve standards of the tribes unfurl'd
Had bid defiance to the warring world.
But grace abus'd brings forth the foulest deeds,
As richest soil the most luxuriant weeds.
Cur'd of the golden calves, their fathers' sin,
They set up self, that idol god within;
View'd a Deliv'rer with disdain and hate,
Who left them still a tributary state;
Seiz'd fast his hand, held out to set them free
From a worse yoke, and nail'd it to the tree:
There was the consummation and the crown,
The flow'r of Israel's infamy full blown;
Thence date their sad declension and their fall,
Their woes not yet repeal'd, thence date them all.
  Thus fell the best instructed in her day,
And the most favour'd land, look where we may.
Philosophy indeed on Grecian eyes
Had pour'd the day, and clear'd the Roman skies;

In other climes perhaps creative Art,
With pow'r surpassing theirs, perform'd her part,
Might give more life to marble, or might fill
The glowing tablets with a juster skill,
Might shine in fable, and grace idle themes
With all th'embroid'ry of poetic dreams;
'Twas theirs alone to dive into the plan,
That Truth and Mercy had reveal'd to man;
And while the World beside, that plan unknown,
Deified useless wood, or senseless stone,
They breath'd in faith their well-directed pray'rs,
And the true God, the God of truth, was theirs.
  Their glory faded, and their race dispers'd,
The last of nations now, though once the first;
They warn and teach the proudest, would they learn,
Keep wisdom, or meet vengeance in your turn:
If we escap'd not, if Heav'n spar'd not us,
Peel'd, scatter'd, and exterminated thus;
If Vice receiv'd her retribution due,
When we were visited, what hope for you?
When God arises with an awful frown
To punish lust, or pluck presumption down;
When gifts perverted, or not duly priz'd,
Pleasure o'ervalued, and his grace despis'd,
Provoke the vengeance of his righteous hand,
To pour down wrath upon a thankless land;
He will be found impartially severe,
Too just to wink, or speak the guilty clear.
  Oh Israel, of all nations most undone!
Thy diadem displac'd, thy sceptre gone;
Thy temple, once thy glory, fall'n and ras'd,
And thou a worshipper e'en where thou mayst;
Thy services, once holy, without spot,
Mere shadows now, their ancient pomp forgot;
Thy Levites, once a consecrated host,
No longer Levites, and their lineage lost,
And thou thyself o'er ev'ry country sown,
With none on Earth that thou canst call thine own;
Cry aloud, thou that sittest in the dust,
Cry to the proud, the cruel, and unjust;
Knock at the gates of nations, rouse their fears;
Say wrath is coming, and the storm appears;
But raise the shrillest cry in British ears.
  What ails thee, restless as the waves that roar,
And fling their foam against thy chalky shore?
Mistress, at least while Providence shall please,
And trident-bearing queen of the wide seas—
Why, having kept good faith, and often shown
Friendship and truth to others, find'st thou none?

Thou that hast set the persecuted free,
None interposes now to succour thee.
Countries indebted to thy pow'r, that shine
With light deriv'd from thee, would smother thine;
Thy very children watch for thy disgrace—
A lawless brood, and curse thee to thy face.
Thy rulers load thy credit, year by year,
With sums Peruvian mines could never clear;
As if, like arches built with skilful hand,
The more 'twere press'd the firmer it would stand.
The cry in all thy ships is still the same,
Speed us away to battle and to fame.
Thy mariners explore the wide expanse,
Impatient to descry the flags of France;
But, though they fight as thine have ever fought,
Return asham'd without the wreaths they sought.
Thy senate is a scene of civil jar,
Chaos of contrarieties at war;
Where sharp and solid, phlegmatic and light,
Discordant atoms meet, ferment, and fight;
Where Obstinacy takes his sturdy stand,
To disconcert what Policy has plann'd;
Where Policy is busied all night long
In setting right what Faction has set wrong;
Where flails of oratory thrash the floor,
That yields them chaff and dust, and nothing more.
Thy rack'd inhabitants repine, complain,
Tax'd till the brow of Labour sweats in vain;
War lays a burden on the reeling state,
And peace does nothing to relieve the weight;
Successive loads succeeding broils impose,
And sighing millions prophesy the close.
Is adverse Providence, when ponder'd well,
So dimly writ, or difficult to spell,
Thou canst not read with readiness and ease
Providence adverse in events like these?
Know then that heav'nly wisdom on this ball
Creates, gives birth to, guides, consummates all;
That, while laborious and quick-thoughted man
Snuffs up the praise of what he seems to plan,
He first conceives, then perfects his design,
As a mere instrument in hands divine:
Blind to the working of that secret pow'r,
That balances the wings of ev'ry hour,
The busy trifler dreams himself alone,
Frames many a purpose, and God works his own.
States thrive and wither as moons wax and wane,
E'en as his will and his decrees ordain;
While honour, virtue, piety, bear sway,

They flourish; and as these decline, decay:
In just resentment of his injur'd laws,
He pours contempt on them and on their cause;
Strikes the rough thread of error right athwart
The web of ev'ry scheme they have at heart;
Bids rottenness invade and bring to dust
The pillars of support, in which they trust,
And do his errand of disgrace and shame
On the chief strength and glory of the frame.
None ever yet impeded what he wrought,
None bars him out from his most secret thought:
Darkness itself before his eye is light,
And hell's close mischief naked in his sight.
  Stand now and judge thyself—Hast thou incurr'd
His anger, who can waste thee with a word,
Who poises and proportions sea and land,
Weighing them in the hollow of his hand,
And in whose awful sight all nations seem
As grasshoppers, as dust, a drop, a dream?
Hast thou (a sacrilege his soul abhors)
Claim'd all the glory of thy prosp'rous wars?
Proud of thy fleets and armies, stol'n the gem
Of his just praise, to lavish it on them?
Hast thou not learn'd, what thou art often told,
A truth still sacred, and believ'd of old,
That no success attends on spears and swords
Unblest, and that the battle is the Lord's?
That courage is his creature; and dismay
The post, that at his bidding speeds away,
Ghastly in feature, and his stamm'ring tongue
With doleful humour and sad presage hung,
To quell the valour of the stoutest heart,
And teach the combatant a woman's part?
That he bids thousands fly when none pursue,
Saves as he will by many or by few,
And claims for ever, as his royal right,
Th'event and sure decision of the fight?
Hast thou, though suckled at fair Freedom's breast,
Exported slav'ry to the conquer'd East?
Pull'd down the tyrants India serv'd with dread,
And rais'd thyself, a greater, in their stead?
Gone thither arm'd and hungry, return'd full,
Fed from the richest veins of the mogul,
A despot big with pow'r obtain'd by wealth,
And that obtain'd by rapine and by stealth?
With Asiatic vices stor'd thy mind,
But left their virtues and thine own behind?
And, having truck'd thy soul, brought home the fee,
To tempt the poor to sell himself to thee?

Hast thou by statue shov'd from its design
The Saviour's feast, his own blest bread and wine,
And made the symbols of atoning grace
An office-key, a picklock to a place,
That infidels may prove their title good
By an oath dipp'd in sacramental blood?
A blot that will be still a blot, in spite
Of all that grave apologists may write;
And though a bishop toil to cleanse the stain,
He wipes and scours the silver cup in vain.
And hast thou sworn on ev'ry slight pretence,
Till perjuries are common as bad pence,
While thousands, careless of the damning sin,
Kiss the book's outside, who ne'er looked within?
Hast thou, when Heav'n has cloth'd thee with disgrace,
And, long provok'd, repaid thee to thy face,
(For thou hast known eclipses, and endur'd
Dimness and anguish, all thy beams obscur'd,
When sin has shed dishonour on thy brow;
And never of a sabler hue than now,)
Hast thou, with heart perverse and conscience sear'd,
Despising all rebuke, still persever'd,
And having chosen evil, scorn'd the voice
That cried, Repent!—and gloried in thy choice?
Thy fastings, when calamity at last
Suggests th'expedient of a yearly fast,
What mean they? Canst thou dream there is a pow'r
In lighter diet at a later hour,
To charm to sleep the threat'ning of the skies,
And hide past folly from all-seeing eyes?
The fast, that wins deliverance, and suspends
The stroke, that a vindictive God intends,
Is to renounce hypocrisy; to draw
Thy life upon the pattern of the law;
To war with pleasure, idoliz'd before;
To vanquish lust, and wear its yoke no more.
All fasting else, whate'er be the pretence,
Is wooing mercy by renew'd offence.
Hast thou within the sin, that in old time
Brought fire from Heav'n, the sex-abusing crime,
Whose horrid perpetration stamps disgrace,
Baboons are free from, upon human race?
Think on the fruitful and well-water'd spot,
That fed the flocks and herds of wealthy Lot,
Where Paradise seem'd still vouchsaf'd on earth,
Burning and scorch'd into perpetual dearth,
Or, in his words who damn'd the base desire,
Suff'ring the vengeance of eternal fire:
Then Nature injur'd, scandaliz'd, defil'd,

Unveil'd her blushing cheek, look'd on, and smil'd;
Beheld with joy the lovely scene defac'd,
And prais'd the wrath that laid her beauties waste.
Far be the thought from any verse of mine,
And farther still the form'd and fix'd design,
To thrust the charge of deeds that I detest,
Against an innocent, unconscious breast:
The man that dares traduce, because he can
With safety to himself, is not a man:
An individual is a sacred mark,
Not to be pierc'd in play, or in the dark;
But public censure speaks a public foe,
Unless a zeal for virtue guide the blow.
The priestly brotherhood, devout, sincere,
From mean self-int'rest and ambition clear,
Their hope in heav'n, servility their scorn,
Prompt to persuade, expostulate, and warn,
Their wisdom pure, and giv'n them from above,
Their usefulness ensur'd by zeal and love,
As meek as the man Moses, and withal
As bold as in Agrippa's presence Paul,
Should fly the world's contaminating touch,
Holy and unpolluted:—are thine such?
Except a few with Eli's spirit blest,
Hophni and Phineas may describe the rest.
Where shall a teacher look, in days like these,
For ears and hearts, that he can hope to please?
Look to the poor—the simple and the plain
Will hear perhaps thy salutary strain:
Humility is gentle, apt to learn,
Speak but the word, will listen and return.
Alas, not so! the poorest of the flock
Are proud, and set their faces as a rock;
Denied that earthly opulence they choose,
God's better gift they scoff at and refuse.
The rich, the produce of a nobler stem,
Are more intelligent at least—try them.
Oh vain inquiry! they without remorse
Are altogether gone a devious course;
When beck'ning Pleasure leads them, wildly stray;
Have burst the bands, and cast the yoke away.
Now borne upon the wings of truth sublime,
Review thy dim original and prime.
This island, spot of unreclaim'd rude earth,
The cradle that receiv'd thee at thy birth,
Was rock'd by many a rough Norwegian blast,
And Danish howlings scar'd thee as they pass'd;
For thou wast born amid the din of arms,
And suck'd a breast that panted with alarms.

While yet thou wast a grov'ling puling chit,
Thy bones not fashion'd, and thy joints not knit,
The Roman taught thy stubborn knee to bow,
Though twice a Cæsar could not bend thee now.
His victory was that of orient light,
When the sun's shafts disperse the gloom of night.
Thy language at this distant moment shows
How much the country to the conqu'ror owes;
Expressive, energetic, and refin'd,
It sparkles with the gems he left behind:
He brought thy land a blessing when he came,
He found thee savage, and he left thee tame;
Taught thee to clothe thy pink'd and painted hide,
And grace thy figure with a soldier's pride;
He sow'd the seeds of order where he went,
Improv'd thee far beyond his own intent,
And, while he rul'd thee by the sword alone,
Made thee at last a warrior like his own.
Religion, if in heav'nly truths attir'd,
Needs only to be seen to be admir'd;
But thine, as dark as witch'ries of the night,
Was form'd to harden hearts and shock the sight;
Thy Druids struck the well-hung harps they bore
With fingers deeply dyed in human gore;
And while the victim slowly bled to death,
Upon the rolling chords rung out his dying breath.
Who brought the lamp, that with awaking beams
Dispell'd thy gloom, and broke away thy dreams,
Tradition, now decrepit and worn out,
Babbler of ancient fables, leaves a doubt:
But still light reach'd thee; and those gods of thine,
Woden and Thor, each tott'ring in his shrine,
Fell broken and defac'd at his own door,
As Dagon in Philistia long before.
But Rome, with sorceries and magic wand,
Soon rais'd a cloud that darken'd ev'ry land;
And thine was smother'd in the stench and fog
Of Tiber's marshes and the papal bog.
Then priests, with bulls and briefs, and shaven crowns,
And griping fists, and unrelenting frowns,
Legates and delegates with pow'rs from hell,
Though heav'nly in pretension, fleec'd thee well;
And to this hour, to keep it fresh in mind,
Some twigs of that old scourge are left behind.*
Thy soldiery, the Pope's well-manag'd pack,
Were train'd beneath his lash, and knew the smack;
And, when he laid them on the scent of blood,

* Which may be found at Doctors' Commons.

Would hunt a Saracen through fire and flood.
Lavish of life, to win an empty tomb,
That prov'd a mint of wealth, a mine to Rome,
They left their bones beneath unfriendly skies,
His worthless absolution all the prize.
Thou wast the veriest slave in days of yore,
That ever dragg'd a chain or tugg'd an oar;
Thy monarchs, arbitrary, fierce, unjust,
Themselves the slaves of bigotry or lust,
Disdain'd thy counsels, only in distress
Found thee a goodly sponge for Pow'r to press.
Thy chiefs, the lords of many a petty fee,
Provok'd and harass'd, in return plagu'd thee;
Call'd thee away from peaceable employ,
Domestic happiness and rural joy,
To waste thy life in arms, or lay it down
In causeless feuds and bick'rings of their own.
Thy parliaments ador'd on bended knees
The sov'reignty they were conven'd to please;
Whate'er was ask'd, too timid to resist,
Complied with, and were graciously dismiss'd;
And if some Spartan soul a doubt express'd,
And, blushing at the tameness of the rest,
Dar'd to suppose the subject had a choice,
He was a traitor by the gen'ral voice.
Oh slave! with pow'rs thou didst not dare exert,
Verse cannot stoop so low as thy desert;
It shakes the sides of splenetic Disdain,
Thou self-entitled ruler of the main,
To trace thee to the date when yon fair sea,
That clips thy shores, had no such charms for thee;
When other nations flew from coast to coast,
And thou hadst neither fleet nor flag to boast.
Kneel now, and lay thy forehead in the dust;
Blush, if thou canst; not petrified, thou must:
Act but an honest and a faithful part;
Compare what then thou wast with what thou art;
And God's disposing providence confess'd,
Obduracy itself must yield the rest.—
Then thou art bound to serve him, and to prove,
Hour after hour, thy gratitude and love.

Has he not hid thee, and thy favour'd land,
For ages safe beneath his shelt'ring hand,
Giv'n thee his blessing on the clearest proof,
Bid nations leagu'd against thee stand aloof,
And charg'd Hostility and Hate to roar
Where else they would, but not upon thy shore?
His pow'r secur'd thee, when presumptuous Spain
Baptiz'd her fleet invincible in vain;

Her gloomy monarch, doubtful and resign'd
To ev'ry pang that racks an anxious mind,
Ask'd of the waves, that broke upon his coast,
What tidings? and the surge replied—All lost!
And when the Stuart leaning on the Scot,
Then too much fear'd, and now too much forgot,
Pierc'd to the very centre of the realm,
And hop'd to seize his abdicated helm,
'Twas but to prove how quickly with a frown
He that had rais'd thee could have pluck'd thee down.
Peculiar is the grace by thee possess'd,
Thy foes implacable, thy land at rest;
Thy thunders travel over earth and seas,
And all at home is pleasure, wealth, and ease.
'Tis thus, extending his tempestuous arm,
Thy Maker fills the nations with alarm,
While his own Heav'n surveys the troubled scene,
And feels no change, unshaken and serene.
Freedom, in other lands scarce known to shine,
Pours out a flood of splendour upon thine;
Thou hast as bright an int'rest in her rays
As ever Roman had in Rome's best days.
True freedom is where no restraint is known,
That Scripture, justice, and good sense disown,
Where only vice and injury are tied,
And all from shore to shore is free beside.
Such freedom is—and Windsor's hoary tow'rs
Stood trembling at the boldness of thy pow'rs,
That won a nymph on that immortal plain
Like her the fabled Phœbus woo'd in vain:
He found the laurel only—happier you
Th'unfading laurel, and the virgin too! *
   Now think, if Pleasure have a thought to spare;
If God himself be not beneath her care;
If Business, constant as the wheels of time,
Can pause an hour to read a serious rhyme;
If the new mail thy merchants now receive,
Or expectation of the next, give leave;
Oh think! if chargeable with deep arrears
For such indulgence gilding all thy years,
How much, though long neglected, shining yet,
The beams of heav'nly truth have swell'd the debt.
When persecuting zeal made royal sport
With tortur'd innocence in Mary's court,
And Bonner, blithe as shepherd at a wake,
Enjoy'd the show, and danc'd about the stake;

* Alluding to the grant of Magna Charta, which was extorted from king John by the barons at Runnymede near Windsor.

The sacred Book, its value understood,
Receiv'd the seal of martyrdom in blood.
Those holy men, so full of truth and grace,
Seem to reflection of a diff'rent race;
Meek, modest, venerable, wise, sincere,
In such a cause they could not dare to fear;
They could not purchase earth with such a prize,
Or spare a life too short to reach the skies.
From them to thee convey'd along the tide,
Their streaming hearts pour'd freely when they died.
Those truths, which neither use nor years impair,
Invite thee, woo thee, to the bliss they share.
What dotage will not vanity maintain?
What web too weak to catch a modern brain?
The moles and bats in full assembly find,
On special search, the keen-ey'd eagle blind.
And did they dream, and art thou wiser now?
Prove it—if better, I submit and bow.
Wisdom and goodness are twin-born, one heart
Must hold both sisters, never seen apart.
So then—as darkness overspread the deep,
Ere Nature rose from her eternal sleep,
And this delightful earth, and that fair sky,
Leap'd out of nothing, call'd by the Most High;
By such a change thy darkness is made light,
Thy chaos order, and thy weakness might;
And He, whose pow'r mere nullity obeys,
Who found thee nothing, form'd thee for his praise
To praise him is to serve him, and fulfil,
Doing and suff'ring, his unquestion'd will;
'Tis to believe what men inspir'd of old,
Faithful, and faithfully inform'd, unfold;
Candid and just, with no false aim in view,
To take for truth what cannot but be true;
To learn in God's own school the Christian part,
And bind the task assign'd thee to thine heart:
Happy the man there seeking and there found,
Happy the nation where such men abound.
  How shall a verse impress thee? by what name
Shall I adjure thee not to court thy shame?
By theirs, whose bright example unimpeach'd
Directs thee to that eminence they reach'd,
Heroes and worthies of days past, thy sires?
Or his, who touch'd their hearts with hallow'd fires?
Their names, alas! in vain reproach an age,
Whom all the vanities they scorn'd engage!
And His, that seraphs tremble at, is hung
Disgracefully on ev'ry trifler's tongue,
Or serves the champion in forensic war

To flourish and parade with at the bar.
Pleasure herself perhaps suggests a plea,
If int'rest move thee, to persuade e'en thee;
By ev'ry charm that smiles upon her face,
By joys possess'd, and joys still held in chase,
If dear society be worth a thought,
And if the feast of freedom cloy thee not,
Reflect that these, and all that seems thine own,
Held by the tenure of his will alone,
Like angels in the service of their Lord,
Remain with thee, or leave thee at his word;
That gratitude and temp'rance in our use
Of what he gives, unsparing and profuse,
Secure the favour, and enhance the joy,
That thankless waste and wild abuse destroy.
But above all reflect, how cheap soe'er
Those rights, that millions envy thee, appear,
And, though resolv'd to risk them, and swim down
The tide of pleasure, heedless of His frown,
That blessings truly sacred, and when giv'n
Mark'd with the signature and stamp of Heav'n,
The word of prophecy, those truths divine,
Which make that Heav'n, if thou desire it, thine,
(Awful alternative! believ'd, belov'd,
Thy glory, and thy shame if unimprov'd,)
Are never long vouchsaf'd, if push'd aside
With cold disgust or philosophic pride!
And that, judicially withdrawn, disgrace,
Error, and darkness occupy their place.
  A world is up in arms, and thou, a spot
Not quickly found, if negligently sought,
Thy soul as ample as thy bounds are small,
Endur'st the brunt, and dar'st defy them all:
And wilt thou join to this bold enterprise
A bolder still, a contest with the skies?
Remember, if He guard thee and secure,
Whoe'er assails thee, thy success is sure;
But if He leave thee, though the skill and pow'r
Of nations sworn to spoil thee and devour,
Were all collected in thy single arm,
And thou couldst laugh away the fear of harm,
That strength would fail, oppos'd against the push
And feeble onset of a pigmy rush.
  Say not (and if the thought of such defence
Should spring within thy bosom, drive it thence)
What nation amongst all my foes is free
From crimes as base as any charg'd on me?
Their measure fill'd, they too shall pay the debt,
Which God, though long forborn, will not forget.

But know that Wrath divine, when most severe,
Makes justice still the guide of his career,
And will not punish, in one mingled crowd,
Them without light, and thee without a cloud.
  Muse, hang this harp upon yon aged beech,
Still murm'ring with the solemn truths I teach;
And while at intervals a cold blast sings
Through the dry leaves, and pants upon the strings;
My soul shall sigh in secret, and lament
A nation scourg'd, yet tardy to repent.
I know the warning song is sung in vain;
That few will hear, and fewer heed the strain;
But if a sweeter voice, and one design'd
A blessing to my country and mankind,
Reclaim the wand'ring thousands, and bring home
A flock so scatter'd and so wont to roam,
Then place it once again between my knees;
The sound of truth will then be sure to please:
And truth alone, where'er my life be cast,
In scenes of plenty, or the pining waste,
Shall be my chosen theme, my glory to the last

HOPE.

. . . . . . doceas iter, et sacra otia pandas.
Virg. En. 6.

Ask what is human life—the sage replies,
With disappointment low'ring in his eyes,
A painful passage o'er a restless flood,
A vain pursuit of fugitive false good,
A scene of fancied bliss and heart-felt care,
Closing at last in darkness and despair,
The poor, inur'd to drudg'ry and distress,
Act without aim, think little, and feel less,
And no where, but in feign'd Arcadian scenes,
Taste happiness, or know what pleasure means.
Riches are pass'd away from hand to hand,
As fortune, vice, or folly may command;
As in a dance the pair that take the lead
Turn downward, and the lowest pair succeed,
So shifting and so various is the plan,
By which Heav'n rules the mix'd affairs of man;
Vicissitude wheels round the motley crowd,
The rich grow poor, the poor become purse-proud;
Bus'ness is labour, and man's weakness such,
Pleasure is labour too, and tires as much,
The very sense of it forgets its use,
By repetition pall'd, by age obtuse.
Youth lost in dissipation we deplore,
Through life's sad remnant, what no sighs restore;
Our years, a fruitless race without a prize,
Too many, yet too few to make us wise.
Dangling his cane about, and taking snuff,
Lothario cries, What philosophic stuff—
O querulous and weak!—whose useless brain
Once thought of nothing, and now thinks in vain;
Whose eye reverted weeps o'er all the past,
Whose prospects shows thee a disheart'ning waste;
Would age in thee resign his wintry reign,
And youth invigorate that frame again,

Renew'd desire would grace with other speech
Joys always priz'd, when plac'd within our reach.
For lift thy palsied head, shake off the gloom
That overhangs the borders of thy tomb,
See Nature gay, as when she first began
With smiles alluring her admirer man ;
She spreads the morning over eastern hills,
Earth glitters with the drops the night distils;
The Sun obedient at her call appears,
To fling his glories o'er the robe she wears;
Banks cloth'd with flow'rs, groves fill'd with sprightly sounds,
Thy yellow tilth, green meads, rocks, rising grounds,
Streams edg'd with osiers, fatt'ning ev'ry field,
Where'er they flow, now seen and now conceal'd;
From the blue rim, where skies and mountains meet,
Down to the very turf beneath thy feet,
Ten thousand charms, that only fools despise,
Or Pride can look at with indiff'rent eyes,
All speak one language, all with one sweet voice
Cry to her universal realm, Rejoice!
Man feels the spur of passions and desires,
And she gives largely more than he requires;
Not that his hours devoted all to Care,
Hollow-ey'd Abstinence, and lean Despair,
The wretch may pine, while to his smell, taste, sight,
She holds a paradise of rich delight;
But gently to rebuke his awkward fear,
To prove that what she gives, she gives sincere;
To banish hesitation, and proclaim
His happiness, her dear, her only aim.
'Tis grave philosophy's absurdest dream,
That Heav'n's intentions are not what they seem.
That only shadows are dispens'd below,
And Earth has no reality but woe.
Thus things terrestial wear a diff'rent hue,
As youth or age persuades; and neither true.
So Flora's wreath through-colour'd crystal seen,
The rose or lily appears blue or green,
But still th'imputed tints are those alone
The medium represents, and not their own.
To rise at noon, sit slipshod and undress'd,
To read the news, or fiddle, as seems best,
Till half the world comes rattling at his door,
To fill the dull vacuity till four;
And, just when ev'ning turns the blue vault grey
To spend two hours in dressing for the day;
To make the sun a bauble without use,
Save for the fruits his heav'nly beams produce;

Quite to forget, or deem it worth no thought,
Who bids him shine, or if he shine or not;
Through mere necessity to close his eyes
Just when the larks and when the shepherds rise;
Is such a life, so tediously the same,
So void of all utility or aim,
That poor *Jonquil* with almost ev'ry breath
Sighs for his exit, vulgarly call'd death:
For he, with all his follies, has a mind
Not yet so blank, or fashionably blind,
But now and then perhaps a feeble ray
Of distant wisdom shoots across his way,
By which he reads, that life without a plan,
As useless as the moment it began,
Serves merely as a soil for discontent
To thrive in; an encumbrance ere half spent.
Oh weariness beyond what asses feel,
That tread the circuit of the cistern wheel;
A dull rotation, never at a stay,
Yesterday's face twin-image of to-day;
While conversation, an exhausted stock,
Grows drowsy as the clicking of a clock.
No need, he cries, of gravity stuff'd out
With academic dignity devout,
To read wise lectures, vanity the text:
Proclaim the remedy, ye learned, next;
For truth self-evident, with pomp impress'd,
Is vanity surpassing all the rest.
   That remedy, not hid in deeps profound,
Yet seldom sought where only to be found,
While passion turns aside from its due scope
Th'inquirer's aim, that remedy is hope.
Life is His gift, from whom whate'er life needs,
With ev'ry good and perfect gift, proceeds;
Bestow'd on man, like all that we partake,
Royally, freely, for his bounty's sake;
Transient indeed, as is the fleeting hour,
And yet the seed of an immortal flow'r;
Design'd in honour of his endless love,
To fill with fragrance his abode above;
No trifle, howsoever short it seem,
And, howsoever shadowy, no dream;
Its value, what no thought can ascertain
Nor all an angel's eloquence explain;
Men deal with life as children with their play,
Who first misuse, then cast their toys away;
Live to no sober purpose, and contend
That their Creator had no serious end.
When God and man stand opposite in view,

Man's disappointment must of course ensue
The just Creator condescends to write,
In beams of inextinguishable light,
His names of wisdom, goodness, pow'r, and love,
On all that blooms below, or shines above;
To catch the wandering notice of mankind,
And teach the world, if not perversely blind,
His gracious attributes, and prove the share
His offspring hold in his paternal care.
If, led from earthly things to things divine,
His creature thwart not his august design,
Then praise is heard instead of reas'ning pride,
And captious cavil and complaint subside.
Nature, employ'd in her allotted place,
Is hand-maid to the purposes of Grace;
By good vouchsaf'd makes known superior good
And bliss not seen by blessings understood:
That bliss, reveal'd in Scripture, with a glow
Bright as the covenant-ensuring bow,
Hires all his feelings with a noble scorn
Of sensual evil, and thus Hope is born.
Hope sets the stamp of vanity on all
That men have deem'd substantial since the fall,
Yet has the wondrous virtue to educe
From emptiness itself a real use;
And while she takes, as at a father's hand,
What health and sober appetite demand,
From fading good derives, with chemic art,
That lasting happiness, a thankful heart.
Hope, with uplifted foot, set free from earth,
Pants for the place of her ethereal birth,
On steady wings sails through th'immense abyss,
Plucks amaranthine joys from bow'rs of bliss,
And crowns the soul, while yet a mourner here,
With wreaths like those triumphant spirits wear.
Hope, as an anchor firm and sure, holds fast
The Christian vessel, and defies the blast.
Hope! nothing else can nourish and secure
His new born virtues, and preserve him pure.
Hope! let the wretch, once conscious of the joy,
Whom now despairing agonies destroy,
Speak, for he can, and none so well as he,
What treasures centre, what delights in thee.
Had he the gems, the spices, and the land
That boasts the treasure, all at his command;
The fragrant grove, th'inestimable mine,
Were light, when weigh'd against one smile of thine.
Though clasp'd and cradled in his nurse's arms,
He shines with all a cherub's artless charms,

Man is the genuine offspring of revolt,
Stubborn and sturdy, a wild ass's colt;
His passions, like the wat'ry stores that sleep
Beneath the smiling surface of the deep,
Wait but the lashes of a wint'ry storm,
To frown and roar, and shake his feeble form.
From infancy through childhood's giddy maze,
Froward at school, and fretful in his plays,
The puny tyrant burns to subjugate
The free republic of the whip-gig state.
If one, his equal in athletic frame,
Or, more provoking still, of nobler name,
Dare step across his arbitrary views,
An Iliad, only not in verse, ensues:
The little Greeks look trembling at the scales,
Till the best tongue, or heaviest hand, prevails.
Now see him launch'd into the world at large;
If priest, supinely droning o'er his charge,
Their fleece his pillow, and his weekly drawl,
Though short, too long, the price he pays for all.
If lawyer, loud, whatever cause he plead,
But proudest of the worst, if that succeed.
Perhaps a grave physician, gath'ring fees,
Punctually paid for length'ning out disease;
No COTTON, whose humanity sheds rays,
That make superior skill his second praise.
If arms engage him, he devotes to sport
His date of life, so likely to be short;
A soldier may be anything, if brave,
So may a tradesman, if not quite a knave.
Such stuff the world is made of; and mankind
To passion, int'rest, pleasure, whim resign'd,
Insist on as if each were his own pope,
Forgiveness, and the privilege of hope.
But Conscience, in some awful silent hour,
When captivating lusts have lost their pow'r,
Perhaps when sickness, or some fearful dream,
Reminds him of religion, hated theme!
Starts from the down, on which she lately slept,
And tells of laws despis'd, at least not kept:
Shows with a pointing finger, but no noise,
A pale procession of past, sinful joys,
All witnesses of blessings foully scorn'd,
And life abus'd, and not to be suborn'd.
Mark these, she says; these summon'd from afar,
Begin their march to meet thee at the bar;
There find a Judge inexorably just,
And perish there, as all presumption must.
Peace be to those (such peace as Earth can give)

Who live in pleasure, dead e'en while they live;
Born capable indeed of heav'nly truth;
But down to latest age, from earliest youth,
Their mind a wilderness through want of care,
The plough of wisdom never ent'ring there.
Peace (if insensibility may claim
A right to the meek honours of her name)
To men of pedigree, their noble race,
Emulous always of the nearest place
To any throne, except the throne of Grace.
Let cottagers and unenlighten'd swains
Revere the laws they dream that Heav'n ordains;
Resort on Sundays to the house of pray'r,
And ask, and fancy they find, blessings there.
Themselves, perhaps, when weary they retreat
T'enjoy cool nature in a country seat,
T'exchange the centre of a thousand trades,
For clumps, and lawns, and temples, and cascades,
May now and then their velvet cushions take,
And seem to pray for good example's sake;
Judging, in charity no doubt, the town
Pious enough, and having need of none.
Kind souls! to teach their tenantry to prize
What they themselves, without remorse, despise:
Nor hope have they, nor fear, of aught to come,
As well for them had prophecy been dumb;
They could have held the conduct they pursue,
Had Paul of Tarsus liv'd and died a Jew;
And truth, propos'd to reas'ners wise as they,
Is a pearl cast—completely cast away.
They die—Death lends them, pleas'd, and as in sport,
All the grim honours of his ghastly court.
Far other paintings grace the chamber now,
Where late we saw the mimic landscape glow:
The busy heralds hang the sable scene
With mournful 'scutcheons, and dim lamps between;
Proclaim their titles to the crowd around,
But they that wore them move not at the sound;
The coronet, plac'd idly at their head,
Adds nothing now to the degraded dead;
And e'en the star, that glitters on the bier,
Can only say—Nobility lies here.
Peace to all such—'twere pity to offend,
By useless censure, whom we cannot mend;
Life without hope can close but in despair,
'Twas there we found them, and must leave them there.
As, when two pilgrims in a forest stray,
Both may be lost, yet each in his own way;
So fares it with the multitudes beguil'd

In vain Opinion's waste and dang'rous wild;
Ten thousand rove the brakes and thorns among,
Some eastward, and some westward, and all wrong.
But here, alas! the fatal diff'rence lies,
Each man's belief is right in his own eyes;
And he that blames what they have blindly chose
Incurs resentment for the love he shows.
Say botanist, within whose province fall
The cedar and the hyssop on the wall,
Of all that deck the lanes, the fields, the bow'rs,
What parts the kindred tribes of weeds and flow'rs?
Sweet scent, or lovely form, or both combin'd,
Distinguish ev'ry cultivated kind;
The want of both denotes a meaner breed,
And Chloe from her garland picks the weed.
Thus hopes of ev'ry sort, whatever sect
Esteem them, sow them, rear them, and protect,
If wild in nature, and not duly found,
Gethsemane! in thy dear hallow'd ground,
That cannot bear the blaze of Scripture light,
Nor cheer the spirit, nor refresh the sight,
Nor animate the soul to Christian deeds,
(Oh cast them from thee!) are weeds, arrant weeds.
Ethelred's house, the centre of six ways,
Diverging each from each, like equal rays,
Himself as bountiful as April rains,
Lord paramount of the surrounding plains,
Would give relief of bed and board to none
But guests that sought it in th' appointed *One*;
And they might enter at his open door,
E'en till his spacious hall would hold no more.
He sent a servant forth by ev'ry road,
To sound his horn, and publish it abroad,
That all might mark—knight, menial, high, and low,
An ord'nance it concern'd them much to know.
If, after all, some headstrong hardy lout
Would disobey, though sure to be shut out,
Could he with reason murmer at his case,
Himself sole author of his own disgrace?
No! the decree was just and without flaw;
And he, that made, had right to make, the law;
His sov'reign pow'r and pleasure unrestrain'd,
The wrong was his who wrongfully complain'd.
Yet half mankind maintain a churlish strife
With Him, the Donor of eternal life,
Because the deed, by which his love confirms
The largess he bestows, prescribes the terms.
Compliance with his will your lot ensures,
Accept it only, and the boon is yours.

And sure it is as kind to smile and give,
As with a frown to say, Do this, and live.
Love is not pedlar's trump'ry bought and sold:
He *will* give freely, or he *will* withhold;
His soul abhors a mercenary thought,
And him as deeply who abhors it not;
He stipulates indeed, but merely this,
That man will freely take an unbought bliss,
Will trust him for a faithful gen'rous part,
Nor set a price upon a willing heart.
Of all the ways that seem to promise fair,
To place you where his saints his presence share,
This only can; for this plain cause, express'd
In terms as plain, Himself has shut the rest.
But oh the strife, the bick'ring, and debate,
The tidings of unpurchas'd Heav'n create!
The flirted fan, the bridle, and the toss,
All speakers, yet all language at a loss.
From stucco'd walls smart arguments rebound;
And beaus, adept in ev'ry thing profound,
Die of disdain, or whistle off the sound.
Such is the clamour of rooks, daws, and kites,
Th'explosion of the levell'd tube excites,
Where mould'ring abbey-walls o'erhang the glade,
And oaks coeval spread a mournful shade;
The screaming nations, hov'ring in mid air,
Loudly resent the strangers freedom there,
And seem to warn him never to repeat
His bold intrusion on their dark retreat.
Adieu, Vinosa cries, ere yet he sips
The purple bumper trembling at his lips,
Adieu to all morality! if Grace
Make works a vain ingredient in the case.
The Christian hope is—Waiter, draw the cork—
If I mistake not—Blockhead! with a fork!
Without good works, whatever some may boast,
Mere folly and delusion—Sir, your toast.
My firm persuasion is, at least sometimes,
That Heav'n will weigh man's virtues and his crimes
With nice attention, in a righteous scale,
And save or damn as these or those prevail.
I plant my foot upon this ground of trust,
And silence ev'ry fear with—God is just.
But if perchance on some dull drizzling day
A thought intrude, that says, or seems to say,
If thus th' important cause is to be tried,
Suppose the beam should dip on the wrong side;
I soon recover from these needless frights,
And God is merciful—sets all to rights.

Thus between justice, as my prime support,
And mercy, fled to as the last resort,
I glide and steal along with Heav'n in view,
And,—pardon me, the bottle stands with you.
  I never will believe, the Col'nel cries,
The sanguinary schemes that some devise,
Who make the good Creator on their plan
A being of less equity than man.
If appetite, or what divines call lust,
Which men comply with, e'en because they must,
Be punished with perdition, who is pure?
Then theirs, no doubt, as well as mine, is sure.
If sentence of eternal pain belong
To ev'ry sudden slip and transient wrong,
Then Heav'n enjoins the fallible and frail
A hopeless task, and damns them if they fail.
My creed (whatever some creed-makers mean
By Athanasian nonsense, or Nicene)—
My creed is, he is safe that does his best,
And death's a doom sufficient for the rest.
  Right, says an ensign; and, for aught I see,
Your faith and mine substantially agree;
The best of ev'ry man's performance here
Is to discharge the duties of his sphere.
A lawyer's dealings should be just and fair,
Honesty shines with great advantage there.
Fasting and pray'r sit well upon a priest,
A decent caution and reserve at least.
A soldier's best is courage in the field,
With nothing here that wants to be conceal'd.
Manly deportment, gallant, easy, gay;
A hand as lib'ral as the light of day.
The soldier thus endow'd, who never shrinks,
Nor closets up his thoughts, whate'er he thinks,
Who scorns to do an injury by stealth,
Must go to Heav'n—and I must drink his health
Sir Smug, he cries, (for lowest at the board,
Just made fifth chaplain of his patron lord,
His shoulders witnessing, by many a shrug,
How much his feelings suffer'd, sat Sir Smug,)
Your office is to winnow false from true;
Come, prophet, drink, and tell us what think you?
  Sighing and smiling as he takes his glass,
Which they that woo preferment rarely pass,
Fallible man, the church-bred youth replies,
Is still found fallible, however wise;
And diff'ring judgments serve but to declare,
That truth lies somewhere, if we knew but where.
Of all it ever was my lot to read,

Of critics now alive, or long since dead,
The book of all the world that charm'd me most
Was,—welladay, the titlepage was lost;
The writer well remarks, a heart that knows
To take with gratitude what Heav'n bestows,
With prudence always ready at our call,
To guide our use of it, is all in all.
Doubtless it is.—To which, of my own store,
I superadd a few essentials more;
But these, excuse the liberty I take,
I wave just now, for conversation's sake—
Spoke like an oracle, they all exclaim,
And add Right Rev'rend to Smug's honour'd name.
And yet our lot is giv'n us in a land,
Where busy arts are never at a stand;
Where Science points her telescopic eye,
Familiar with the wonders of the sky;
Where bold Inquiry, diving out of sight,
Brings many a precious pearl of truth to light;
Where nought eludes the persevering quest
That fashion, taste, or luxury, suggest.
But, above all, in her own light array'd,
See Mercy's grand apocalypse display'd!
The sacred book no longer suffers wrong,
Bound in the fetters of an unknown tongue;
But speaks with plainness, art could never mend,
What simplest minds can soonest comprehend.
God gives the word, the preachers throng around,
Live from his lips, and spread the glorious sound:
That sound bespeaks Salvation on her way,
The trumpet of a life-restoring day;
'Tis heard where England's eastern glory shines,
And in the gulfs of her Cornubian mines.
And still it spreads. See Germany send forth
Her sons* to pour it on the farthest north;
Fir'd with a zeal peculiar, *they* defy
The rage and rigour of a polar sky,
And plant successfully sweet Sharon's rose
On icy plains, and in eternal snows.
O blest within th'inclosure of your rocks,
Nor herds have ye to boast, nor bleating flocks;
No fertilizing streams your fields divide,
That show revers'd the villas on their side;
No groves have ye; no cheerful sound of bird,
Or voice of turtle in your land is heard;
Nor grateful eglantine regales the smell
Of those, that walk at ev'ning where ye dwell:

* The Moravian Missionaries in Greenland. *See* Krantz.

But Winter, arm'd with terrors here unknown,
Sits absolute on his unshaken throne;
Piles up his stores amidst the frozen waste,
And bids the mountains he has built stand fast;
Beckons the legions of his storms away
From happier scenes, to make your land a prey;
Proclaims the soil a conquest he has won,
And scorns to share it with the distant sun.
Yet Truth is yours, remote, unenvied isle!
And Peace, the genuine offspring of her smile;
The pride of letter'd Ignorance, that binds
In chains of error our accomplish'd minds,
That decks, with all the splendour of the true,
A false religion, is unknown to you.
Nature, indeed, vouchsafes for our delight
The sweet vicissitudes of day and night;
Soft airs and genial moisture feed and cheer
Field, fruit, and flow'r, and ev'ry creature here;
But brighter beams than his who fires the skies,
Have ris'n at length on your admiring eyes,
That shoot into your darkest caves the day,
From which our nicer optics turn away.
  Here see th'encouragement Grace gives to vice,
The dire effect of mercy without price!
What were they? what some fools are made by art,
They were by nature, atheists, head and heart.
The gross idolatry blind heathens teach
Was too refin'd for them, beyond their reach.
Not e'en the glorious Sun, though men revere
The monarch most, that seldom will appear,
And though his beams, that quicken where they shine,
May claim some right to be esteem'd divine,
Not e'en the sun, desirable as rare,
Could bend one knee, engage one vot'ry there;
They were, what base Credulity believes
True Christians are, dissemblers, drunkards, thieves.
The full-gorg'd savage, at his nauseous feast,
Spent half the darkness, and snor'd out the rest,
Was one, whom Justice, on an equal plan,
Denouncing death upon the sins of man,
Might almost have indulg'd with an escape,
Chargeable only with a human shape.
What are they now?—Morality may spare
Her grave concern, her kind suspicions there:
The wretch, who once sang wildly, danc'd, and laugh'd,
And suck'd in dizzy madness with his draught,
Has wept a silent flood, revers'd his ways,
Is sober, meek, benevolent, and prays,
Feeds sparingly, communicates his store,

Abhors the craft he boasted of before,
And he that stole, has learn'd to steal no more.
Well spake the prophet, Let the desert sing,
Where sprang the thorn, the spiry fir shall spring,
And where unsightly and rank thistles grew,
Shall grow the myrtle and luxuriant yew.
Go now, and with important tone demand
On what foundation virtue is to stand,
If self-exalting claims be turn'd adrift,
And grace be grace indeed, and life a gift;
The poor reclaim'd inhabitant, his eyes
Glist'ning at once with pity and surprise,
Amaz'd that shadows should obscure the sight
Of one, whose birth was in a land of light,
Shall answer, Hope, sweet Hope, has set me free,
And made all pleasures else mere dross to me.
These, amidst scenes as waste as if denied
The common care that waits on all beside,
Wild as if Nature there, void of all good,
Play'd only gambols in a frantic mood,
(Yet charge not heav'nly skill with having plann'd
A plaything world, unworthy of his hand,)
Can see his love, though secret evil lurks
In all we touch, stamp'd plainly on his works,
Deem life a blessing with its num'rous woes,
Nor spurn away a gift a God bestows.
Hard task, indeed, o'er arctic seas to roam!
Is hope exotic? grows it not at home?
Yes, but an object, bright as orient morn,
May press the eye too closely to be borne;
A distant virtue we can all confess,
It hurts our pride, and moves our envy, less.
Leuconomus (beneath well-sounding Greek
I slur a name a poet must not speak)
Stood pilloried on Infamy's high stage,
And bore the pelting score of half an age;
The very butt of Slander, and the blot
For ev'ry dart that Malice ever shot.
The man that mention'd *him* at once dismiss'd
All mercy from his lips, and sneer'd and hiss'd;
His crimes were such as Sodom never knew,
And Perjury stood up to swear all true;
His aim was mischief, and his zeal pretence,
His speech rebellion against common sense;
A knave, when tried on honesty's plain rule;
And when by that of reason, a mere fool;
The World's best comfort was, his doom was pass'd;
Die when he might, he must be damn'd at last.
Now, Truth, perform thine office; waft aside

The curtain drawn by Prejudice and Pride,
Reveal (the man is dead) to wond'ring eyes
This more than monster, in his proper guise.
He lov'd the World that hated him: the tear
That dropp'd upon his Bible was sincere:
Assail'd by scandal and the tongue of strife,
His only answer was a blameless life;
And he that forg'd, and he that threw the dart,
Had each a brother's int'rest in his heart.
Paul's love of Christ, and steadiness unbrib'd,
Were copies close in him, and well transcrib'd.
He follow'd Paul; his zeal a kindred flame,
His apostolic charity the same.
Like him, cross'd cheerfully tempestuous seas,
Forsaking country, kindred, friends, and ease;
Like him he labour'd, and like him content
To bear it, suffer'd shame where'er he went.
Blush, Calumny! and write upon his tomb,
If honest Eulogy can spare thee room,
Thy deep repentance of thy thousand lies,
Which, aim'd at him, have pierc'd th'offended skies!
And say, Blot out my sin, confess'd, deplor'd,
Against thine image, in thy saint, O Lord!
No blinder bigot, I maintain it still,
Than he who must have pleasure, come what will:
He laughs, whatever weapon Truth may draw,
And deems her sharp artillery mere straw.
Scripture indeed is plain; but God and he
On Scripture ground are sure to disagree;
Some wiser rule must teach him how to live,
Than this his Maker has seen fit to give;
Supple and flexible as Indian cane,
To take the bend his appetites ordain;
Contriv'd to suit frail Nature's crazy case,
And reconcile his lusts with saving grace.
By this, with nice precision of design,
He draws upon life's map a zigzag line,
That shows how far 'tis safe to follow sin,
And where his danger and God's wrath begin.
By this he forms, as pleas'd he sports along,
His well-pois'd estimate of right and wrong;
And finds the modish manners of the day,
Though loose, as harmless as an infant's play.
Build by whatever plan Caprice decrees,
With that materials, on what ground you please;
Your hope shall stand unblam'd, perhaps admir'd,
If not that hope the Scripture has requir'd.
The strange conceits, vain projects, and wild dreams,
With which hypocrisy for ever teems.

(Though other follies strike the public eye,
And raise a laugh,) pass unmolested by;
But if, unblameable in word and thought,
A *man* arise, a man whom God has taught,
With all Elijah's dignity of tone,
And all the love of the beloved John,
To storm the citadels they build in air,
And smite th'untemper'd wall; 'tis death to spare.
To sweep away all refuges of lies,
And place, instead of quirks themselves devise,
Lama Sabacthani before their eyes;
To prove, that without Christ all gain is loss,
All hope despair, that stands not on his cross;
Except the few his God may have impress'd,
A tenfold frenzy seizes all the rest.
  Throughout mankind, the Christian kind at least,
There dwells a consciousness in ev'ry breast,
That folly ends where genuine hope begins,
And he that finds his Heav'n must lose his sins.
Nature opposes with her utmost force
This riving stroke, this ultimate divorce;
And, while religion seems to be her view,
Hates with a deep sincerity *the true*:
For this, of all that ever influenc'd man,
Since Abel worshipp'd, or the world began,
This only spares no lust, admits no plea,
But makes him, if at all, completely free;
Sounds forth the signal, as she mounts her car,
Of an eternal, universal war;
Rejects all treaty, penetrates all wiles,
Scorns with the same indiff'rence frowns and smiles;
Drives through the realms of Sin, where Riot reels,
And grinds his crown beneath her burning wheels!
Hence all that is in man, pride, passion, art,
Pow'rs of the mind, and feelings of the heart,
Insensible of Truth's almighty charms,
Starts at her first approach, and sounds to arms!
While Bigotry, with well-dissembled fears,
His eyes shut fast, his fingers in his ears,
Mighty to parry and push by God's word,
With senseless noise, his argument the sword,
Pretends a zeal for godliness and grace,
And spits abhorrence in the Christian's face.
  Parent of Hope, immortal Truth! make known
Thy deathless wreaths, and triumphs all thine own:
The silent progress of thy pow'r is such,
Thy means so feeble, and despis'd so much,
That few believe the wonders thou hast wrought,
And none can teach them, but whom thou hast taught.

O see me sworn to serve thee, and command
A painter's skill into a poet's hand,
That, while I trembling trace a work divine,
Fancy may stand aloof from the design,
And light, and shade, and ev'ry stroke be thine.
If ever thou hast felt another's pain,
If ever when he sigh'd hast sigh'd again,
If ever on thy eyelid stood the tear,
That pity had engender'd, drop one here.
This man was happy—had the World's good word,
And with it ev'ry joy it can afford;
Friendship and love seem'd tenderly at strife,
Which most should sweeten his untroubled life;
Politely learn'd, and of a gentle race,
Good breeding and good sense gave all a grace,
And whether at the toilette of the fair,
He laugh'd and trifled, made him welcome there,
Or if in masculine debate he shar'd,
Ensur'd him mute attention and regard.
Alas how chang'd! Expressive of his mind,
His eyes are sunk, arms folded, head reclin'd;
Those awful syllables, Hell, death, and sin,
Though whisper'd, plainly tell what works within;
That Conscience there performs her proper part,
And writes a doomsday sentence on his heart;
Forsaking, and forsaken of all friends,
He now perceives where earthly pleasure ends;
Hard task! for one who lately knew no care,
And harder still as learnt beneath despair;
His hours no longer pass unmark'd away,
A dark importance saddens ev'ry day;
He hears the notice of the clock perplex'd,
And cries, Perhaps eternity strikes next;
Sweet music is no longer music here,
And laughter sounds like madness in his ear:
His grief the World of all her pow'r disarms,
Wine has no taste, and beauty has no charms:
God's holy word, once trivial in his view,
Now by the voice of his experience true,
Seems, as it is, the fountain whence alone
Must spring that hope he pants to make his own.
Now let the bright reverse be known abroad;
Say man's a worm, and pow'r belongs to God.
As when a felon, whom his country's laws
Have justly doom'd for some atrocious cause,
Expects in darkness and heart-chilling fears,
The shameful close of all his misspent years;
If chance, on heavy pinions slowly borne,
A tempest usher in the dreadful morn,

Upon his dungeon walls the lightnings play,
The thunder seems to summon him away,
The warder at the door his key applies,
Shoots back the bolt, and all his courage dies:
If then, just then, all thoughts of mercy lost,
When Hope, long ling'ring, at last yields the ghost,
The sound of pardon pierce his startled ear,
He drops at once his fetters and his fear;
A transport glows in all he looks and speaks,
And the first thankful tears bedew his cheeks.
Joy, far superior joy, that much outweighs
The comfort of a few poor added days,
Invades, possesses, and o'erwhelms the soul
Of him, whom Hope has with a touch made whole
'Tis Heav'n, all Heav'n descending on the wings
Of the glad legions of the King of kings;
'Tis more—'tis God diffus'd through ev'ry part,
'Tis God himself triumphant in his heart.
O welcome now the Sun's once hated light,
His noonday beams were never half so bright
Not kindred minds alone are call'd t'employ
Their hours, their days, in list'ning to his joy;
Unconscious nature, all that he surveys,
Rocks, groves, and streams, must join him in his praise.
 These are thy glorious works, eternal Truth,
The scoff of wither'd age and beardless youth;
These move the censure and illib'ral grin
Of fools, that hate thee and delight in sin:
But these shall last when night has quench'd the pole,
And Heav'n is all departed as a scroll.
And when, as Justice has long since decreed,
This Earth shall blaze, and a new world succeed,
Then these thy glorious works, and they who share
That hope, which can alone exclude despair,
Shall live exempt from weakness and decay,
The brightest wonders of an endless day.
 Happy the bard, (if that fair name belong
To him, that blends no fable with his song,)
Whose lines uniting, by an honest art,
The faithful monitor's and poet's part,
Seek to delight, that they may mend mankind,
And, while they captivate, inform the mind:
Still happier, if he till a thankful soil,
And fruit reward his honourable toil:
But happier far, who comfort those, that wait
To hear plain truth at Judah's hallow'd gate:
Their language simple, as their manners meek,
No shining ornaments have they to seek;
Nor labour they, nor time nor talents waste,

In sorting flow'rs to suit a fickle taste;
But while they speak the wisdom of the skies,
Which art can only darken and disguise,
Th' abundant harvest, recompense divine,
Repays their work—the gleaning only mine.

CHARITY.

"Quo nihil majus meliusve terris
Fata donavê, bonique divi;
Nec dabunt, quamvis redeant in aurum
Tempora priscum."—
Hor. Lib. iv. Od. 2.

Fairest and foremost of the train, that wait
On man's most dignified and happiest state,
Whether we name thee Charity or Love,
Chief grace below, and all in all above,
Prosper (I press thee with a pow'rful plea)
A task I venture on, impell'd by thee:
O never seen but in thy blest effects,
Or felt but in the soul that Heav'n selects;
Who seeks to praise thee, and to make thee known
To other hearts, must have thee in his own.
Come, prompt me with benevolent desires,
Teach me to kindle at thy gentle fires,
And, though disgrac'd and slighted, to redeem
A poet's name, by making thee the theme.
God, working ever on a social plan,
By various ties attaches man to man:
He made at first, though free and unconfin'd,
One man the common father of the kind;
That ev'ry tribe, though plac'd as he sees best,
Where seas or deserts part them from the rest,
Diff'ring in language, manners, or in face,
Might feel themselves allied to all the race.
When Cook—lamented, and with tears as just
As ever mingled with heroic dust,—
Steer'd Britain's oak into a world unknown,
And in his country's glory sought his own,
Wherever he found man, to nature true,
The rights of man were sacred in his view;
He sooth'd with gifts, and greeted with a smile,
The simple native of the new-found isle;
He spurn'd the wretch, that slighted or withstood

The tender argument of kindred blood,
Nor would endure, that any should control
His freeborn brethren of the southern pole.
  But though some nobler minds a law respect,
That none shall with impunity neglect,
In baser souls unnumber'd evils meet,
To thwart its influence, and its end defeat.
While Cook is lov'd for savage lives he sav'd,
See Cortez odious for a world enslav'd!
Where wast thou then, sweet Charity? where then,
Thou tutelary friend of helpless men?
Wast thou in monkish cells and nunn'ries found,
Or building hospitals on English ground?
No—Mammon makes the World his legatee
Through fear, not love; and Heav'n abhors the fee.
Wherever found, (and all men need thy care,)
Nor age nor infancy could find thee there.
The hand, that slew till it could slay no more,
Was glued to the sword-hilt with Indian gore.
Their prince, as justly seated on his throne
As vain imperial Philip on his own,
Trick'd out of all his royalty by art,
That stripp'd him bare, and broke his honest heart,
Died by the sentence of a shaven priest,
For scorning what they taught him to detest.
How dark the veil, that intercepts the blaze
Of Heav'n's mysterious purposes and ways!
God stood not, though he seem'd to stand, aloof;
And at this hour the conqu'ror feels the proof:
The wreath he won drew down an instant curse,
The fretting plague is in the public purse,
The canker'd spoil corrodes the pining state,
Starv'd by that indolence their mines create.
  Oh could their ancient Incas rise again,
How would they take up Israel's taunting strain!
Art then too fall'n Iberia? Do we see
The robber and the murd'rer weak as we?
Thou, that hast wasted Earth, and dar'd despise
Alike the wrath and mercy of the skies,
Thy pomp is in the grave, thy glory laid
Low in the pits thine avarice has made.
We come with joy from our eternal rest,
To see th' oppressor in his turn oppress'd.
Art thou the god, the thunder of whose hand
Roll'd over all our desolated land,
Shook principalities and kingdoms down,
And made the mountains tremble at his frown?
The sword shall light upon thy boasted pow'rs,
And waste them, as thy sword has wasted ours.

'Tis thus Omnipotence his law fulfils,
And Vengeance executes what Justice wills.
Again—the band of commerce was design'd
T'associate all the branches of mankind;
And if a boundless plenty be the robe,
Trade is the golden girdle of the globe.
Wise to promote whatever end he means,
God opens fruitful nature's various scenes:
Each climate needs what other climes produce,
And offers something to the gen'ral use;
No land but listens to the common call,
And in return receives supply from all.
This genial intercourse, and mutual aid,
Cheers what were else an universal shade,
Calls Nature from her ivy-mantled den,
And softens human rock-work into men.
Ingenious Art, with her expressive face,
Steps forth to fashion and refine the race;
Not only fills Necessity's demand,
But overcharges her capacious hand:
Capricious Taste itself can crave no more,
Than she supplies from her abounding store;
She strikes out all that luxury can ask,
And gains new vigour at her endless task.
Hers is the spacious arch, the shapely spire,
The painter's pencil, and the poet's lyre;
From her the canvass borrows light and shade,
And verse, more lasting, hues that never fade.
She guides the finger o'er the dancing keys,
Gives difficulty all the grace of ease,
And pours a torrent of sweet notes around,
Fast as the thirsting ear can drink the sound.
These are the gift of Art, and Art thrives most
Where commerce has enrich'd the busy coast;
He catches all improvements in his flight,
Spreads foreign wonders in his country's sight,
Imports what others have invented well,
And stirs his own to match them, or excel.
'Tis thus reciprocating, each with each,
Alternately the nations learn and teach;
While Providence enjoins to ev'ry soul
An union with the vast terraqueous whole.
Heav'n speed the canvass, gallantly unfurl'd
To furnish and accomodate a world,
To give the pole the produce of the sun,
And knit th'unsocial climates into one.—
Soft airs and gentle heavings of the wave
Impel the fleet, whose errand is to save,
To succour wasted regions, and replace

The smile of Opulence in Sorrow's face.—
Let nothing adverse, nothing unforeseen,
Impede the bark, that ploughs the deep serene,
Charg'd with a freight transcending in its worth
The gems of India, Nature's rarest birth,
That flies, like Gabriel on his Lord's commands,
A herald of God's love to pagan lands.
But ah! what wish can prosper, or what pray'r,
For merchants rich in cargoes of despair,
Who drive a loathsome traffic, gauge, and span,
And buy the muscles and the bones of man!
The tender ties of father, husband, friend,
All bonds of nature in that moment end;
And each endures, while yet he draws his breath,
A stroke as fatal as the scythe of Death.
The sable warrior, frantic with regret
Of her he loves, and never can forget,
Loses in tears the far-receding shore,
But not the thought, that they must meet no more:
Depriv'd of her and freedom at a blow,
What has he left that he can yet forego?
Yes, to deep sadness sullenly resign'd,
He feels his body's bondage in his mind;
Puts off his gen'rous nature; and, to suit
His manners with his fate, puts on the brute.
O most degrading of all ills, that wait
On many a mourner in his best estate!
All other sorrows Virtue may endure,
And find submission more than half a cure;
Grief is itself a med'cine, and bestow'd
T'improve the fortitude that bears the load,
To teach the wand'rer, as his woes increase,
The path of Wisdom, all whose paths are peace;
But slav'ry!—Virtue dreads it as her grave:
Patience itself is meanness in a slave:
Or if the will and sov'reignty of God
Bid suffer it a while, and kiss the rod,
Wait for the dawning of a brighter day,
And snap the chain the moment when you may.
Nature imprints upon whate'er we see
That has a heart and life in it, Be free
The beasts are charter'd—neither age nor force
Can quell the love of freedom in a horse:
He breaks the cord that held him at the rack;
And, conscious of an unencumber'd back,
Snuffs up the morning air, forgets the rein;
Loose fly his forelock and his ample mane;
Responsive to the distant neigh he neighs;
Nor stops till, overleaping all delays,

He finds the pasture where his fellows graze.
  Canst thou, and honor'd with a Christian name,
Buy what is woman-born, and feel no shame;
Trade in the blood of innocence, and plead
Expedience as a warrant for the deed?
So may the wolf, whom famine has made bold,
To quit the forest and invade the fold:
So may the ruffian, who, with ghostly glide,
Dagger in hand, steals close to your bed-side;
Not he, but his emergence forc'd the door,
He found it inconvenient to be poor.
Has God then given its sweetness to the cane,
Unless his laws be trampled on—in vain?
Built a brave world, which cannot yet subsist,
Unless his right to rule it be dismiss'd?
Impudent blasphemy! So Folly pleads,
And, Av'rice being judge, with ease succeeds.
  But grant the plea, and let it stand for just,
That man make man his prey, because he *must*;
Still there is room for pity to abate,
And soothe the sorrows of so sad a state.
A Briton knows, or if he knows it not,
The Scripture plac'd within his reach, he ought,
That souls have no discriminating hue,
Alike important in their Maker's view;
That none are free from blemish since the fall,
And Love divine has paid one price for all.
The wretch, that works and weeps without relief
Has one that notices his silent grief.
He from whose hands alone all pow'r proceeds,
Ranks its abuse among the foulest deeds,
Considers *all* injustice with a frown;
But *marks* the man that treads his fellow down.
Begone—the whip and bell in that hard hand
Are hateful ensigns of usurp'd command.
Not Mexico could purchase kings a claim
To scourge him, weariness his only blame.
Remember Heav'n has an avenging rod:
To smite the poor is treason against God.
  Trouble is grudgingly and hardly brook'd,
While life's sublimest joys are overlook'd:
We wander o'er a sunburnt thirsty soil,
Murm'ring and weary of our daily toil,
Forget t'enjoy the palm-tree's offer'd shade,
Or taste the fountain in the neighbouring glade:
Else who would lose, that had the pow'r t' improve,
Th' occasion of transmuting fear to love?
O 'tis a godlike privilege to save,
And he that scorns it is himself a slave.

Inform his mind; one flash of heav'nly day
Would heal his heart, and melt his chains away.
"Beauty for ashes" is a gift indeed,
And slaves, by truth enlarg'd, are doubly freed.
Then would he say, submissive at thy feet,
While gratitude and love made service sweet,—
My dear deliv'rer out of hopeless night,
Whose bounty bought me but to give me light,
I was a bondman on my native plain,
Sin forg'd, and Ignorance made fast, the chain;
Thy lips have shed instruction as the dew,
Taught me what path to shun, and what pursue;
Farewell my former joys! I sigh no more
For Africa's once loved, benighted shore;
Serving a benefactor I am free;
At my best home, if not exil'd from thee.
Some men make gain a fountain, whence proceeds
A stream of lib'ral and heroic deeds;
The swell of pity, not to be confin'd
Within the scanty limits of the mind,
Disdains the bank, and throws the golden sands,
A rich deposit, on the bord'ring lands:
These have an ear for his paternal call,
Who makes some rich for the supply of all;
God's gift with pleasure in his praise employ;
And *Thornton* is familiar with the joy.
O could I worship aught beneath the skies,
That earth has seen, or fancy can devise,
Thine altar, sacred Liberty, should stand,
Built by no mercenary vulgar hand,
With fragrant turf, and flow'rs as wild and fair
As ever dress'd a bank, or scented summer air.
Duly, as ever on the mountain's height
The peep of Morning shed a dawning light,
Again, when Ev'ning, in her sober vest,
Drew the gray curtain of the fading west,
My soul should yield thee willing thanks and praise,
For the chief blessings of my fairest days:
But t were sacrilege—praise is not thine,
But his who gave thee, and preserves thee mine:
Else I would say, and as I spake bid fly
A captive bird into the boundless sky,
This triple realm adores thee—thou art come
From Sparta hither, and art here at home.
We feel thy force still active, at this hour
Enjoy immunity from priestly pow'r,
While Conscience, happier than in ancient years,
Owns no superior but the God she fears.
Propitious spirit! yet expunge a wrong

Thy rights have suffer'd, and our land, too long.
Teach mercy to ten thousand hearts, that share
The fears and hopes of a commercial care.
Prisons expect the wicked, and were built
To bind the lawless, and to punish guilt;
But shipwreck, earthquake, battle, fire, and flood,
Are mighty mischiefs, not to be withstood;
And honest Merit stands on slipp'ry ground,
Where covert guile and artifice abound.
Let just Restraint, for public peace design'd,
Chain up the wolves and tigers of mankind;
The foe of virtue has no claim to thee,
But let insolvent Innocence go free.
  Patron of else the most despis'd of men,
Accept the tribute of a stranger's pen;
Verse, like the laurel, its immortal meed,
Should be the guerdon of a noble deed;
I may alarm thee, but I fear the shame
(Charity chosen as my theme and aim)
I must incur, forgetting *Howard's* name.
Blest with all wealth can give thee, to resign
Joys doubly sweet to feelings quick as thine,
To quit the bliss thy rural scenes bestow,
To seek a nobler amidst scenes of woe,
To traverse seas, range kingdoms, and bring home,
Not the proud monuments of Greece or Rome,
But knowledge such as only dungeons teach,
And only sympathy like thine could reach;
That grief, sequester'd from the public stage,
Might smooth her feathers, and enjoy her cage;
Speaks a divine ambition, and a zeal,
The boldest patriot might be proud to feel.
O that the voice of clamor and debate,
That pleads for peace till it disturbs the state,
Were hush'd in favor of thy gen'rous plea,
The poor thy clients, and Heav'n's smile thy fee!
Philosophy, that does not dream or stray,
Walks arm in arm with Nature all his way;
Compasses earth, dives into it, ascends
Whatever steep Inquiry recommends,
Sees planetary wonders smoothly roll
Round other systems under her control,
Drinks wisdom at the milky stream of light,
That cheers the silent journey of the night,
And brings at his return a bosom charg'd
With rich instruction, and a soul enlarg'd.
The treasur'd sweets of the capacious plan,
That Heav'n spreads wide before the view of man,
All prompt his pleas'd pursuit, and to pursue

Still prompt him, with a pleasure always new;
He too has a connecting pow'r, and draws
Man to the centre of the common cause,
Aiding a dubious and deficient sight
With a new medium and a purer light.
All truth is precious, if not all divine;
And what dilates the pow'rs must needs refine.
He reads the skies, and, watching ev'ry change,
Provides the faculties an ampler range;
And wins mankind, as his attempts prevail,
A prouder station on the gen'ral scale.
But Reason still, unless divinely taught,
Whate'er she learns, learns nothing as she ought;
The lamp of revelation only shows,
What human wisdom cannot but oppose,
That man, in nature's richest mantle clad
And grac'd with all philosophy can add,
Though fair without, and luminous within,
Is still the progeny and heir of sin.
Thus taught, down falls the plumage of his pride;
He feels his need of an unerring guide,
And knows that falling he shall rise no more,
Unless the pow'r that bade him stand restore.
This is indeed philosophy; this known
Makes wisdom, worthy of the name, his own;
And, without this, whatever he discuss;
Whether the space between the stars and us;
Whether he measure earth, compute the sea;
Weigh sunbeams, carve a fly, or spit a flea;
The solemn trifler with his boasted skill
Toils much, and is a solemn trifler still:
Blind was he born, and his misguided eyes
Grown dim in trifling studies, blind he dies.
Self-knowledge truly learn'd of course implies
The rich possession of a nobler prize;
For self to self, and God to man reveal'd,
(Two themes to Nature's eye for ever seal'd)
Are taught by rays, that fly with equal pace
From the same centre of enlight'ning grace.
Here stay thy foot; how copious, and how clear,
Th' o'erflowing well of Charity springs here!
Hark! 'tis the music of a thousand rills,
Some thro' the groves, some down the sloping hills,
Winding a secret or an open course,
And all supplied from an eternal source.
The ties of Nature do but feebly bind;
And Commerce partially reclaims mankind;
Philosophy, without his heav'nly guide,
May blow up self-conceit, and nourish pride;

But, while his promise is the reas'ning part,
Has still a veil of midnight on his heart:
'Tis Truth divine, exhibited on earth,
Gives Charity her being and her birth.
Suppose (when thought is warm and fancy flows,
What will not argument sometimes suppose?)
An isle possess'd by creatures of our kind,
Endued with reason, yet by nature blind.
Let Supposition lend her aid once more,
And land some grave optician on the shore:
He claps his lens, if haply they may see,
Close to the part where vision ought to be;
But finds, that, though his tubes assist the sight,
They cannot give it, or make darkness light.
He reads wise lectures, and describes aloud
A sense they know not, to the wond'ring crowd;
He talks of light, and the prismatic hues,
As men of depth in erudition use;
But all he gains for his harangue is—Well,——
What monstrous lies some travellers will tell!
The soul whose sight all-quick'ning grace renews,
Takes the resemblance of the good she views,
As diamonds, stripp'd of their opaque disguise,
Reflect the noonday glory of the skies.
She speaks of him, her author, guardian, friend,
Whose love knew no beginning, knows no end,
In language warm as all that love inspires,
And in the glow of her intense desires,
Pants to communicate her noble fires.
She sees a worl l stark blind to what employs
Her eager thought, and feeds her flowing joys;
Though Wisdom hail them, heedless of her call,
Flies to save some, and feels a pang for all:
Herself as weak as her support is strong,
She feels that frailty she denied so long;
And, from a knowledge of her own disease,
Learns to compassionate the sick she sees.
Here see, acquitted of all vain pretence,
The reign of genuine Charity commence.
Though scorn repay her sympathetic tears,
She still is kind, and still she perseveres;
The truth she loves a sightless world blaspheme,
'Tis childish dotage, a delirious dream;
The danger they discern not, they deny;
Laugh at their only remedy, and die.
But still a soul thus touch'd can never cease,
Whoever threatens war, to speak of peace.
Pure in her aim, and in her temper mild,
Her wisdom seems the weakness of a child:

She makes excuses where she might condemn,
Revil'd by those that hate her, prays for them;
Suspicion lurks not in her artless breast,
The worst suggested, she believes the best;
Not soon provok'd, however stung and teas'd,
And, if perhaps made angry, soon appeas'd;
She rather waves than will dispute her right,
And, injur'd, makes forgiveness her delight.
Such was the portrait an apostle drew,
The bright original was one he knew;
Heav'n held his hand, the likeness must be true.
When one, that holds communion with the skies,
Has fill'd his urn where these pure waters rise,
And once more mingles with us meaner things,
'Tis e'en as if an angel shook his wings;
Immortal fragrance fills the circuit wide,
That tells us whence his treasures are supplied.
So when a ship, well freighted with the stores
The sun matures on India's spicy shores,
Has dropp'd her anchor, and her canvass furl'd,
In some safe haven of our western world,
'Twere vain inquiry to what port she went,
The gale informs us, laden with the scent.
Some seek, when queasy conscience has its qualms,
To lull the painful malady with arms;
But charity not feign'd intends alone
Another's good—theirs centres in their own;
And, too short-liv'd to reach the realms of peace,
Must cease for ever when the poor shall cease.
Flavia, most tender of her own good name,
Is rather careless of her sister's fame:
Her superfluity the poor supplies,
But, if she touch a character, it dies.
The seeming virtue weigh'd against the vice,
She deems all safe, for she has paid the price:
No charity but alms aught values she,
Except in porc'lain on her mantel-tree.
How many deeds, with which the world has rung,
From Pride, in league with Ignorance, have sprung!
But God o'errules all human follies still,
And bends the tough materials to his will.
A conflagation, or a wintry flood,
Has left some hundreds without home or food;
Extravagance and Av'rice shall subscribe,
While fame and self-complacence are the bribe.
The brief proclaim'd, it visits ev'ry pew,
But first the squire's, a compliment but due:
With slow deliberation he unties
His glitt'ring purse, that envy of all eyes

And, while the clerk just puzzles out the psalm,
Glides guinea behind guinea in his palm;
Till finding, what he might have found before,
A smaller piece amidst the precious store,
Pinch'd close between his finger and his thumb,
He half exhibits, and then drops the sum.
Gold to be sure!—Throughout the town 'tis told,
How the good squire gives never less than gold,
From motives such as his, though not the best,
Springs in due time supply for the distress'd;
Not less effectual than what love bestows,
Except that office clips it as it goes.
But lest I seem to sin against a friend,
And wound the grace I mean to recommend,
(Though vice derided with a just design
Implies no trespass against love divine,)
Once more I would adopt the graver style,
A teacher should be sparing of his smile.
Unless a love of virtue light the flame,
Satire is, more than those he brands, to blame;
He hides behind a magisterial air
His own offences, and strips others bare;
Affects indeed a most humane concern,
That men, if gently tutor'd, will not learn;
That mulish Folly, not to be reclaim'd
By softer methods, must be made asham'd;
But (I might instance in St. Patrick's dean)
Too often rails to gratify his spleen.
Most sat'rists are indeed a public scourge;
Their mildest physic is a farrier's purge;
Their acrid temper turns, as soon as stirr'd,
The milk of their good purpose all to curd.
Their zeal begotten, as their works rehearse,
By lean despair upon an empty purse,
The wild assassins start into the street,
Prepar'd to poniard whomsoe'er they meet.
No skill in swordmanship, however just,
Can be secure against a madman's thrust;
And even Virtue, so unfairly match'd,
Although immortal, may be prick'd or scratchd.
When Scandal has new minted an old lie,
Or tax'd invention for a fresh supply,
'Tis call'd a satire, and the world appears
Gath'ring around it with erected ears:
A thousand names are toss'd into the crowd;
Some whisper'd softly, and some twang'd aloud;
Just as the sapience of an author's brain
Suggests it safe or dang'rous to be plain.
Strange! how the frequent interjected dash

Quickens a market, and helps off the trash;
Th'important letters, that include the rest,
Serve as a key to those that are suppress'd;
Conjecture gripes the victims in his paw,
The world is charm'd, and Scrib escapes the law.
So, when the cold damp shades of night prevail,
Worms may be caught by either head or tail;
Forcibly drawn from many a close recess,
They meet with little pity, no redress;
Plung'd in the stream they lodge upon the mud,
Food for the famish'd rovers of the flood.
All zeal for a reform, that gives offence
To peace and charity, is mere pretence:
A bold remark, but which, if well applied,
Would humble many a tow'ring poet's pride.
Perhaps the man was in a sportive fit,
And had no other play-place for his wit;
Perhaps enchanted with the love of fame,
He sought the jewel in his neighbour's shame;
Perhaps—whatever end he might pursue,
The cause of virtue could not be his view.
At ev'ry stroke wit flashes in our eyes;
The turns are quick, the polish'd points surprise,
But shine with cruel and tremendous charms,
That, while they please, possess us with alarms;
So have I seen (and hasten'd to the sight
On all the wings of holiday delight),
Where stands that monument of ancient pow'r,
Nam'd, with emphatic dignity, the Tow'r,
Guns, halberts, swords, and pistols, great and small,
In starry forms dispos'd upon the wall;
We wonder, as we gazing stand below,
That brass and steel should make so fine a show;
But though we praise th'exact designer's skill,
Accounts them implements of mischief still.
No works shall find acceptance in that day,
When all disguises shall be rent away,
That square not truly with the Scripture plan,
Nor spring from love to God, or love to man.
As he ordains things sordid in their birth
To be resolv'd into their parent earth;
And, though the soul shall seek superior orbs,
Whate'er this world produces, it absorbs;
So self starts nothing, but what tends apace
Home to the goal, where it began the race.
Such as our motive is, our aim must be;
If this be servile, that can ne'er be free:
If self employ us, whatsoe'er is wrought,
We glorify that self, not him we ought;

Such virtues had need prove their own reward,
The judge of all men owes them no regard.
True Charity, a plant divinely nurs'd,
Fed by the love from which it rose at first,
Thrives against hope, and, in the rudest scene,
Storms but enliven its unfading green:
Exub'rant is the shadow it supplies,
Its fruit on earth, its growth above the skies.
To look at Him, who form'd us and redeem'd,
So glorious now, though once so disesteem'd,
To see a God stretch forth his human hand,
T'uphold the boundless scenes of his command;
To recollect, that, in a form like ours,
He bruis'd beneath his feet th'infernal pow'rs,
Captivity led captive, rose to claim
The wreath he won so dearly in our name;
That, thron'd above all height, he condescends
To call the few that trust in him his friends;
That, in the Heav'n of heav'ns, that space he deems
Too scanty for th'exertion of his beams,
And shines, as if impatient to bestow
Life and a kingdom upon worms below;
That sight imparts a never-dying flame,
Though feeble in degree, in kind the same.
Like him the soul, thus kindled from above,
Spreads wide her arms of universal love;
And, still enlarg'd as she receives the grace,
Includes creation in her close embrace.
Behold a Christian! and without the fires
The founder of that name alone inspires,
Though all accomplishment, all knowledge meet,
To make the shining prodigy complete,
Whoever boasts that name—behold a cheat!
Were love, in these the world's last doting years,
As frequent as the want of it appears,
The churches warm'd, they would no longer hold
Such frozen figures, stiff as they are cold;
Relenting forms would lose their pow'r, or cease;
And e'en the dipp'd and sprinkled live in peace:
Each heart would quit its prison in the breast,
And flow in free communion with the rest.
The statesman, skill'd in projects dark and deep,
Might burn his useless Machiavel, and sleep;
His budget often fill'd, yet always poor,
Might swing at ease behind his study door,
No longer prey upon our annual rents,
Or scare the nation with its big contents:
Disbanded legions freely might depart,
And slaying man would cease to be an art.

No learned disputants would take the field,
Sure not to conquer, and sure not to yield;
Both sides deceiv'd, if rightly understood,
Pelting each other for the public good.
Did charity prevail, the press would prove
A vehicle of virtue, truth, and love;
And I might spare myself the pains to show
What few can learn, and all suppose they know.
Thus have I thought to grace a serious lay
With many a wild, indeed, but flow'ry spray,
In hopes to gain, what else I must have lost,
Th'attention pleasure has so much engross'd.
But if, unhappily deceiv'd, I dream,
And prove too weak for so divine a theme,
Let Charity forgive me a mistake,
That zeal, not vanity, has chanc'd to make,
And spare the poet for his subject's sake.

CONVERSATION.

" Nam neque me tantum venientis sibilus austri,
Nec percussa juvant fluctu tam litora, nec quæ
Saxosas inter decurrunt flumina valles."
Virg. Ecl. 5.

Though nature weigh our talents, and dispense
To ev'ry man his modicum of sense,
And Conversation in its better part
May be esteem'd a gift, and not an art,
Yet much depends, as in the tiller's toil,
On culture, and the sowing of the soil.
Words learn'd by rote a parrot may rehearse,
But talking is not always to converse;
Not more distinct from harmony divine,
The constant creaking of a country sign.
As alphabets in ivory employ,
Hour after hour, the yet unletter'd boy,
Sorting and puzzling with a deal of glee
Those seeds of science call'd his A B C;
So language in the mouths of the adult,
Witness its insignificant result,
Too often proves an implement of play,
A toy to sport with, and pass time away.
Collect at ev'ning what the day brought forth,
Compress the sum into its solid worth,
And if it weighed th' importance of a fly,
The scales are false, or algebra a lie.
Sacred interpreter of human thought,
How few respect or use thee as they ought!
But all shall give account of ev'ry wrong,
Who dare dishonour or defile the tongue;
Who prostitute it in the cause of vice,
Or sell their glory at a market-price;
Who vote for hire, or point it with lampoon,
The dear-bought placeman, and the cheap buffoon
There is a prurience in the speech of some,
Wrath stays him, or else God would strike them dumb.

His wise forbearance has their end in view,
They fill their measure, and receive their due.
The heathen law-givers of ancient days,
Names almost worthy of a Christian's praise,
Would drive them forth from the resort of men,
And shut up ev'ry satyr in his den.
O come not ye near innocence and truth,
Ye worms that eat into the bud of youth!
Infectious as impure, your blighting pow'r
Taints in its rudiments the promis'd flow'r,
Its odour perish'd, and its charming hue,
Thenceforth 'tis hateful, for it smells of you.
Not e'en the vigorous and headlong rage
Of adolescence, or a firmer age,
Affords a plea allowable or just
For making speech the pamperer of lust;
But when the breath of age commits the fault,
'Tis nauseous as the vapour of a vault.
So wither'd stumps disgrace the sylvan scene,
No longer fruitful, and no longer green;
The sapless wood, divested of the bark,
Grows fungous, and takes fire at ev'ry spark.
Oaths terminate, as Paul observes, all strife—
Some men have surely then a peaceful life;
Whatever subject occupy discourse,
The feats of Vestris, or the naval force,
Asseveration blust'ring in your face
Makes contradiction such a hopeless case:
In ev'ry tale they tell, or false or true,
Well known, or such as no man ever knew,
They fix attention, heedless of your pain,
With oaths like rivets forc'd into the brain;
And e'en when sober truth prevails throughout,
They swear it, till affirmance breeds a doubt.
A Persian, humble servant of the sun,
Who, though devout, yet bigotry had none,
Hearing a lawyer, grave in his address,
With adjurations ev'ry word impress,
Suppos'd the man a bishop, or, at least,
God's name so much upon his lips, a priest;
Bow'd at the close with all his graceful airs,
And begg'd an int'rest in his frequent pray'rs.
Go, quit the rank to which ye stood preferr'd,
Henceforth associate in one common herd;
Religion, virtue, reason, common sense,
Pronounce your human form a false pretence;
A mere disguise, in which a devil lurks,
Who yet betrays his secret by his works.
Ye pow'rs who rule the tongue, if such there are,

And make colloquial happiness your care,
Preserve me from the thing I dread and hate,
A duel in the form of a debate.
The clash of arguments and jar of words,
Worse than the mortal brunt of rival swords,
Decide no question with their tedious length,
For opposition gives opinion strength.
Divert the champions prodigal of breath;
And put the peaceably-dispos'd to death.
O thwart me not, sir Soph, at ev'ry turn,
Nor carp at ev'ry flaw you may discern;
Though syllogisms hang not on my tongue,
I am not surely always in the wrong;
'Tis hard if all is false that I advance,
A fool must now and then be right by chance.
Not that all freedom of dissent I blame;
No—there I grant the privilege I claim.
A disputable point is no man's ground:
Rove where you please, 'tis common all around.
Discourse may want an animated—No,
To brush the surface, and to make it flow;
But still remember, if you mean to please,
To press your point with modesty and ease.
The mark, at which my juster aim I take,
Is contradiction for its own dear sake.
Set your opinion at whatever pitch,
Knots and impediments make something hitch;
Adopt his own, 'tis equally in vain,
Your thread of argument is snapp'd again;
The wrangler, rather than accord with you,
Will judge himself deceiv'd, and prove it too.
Vociferated logic kills me quite,
A noisy man is always in the right:
I twirl my thumbs, fall back into my chair,
Fix on the wainscot a distressful stare,
And, when I hope his blunders are all out,
Reply discreetly—To be sure—no doubt!
Dubius is such a scrupulous good man—
Yes—you may catch him tripping, if you can.
He would not, with a peremptory tone,
Assert the nose upon his face his own;
With hesitation admirably slow,
He humbly hopes—presumes—it may be so.
His evidence, if he were call'd by law
To swear to some enormity he saw,
For want of prominence and just relief,
Would hang an honest man, and save a thief.
Through constant dread of giving truth offence,
He ties up all his hearers in suspense;

Knows what he knows, as if he knew it not;
What he remembers, seems to have forgot;
His sole opinion, whatsoe'er befall,
Cent'ring at last in having none at all.
Yet, though he tease and balk your list'ning ear
He makes one useful point exceeding clear;
Howe'er ingenious on his darling theme
A sceptic in philosophy may seem,
Reduc'd to practice, his beloved rule
Would only prove him a consummate fool;
Useless in him alike both brain and speech,
Fate having plac'd all truth above his reach,
His ambiguities his total sum,
He might as well be blind, and deaf, and dumb.
Where men of judgment creep and feel their way,
The positive pronounce without dismay;
Their want of light and intellect supplied
By sparks absurdity strikes out of pride.
Without the means of knowing right from wrong,
They always are decisive, clear, and strong;
Where others toil with philosophic force,
Their nimble nonsense takes a shorter course;
Flings at your head conviction in the lump,
And gains remote conclusions at a jump:
Their own defect, invisible to them,
Seen in another, they at once condemn;
And, though self-idoliz'd in ev'ry case,
Hate their own likeness in a brother's face.
The cause is plain, and not to be denied,
The proud are always most provok'd by pride;
Few competitions but engender spite;
And those the most, where neither has a right.
The point of honor has been deem'd of use,
To teach good manners, and to curb abuse;
Admit it true, the consequence is clear,
Our polish'd manners are a mask we wear,
And, at the bottom, barb'rous still and rude,
We are restrain'd, indeed, but not subdued.
The very remedy, however sure,
Springs from the mischief it intends to cure,
And savage in its principle appears,
Tried, as it should be, by the fruit it bears.
'Tis hard, indeed, if nothing will defend
Mankind from quarrels but their fatal end;
That now and then a hero must decease,
That the surviving world may live in peace.
Perhaps at last close scrutiny may show
The practice dastardly, and mean, and low;
That men engage in it compell'd by force,

And fear, not courage, is its proper source;
The fear of tyrant custom, and the fear
Lest fops should censure us, and fools should sneer.
At least, to trample on our Maker's laws,
And hazard life for any or no cause,
To rush into a fix'd eternal state
Out of the very flames of rage and hate,
Or send another shiv'ring to the bar
With all the guilt of such unnat'ral war,
Whatever Use may urge, or Honor plead,
On Reason's verdict is a madman's deed.
Am I to set my life upon a throw,
Because a bear is rude and surly? No—
A moral, sensible, and well-bred man
Will not affront me; and no other can.
Were I empow'r'd to regulate the lists,
They should encounter with well-loaded fists;
A Trojan combat would be something new,
Let *Dares* beat *Entellus* black and blue;
Then each might show, to his admiring friends,
In honorable bumps his rich amends,
And carry in contusions of his skull,
A satisfactory receipt in full.
  A story, in which native humor reigns,
Is often useful, always entertains:
A graver fact, enlisted on your side,
May furnish illustration, well applied;
But sedentary weavers of long tales
Give me the fidgets, and my patience fails.
'Tis the most asinine employ on earth,
To hear them tell of parentage and birth,
And echo conversations, dull and dry,
Embellish'd with—*He said*, and *So said I*.
At ev'ry interview their route the same,
The repetition makes attention lame;
We bustle up with unsuccessful speed,
And in the saddest part cry—*Droll indeed!*
The path of narrative with care pursue,
Still making probability your clew:
On all the vestiges of truth attend,
And let *them* guide you to a decent end.
Of all ambitions man may entertain,
The worst, that can invade a sickly brain,
Is that, which angles hourly for surprise,
And baits its hook with prodigies and lies.
Credulous infancy, or age as weak,
Are fittest auditors for such to seek,
Who to please others will themselves disgrace,
Yet please not, but affront you to your face.

A great retailer of this curious ware
Having unloaded and made many stare,
Can this be true?—an arch observer cries,
Yes, (rather mov'd) I saw it with these eyes;
Sir! I believe it on that ground alone;
I could not, had I seen it with my own.
A tale should be judicious, clear, succinct;
The language plain, and incidents well link'd;
Tell not as new what ev'ry body knows,
And, new or old, still hasten to a close;
There, cent'ring in a focus round and neat,
Let all your rays of information meet.
What neither yields us profit nor delight
Is like a nurse's lullaby at night;
Guy Earl of Warwick, and fair Eleanore,
Or giant-killing Jack, would please me more.
The pipe, with solemn interposing puff,
Makes half a sentence at a time enough;
The dozing sages drop the drowsy strain,
Then pause, and puff—and speak, and pause again.
Such often, like the tube they so admire,
Important triflers! have more smoke than fire.
Pernicious weed! whose scent the fair annoys,
Unfriendly to society's chief joys,
Thy worst effect is banishing for hours
The sex, whose presence civilizes ours:
Thou art indeed the drug a gard'ner wants,
To poison vermin that infests his plants;
But are we so to wit and beauty blind,
As to despise the glory of our kind
And show the softest minds and fairest forms
As little mercy, as he grubs and worms?
They dare not wait the riotous abuse,
Thy thirst-creating steams at length produce,
When wine has giv'n indecent language birth,
And forc'd the floodgates of licentious mirth;
For sea-born Venus her attachment shows
Still to that element from which she rose,
And with a quiet, which no fumes disturb,
Sips meek infusions of a milder herb.
Th'emphatic speaker dearly loves t'oppose
In contact inconvenient, nose to nose.
As if the gnomon on his neighbour's phiz,
Touch'd with the magnet, had attracted his.
His whisper'd theme, dilated and at large,
Proves after all a wind-gun's airy charge,
An extract of his diary—no more,
A tasteless journal of the day before.
He walk'd abroad, o'ertaken in the rain,

Call'd on a friend, drank tea, stepp'd home again,
Resum'd his purpose, had a world of talk
With one he stumbled on, and lost his walk.
I interrupt him with a sudden bow,
Adieu, dear sir! lest you should lose it now.
I cannot talk with civet in the room,
A fine puss-gentleman that's all perfume;
The sight's enough—no need to smell a beau—
Who thrusts his nose into a raree show?
His odoriferous attempts to please
Perhaps might prosper with a swarm of bees;
But we that make no honey, though we sting,
Poets, are sometimes apt to maul the thing.
'Tis wrong to bring into a mix'd resort,
What makes some sick, and others *à-la-mort*:
An argument of cogence, we may say,
Why such an one should keep himself away.
A graver coxcomb we may sometimes see,
Quite as absurd, though not so light as he:
A shallow brain behind a serious mask,
An oracle within an empty cask,
The solemn fop; significant and budge;
A fool with judges, amongst fools a judge;
He says but little, and that little said
Owes all its weight, like loaded dice, to lead.
His wit invites you by his looks to come,
But when you knock, it never is at home.
'Tis like a parcel sent you by the stage,
Some handsome present, as your hopes presage;
'Tis heavy, bulky, and bids fair to prove
An absent friend's fidelity and love;
But when unpack'd, your disappointment groans
To find it stuff'd with brickbats, earth, and stones.
Some men employ their health, an ugly trick,
In making known how oft they have been sick,
And give us in recitals of disease
A doctor's trouble, but without the fees;
Relate how many weeks they kept their bed,
How an emetic or cathartic sped;
Nothing is slightly touch'd, much less forgot,
Nose, ears, and eyes, seem present on the spot.
Now the distemper, spite of draught or pill,
Victorious seem'd, and now the doctor's skill;
And now— alas for unforeseen mishaps!
They put on a damp nightcap and relapse;
They thought they must have died, they were so bad;
Their peevish hearers almost wish they had.
Some fretful tempers wince at ev'ry touch,
You always do too little or too much:

You speak with life, in hopes to entertain,
Your elevated voice goes through the brain;
You fall at once into a lower key,
That's worse—the drone-pipe of an humble bee.
The southern sash admits too strong a light,
You rise and drop the curtain—now 'tis night.
He shakes with cold—you stir the fire and strive
To make a blaze—that's roasting him alive.
Serve him with venison, and he chooses fish;
With sole—that's just the sort he does not wish.
He takes what he at first profess'd to loath,
And in due time feeds heartily on both;
Yet still, o'erclouded with a constant frown,
He does not swallow, but he gulps it down.
Your hope to please him vain on ev'ry plan,
Himself should work that wonder, if he can—
Alas! his efforts double his distress,
He likes yours little, and his own still less.
Thus always teasing others, always teas'd,
His only pleasure is—to be displeas'd.
 I pity bashful men, who feel the pain
Of fancied scorn and undeserv'd disdain,
And bear the marks upon a blushing face
Of needless shame, and self-impos'd disgrace.
Our sensibilties are so acute,
The fear of being silent makes us mute.
We sometimes think we could a speech produce
Much to the purpose, if our tongues were loose;
But being tried, it dies upon the lip,
Faint as a chicken's note that has the pip:
Our wasted oil unprofitably burns,
Like hidden lamps in old sepulchral urns.
Few Frenchmen of this evil have complain'd;
It seems as if we Britons were ordain'd,
By way of wholesome curb upon our pride,
To fear each other, fearing none beside.
The cause perhaps inquiry may descry,
Self-searching with an introverted eye,
Conceal'd within an unsuspected part,
The vainest corner of our own vain heart:
For ever aiming at the world's esteem,
Our self-importance ruins its own scheme;
In other eyes our talents rarely shown,
Become at length so splendid in our own,
We dare not risk them into public view,
Lest they miscarry of what seems their due.
True modesty is a discerning grace,
And only blushes in the proper place;
But counterfeit is blind, and sculks through fear,

Where 'tis a shame to be asham'd t'appear:
Humility the parent of the first,
The last by vanity produc'd and nurs'd.
The circle form'd, we sit in silent state,
Like figures drawn upon a dial-plate;
Yes ma'am, and no ma'am, utter'd softly show,
Ev'ry five minutes how the minutes go;
Each individual, suff'ring a constraint
Poetry may, but colours cannot paint;
As if in close committe on the sky,
Reports it hot or cold, or wet or dry;
And finds a changing clime a happy source
Of wise reflection, and well tim'd discourse.
We next inquire, but softly and by stealth,
Like conservators of the public health,
Of epidemic throats, if such there are,
And coughs and rheums, and phthisic, and catarrh.
That theme exhausted, a wide chasm ensues,
Fill'd up at last with interesting news,
Who danc'd with whom, and who are like to wed,
And who is hang'd, and who is brought to bed:
But fear to call a more important cause,
As if t'were treason against English laws.
The visit paid, with ecstasy we come,
As from a sev'n years transportation, home,
And there resume an unembarrass'd brow,
Recov'ring what we lost we know not how,
The faculties, that seem'd reduc'd to nought,
Expression and the privilege of thought.
  The reeking, roaring hero of the chase,
I give him over as a desperate case.
Physicians write in hopes to work a cure,
Never, if honest ones, when death is sure;
And though the fox he follows may be tam'd,
A mere fox-foll'wer never is reclaim'd.
Some farrier should prescribe his proper course,
Whose only fit companion is his horse;
Or if, deserving of a better doom,
The noble beast judge otherwise, his groom.
Yet e'en the rogue that serves him, though he stand,
To take his honor's orders, cap in hand,
Prefers his fellow-grooms with much good sense,
Their skill a truth, his master's a pretence.
If neither horse nor groom affect the squire,
Where can at last his jockeyship retire?
O to the club, the scene of savage joys,
The school of coarse good fellowship and noise;
There, in the sweet society of those,
Whose friendship from his boyish years he chose,

Let him improve his talent if he can,
Till none but beasts acknowledge him a man.
Man's heart had been impenetrably seal'd,
Like theirs that cleave the flood or graze the field,
Had not his Maker's all-bestowing hand
Giv'n him a soul, and bade him understand;
The reas'ning pow'r vouchsaf'd of course inferr'd
The pow'r to clothe that reason with his word;
For all is perfect, that God works on earth,
And he, that gives conception, aids the birth.
If this be plain, 'tis plainly understood,
What uses of his boon the Giver would.
The Mind, dispatch'd upon her busy toil,
Should range where Providence has bless'd the soil;
Visiting ev'ry flow'r with labour meet,
And gath'ring all her treasures sweet by sweet,
She should imbue the tongue with what she sips,
And shed the balmy blessing on the lips,
That good diffus'd may more abundant grow,
And speech may praise the pow'r that bids it flow.
Will the sweet warbler of the livelong night,
That fills the list'ning lover with delight,
Forget his harmony, with rapture heard,
To learn the twitt'ring of a meaner bird?
Or make the parrot's mimicry his choice,
That odious libel on a human voice?
No—Nature, unsophisticate by man,
Starts not aside from her Creator's plan;
The melody, that was at first design'd
To cheer the rude forefathers of mankind,
Is note for note deliver'd in our ears,
In the last scene of her six thousand years.
Yet Fashion, leader of a chatt'ring train,
Whom man, for his own hurt, permits to reign,
Who shifts and changes all things but his shape,
And would degrade her vot'ry to an ape,
The fruitful parent of abuse and wrong,
Holds a usurp'd dominion o'er his tongue;
There sits and prompts him with his own disgrace,
Prescribes the theme, the tone, and the grimace,
And, when accomplish'd in her wayward school,
Calls gentleman whom she has made a fool.
'Tis an unalterable fix'd decree,
That none could frame or ratify but she,
That heav'n and hell, and righteousness and sin,
Snares in his path, and foes that lurk within,
God and his attributes (a field of day
Where 'tis an angel's happiness to stray,)
Fruits of his love, and wonders of his might,

Be never nam'd in ears esteem'd polite,
That he who dares, when she forbids, be grave,
Shall stand proscrib'd, a madman or a knave,
A close designer not to be believ'd,
Or, if excus'd that charge, at least deceiv'd.
Oh folly worthy of the nurses lap,
Give it the breast, or stop its mouth with pap!
Is it incredible, or can it seem,
A dream to any, except those that dream,
That man should love his Maker, and *that* fire,
Warming his heart, should at his lips transpire?
Know then, and modesty let fall your eyes,
And veil your daring crest that braves the skies;
That air of insolence affronts your God,
You need his pardon, and provoke his rod:
Now, in a posture that becomes you more
Than that heroic strut assum'd before,
Know, your arrears with ev'ry hour accrue
For mercy shown, while wrath is justly due.
The time is short, and there are souls on earth,
Though future pain may serve for present mirth,
Acquainted with the woes, that fear or shame,
By Fashion taught, forbade them once to name,
And, having felt the pangs you deem a jest,
Have prov'd them truths too big to be express'd.
Go seek on revelation's hallow'd ground,
Sure to succeed, the remedy they found;
Touch'd by that pow'r that you have dar'd to mock,
That makes seas stable, and dissolves the rock,
Your heart shall yield a life-renewing stream,
That fools, as you have done, shall call a dream.
It happen'd on a solemn eventide,
Soon after He that was our Surety died,
Two bosom friends, each pensively inclin'd,
The scene of all those sorrows left behind,
Sought their own village, busied as they went
In musings worthy of the great event:
They spake of him they lov'd, of him whose life,
Though blameless, had incurr'd perpetual strife,
Whose deeds had left, in spite of hostile arts,
A deep memorial graven on their hearts.
The recollection, like a vein of ore,
The farther trac'd, enrich'd them still the more;
They thought him, and they justly thought him, one
Sent to do more than he appear'd t' have done;
T' exalt a people, and to place them high
Above all else, and wonder'd he should die.
Ere yet they brought their journey to an end,
A stranger join'd them, courteous as a friend,

And ask'd them, with a kind, engaging air,
What their affliction was, and begg'd a share.
Inform'd, he gather'd up the broken thread,
And, truth and wisdom gracing all he said,
Explain'd, illustrated, and search'd so well
The tender theme, on which they chose to dwell,
That, reaching home, The night, they said, is near,
We must not now be parted, sojourn here—
The new acquaintance soon become a guest,
And, made so welcome at their simple feast,
He bless'd the bread, but vanish'd at the word,
And left them both exclaiming, 'Twas the Lord!
Did not our hearts feel all he deign'd to say?
Did not they burn within us by the way?
Now theirs was converse, such as it behoves
Man to maintain, and such as God approves:
Their views, indeed, were indistinct and dim,
But yet successful, being aim'd at him.
Christ and his character their only scope,
Their object, and their subject and their hope,
They felt what it became them much to feel,
And, wanting him to loose the sacred seal,
Found him as prompt, as their desire was true,
To spread the newborn glories in their view.
Well—what are ages and the lapse of time,
Match'd against truths, as lasting as sublime;
Can length of years on God himself exact?
Or make that fiction, which was once a fact?
No—marble and recording brass decay,
And, like the graver's mem'ry, pass away;
The works of man inherit, as is just,
Their author's frailty, and return to dust:
But truth divine for ever stands secure,
Its head is guarded, as its base is sure;
Fix'd in the rolling flood of endless years,
The pillar of th'eternal plan appears,
The raving storm and dashing wave defies,
Built by that architect who built the skies.
Hearts may be found, that harbour at this hour
That love of Christ, and all its quick'ning pow'r
And lips unstain'd by folly or by strife,
Whose wisdom, drawn from the deep well of life,
Tastes of its healthful origin, and flows
A Jordan for th'ablution of our woes.
O days of heav'n, and nights of equal praise,
Serene and peaceful as those heav'nly days,
When souls drawn upwards in communion sweet,
Enjoy the stillness of some close retreat,
Discourse, as if releas'd and safe at home,

Of dangers past, and wonders yet to come,
And spread the sacred treasures of the breast
Upon the lap of covenanted Rest.
What, always dreaming over heav'nly things,
Like angel-heads in stone with pigeon-wings?
Canting and whining out all day the word,
And half the night? Fanatic and absurd!
Mine be the friend less frequent in his pray'rs,
Who makes no bustle with his soul's affairs,
Whose wit can brighten up a wintry day,
And chase the splenetic dull hours away;
Content on earth in earthly things to shine,
Who waits for heav'n ere he becomes divine,
Leaves saints t'enjoy those altitudes they teach,
And plucks the fruit plac'd more within his reach.
Well spoken, advocate of sin and shame,
Known by thy bleating, Ignorance thy name.
Is sparkling wit the World's exclusive right?
The fix'd fee-simple of the vain and light?
Can hopes of heav'n, bright prospects of an hour,
That come to waft us out of Sorrow's pow'r,
Obscure or quench a faculty, that finds
Its happiest soil in the serenest minds?
Religion curbs indeed its wanton play,
And brings the trifler under rig'rous sway,
But gives it usefulness unknown before,
And, purifying, makes it shine the more.
A Christian's wit is inoffensive light,
A beam that aids, but never grieves the sight;
Vig'rous in age as in the flush of youth,
'Tis always active on the side of truth;
Temp'rance and peace insure its healthful state,
And make it brightest at its latest date.
Oh I have seen (nor hope perhaps in vain,
Ere life go down, to see such sights again)
A vet'ran warrior in the Christian field,
Who never saw the sword he could not wield;
Grave without dulness, learned without pride,
Exact, yet not precise, though meek, keen-ey'd;
A man that would have foil'd at their own play
A dozen would-be's of the modern day;
Who, when occasion justified its use,
Had wit as bright as ready to produce,
Could fetch from records of an earlier age,
Or from philosophy's enlighten'd page,
His rich materials, and regale your ear
With strains it was a privilege to hear:
Yet, above all, his luxury is supreme,
And his chief glory, was the Gospel theme;

There he was copious as old Greece or Rome,
His happy eloquence seem'd there at home,
Ambitious not to shine or to excel,
But to treat justly what he lov'd so well.
It moves me more perhaps than folly ought,
When some green heads, as void of wit as thought,
Suppose *themselves* monopolists of sense,
And wiser men's ability pretence.
Though time will wear us, and we must grow old,
Such men are not forgot as soon as cold;
Their fragrant mem'ry will outlast their tomb,
Embalm'd for ever in its own perfume.
And to say truth, though in its early prime,
And when unstain'd with any grosser crime,
Youth has a sprightliness and fire to boast,
That in the valley of decline are lost,
And Virtue with peculiar charms appears,
Crown'd with the garland of life's blooming years;
Yet Age, by long experience well inform'd,
Well read, well temper'd, with religion warm'd,
That fire abated, which impels rash Youth,
Proud of his speed, to overshoot the truth,
As time improves the grape's authentic juice,
Mellows and makes the speech more fit for use,
And claims a rev'rence in its short'ning day,
That 'tis an honor and a joy to pay.
The fruits of Age, less fair, are yet more sound,
Than those a brighter season pours around;
And, like the stores autumnal suns mature,
Through wintry rigors unimpair'd endure.
What is fanatic frenzy, scorn'd so much,
And dreaded more than a contagious touch?
I grant it dang'rous, and approve your fear,
That fire is catching if you draw too near;
But sage observers oft mistake the flame,
And give true piety that odious name.
To tremble (as the creature of an hour
Ought at the view of an almighty pow'r)
Before his presence, at whose awful throne
All tremble in all worlds, except our own,
To supplicate his mercy, love his ways,
And prize them above pleasure, wealth, or praise,
Though common sense, allow'd a casting voice,
And free from bias, must approve the choice,
Convicts a man fanatic in th'extreme,
And wild as madness in the world's esteem.
But that disease, when soberly defin'd,
Is the false fire of an o'erheated mind;
It views the truth with a distorted eye,

And either warps or lays it useless by;
'Tis narrow, selfish, arrogant, and draws
Its sordid nourishment from man's applause;
And while at heart sin unrelinquish'd lies,
Presumes itself chief fav'rite of the skies.
'Tis such a light as putrefaction breeds
In fly-blow'n flesh, whereon the maggot feeds,
Shines in the dark, but, usher'd into day,
The stench remains, the lustre dies away.
True bliss, if man may reach it, is compos'd
Of hearts in union mutually disclos'd;
And, farewell else all hope of pure delight,
Those hearts should be reclaim'd, renew'd, upright.
Bad men, profaning friendship's hallow'd name,
Form, in its stead, a covenant of shame,
A dark confed'racy against the laws
Of virtue, and religion's glorious cause:
They build each other up with dreadful skill,
As bastions set point blank against God's will;
Enlarge and fortify the dread redoubt,
Deeply resolved to shut a Saviour out;
Call legions up from hell to back the deed;
And, curs'd with conquest, finally succeed.
But souls, that carry on a blest exchange
Of joys, they meet with in their heav'nly range,
And with a fearless confidence make known
The sorrows, sympathy esteems its own,
Daily derive increasing light and force
From such communion in their pleasant course,
Feel less the journey's roughness and its length,
Meet their opposers with united strength,
And, one in heart, in int'rest, and design,
Gird up each other to the race divine.
But Conversation, choose what theme we may,
And chiefly when religion leads the way,
Should flow, like waters after summer show'rs,
Not as if rais'd by mere mechanic pow'rs.
The Christian, in whose soul, though now distress'd,
Lives the dear thoughts of joys he once possess'd,
When all his glowing language issu'd forth
With God's deep stamp upon its current worth,
Will speak without disguise, and must impart,
Sad as it is, his undissembling heart,
Abhors constraint, and dares not feign a zeal,
Or seem to boast a fire he does not feel.
The song of Zion is a tasteless thing,
Unless, when rising on a joyful wing,
The soul can mix with the celestial bands,
And give the strain the compass it demands.

Strange tidings these to tell a world, who treat
All but their own experience as deceit!
Will they believe, though credulous enough
To swallow much upon much weaker proof,
That there are blest inhabitants of earth,
Partakers of a new ethereal birth,
Their hopes, desires, and purposes estrang'd
From things terrestial, and divinely chang'd,
Their very language, of a kind, that speaks
The soul's sure int'rest in the good she seeks,
Who deal with Scripture, its importance felt,
As Tully with philosophy once dealt,
And in the silent watches of the night,
And through the scenes of toil-renewing light,
The social walk, or solitary ride,
Keep still the dear companion at their side?
No—shame upon a self-disgracing age,
God's work may serve an ape upon a stage
With such a jest, as fill'd with hellish glee
Certain invisibles as shrewd as he;
But veneration or respect finds none,
Save from the subjects of that work alone.
The World grown old her deep discernment shows,
Claps spectacles on her sagacious nose,
Peruses closely the true Christian's face,
And finds it a mere mask of sly grimace;
Usurps God's office, lays his bosom bare,
Vnd finds hypocrisy close lurking there;
And, serving God herself through mere constraint,
Concludes his unfeign'd love of him a feint.
And yet, God knows, look human nature through,
(And in due time the World shall know it too)
That since the flow'rs of Eden felt the blast,
That after man's defection laid all waste,
Sincerity tow'rds the heart-searching God
Has made the new-born creature her abode,
Nor shall be found in unregen'rate souls,
Till the last fire burn all between the poles.
Sincerity! why 'tis his only pride,
Weak and imperfect in all grace beside,
He knows that God demands his heart entire,
And gives him all his just demands require.
Without it his pretensions were as vain,
As having it he deems the World's disdain;
That great defect would cost him not alone
Man's favorable judgment, but his own;
His birthright shaken, ana no longer clear,
Than while his conduct proves his heart sincere.
Retort the charge, and let the World be told

She boasts a confidence she does not hold;
That, conscious of her crimes, she feels instead
A cold misgiving, and a killing dread:
That while in health the ground of her support
Is madly to forget that life is short;
That sick she trembles, knowing she must die,
Her hope presumption, and her faith a lie;
That while she dotes, and dreams that she believes,
She mocks her Maker, and herself deceives,
Her utmost reach, historical assent,
The doctrines warp'd to what they never meant;
That truth itself is in her head as dull
And useless as a candle in a scull,
And all her love of God a groundless claim,
A trick upon the canvass, painted flame.
Tell her again, the sneer upon her face,
And all her censures of the work of grace,
Are insincere, meant only to conceal
A dread she would not, yet is forc'd to feel;
That in her heart the Christian she reveres,
And while she seems to scorn him, only fears.
 A poet does not work by square or line,
As smiths and joiners perfect a design;
At least we moderns, our attention less,
Beyond th'example of our sires digress,
And claim a right to scamper and run wide,
Wherever chance, caprice, or fancy guide.
The World and I fortuitously met;
I ow'd a trifle, and have paid the debt;
She did no wrong, I recompens'd the deed,
And, having struck the balance, now proceed.
Perhaps, however, as some years have pass'd,
Since she and I convers'd together last,
And I have liv'd recluse in rural shades,
Which seldom a distinct report pervades,
Great changes and new manners have occurr'd,
And blest reforms, that I have never heard,
And she may now be as discreet and wise,
As once absurd in all discerning eyes.
Sobriety perhaps may now be found,
Where once Intoxication press'd the ground;
The subtle and injurious may be just,
And he grown chaste, that was the slave of lust;
Arts once esteem'd may be with shame dismiss'd;
Charity may relax the miser's fist;
The gamester may have cast his cards away,
Forgot to curse, and only kneel to pray.
It has indeed been told me (with what weight,
How credibly, 'tis hard for me to state)

That fables old, that seem'd for ever mute,
Reviv'd are hast'ning into fresh repute,
And gods and goddesses, discarded long
Like useless lumber, or a stroller's song,
Are bringing into vogue their heathen train,
And Jupiter bids fair to rule again;
That certain feasts are instituted now,
Where Venus hears the lover's tender vow;
That all Olympus through the country roves,
To consecrate our few remaining groves,
And Echo learns politely to repeat
The praise of names for ages obsolete:
That having prov'd the weakness, it should seem,
Of revelation's ineffectual beam,
To bring the passions under sober sway,
And give the moral springs their proper play,
They mean to try what may at last be done,
By stout substantial gods of wood and stone,
And whether Roman rites may not produce
The virtues of old Rome for English use.
May such success attend the pious plan,
May Mercury once more embellish man,
Grace him again with long-forgotten arts,
Reclaim his taste, and brighten up his parts,
Make him athletic, as in days of old,
Learn'd at the bar, in the palæstra bold,
Divest the rougher sex of female airs,
And teach the softer not to copy theirs:
The change shall please, nor shall it matter aught
Who works the wonder, if it be but wrought.
'Tis time, however, if the case stands thus,
For us plain folks, and all who side with us,
To build our altar, confident and bold,
And say as stern Elijah said of old,
The strife now stands upon a fair award,
If Israel's Lord be God, then serve the Lord:
If he be silent, faith is all a whim,
Then Baal is the God, and worship him.
Digression is so much in modern use,
Thought is so rare, and fancy so profuse,
Some never seem so wide of their intent,
As when returning to the theme they meant;
As mendicants, whose business is to roam,
Make ev'ry parish but their own their home.
Though such continual zigzags in a book,
Such drunken reelings have an awkward look,
And I had rather creep to what is true,
Than rove and stagger with no mark in view;
Yet to consult a little, seem'd no crime,

The freakish humor of the present time:
But now to gather up what seems dispers'd,
And touch the subject I design'd at first,
May prove, through much beside the rules of art,
Best for the public, and my wisest part.
And first, let no man charge me, that I mean
To clothe in sable ev'ry social scene,
And give good company a face severe,
As if they met around a father's bier;
For tell some men, that pleasure all their bent,
And laughter all their work, is life misspent,
Their wisdom bursts into this sage reply,
Then mirth is sin, and we should always cry.
To find the medium asks some share of wit,
And therefore 'tis a mark fools never hit.
But though life's valley be a vale of tears,
A brighter scene beyond that vale appears,
Whose glory, with a light that never fades,
Shoots between scatter'd rocks and op'ning shades,
And, while it shows the land the soul desires,
The language of the land she seeks inspires.
Thus touch'd, the tongue receives a sacred cure
Of all that was absurd, profane, impure;
Held within modest bounds, the tide of speech
Pursues the course that Truth and Nature teach;
No longer labours merely to produce
The pomp of sound, or tinkle without use:
Where'er it winds, the salutary stream,
Sprightly and fresh, enriches ev'ry theme,
While all the happy man possess'd before,
The gift of nature, or the classic store,
Is made subservient to the grand design,
For which Heav'n form'd the faculty divine,
So, should an idiot, while at large he strays,
Find the sweet lyre, on which an artist plays,
With rash and awkward force the chords he shakes,
And grins with wonder at the jar he makes;
But let the wise and well-instructed hand
Once take the shell beneath his just command,
In gentle sound it seems as it complain'd
Of the rude injuries it late sustain'd,
Till tun'd at length to some immortal song,
It sounds Jehovah's name, and pours his praise along.

RETIREMENT.

. . . . . . studiis florens ignobilis otî.
Virg. Geor. lib. 4.

Hackney'd in business, wearied at that oar,
Which thousands, once fast chain'd to, quit no more,
But which, when life at ebb runs weak and low,
All wish, or seem to wish, they could forego;
The statesman, lawyer, merchant, man of trade,
Pants for the refuge of some rural shade,
Where, all his long anxieties forgot
Amid the charms of a sequester'd spot,
Or recollected only to gild o'er,
And add a smile to what was sweet before,
He may possess the joys he thinks he sees,
Lay his old age upon the lap of Ease,
Improve the remnant of his wasted span,
And, having liv'd a trifler, die a man.
Thus Conscience pleads her cause within the breast,
Though long rebell'd against, not yet suppress'd,
And calls a creature form'd for God alone,
For Heav'ns high purposes, and not his own,
Calls him away from selfish ends and aims,
From what debilitates and what inflames,
From cities humming with a restless crowd,
Sordid as active, ignorant as loud,
Whose highest praise is that they live in vain,
The dupes of pleasure, or the slaves of gain,
Where works of man are cluster'd close around,
And works of God are hardly to be found,
To regions where, in spite of sin and woe,
Traces of Eden are still seen below,
Where mountain, river, forest, field, and grove,
Remind him of his Maker's pow'r and love.
'Tis well if, look'd for at so late a day,
In the last scene of such a senseless play,
True wisdom will attend his feeble call,
And grace his action ere the curtain fall.

Souls, that have long despis'd their heav'nly birth,
Their wishes all impregnated with earth,
For threescore years employ'd with ceaseless care
In catching smoke and feeding upon air,
Conversant only with the ways of men,
Rarely redeem the short remaining ten.
Invet'rate habits choke th'unfruitful heart,
Their fibres penetrate its tend'rest part,
And, draining its nutritious pow'rs to feed
Their noxious growth, starve ev'ry better seed.
Happy, if full of days—but happier far,
If, ere we yet discern life's ev'ning star,
Sick of the service of a world, that feeds
Its patient drudges with dry chaff and weeds,
We can escape from Custom's idiot sway,
To serve the Sovereign we were born t'obey.
Then sweet to muse upon his skill display'd
(Infinite skill) in all that he has made!
To trace in Nature's most minute design
The signature and stamp of pow'r divine,
Contrivance intricate, express'd with ease,
Where unassisted sight no beauty sees,
The shapely limb and lubricated joint
Within the small dimensions of a point,
Muscle and nerve miraculously spun,
His mighty work, who speaks, and it is done,
Th' invisible in things scarce seen reveal'd,
To whom an atom is an ample field;
To wonder at a thousand insect forms,
These hatch'd, and those resuscitated worms,
New life ordain'd and brighter scenes to share,
Once prone on earth, now buoyant upon air,
Whose shape would make them, had they bulk and size,
More hideous foes than fancy can devise;
With helmet-heads and dragon-scales adorn'd,
The mighty myriads, now securely scorn'd,
Would mock the majesty of man's high birth,
Despise his bulwarks, and unpeople earth.
Then with a glance of fancy to survey,
Far as the faculty can stretch away,
Ten thousand rivers pour'd at his command
From urns, that never fail, through ev'ry land;
These like a deluge with impetuous force,
Those winding modestly a silent course;
The cloud-surmounting Alps, the fruitful vales;
Seas, on which ev'ry nation spreads her sails;
The sun, a world whence other worlds drink light,
The crescent moon, the diadem of night;
Stars countless, each in his appointed place,

Fast anchor'd in the deep abyss of space—
At such a sight to catch the poet's flame,
And with a rapture like his own exclaim,
These are thy glorious works, thou source of good,
How dimly seen, how faintly understood!
Thine, and upheld by thy paternal care,
This universal frame, thus wondrous fair;
Thy pow'r divine, and bounty beyond thought,
Ador'd and prais'd in all that thou hast wrought.
Absorb'd in that immensity I see,
I shrink abas'd, and yet aspire to thee;
Instruct me, guide me to that heav'nly day,
Thy words more clearly than thy works display,
That, while thy truths my grosser thoughts refine,
I may resemble thee, and call thee mine.
O blest proficiency! surpassing all,
That men erroneously their glory call,
The recompense that arts or arms can yield,
The bar, the senate, or the tented field.
Compar'd with this sublimest life below,
Ye kings and rulers, what have courts to show?
Thus studied, us'd and consecrated thus,
On earth what is, seems form'd indeed for us:
Not as the plaything of a froward child,
Fretful unless diverted and beguil'd,
Much less to feed and fan the fatal fires
Of pride, ambition, or impure desires,
But as a scale, by which the soul ascends
From mighty means to more important ends,
Securely, though by steps but rarely trod,
Mounts from inferior beings up to God,
And sees, by no fallacious light or dim,
Earth made for man, and man himself for him.
Not that I mean t'approve, or would enforce,
A superstitious and monastic course:
Truth is not local, God alike pervades
And fills the world of traffic and the shades,
And may be fear'd amidst the busiest scenes,
Or scorn'd where business never intervenes.
But 'tis not easy with a mind like ours,
Conscious of weakness in its noblest pow'rs,
And in a world where, other ills apart,
The roving eye misleads the careless heart,
To limit Thought, by nature prone to stray
Wherever freakish Fancy points the way;
To bid the pleadings of Self-love be still,
Resign our own and seek our Maker's will;
To spread the page of Scripture, and compare
Our conduct with the laws engraven there;

To measure all that passes in the breast,
Faithfully, fairly, by that sacred test;
To dive into the secret deeps within,
To spare no passion and no fav'rite sin,
And search the themes, important above all,
Ourselves, and our recov'ry from our fall.
But leisure, silence, and a mind releas'd
From anxious thoughts how wealth may be increas'd,
How to secure, in some propitious hour,
The point of int'rest or the post of pow'r,
A soul serene, and equally retir'd
From objects too much dreaded or desir'd,
Safe from the clamors of perverse dispute,
At least are friendly to the great pursuit.
Op'ning the map of God's extensive plan,
We find a little isle, this life of man;
Eternity's unknown expanse appears
Circling around and limiting his years.
The busy race examine and explore
Each creek and cavern of the dang'rous shore,
With care collect what in their eyes excels,
Some shining pebbles, and some weeds and shells;
Thus laden, dream that they are rich and great,
And happiest he that groans beneath his weight.
The waves o'ertake them in their serious play,
And ev'ry hour sweeps multitudes away;
They shriek and sink, survivors start and weep,
Pursue their sport, and follow to the deep.
A few forsake the throng; with lifted eyes
Ask wealth of Heav'n, and gain a real prize,
Truth, wisdom, grace, and peace like that above,
Seal'd with his signet whom they serve and love;
Scorn'd by the rest, with patient hope they wait
A kind release from their imperfect state,
And unregretted are soon snatch'd away
From scenes of sorrow into glorious day.
Nor these alone prefer a life recluse,
Who seek retirement for its proper use;
The love of change, that lives in ev'ry breast,
Genius and temper, and desire of rest,
Discordant motives in one centre meet,
And each inclines its vot'ry to retreat.
Some minds by nature are averse to noise,
And hate the tumult half the world enjoys,
The lure of av'rice, or the pompous prize,
That courts display before ambitious eyes;
The fruits that hang on pleasure's flow'ry stem,
Whate'er enchants them, are no snares to them.
To them the deep recess of dusky groves,

Or forest, where the deer securely roves,
The fall of waters, and the song of birds,
And hills that echo to the distant herds,
Are luxuries excelling all the glare
The world can boast, and her chief fav'rites share.
With eager step, and carelessly array'd,
For such a cause the poet seeks the shade,
From all he sees he catches new delight,
Pleas'd Fancy claps her pinions at the sight,
The rising or the setting orb of day,
The clouds that flit, or slowly float away,
Nature in all the various shapes she wears,
Frowning in storms, or breathing gentle airs;
The snowy robe her wintry state assumes,
Her summer heats, her fruits, and her perfumes;
All, all alike transport the glowing bard,
Success in rhyme his glory and reward.
O Nature! whose Elysian scenes disclose
His bright perfections, at whose word they rose,
Next to that pow'r, who form'd thee and sustains,
Be thou the great inspirer of my strains.
Still, as I touch the lyre, do thou expand
Thy genuine charms, and guide an artless hand,
That I may catch a fire but rarely known,
Give useful light, though I should miss renown,
And, poring on thy page, whose ev'ry line
Bears proof of an intelligence divine,
May feel a heart enrich'd by what it pays,
That builds its glory on its Maker's praise.
Wo to the man, whose wit disclaims its use,
Glitt'ring in vain, or only to seduce,
Who studies nature with a wanton eye,
Admires the work, but slips the lesson by;
His hours of leisure and recess employs
In drawing pictures of forbidden joys,
Retires to blazon his own worthless name,
Or shoot the careless with a surer aim.
  The lover too shuns business and alarms,
Tender idolater of absent charms.
Saints offer nothing in their warmest pray'rs,
That he devotes not with a zeal like theirs;
'Tis consecration of his heart, soul, time,
And ev'ry thought that wanders is a crime.
In sighs he worships his supremely fair,
And weeps a sad libation in despair;
Adores a creature, and, devout in vain,
Wins in return an answer of disdain.
As woodbine weds the plant within her reach,
Rough elm, or smooth-grain'd ash, or glossy beech,

In spiral rings ascends the trunk, and lays
Her golden tassels on the leafy sprays,
But does a mischief while she lends a grace,
Strait'ning its growth by such a strict embrace;
So love, that clings around the noblest minds,
Forbids th' advancement of the soul he binds;
The suitor's air indeed he soon improves,
And forms it to the taste of her he loves,
Teaches his eyes a language, and no less
Refines his speech, and fashions his address;
But farewell promises of happier fruits,
Manly designs, and learning's grave pursuits;
Girt with a chain he cannot wish to break,
His only bliss is sorrow for her sake;
Who will may pant for glory, and excel,
Her smile his aim, all higher aims farewell!
Thyrsis, Alexis, or whatever name
May least offend against so pure a flame,
Though sage advice of friends the most sincere
Sounds harshly in so delicate an ear,
And lovers, of all creatures, tame or wild,
Can least brook management, however mild;
Yet let a poet (poetry disarms
The fiercest animals with magic charms)
Risk an intrusion on thy pensive mood,
And woo and win thee to thy proper good.
Pastoral images and still retreats,
Umbrageous walks and solitary seats,
Sweet birds in concert with harmonious streams
Soft airs, nocturnal vigils, and day dreams,
Are all enchantments in a case like thine,
Conspire against thy peace with one design,
Soothe thee to make thee but a surer prey,
And feed the fire that wastes thy pow'rs away.
Up—God has form'd thee with a wiser view,
Not to be led in chains, but to subdue;
Calls thee to cope with enemies, and first
Points out a conflict with thyself, the worst.
Woman indeed, a gift he would bestow
When he design'd a Paradise below,
The richest earthly boon his hands afford,
Deserves to be belov'd, but not ador'd.
Post away swiftly to more active scenes,
Collect the scatter'd truths that study gleans,
Mix with the world, but with its wiser part,
No longer give an image all thine heart;
Its empire is not hers, nor is it thine,
'Tis God's just claim, prerogative divine.
Virtuous and faithful HEBERDEN, whose skill

Attemps no task it cannot well fulfil,
Gives melancholy up to Nature's care,
And sends the patient into purer air.
Look where he comes—in this embow'r'd alcove
Stand close conceal'd, and see a statue move:
Lips busy, and eyes fix'd, foot falling slow,
Arms hanging idly down, hands clasp'd below,
Interpret to the marking eye distress,
Such as its symptoms can alone express.
That tongue is silent now; that silent tongue
Could argue once, could jest or join the song,
Could give advice, could censure or commend,
Or charm the sorrows of a drooping friend.
Renounc'd alike its office and its sport,
Its brisker and its graver strains fall short;
Both fail beneath a fever's secret sway,
And like a summer brook are past away.
This is a sight for Pity to peruse,
Till she resemble faintly what she views,
Till Sympathy contract a kindred pain,
Pierc'd with the woes that she laments in vain.
This, of all maladies that man infest,
Claims most compassion, and receives the least:
Job felt it, when he groan'd beneath the rod
And the barb'd arrows of a frowning God;
And such emollients as his friends could spare,
Friends such as his for modern Jobs prepare.
Blest, rather curst, with hearts that never feel,
Kept snug in caskets of close-hammer'd steel,
With mouths made only to grin wide and eat,
And minds, that deem derided pain a treat,
With limbs of British oak, and nerves of wire,
And wit that puppet-prompters might inspire,
Their sov'reign nostrum is a clumsy joke
On pangs enforc'd with God's severest stroke.
But with a soul, that ever felt the sting
Of sorrow, sorrow is a sacred thing:
Not to molest, or irritate, or raise
A laugh at his expense, is slender praise;
He, that has not usurp'd the name of man,
Does all, and deems too little all, he can,
T'assuage the throbbings of the fester'd part,
And staunch the bleedings of a broken heart.
'Tis not, as heads that never ache, suppose,
Forg'ry of fancy, and a dream of woes;
Man is a harp, whose chords elude the sight,
Each yielding harmony dispos'd aright;
The screws revers'd (a task which, if he please,
God in a moment executes with ease,)

Ten thousand thousand strings at once go loose,
Lost, till he tune them, all their pow'r and use.
Then neither heathy wilds, nor scenes as fair
As ever recompens'd the peasant's care,
Nor soft declivities with tufted hills,
Nor view of waters turning busy mills,
Parks in which Art preceptress Nature weds,
Nor gardens interspers'd with flow'ry beds,
Nor gales, that catch the scent of blooming groves,
And waft it to the mourner as he roves,
Can call up life into his faded eye,
That passes all he sees unheeded by;
No wounds like those a wounded spirit feels,
No cure for such, till God, who makes them, heals.
And thou, sad suff'rer under nameless ill,
That yields not to the touch of human skill,
Improve the kind occasion, understand
A Father's frown, and kiss his chast'ning hand.
To thee the dayspring, and the blaze of noon,
The purple ev'ning and resplendent moon,
The stars, that, sprinkled o'er the vault of night,
Seem drops descending in a show'r of light,
Shine not, or undesir'd and hated shine,
Seen through the medium of a cloud like thine:
Yet seek him, in his favor life is found,
All bliss beside a shadow or a sound:
Then heav'n, eclips'd so long, and this dull earth,
Shall seem to start into a second birth;
Nature, assuming a more lovely face,
Borrowing a beauty from the works of grace,
Shall be despis'd and overlook'd no more,
Shall fill thee with delight unfelt before,
Impart to things inanimate a voice,
And bid her mountains and her hills rejoice;
The sound shall run along the winding vales,
And thou enjoy an Eden ere it fails.
  Ye groves (the statesman at his desk exclaims,
Sick of a thousand disappointed aims),
My patrimonial treasure and my pride,
Beneath your shades your gray possessor hide,
Receive me languishing for that repose
The servant of the public never knows.
Ye saw me once (ah, those regretted days,
When boyish innocence was all my praise!)
Hour after hour delightfully allot
To studies then familiar, since forgot,
And cultivate a taste for ancient song,
Catching its ardor as I mus'd along;
Nor seldom, as propitious Heav'n might send,

What once I valu'd and could boast, a friend,
Were witnesses how cordially I press'd
His undissembling virtue to my breast;
Receive me now, not incorrupt as then,
Nor guiltless of corrupting other men,
But vers'd in arts, that, while they seem to stay
A falling empire, hasten its decay.
To the fair haven of my native home,
The wreck of what I was, fatigued I come;
For once I can approve the patriot's voice,
And make the course he recommends my choice:
We meet at last in one sincere desire,
His wish and mine both prompt me to retire.
'Tis done—he steps into the welcome chaise,
Lolls at his ease behind four handsome bays,
That whirl away from business and debate
The disencumber'd Atlas of the state.
Ask not the boy, who, when the breeze of morn
First shakes the glitt'ring drops from ev'ry thorn,
Unfolds his flock, then under bank or bush
Sits linking cherry-stones, or platting rush,
How fair is Freedom?—he was always free:
To carve his rustic name upon a tree,
To snare the mole, or with ill-fashion'd hook
To draw th'incautious minnow from the brook,
Are life's prime pleasures in his simple view,
His flock the chief concern he ever knew;
She shines but little in his heedless eyes,
The good we never miss we rarely prize:
But ask the noble drudge in state affairs,
Escap'd from office and its constant cares,
What charms he sees in Freedom's smile express'd,
In Freedom lost so long, now repossess'd;
The tongue, whose strains were cogent as commands,
Rever'd at home, and felt in foreign lands,
Shall own itself a stamm'rer in that cause,
Or plead its silence as its best applause.
He knows indeed that whether dress'd or rude
Wild without art or artfully subdued,
Nature in ev'ry form inspires delight,
But never mark'd her with so just a sight.
Her hedge-row shrubs, a variegated store,
With woodbine and wild roses mantled o'er,
Green balks and furrow'd lands, the stream, that spreads
Its cooling vapor o'er the dewy meads,
Downs, that almost escape th'inquiring eye,
That melt and fade into the distant sky,
Beauties he lately slighted as he pass'd,
Seem all created since he travell'd last.

Master of all th'enjoyments he design'd,
No rough annoyance rankling in his mind,
What early philosophic hours he keeps,
How regular his meals, how sound he sleeps!
Not sounder he, that on the mainmast head,
While morning kindles with a windy red,
Begins a long look-out for distant land,
Nor quits till ev'ning watch his giddy stand,
Then swift descending with a seaman's haste,
Slips to his hammock, and forgets the blast.
He chooses company, but not the squires,
Whose wit is rudeness, whose good-breeding tires;
Nor yet the parson's who would gladly come,
Obsequious when abroad, though proud at home;
Nor can he much affect the neighb'ring peer,
Whose toe of emulation treads too near;
But wisely seeks a more convenient friend,
With whom, dismissing forms, he may unbend!
A man, whom marks of condescending grace
Teach, while they flatter him, his proper place;
Who comes when call'd, and at a word withdraws,
Speaks with reserve, and listens with applause;
Some plain mechanic, who, without pretence
To birth or wit, nor gives nor takes offence;
On whom he rests well-pleas'd his weary pow'rs,
And talks and laughs away his vacant hours.
The tide of life, swift always in its course,
May run in cities with a brisker force,
But no where with a current so serene,
Or half so clear, as in the rural scene.
Yet how fallacious is all earthly bliss,
What obvious truths the wisest heads may miss;
Some pleasures live a month, and some a year,
But short the date of all we gather here;
No happiness is felt, except the true,
That does not charm the more for being new.
This observation, as it chanc'd, not made,
Or, if the thought occurr'd, not duly weigh'd,
He sighs—for after all by slow degrees
The spot he lov'd has lost the pow'r to please;
To cross his ambling pony day by day,
Seems at the best but dreaming life away;
The prospect, such as might enchant despair,
He views it not, or sees no beauty there;
With aching heart, and discontented looks,
Returns at noon to billiards or to books,
But feels, while grasping at his faded joys,
A secret thirst of his renounc'd employs.
He chides the tardiness of ev'ry post,

Pants to be told of battles won or lost,
Blames his own indolence, observes, though late,
'Tis criminal to leave a sinking state,
Flies to the levee, and, receiv'd with grace,
Kneels, kisses hands, and shines again in place.
Suburban villas, highway-side retreats,
That dread th'encroachment of our growing streets,
Tight boxes neatly sash'd, and in a blaze
With all a July's sun's collected rays,
Delight the citizen, who, gasping there,
Breathes clouds of dust, and calls it country air.
O sweet retirement, who would balk the thought,
That could afford retirement, or could not?
'Tis such an easy walk, so smooth and straight,
The second milestone fronts the garden gate;
A step if fair, and, if a show'r approach,
You find safe shelter in the next stage-coach.
There, prison'd in a parlor snug and small,
Like bottled wasps upon a southern wall,
The man of business and his friends compress'd
Forget their labours, and yet find no rest;
But still 'tis rural—trees are to be seen
From ev'ry window, and the fields are green;
Ducks paddle in the pond before the door,
And what could a remoter scene show more?
A sense of elegance we rarely find
The portion of a mean or vulgar mind,
And ignorance of better things makes man,
Who cannot much, rejoice in what he can;
And he, that deems his leisure well bestow'd
In contemplation of a turnpike road,
Is occupied as well, employs his hours
As wisely, and as much improves his pow'rs,
As he, that slumbers in pavilions grac'd
With all the charms of an accomplish'd taste.
Yet hence, alas! insolvencies; and hence
Th'unpitied victim of ill-judged expense,
From all his wearisome engagements freed,
Shakes hands with business, and retires indeed.
Your prudent grand-mammas, ye modern belles,
Content with Bristol, Bath, and Tunbridge-wells,
When health requir'd it would consent to roam,
Else more attached to pleasures found at home.
But now alike, gay widow, virgin, wife,
Ingenious to diversify dull life,
In coaches, chaises, caravans, and hoys,
Fly to the coast for daily, nightly joys;
And all, impatient of dry land, agree
With one consent to rush into the sea.—

Ocean exhibits, fathomless and broad,
Much of the pow'r and majesty of God.
He swathes about the swelling of the deep,
That shines and rests, as infants smile and sleep;
Vast as it is, it answers as it flows
The breathings of the lightest air that blows;
Curling and whit'ning over all the waste,
The rising waves obey th'increasing blast,
Abrupt and horrid as the tempest roars,
Thunder and flash upon the stedfast shores,
Till he, that rides the whirlwind, checks the rein,
Then all the world of waters sleeps again.—
Nereids or Dryads, as the fashion leads,
Now in the floods, now panting in the meads,
Vot'ries of Pleasure still, where'er she dwells,
Near barren rocks, in palaces, or cells,
O grant a poet leave to recommend
(A poet fond of Nature, and your friend)
Her slighted works to your admiring view;
Her works must needs excel, who fashion'd you.
Would ye, when rambling in your morning ride,
With some unmeaning coxcomb at your side,
Condemn the prattler for his idle pains,
To waste unheard the music of his strains,
And, deaf to all th'impertinence of tongue,
That, while it courts, affronts and does you wrong,
Mark well the finish'd plan without a fault,
The seas globose and huge, th'o'erarching vault,
Earth's millions daily fed, a world employ'd
In gath'ring plenty yet to be enjoy'd,
Till gratitude grew vocal in the praise
Of God, beneficient in all his ways;
Grac'd with such wisdom, how would beauty shine!
Ye want but that to seem indeed divine.
  Anticipated rents, and bills unpaid,
Force many a shining youth into the shade,
Not to redeem his time, but his estate,
And play the fool, but at a cheaper rate.
There, hid in loath'd obscurity, remov'd
From pleasures left, but never more belov'd,
He just endures, and with a sickly spleen
Sighs o'er the beauties of the charming scene.
Nature indeed looks prettily in rhyme;
Streams tinkle sweetly in poetic chime:
The warblings of the blackbird, clear and strong,
Are musical enough in Thomson's song;
And Cobham's groves, and Windsor's green retreats,
When Pope describes them, have a thousand sweets;
He likes the country, but in truth must own

Most likes it, when he studies it in town.
  Poor Jack—no matter who—for when I blame,
I pity, and must therefore sink the name,
Liv'd in his saddle, lov'd the chase, the course,
And always, ere he mounted, kiss'd his horse.
The estate, his sires had own'd in ancient years,
Was quickly distanc'd, match'd against a peer's.
Jack vanish'd, was regretted and forgot;
'Tis wild good-nature's never-failing lot.
At length, when all had long suppos'd him dead,
By cold submersion, razor, rope, or lead,
My lord, alighting at his usual place,
The Crown, took notice of an ostler's face.
Jack knew his friend, but hop'd in that disguise
He might escape the most observing eyes,
And whistling, as if unconcern'd and gay,
Curried his nag, and look'd another way.
Convinc'd at last, upon a nearer view,
'T was he, the same, the very Jack he knew,
O'erwhelm'd at once with wonder, grief, and joy,
He press'd him much to quit his base employ;
His countenance, his purse, his heart, his hand,
Influence and pow'r, were all at his command:
Peers are not always gen'rous as well-bred,
But Granby was, meant truly what he said.
Jack bow'd, and was oblig'd—confess'd 'twas strange,
That so retir'd he should not wish a change,
But knew no medium between guzzling beer,
And his old stint—three thousand pound a-year.
  Thus some retire to nourish hopeless woe;
Some seeking happiness not found below;
Some to comply with humor, and a mind
To social scenes by nature discinclin'd;
Some sway'd by fashion, some by deep disgust;
Some self-impov'rish'd, and because they must;
But few, that court Retirement, are aware
Of half the toils they must encounter there.
  Lucrative offices are seldom lost
For want of pow'r proportion'd to the post:
Give e'en a dunce th' employment he desires,
And he soon finds the talents it requires;
A business with an income at its heels
Furnishes always oil for its own wheels.
But in his arduous enterprise to close
His active years with indolent repose,
He finds the labors of that state exceed
His utmost faculties, severe indeed.
'T is easy to resign a toilsome place,
But not to manage leisure with a grace;

Absence of occupation is not rest,
A mind quite vacant is a mind distress'd.
The vet'ran steed, excus'd his task at length,
In kind compassion of his failing strength,
And turn'd into the park or mead to graze,
Exempt from future service all his days,
There feels a pleasure perfect in its kind,
Ranges at liberty, and snuffs the wind:
But when his lord would quit the busy road,
To taste a joy like that he had bestow'd,
He proves, less happy than his favor'd brute,
A life of ease a difficult pursuit.
Thought, to the man that never thinks, may seem
As natural as when asleep to dream;
But reveries (for human minds will act)
Spacious in show, impossible in fact,
Those flimsy webs, that break as soon as wrought,
Attain not to the dignity of thought:
Nor yet the swarms, that occupy the brain,
Where dreams of dress, intrigue, and pleasure reigns;
Nor such as useless conversation breeds,
Or lust engenders, and indulgence feeds.
Whence, and what are we? to what end ordain'd?
What means the drama by the world sustain'd?
Business or vain amusement, care or mirth,
Divide the frail inhabitants of earth.
Is duty a mere sport, or an employ?
Life an intrusted talent, or a toy?
Is there, as reason, conscience, Scripture, say,
Cause to provide for a great future day,
When, earth's assign'd duration at an end,
Man shall be summon'd and the dead attend?
The trumpet—will it sound, the curtain rise,
And show th'august tribunal of the skies;
Where no prevarication shall avail,
Where eloquence and artifice shall fail,
The pride of arrogant distinctions fall,
And conscience and our conduct judge us all?
Pardon me, ye that give the midnight oil
To learned cares, or philosophic toil,
Though I revere your honorable names,
Your useful labours and important aims,
And hold the world indebted to your aid,
Enrich'd with the discov'ries ye have made;
Yet let me stand excus'd, if I esteem
A mind employ'd on so sublime a theme,
Pushing her bold inquiry to the date
And outline of the present transient state,
And, after poising her advent'rous wings,

Settling at last upon eternal things,
Far more intelligent, and better taught
The strenuous use of profitable thought,
Than ye, when happiest, and enlightened most,
And highest in renown, can justly boast.
A mind unnerv'd, or indispos'd to bear
The weight of subjects worthiest of her care,
Whatever hopes a change of scene inspires,
Must change her nature, or in vain retires.
An idler is a watch, that wants both hands,
As useless if it goes, as when it stands.
Books therefore, not the scandal of the shelves,
In which lewd sensualists print out themselves;
Nor those, in which the stage gives vice a blow,
With what success let modern manners show;
Nor his, who, for the bane of thousands born,
Built God a church, and laugh'd his word to scorn,
Skilful alike to seem devout and just,
And stab religion with a sly side-thrust;
Nor those of learn'd philologists, who chase
A panting syllable through time and space,
Start it at home, and hunt it in the dark,
To Gaul, to Greece, and into Noah's ark;
But such as Learning without false pretence,
The friend of Truth, th'associate of sound Sense,
And such as, in the zeal of good design,
Strong judgment lab'ring in the Scripture mine,
All such as manly and great souls produce,
Worthy to live, and of eternal use:
Behold in these what leisure hours demand,
Amusement and true knowledge hand in hand.
Luxury gives the mind a childish cast,
And, while she polishes, perverts the taste;
Habits of close attention, thinking heads,
Become more rare as dissipation spreads,
Till authors hear at length one gen'ral cry,—
Tickle and entertain us, or we die.
The loud demand, from year to year the same,
Beggars Invention, and makes Fancy lame;
Till farce itself, most mournfully jejune,
Calls for the kind assistance of a tune;
And novels (witness ev'ry month's review)
Belie their name, and offer nothing new.
The mind, relaxing into needful sport,
Should turn to writers of an abler sort,
Whose wit well manag'd, and whose classic style,
Give truth a lustre, and make wisdom smile.
Friends (for I cannot stint, as some have done,
Too rigid in my view, that name to one;

Though one, I grant it, in the gen'rous breast
Will stand advanc'd a step above the rest:
Flow'rs by that name promiscuously we call,
But one, the rose, the regent of them all)—
Friends, not adopted with a schoolboy's haste,
But chosen with a nice discerning taste,
Well-born, well-disciplin'd, who, plac'd apart
From vulgar minds, have honor much at heart,
And, though the world may think th'ingredients odd,
The love of virtue, and the fear of God!
Such friends prevent what else would soon succeed,
A temper rustic as the life we lead,
And keep the polish of the manners clean
As theirs who bustle in the busiest scenes;
For solitude, however some may rave,
Seeming a sanctuary, proves a grave,
A sepulchre in which the living lie,
Where all good qualities grow sick and die.
I praise the Frenchman,* his remark was shrewd—
How sweet, how passing sweet, is solitude!
But grant me still a friend in my retreat,
Whom I may whisper—solitude is sweet.
Yet neither these delights, nor aught beside,
That appetite can ask, or wealth provide,
Can save us always from a tedious day,
Or shine the dulness of still life away;
Divine communion, carefully enjoy'd,
Or sought with energy, must fill the void.
O sacred art, to which alone life owes
Its happiest seasons, and a peaceful close,
Scorn'd in a world, indebted to that scorn
For evils daily felt and hardly borne,
Not knowing thee, we reap with bleeding hands
Flow'rs of rank odor upon thorny lands,
And, while Experience cautions us in vain,
Grasp seeming happiness, and find it pain.
Despondence, self-deserted in her grief,
Lost by abandoning her own relief,
Murmuring and ungrateful Discontent,
That scorns afflictions mercifully meant,
Those humors, tart as wines upon the fret,
Which idleness and weariness beget;
These, and a thousand plagues, that haunt the breast,
Fond of the phantom of an earthly rest,
Divine communion chases, as the day
Drives to their dens th'obedient beasts of prey.
See Judah's promis'd king, bereft of all,

* Bruyere.

Driv'n out an exile from the face of Saul,
To distant caves the lonely wand'rer flies,
To seek that peace a tyrant's frown denies.
Hear the sweet accents of his tuneful voice,
Hear him, o'erwelm'd with sorrow, yet rejoice;
No womanish or wailing grief has part,
No, not a moment, in his royal heart;
'Tis manly music, such as martyrs make,
Suff'ring with gladness for a Saviour's sake:
His soul exults, hope animates his lays,
The sense of mercy kindles into praise,
And wilds, familiar with a lion's roar,
Ring with ecstatic sounds unheard before:
'Tis love like his, that can alone defeat
The foes of man, or make a desert sweet.
Religion does not censure or exclude
Unnumber'd pleasures harmlessly pursued;
To study culture, and with artful toil
To meliorate and tame the stubborn soil;
To give dissimilar yet fruitful lands
The grain, or herb, or plant that each demands;
To cherish virtue in an humble state,
And share the joys your bounty may create;
To mark the matchless workings of the pow'r
That shuts within its seed the future flow'r,
Bids these in elegance of form excel,
In color these, and those delight the smell,
Sends Nature forth the daughter of the skies,
To dance on earth, and charm all human eyes;
To teach the canvass innocent deceit,
Or lay the landscape on the snowy sheet—
These, these are arts pursued without a crime
That leave no stain upon the wing of Time.
Me poetry (or rather notes that aim
Feebly and vainly at poetic fame)
Employs, shut out from more important views,
Fast by the banks of the slow winding Ouse;
Content if thus sequester'd I may raise
A monitor's though not a poet's praise,
And while I teach an art too little known,
To close life wisely, may not waste my own.

THE YEARLY DISTRESS,

OR TITHING TIME AT STOCK, IN ESSEX.

Verses addressed to a country clergyman complaining of the disagreeableness of the day annually appointed for receiving the dues at the parsonage.

Come, ponder well, for 'tis no jest,
  To laugh it would be wrong,
The troubles of a worthy priest
  The burthen of my song.

This priest he merry is and blithe
  Three quarters of a year,
But oh! it cuts him like a scythe,
  When tithing time draws near.

He then is full of fright and fears,
  As one at point to die,
And long before the day appears
  He heaves up many a sigh.

For then the farmers come jog, jog,
  Along the miry road,
Each heart as heavy as a log,
  To make their payments good.

In sooth, the sorrow of such days
  Is not to be express'd,
When he that takes and he that pays
  Are both alike distress'd.

Now all unwelcome at his gates
  The clumsy swains alight,
With rueful faces and bald pates—
  He trembles at the sight.

And well he may, for well he knows
 Each bumpkin of the clan,
Instead of paying what he owes,
 Will cheat him if he can.

So in they come—each makes his leg,
 And flings his head before,
And looks as if he came to beg,
 And not to quit a score.

"And how does miss and madam do,
 "The little boy and all?"
"All tight and well. And how do you,
 "Good Mr. What-d'ye-call?"

The dinner comes, and down they sit:
 Were e'er such hungry folk?
There's little talking, and no wit;
 It is no time to joke.

One wipes his nose upon his sleeve,
 One spits upon the floor,
Yet, not to give offence or grieve,
 Holds up the cloth before.

The punch goes round, and they are dull
 And lumpish still as ever;
Like barrels with their bellies full,
 They only weigh the heavier.

At length the busy time begins.
 "Come, neighbours, we must wag—"
The money chinks, down drop their chins,
 Each lugging out his bag.

One talks of mildew and of frost,
 And one of storms of hail,
And one of pigs, that he has lost
 By maggots at the tail.

Quoth one, "A rarer man than you
 "In pulpit none shall hear:
"But yet, methinks, to tell you true,
 "You sell it plaguy dear."

O why are farmers made so coarse,
 Or clergy made so fine?

A kick, that scarce would move a horse,
  May kill a sound divine.

Then let the boobies stay at home;
  'Twould cost him, I dare say,
Less trouble taking twice the sum,
  Without the clowns that pay.

SONNET

ADDRESSED TO HENRY COWPER, ESQ.
On his emphatical and interesting Delivery of the Defence of Warren Hastings, Esq., in the House of Lords.

COWPER, whose silver voice, task'd sometimes hard,
  Legends prolix delivers in the ears
  (Attentive when thou read'st) of England's peers,
Let verse at length yield thee thy just reward.

Thou wast not heard with drowsy disregard,
  Expending late on all that length of plea
  Thy gen'rous pow'rs; but silence honor'd thee,
Mute as e'er gaz'd on orator or bard.

Thou art not voice alone, but hast beside
  Both heart and head: and couldst with music sweet
    Of Attic phrase and senatorial tone,
Like thy renown'd forefathers, far and wide
  Thy fame diffuse, prais'd not for utt'rance meet
    Of *Others'* speech, but magic of *thy own*.

LINES

ADDRESSED TO DR. DARWIN, AUTHOR OF
" The Botanic Garden."

Two Poets* (poets, by report,
 Not oft so well agree),
Sweet Harmonist of Flora's court!
 Conspire to honor Thee.

They best can judge a poet's worth,
 Who oft themselves have known
The pangs of a poetic birth
 By labors of their own.

We therefore pleas'd extol thy song
 Though various yet complete,
Rich in embellishment as strong,
 And learned as 'tis sweet.

No envy mingles with our praise,
 Though, could our hearts repine
At any poet's happier lays,
 They would—they must at thine.

But we, in mutual bondage knit
 Of friendship's closest tie,
Can gaze on even Darwin's wit
 With an unjaundic'd eye

And deem the Bard, whoe'er he be,
 And howsoever known,
Who would not twine a wreath for Thee,
 Unworthy of his own.

---

* Alluding to the poem by Mr. Hayley, which accompanied these lines.

ON

MRS. MONTAGU'S FEATHER-HANGINGS.

The birds put off their ev'ry hue,
To dress a room for Montagu.
The Peacock sends his heav'nly dyes,
His *rainbows* and his *starry eyes* ;
The Pheasant plumes, which round infold
His mantling neck with downy gold ;
The Cock his arch'd tail's azure show ;
And, river-blanch'd, the Swan his snow.
All tribes beside of Indian name,
That glossy shine, or vivid flame,
Where rises, and where sets the day,
Whate'er they boast of rich and gay,
Contribute to the gorgeous plan,
Proud to advance it all they can.
This plumage neither dashing show'r,
Nor blasts, that shake the dripping bow'r,
Shall drench again or discompose,
But, screen'd from ev'ry storm that blows,
It boasts a splendor ever new,
Safe with protecting Montagu.
To the same patroness resort,
Secure of favor at her court,
Strong Genius, from whose forge of thought
Forms rise, to quick perfection wrought,
Which, though new-born, with vigor move,
Like Pallas springing arm'd from Jove—
Imagination scatt'ring round
Wild roses over furrow'd ground,
Which Labor of his frown beguile,
And teach Philosophy a smile—
Wit flashing on Religion's side,
Whose fires, to sacred Truth applied,
The gem, though luminous before,
Obtrude on human notice more,
Like sunbeams on the golden height
Of some tall temple playing bright—
Well-tutor'd Learning, from his books
Dismiss'd with grave, not haughty, looks,
Their order on his shelves exact,

Not more harmonious or compact
Than that, to which he keeps confin'd
The various treasures of his mind—
All these to Montagu's repair,
Ambitious of a shelter there.
There Genius, Learning, Fancy, Wit,
Their ruffled plumage calm refit,
(For stormy troubles loudest roar
Around their flight who highest soar)
And in her eye, and by her aid,
Shine safe without a fear to fade.
She thus maintains divided sway
With yon bright regent of the day;
The plume and poet both, we know,
Their lustre to his influence owe;
And she the works of Phoebus aiding,
Both poet saves and plume from fading.

VERSES

Supposed to be written by Alexander Selkirk, during his solitary abode in the Island of Juan Fernandez.

I am monarch of all I survey,
My right there is none to dispute;
From the centre all round to the sea,
I am lord of the fowl and the brute.
O Solitude! where are the charms
That sages have seen in thy face?
Better dwell in the midst of alarms,
Than reign in this horrible place.

I am out of humanity's reach,
I must finish my journey alone,
Never hear the sweet music of speech,
I start at the sound of my own.
The beasts, that roam over the plain,
My form with indifference see;
They are so unacquainted with man,
Their tameness is shocking to me.

Society, friendship, and love,
Divinely bestow'd upon man,
O, had I the wings of a dove,
How soon would I taste you again!

My sorrows I then might assauge
  In the ways of religion and truth,
Might learn from the wisdom of age,
  And be cheer'd by the sallies of youth.

Religion! what treasure untold
  Resides in that heavenly word!
More precious than silver and gold,
  Or all that this earth can afford.
But the sound of the church-going bell
  These valleys and rocks never heard,
Never sigh'd at the sound of a knell,
  Or smil'd when a sabbath appear'd.

Ye winds, that have made me your sport,
  Convey to this desolate shore
Some cordial endearing report
  Of a land I shall visit no more.
My friends, do they now and then send
  A wish or a thought after me?
O tell me I yet have a friend,
  Though a friend I am never to see.

How fleet is a glance of the mind!
  Compar'd with the speed of its flight,
The tempest itself lags behind,
  And the swift-winged arrows of light
When I think of my own native land,
  In a moment I seem to be there;
But alas! recollection at hand
  Soon hurries me back to despair.

But the sea-fowl is gone to her nest,
  The beast is laid down in his lair;
Even here is a season of rest,
  And I to my cabin repair.
There's mercy in ev'ry place,
  And mercy, encouraging thought!
Gives even affliction a grace,
  And reconciles man to his lot.

ON THE PROMOTION OF

EDWARD THURLOW, ESQ.

TO THE LORD HIGH CHANCELLORSHIP OF ENGLAND.

Round Thurlow's head in early youth,
   And in his sportive days,
Fair Science pour'd the light of truth,
   And Genius shed his rays.

See! with united wonder cried
   Th' experienc'd and the sage,
Ambition in a boy supplied
   With all the skill of age!

Discernment, eloquence, and grace
   Proclaim him born to sway
The balance in the highest place,
   And bear the palm away.

The praise bestow'd was just and wise;
   He sprang impetuous forth
Secure of conquest, where the prize
   Attends superior worth.

So the best courser on the plain
   Ere yet he starts is known,
And does but at a goal obtain
   What all had deem'd his own

ODE TO PEACE.

Come, peace of mind, delightful guest!
Return, and make thy downy nest
   Once more in this sad heart:
Nor riches I nor pow'r pursue,
Nor hold forbidden joys in view;
   We therefore need not part.

Where wilt thou dwell, if not with me,
From av'rice and ambition free,
And pleasure's fatal wiles?
For whom, alas! dost thou prepare
The sweets that I was wont to share,
The banquet of thy smiles?

The great, the gay, shall they partake
The heav'n, that thou alone canst make?
And wilt thou quit the stream,
That murmers through the dewy mead,
The grove and the sequester'd shed,
To be a guest with them?

For thee I panted, thee I priz'd,
For thee I gladly sacrific'd
Whate'er I lov'd before;
And shall I see thee start away,
And helpless, hopeless, hear thee say—
Farewell! we meet no more?

HUMAN FRAILTY.

Weak and irresolute is man;
The purpose of to-day,
Woven with pains into his plan,
To-morrow rends away.

The bow well bent, and smart the spring,
Vice seems already slain;
But Passion rudely snaps the string,
And it revives again.

Some foe to his upright intent
Finds out his weaker part;
Virtue engages his assent,
But Pleasure wins his heart.

'Tis here the folly of the wise
Through all his art we view;
And, while his tongue the charge denies,
His conscience owns it true.

Bound on a voyage of awful length
And dangers little known,
A stranger to superior strength,
Man vainly trusts his own.

But oars alone can ne'er prevail,
  To reach the distant coast;
The breath of heav'n must swell the sail,
  Or all the toil is lost.

THE MODERN PATRIOT.

Rebellion is my theme all day;
  I only wish 'twould come
(As who knows but perhaps it may?)
  A little nearer home.

Yon roaring boys, who rave and figh
  On t'other side th'Atlantic,
I always held them in the right,
  But most so when most frantic.

When lawless mobs insult the court,
  That man shall be my toast,
If breaking windows be the sport,
  Who bravely breaks the most.

But O! for him my fancy culls
  The choicest flow'rs she bears,
Who constitutionally pulls
  Your house about your ears.

Such civil broils are my delight,
  Though some folks can't endure them,
Who say the mob are mad outright,
  And that a rope must cure them.

A rope! I wish we patriots had
  Such strings for all who need 'em—
What! hang a man for going mad!
  Then farewell British freedom.

ON OBSERVING SOME

NAMES OF LITTLE NOTE

RECORDED IN

THE BIOGRAPHIA BRITANNICA

Oh, fond attempt to give a deathless lot
To names ignoble, born to be forgot!
In vain, recorded in historic page,
They court the notice of a future age:
Those twinkling tiny lustres of the land
Drop one by one from Fame's neglecting hand;
Lethæan gulfs receive them as they fall,
And dark oblivion soon absorbs them all.
So when a child, as playful children use,
Has burnt to tinder a stale last year's news,
The flame extinct, he views the roving fire—
There goes my lady, and there goes the squire,
There goes the parson, oh illustrious spark!
And there, scarce less illustrious, goes the clerk!

REPORT

OF AN ADJUDGED CASE, NOT TO BE FOUND IN

ANY OF THE BOOKS.

Between Nose and Eyes a strange contest arose,
The spectacles set them unhappily wrong;
The point in dispute was, as all the world knows,
To which the said spectacles ought to belong.

So Tongue was the lawyer, and argued the cause
With a great deal of skill, and a wigfull of learning;
While chief baron Ear sat to balance the laws,
So fam'd for his talent in nicely discerning.

In behalf of the Nose it will quickly appear,
  And your lordship, he said, will undoubtedly find,
That the Nose has had spectacles always in wear,
  Which amounts to possession time out of mind.

Then holding the spectacles up to the court—
  Your lordship observes they are made with a straddle,
As wide as the ridge of the Nose is; in short,
  Design'd to sit close to it, just like a saddle.

Again, would your lordship a moment suppose
  ('Tis a case that has happen'd, and may be again)
That the visage or countenance had not a nose,
  Pray who would, or who could, wear spectacles then?

On the whole it appears, and my argument shows,
  With a reasoning the court will never condemn,
That the spectacles plainly were made for the Nose,
  And the Nose was as plainly intended for them.

Then shifting his side (as a lawyer knows how),
  He pleaded again in behalf of the Eyes:
But what were his arguments few people know,
  For the court did not think they were equally wise.

So his lordship decreed with a grave solemn tone,
  Decisive and clear, without one *if* or *but*—
That, whenever the Nose put his spectacles on,
  By daylight or candlelight—Eyes should be shut!

ON THE BURNING OF LORD MANSFIELD'S LIBRARY,

TOGETHER WITH HIS MSS.

by the mob, in the month of June, 1780.

So then—the Vandals of our isle,
  Sworn foes to sense and law,
Have burnt to dust a nobler pile
  Than ever Roman saw!

And MURRAY sighs o'er Pope and Swift,
  And many a treasure more,
The well-judg'd purchase, and the gift,
  That grac'd his letter'd store.

Their pages mangled, burnt and torn,
The loss was *his alone* ;
But ages yet to come shall mourn.
The burning of *his own.*

ON THE SAME.

When wit and genius meet their doom
In all devouring flame,
They tell us of the fate of Rome,
And bid us fear the same.

O'er MURRAY'S loss the Muses wept,
They felt the rude alarm,
Yet bless'd the guardian care that kept
His sacred head from harm.

There Mem'ry, like the bee, that's fed
From Flora's balmy store,
The quintessence of all he read
Had treasur'd up before.

The lawless herd, with fury blind,
Have done him cruel wrong ;
The flow'rs are gone—but still we find
The honey on his tongue

THE LOVE OF THE WORLD REPROVED

OR

HYPOCRISY DETECTED *.

Thus says the prophet of the Turk,
Good Mussulman, abstain from pork ;
There is a part in ev'ry swine
No friend or follower of mine
May taste, whate'er his inclination,
On pain of excommunication.

* It may be proper to inform the reader, that this piece has already appeared in print, having found its way, though with some unnecessary additions by an unknown hand, into the Leed's Journal, without the author's privity.

Such Mahomet's mysterious charge,
And thus he left the point at large.
Had he the sinful part express'd,
They might with safety eat the rest;
But for one piece they thought it hard
From the whole hog to be debarr'd;
And set their wit at work to find
What joint the prophet had in mind.
Much controversy straight arose,
These choose the back, the belly those;
By some 'tis confidently said
He meant not to forbid the head;
While others at that doctrine rail
And piously prefer the tail.
Thus, conscience freed from ev'ry clog,
Mahometans eat up the hog.
You laugh—'tis well—The tale applied
May make you laugh on t'other side.
Renounce the world—the preacher cries.
We do—a multitude replies.
While one as innocent regards
A snug and friendly game at cards;
And one, whatever you may say,
Can see no evil in a play;
Some love a concert, or a race;
And others shooting, and the chace.
Revil'd and lov'd, renounc'd and follow'd,
Thus, bit by bit, the world is swallow'd;
Each thinks his neighbour makes too free,
Yet likes a slice as well as he;
With sophistry their sauce they sweeten,
Till quite from tail to snout 'tis eaten.

ON THE DEATH OF
MRS. (now LADY) THROCKMORTON'S
BULFINCH.

Ye nymphs! if e'er your eyes were red
With tears o'er hapless fav'rites shed,
O share Maria's grief!
Her fav'rite, even in his cage,
(What will not hunger's cruel rage?)
Assassin'd by a thief.

Where Rhenus strays his vines among,
The egg was laid from which he sprung;
  And, though by nature mute,
Or only with a whistle blest,
Well-taught he all the sounds express'd
  Of flagelet or flute.

The honors of his ebon poll
Were brighter than the sleekest mole;
  His bosom of the hue
With which Aurora decks the skies,
When piping winds shall soon arise,
  To sweep away the dew.

Above, below, in all the house,
Dire foe alike of bird and mouse,
  No cat had leave to dwell;
And Bully's cage supported stood
On props of smoothest-shaven wood,
  Large built, and lattic'd well.

Well-lattic'd—but the grate, alas!
Not rough with wire of steel or brass,
  For Bully's plumage sake,
Cut smooth with wands from Ouse's side,
With which, when neatly peel'd and dried,
  The swains their baskets make.

Night veil'd the pole, all seem'd secure:
When led by instinct sharp and sure,
  Subsistence to provide,
A beast forth sallied on the scout,
Long-back'd, long tail'd, with whisker'd snout,
  And badger-color'd hide.

He, ent'ring at the study door,
Its ample area 'gan explore;
  And something in the wind
Conjectur'd, sniffing round and round,
Better than all the books he found,
  Food chiefly for the mind.

Just then, by adverse fate impress'd,
A dream disturb'd poor Bully's rest;
  In sleep he seem'd to view
A rat fast clinging to the cage,
And, screaming at the sad presage,
  Awoke and found it true.

For, aided both by ear and scent,
Right to his mark the monster went—
    Ah! muse, forbear to speak
Minute the horrors that ensued;
His teeth were strong, the cage was wood—
    He left poor Bully's beak.

O had he made that too his prey;
That beak, whence issued many a lay
    Of such mellifluous tone,
Might have repaid him well, I wote
For silencing so sweet a throat,
    Fast stuck within his own.

Maria weeps—the Muses mourn—
So when, by Bacchanalians torn,
    On Thracian Hebrus' side
The tree-enchanter Orpheus fell,
His head alone remain'd to tell
    The cruel death he died.

THE ROSE.

The rose had been wash'd, just wash'd in a show'r,
  Which Mary to Anna convey'd,
The plentiful moisture encumber'd the flow'r,
  And weigh'd down its beautiful head.

The cup was all fill'd, and the leaves were all wet,
  And it seem'd to a fanciful view,
To weep for the buds it had left with regret,
  On the flourishing bush where it grew.

I hastily seiz'd it, unfit as it was
  For a nosegay, so dripping and drown'd,
And swinging it rudely, too rudely, alas!
  I snapp'd it, it fell to the ground.

And such, I exclaim'd, is the pitiless part
  Some act by the delicate mind,
Regardless of wringing and breaking a heart
  Already to sorrow resign'd.

This elegant rose, had I shaken it less,
  Might have bloom'd with its owner a while;
And the tear, that is wip'd with a little address,
  May be follow'd perhaps by a smile.

THE DOVES.

Reas'ning at ev'ry step he treads,
Man yet mistakes his way,
While meaner things, whom instinct leads,
Are rarely known to stray.

One silent eve I wander'd late,
And heard the voice of love;
The turtle thus address'd her mate,
And sooth'd the list'ning dove:

Our mutual bond of faith and truth
No time shall disengage,
Those blessings of our early youth
Shall cheer our latest age:

While innocence without disguise,
And constancy sincere,
Shall fill the circles of those eyes,
And mine can read them there;

Those ills, that wait on all below,
Shall ne'er be felt by me,
Or gently felt, and only so,
As being shar'd with thee.

When lightnings flash among the trees,
Or kites are hov'ring near,
I fear lest thee alone they seize,
And know no other fear.

'Tis then I feel myself a wife,
And press thy wedded side,
Resolv'd a union form'd for life
Death never shall divide.

But oh! if fickle and unchaste,
(Forgive a transient thought)
Thou could become unkind at last,
And scorn thy present lot,

No need of lightnings from on high,
Or kites with cruel beak;
Denied th'endearments of thine eye,
This widow'd heart would break.

Thus sang the sweet sequester'd bird,
  Soft as the passing wind;
And I recorded what I heard,
  A lesson for mankind.

A FABLE.

A raven, while with glossy breast
Her new-laid eggs she fondly press'd,
And, on her wickerwork high mounted,
Her chickens prematurely counted,
(A fault philosophers might blame
If quite exempted from the same,)
Enjoy'd at ease the genial day;
'Twas April, as the bumpkins say,
The legislature call'd it May.
But suddenly a wind as high,
As ever swept a winter sky,
Shook the young leaves about her ears,
And fill'd her with a thousand fears,
Lest the rude blast should snap the bough,
And spread her golden hopes below.
But just at eve the blowing weather
And all her fears were hush'd together:
And now, quoth poor unthinking Ralph,
'Tis over, and the brood is safe;
(For ravens, though as birds of omen
They teach both conj'rers and old women,
To tell us what is to befall,
Can't prophesy themselves at all.)
The morning came, when neighbour Hodge,
Who long had mark'd her airy lodge
And destin'd all the treasure there
A gift to his expecting fair,
Climb'd like a squirrel to his dray,
And bore the worthless prize away.

MORAL.

'Tis Providence alone secures
In ev'ry change both mine and yours:
Safety consists not in escape
From dangers of a frightful shape;
An earthquake may be bid to spare
The man, that's strangled by a hair.

Fate steals along with silent tread,
Found oft'nest in what least we dread;
Frowns in the storm with angry brow,
But in the sunshine strikes the blow.

A COMPARISON.

The lapse of time and rivers is the same,
Both speed their journey with a restless stream;
The silent pace, with which they steal away,
No wealth can bribe, nor pray'rs persuade to stay;
Alike irrevocable both when past,
And a wide ocean swallows both at last.
Though each resemble each in ev'ry part,
A diff'rence strikes at length the musing heart:
Streams never flow in vain; where streams abound
How laughs the land with various plenty crown'd!
But time, that should enrich the nobler mind,
Neglected, leaves a weary waste behind.

ANOTHER.

ADDRESSED TO A YOUNG LADY.

Sweet stream, that winds through yonder glade,
Apt emblem of a virtuous maid—
Silent and chaste she steals along,
Far from the world's gay busy throng;
With gentle yet prevailing force,
Intent upon her destin'd course;
Graceful and useful all she does,
Blessing and blest where'er she goes,
Pure-bosom'd as that wat'ry glass,
And heav'n reflected in her face.

THE POETS NEW-YEAR'S GIFT.

To MRS. (now LADY) THROCKMORTON.

Maria! I have ev'ry good
For thee wish'd many a time,
Both sad and in a cheerful mood,
But never yet in rhyme.

To wish thee fairer is no need,
More prudent, or more sprightly,
Or more ingenious, or more freed
From temper-flaws unsightly.

What favor then, not yet possess'd,
Can I for thee require,
In wedded love already blest,
To thy whole heart's desire;

None here is happy but in part:
Full bliss is bliss divine:
There dwells some wish in ev'ry heart,
And doubtless one in thine.

That wish, on some fair future day,
Which Fate shall brightly gild,
('Tis blameless, be it what it may,)
I wish it all fulfill'd.

ODE TO APOLLO.

ON AN INKGLASS ALMOST DRIED IN THE SUN.

Patron of all those luckless brains,
That, to the wrong side leaning,
Indite much metre with much pains,
And little or no meaning:

Ah why, since oceans, rivers, streams,
That water all the nations,
Pay tribute to thy glorious beams,
In constant exhalations,

Why, stooping from the noon of day,
  Too covetous of drink,
Apollo, hast thou stol'n away
  A poet's drop of ink?

Upborne into the viewless air,
  It floats a vapor now,
Impell'd through regions dense and rare,
  By all the winds that blow.

Ordain'd perhaps, ere summer flies,
  Combin'd with millions more,
To form an Iris in the skies,
  Though black and foul before.

Illustrious drop! and happy then
  Beyond the happiest lot,
Of all that ever pass'd my pen,
  So soon to be forgot!

Phoebus, if such be thy design,
  To place it in thy bow,
Give wit, that what is left may shine
  With equal grace below.

PAIRING TIME ANTICIPATED.

A FABLE.

  I shall not ask Jean Jacques Rousseau,*
If birds confabulate or no;
'Tis clear, that they were always able
To hold discourse, at least in fable;
And e'en the child, who knows no better
Than to interpret by the letter,
A story of a cock and bull,
Must have a most uncommon skull.
  It chanc'd then, on a winter's day,
But warm, and bright, and calm as May,
The birds, conceiving a design
To forestal sweet St. Valentine,

* It was one of the whimsical speculations of this philosopher, that all fables which ascribe reason and speech to animals should be withheld from children, as being only vehicles of deception. But what child was ever deceived by them, or can be, against the evidence of his senses?

In many an orchard, copse, and grove,
Assembled on affairs of love,
And with much twitter and much chatter,
Began to agitate the matter.
At length a Bulfinch, who could boast
More years and wisdom than the most,
Entreated, op'ning wide his beak,
A moment's liberty to speak;
And, silence publicly enjoin'd,
Deliver'd briefly thus his mind:
  My friends! be cautious how ye treat
The subject upon which we meet;
I fear we shall have winter yet.
  A Finch, whose tongue knew no control,
With golden wing, and satin poll,
A last year's bird, who ne'er had tried
What marriage means, thus pert replied:
  Methinks the gentleman, quoth she,
Opposite in the apple-tree,
By his good will would keep us single
Till yonder heav'n and earth shall mingle,
Or (which is likelier to befall)
Till death exterminate us all.
I marry without more ado,
My dear Dick Redcap, what say you?
  Dick heard, and tweedling, ogling, bridling,
Turning short round, strutting and sideling,
Attested, glad, his approbation
Of an immediate conjugation.
Their sentiments so well express'd,
Influenc'd mightily the rest;
All pair'd, and each pair built a nest.
  But though the birds were thus in haste,
The leaves came on not quite so fast,
And Destiny, that sometimes bears
An aspect stern on man's affairs,
Not altogether smil'd on theirs.
The wind, of late breath'd gently forth,
Now shifted east, and east by north;
Bare trees and shrubs but ill, you know,
Could shelter them from rain or snow,
Stepping into their nests, they paddled,
Themselves were chill'd, their eggs were addled;
Soon ev'ry father-bird and mother
Grew quarrelsome, and peck'd each other,
Parted without the least regret,
Except that they had ever met,
And learn'd in future to be wiser,
Than to neglect a good adviser

MORAL.

Misses! the tale that I relate
  This lesson seems to carry—
Choose not alone a proper mate,
  But proper time to marry.

THE DOG AND THE WATER-LILY

NO FABLE.

The noon was shady, and soft airs
  Swept Ouse's silent tide,
When, 'scap'd from literary cares,
  I wander'd on his side.

My spaniel, prettiest of his race,
  And high in pedigree,
(Two nymphs* adorn'd with ev'ry grace
  That spaniel found for me,)

Now wanton'd lost in flags and reeds,
  Now starting into sight,
Pursued the swallow o'er the meads
  With scarce a slower flight.

It was the time when Ouse display'd
  His lilies newly blown;
Their beauties I intent survey'd,
  And one I wish'd my own.

With cane extended far I sought
  To steer it close to land;
But still the prize, though nearly caught,
  Escap'd my eager hand.

Beau mark'd my unsuccessful pains
  With fix'd considerate face,
And puzzling set his puppy brains
  To comprehend the case.

But with a cherup clear and strong,
  Dispersing all his dream,
I thence withdrew, and follow'd long
  The windings of the stream.

* Sir Robert Gunning's daughters.

My ramble ended, I return'd;
Beau, trotting far before,
The floating wreath again discern'd
And plunging left the shore.

I saw him with that lily cropp'd
Impatient swim to meet
My quick approach, and soon he dropp'd
The treasure at my feet.

Charm'd with the sight, the world, I cried,
Shall hear of this thy deed:
My dog shall mortify the pride
Of man's superior breed:

But chief myself I will enjoin,
Awake at duty's call,
To show a love as prompt as thine
To Him who gives me all.

THE POET, THE OYSTER, AND SENSITIVE PLANT.

An Oyster, cast upon the shore,
Was heard, though never heard before,
Complaining in a speech well worded—
And worthy thus to be recorded:—
Ah, hapless wretch! condemn'd to dwell
For ever in my native shell;
Ordain'd to move when others please,
Not for my own content or ease;
But toss'd and buffeted about,
Now *in* the water and now *out*.
'Twere better to be born a stone,
Of ruder shape, and feeling none,
Than with a tenderness like mine,
And sensibilities so fine!
I envy that unfeeling shrub,
Fast-rooted against ev'ry rub.
The plant he meant grew not far off,
And felt the sneer with scorn enough;
Was hurt, disgusted, mortified,
And with asperity replied.
When, cry the botanists, and stare,
Did plants call'd sensitive grow there?

No matter when—a poet's muse is
To make them grow just where she chooses.
  You shapeless nothing in a dish,
You that are but almost a fish,
I scorn your coarse insinuation,
And have most plentiful occasion,
To wish myself the rock I view,
Or such another dolt as you:
For many a grave and learned clerk,
And many a gay unletter'd spark,
With curious touch examines me,
If I can feel as well as he;
And when I bend, retire, and shrink,
Says—Well, 'tis more than one would think!
Thus life is spent (oh fie upon't!)
In being touch'd, and crying—Don't!
  A poet, in his ev'ning walk,
O'erheard and check'd this idle talk.
And your fine sense, he said, and yours,
Whatever evil it endures,
Deserves not, if so soon offended,
Much to be pitied or commended.
Disputes, though short, are far too long,
Where both alike are in the wrong;
Your feelings in their full amount,
Are all upon your own account.
  You, in your grotto-work enclos'd,
Complain of being thus expos'd;
Yet nothing feel in that rough coat,
Save when the knife is at your throat,
Wherever driv'n by wind or tide,
Exempt from ev'ry ill beside.
And as for you, my Lady Squeamish,
Who reckon ev'ry touch a blemish,
If all the plants, that can be found
Embellishing the scene around,
Should droop and wither where they grow,
You would not feel at all—not you.
The noblest minds their virtue prove
By pity, sympathy, and love:
These, these are feelings truly fine,
And prove their owner half divine.
  His censure reach'd them as he dealt it,
And each by shrinking show'd he felt it.

THE SHRUBBERY.

WRITTEN IN A TIME OF AFFLICTION.

Oh, happy shades—to me unblest!
  Friendly to peace, but not to me!
How ill the scene that offers rest,
  And heart that cannot rest, agree!

This glassy stream, that spreading pine,
  Those alders quiv'ring to the breeze,
Might soothe a soul less hurt than mine,
  And please, if any thing could please.

But fix'd unalterable Care
  Foregoes not what she feels within,
Shows the same sadness ev'ry where,
  And slights the season and the scene.

For all that pleas'd in wood or lawn,
  While Peace possess'd these silent bow'rs,
Her animating smile withdrawn,
  Has lost its beauties and its pow'rs.

The saint or moralist should tread
  This moss-grown alley musing, slow;
They seek like me the secret shade,
  But not like me to nourish woe!

Me fruitful scenes and prospects waste
  Alike admonish not to roam;
These tell me of enjoyments past,
  And those of sorrows yet to come.

THE WINTER NOSEGAY.

What Nature, alas! has denied
  To the delicate growth of our isle,
Art has in a measure supplied,
  And Winter is deck'd with a smile
See, Mary, what beauties I bring
  From the shelter of that sunny shed,
Where the flow'rs have the charms of the spring,
  Though abroad they are frozen and dead.

'Tis a bow'r of Arcadian sweets,
  Where Flora is still in her prime,
A fortress to which she retreats
  From the cruel assaults of the clime
While Earth wears a mantle of snow,
  These pinks are as fresh and as gay,
As the fairest and sweetest that blow
  On the beautiful bosom of May.

See how they have safely surviv'd
  The frowns of a sky so severe;
Such Mary's true love, that has liv'd
  Through many a turbulent year.
The charms of the late blowing rose
  Seem grac'd with a livelier hue,
And the winter of sorrow best shows
  The truth of a friend such as you.

MUTUAL FORBEARANCE

NECESSARY TO THE HAPPINESS OF THE MARRIED STATE.

  The lady thus address'd her spouse :—
What a mere dungeon is this house!
By no means large enough; and was it,
Yet this dull room, and that dark closet,
Those hangings with their worn-out graces,
Long beards, long noses, and pale faces,
Are such an antiquated scene,
They overwhelm me with the spleen.
Sir Humphrey, shooting in the dark,
Makes answer quite beside the mark:
No doubt, my dear, I bade him come,
Engag'd myself to be at home,
And shall expect him at the door,
Precisely when the clock strikes four.
  You are so deaf, the lady cried,
(And rais'd her voice, and frown'd beside,)
You are so sadly deaf, my dear,
What shall I do to make you hear?
  Dismiss poor Harry! he replies;
Some people are more nice than wise:

For one slight trespass all this stir?
What if he did ride whip and spur,
'Twas but a mile—your fav'rite horse
Will never look one hair the worse.
Well, I protest 'tis past all bearing—
Child! I am rather hard of hearing—
Yes, truly; one must scream and bawl:
I tell you, you can't hear at all!
Then, with a voice exceeding low,
No matter if you hear or no.
Alas! and is domestic strife,
That sorest ill of human life,
A plague so little to be fear'd,
As to be wantonly incurr'd,
To gratify a fretful passion,
On ev'ry trivial provocation?
The kindest and the happiest pair
Will find occasion to forbear;
And something, ev'ry day they live,
To pity, and perhaps forgive.
But if infirmities, that fall
In common to the lot of all,
A blemish or a sense impair'd,
Are crimes so little to be spar'd,
Then farewell all that must create
The comfort of the wedded state;
Instead of harmony, 'tis jar,
And tumult, and intestine war.
The love that cheers life's latest stage,
Proof against sickness and old age,
Preserv'd by virtue from declension,
Becomes not weary of attention;
But lives, when that exterior grace,
Which first inspir'd the flame, decays.
'Tis gentle, delicate, and kind,
To faults compassionate or blind,
And will with sympathy endure
Those evils, it would gladly cure:
But angry, coarse, and harsh expression
Shows love to be a mere profession;
Proves that the heart is none of his,
Or soon expels him if it is.

THE NEGRO'S COMPLAINT.

Forc'd from home and all its pleasures,
  Afric's coast I left forlorn;
To increase a stranger's treasures,
  O'er the raging billows borne.
Men from England bought and sold me,
  Paid my price in paltry gold;
But, though slave they have enroll'd me,
  Minds are never to be sold.

Still in thought as free as ever,
  What are England's rights, I ask,
Me from my delights to sever,
  Me to torture, me to task?
Fleecy locks and black complexion
  Cannot forfeit Nature's claim;
Skins may differ, but affection
  Dwells in white and black the same.

Why did all-creating Nature
  Make the plant, for which we toil?
Sighs must fan it, tears must water,
  Sweat of ours must dress the soil.
Think, ye masters iron-hearted,
  Lolling at your jovial boards;
Think how many backs have smarted
  For the sweets your cane affords.

Is there, as ye sometimes tell us,
  Is there one, who reigns on high?
Has he bid you buy and sell us,
  Speaking from his throne the sky?
Ask him, if your knotted scourges,
  Matches, blood-extorting screws,
Are the means that duty urges,
  Agents of his will to use?

Hark! he answers—wild tornadoes,
  Strewing yonder sea with wrecks;
Wasting towns, plantations, meadows,
  Are the voice, with which he speaks.
He, foreseeing what vexations
  Afric's sons should undergo,
Fix'd their tyrants' habitations
  Where his whirlwinds answer—no.

By our blood in Afric wasted,
  Ere our necks receiv'd the chain,
By the mis'ries that we tasted,
  Crossing in your barks the main;
By our suff'rings, since ye brought us
  To the man-degrading mart;
All, sustain'd by patience, taught us
  Only by a broken heart:

Deem our nation brutes no longer,
  Till some reason ye shall find
Worthier of regard, and stronger
  Than the color of our kind.
Slaves of gold, whose sordid dealings
  Tarnish all your boasted pow'rs,
Prove that you have human feelings,
  Ere you proudly question ours!

PITY FOR POOR AFRICANS.

'Video meliora proboque,
Deteriora sequor.'—

I own I am shock'd at the purchase of slaves,
And fear those who buy them and sell them, are knaves;
What I hear of their hardships, their tortures, and groans,
Is almost enough to draw pity from stones.

I pity them greatly, but I must be mum,
For how could we do without sugar and rum?
Especially sugar, so needful we see?
What, give up our desserts, our coffee, and tea!

Besides, if we do, the French, Dutch, and Danes,
Will heartily thank us, no doubt, for our pains;
If we do not buy the poor creatures, they will,
And tortures and groans will be multiplied still.

If foreigners likewise would give up the trade,
Much more in behalf of your wish might be said;
But, while they get riches by purchasing blacks,
Pray tell me why we may not also go snacks?

Your scruples and arguments bring to my mind
A story so pat, you may think it is coin'd,
On purpose to answer you, out of my mint;
But I can assure you I saw it in print.

A youngster at school, more sedate than the rest,
Had once his integrity put to the test;
His comrades had plotted an orchard to rob,
And ask'd him to go and assist in the job.

He was shock'd, sir, like you, and answer'd—'Oh no!
What! rob our good neighbour! I pray you don't go;
Besides, the man's poor, his orchard's his bread,
Then think of his children, for they must be fed.'

'You speak very fine, and you look very grave,
But apples we want, and apples we'll have;
If you will go with us, you shall have a share,
If not, you shall have neither apple nor pear.'

They spoke, and Tom ponder'd—'I see they will go:
Poor man! what a pity to injure him so!
Poor man! I would save him his fruit if I could,
But staying behind will do him no good.

'If the matter depended alone upon me,
His apples might hang, till they dropp'd from the tree;
But, since they will take them, I think I'll go too,
He will lose none by me, though I get a few.'

His scruples thus silenc'd; Tom felt more at ease,
And went with his comrades the apples to seize;
He blam'd and protested, but join'd in the plan:
He shar'd in the plunder, but pitied the man.

THE MORNING DREAM.

'Twas in the glad season fo spring,
  Asleep at the dawn of the day,
I dream'd what I cannot but sing,
  So pleasant it seem'd as I lay.
I dream'd, that, on ocean afloat,
  Far hence to the westward I sail'd,
While the billows high-lifted the boat;
  And the fresh-blowing breeze never fail'd.

In the steerage a woman I saw,
  Such at least was the form that she wore,
Whose beauty impress'd me with awe,
  Ne'er taught me by woman before.
She sat, and a shield at her side
  Shed light, like a sun on the waves,
And, smiling divinely, she cried—
  'I go to make freemen of slaves.'—

Then raising her voice to a strain
  The sweetest that ear ever heard,
She sung of the slave's broken chain,
  Wherever her glory appear'd.
Some clouds, which had over us hung,
  Fled, chas'd by her melody clear,
And methought while she liberty sung,
  'Twas liberty only to hear.*

Thus swiftly dividing the flood,
  To a slave-cultur'd island we came,
Where, a demon, her enemy, stood—
  Oppression his terrible name.
In his hand, as the sign of his sway,
  A scourge hung with lashes he bore,
And stood looking out for his prey
  From Africa's sorrowful shore.

But soon as approaching the land
  That goddess-like woman he view'd,
The scourge he let fall from his hand,
  With blood of his subjects imbru'd.
I saw him both sicken and die,
  And the moment the monster expir'd,
Heard shouts that ascended the sky,
  For thousands with rapture inspir'd.

Awaking, how could I but muse
  At what such a dream should betide?
But soon my ear caught the glad news,
  Which serv'd my weak thought for a guide—
That Britannia, renown'd o'er the waves
  For the hatred she ever has shown
To the black-sceptred rulers of slaves,
  Resolves to have none of her own.

THE NIGHTINGALE AND GLOW-WORM.

A Nightingale, that all day long
Had cheer'd the village with his song,
Nor yet at eve his note suspended,
Nor yet when eventide was ended,
Began to feel, as well he might,
The keen demands of appetite;
When, looking eagerly around,
He spied far off, upon the ground,

A something shining in the dark,
And knew the glow-worm by his spark;
So, stooping down from hawthorn top,
He thought to put him in his crop.
The worm, aware of his intent,
Harangu'd him thus, right eloquent—

Did you admire my lamp, quoth he,
As much as I your minstrelsy,
You would abhor to do me wrong,
As much as I to spoil your song;
For 'twas the selfsame pow'r divine
Taught you to sing, and me to shine;
That you with music, I with light,
Might beautify and cheer the night.
The songster heard his short oration,
And, warbling out his approbation,
Releas'd him, as my story tells,
And found a supper somewhere else.

Hence jarring sectaries may learn
Their real int'rest to discern;
That brother should not war with brother,
And worry and devour each other:
But sing and shine by sweet consent,
Till life's poor transient night is spent,
Respecting in each other's case
The gifts of nature and of grace.

Those Christians best deserve the name,
Who studiously make peace their aim;
Peace both the duty and the prize
Of him that creeps and him that flies

ON A GOLDFINCH,

STARVED TO DEATH IN HIS CAGE.

Time was when I was free as air,
The thistle's downy seed my fare,
My drink the morning dew;
I perch'd at will on ev'ry spray,
My form genteel, my plumage gay,
My stra'ns for ever new.

But gaudy plumage, sprightly strain,
And form genteel, were all in vain,
And of a transient date;
For caught, and cag'd, and starv'd to death,
In dying sighs my little breath
Soon pass'd the wiry grate.

Thanks, gentle swain, for all my woes,
And thanks for this effectual close
And cure of ev'ry ill;
More cruelty could none express;
And I, if you had shown me less,
Had been your pris'ner still.

THE
PINEAPPLE AND THE BEE.

The pineapples, in triple row,
Were basking hot, and all in blow;
A bee of most discerning taste,
Perceiv'd the fragrance as he pass'd,
On eager wing the spoiler came,
And search'd for crannies in the frame,
Urg'd his attempt on ev'ry side,
To ev'ry pane his trunk applied;
But still in vain, the frame was tight,
And only pervious to the light:
Thus having wasted half the day,
He trimm'd his flight another way.
Methinks, I said, in thee I find
The sin and madness of mankind.
To joys forbidden man aspires,
Consumes his soul with vain desires;
Folly the spring of his pursuit,
And disappointment all the fruit.
While Cynthio ogles, as he passes,
The nymph between two chariot glasses,
She is the pineapple, and he
The silly unsuccessful bee.
The maid, who views with pensive air
The show-glass fraught with glitt'ring ware,
Sees watches, bracelets, rings, and lockets,
But sighs at thought of empty pockets;

Like thine, her appetite is keen,
But ah, the cruel glass between!
Our dear delights are often such,
Expos'd to view, but not to touch;
The sight our foolish heart inflames,
We long for pineapples in frames;
With hopeless wish one looks and lingers;
One breaks the glass, and cuts his fingers:
But they whom truth and wisdom lead,
Can gather honey from a weed.

HORACE.

Book II. Ode X.

Receive, dear friend, the truths I teach,
So shalt thou live beyond the reach
   Of adverse Fortune's pow'r;
Not always tempt the distant deep,
Nor always timorously creep
   Along the treach'rous shore.

He, that holds fast the golden mean,
And lives contentedly between
   The little and the great,
Feels not the wants that pinch the poor,
Nor plagues that haunt the rich man's door,
   Imbitt'ring all his state.

The tallest pines feel most the pow'r
Of wintry blasts; the loftiest tow'r
   Comes heaviest to the ground;
The bolts, that spare the mountain's side,
His cloud-capt eminence divide,
   And spread the ruin round.

The well inform'd philosopher
Rejoices with a wholesome fear,
   And hopes, in spite of pain;
If Winter bellow from the north,
Soon the sweet Spring comes dancing forth,
   And Nature laughs again.

What if thine heav'n be overcast,
The dark appearance will not last;
Expect a brighter sky.
The God that strings the silver bow,
Awakes sometimes the muses too,
And lays his arrows by.

If hind'rances obstruct thy way,
Thy magnanimity display,
And let thy strength be seen;,
But O! if fortune fill thy sail
With more than a propitious gale,
Take half thy canvass in.

A REFLECTION.

ON THE FOREGOING ODE.

And is this all? Can Reason do no more,
Than bid me shun the deep, and dread the shore?
Sweet moralist! afloat on life's rough sea,
The Christian has an art unknown to thee.
He holds no parley with unmanly fears;
Where duty bids, he confidently steers,
Faces a thousand dangers at her call,
And, trusting in his God, surmounts them all.

THE LILY AND THE ROSE.

The nymph must lose her female friend,
If more admir'd than she—
But where will fierce contention end,
If flow'rs can disagree?

Within the garden's peaceful scene
Appear'd two lovely foes,
Aspiring to the rank of queen,
The Lily and the Rose.

The Rose soon redden'd into rage,
And, swelling with disdain,
Appeal'd to many a poet's page
To prove her right to reign.

The Lily's height bespoke command,
A fair imperial flow'r;
She seem'd design'd for Flora's hand,
The sceptre of her pow'r.

This civil bick'ring and debate
The goddess chanc'd to hear,
And flew to save, ere yet too late,
The pride of the parterre.

Yours is, she said, the nobler hue,
And yours the statelier mien;
And, till a third surpasses you,
Let each be deem'd a queen.

Thus, sooth'd and reconcil'd, each seeks
The fairest British fair:
The seat of empire is her cheeks,
They reign united there.

IDEM LATINE REDDITUM.

Heu inimicitias quoties parit æmula forma,
Quam raro pulchræ pulchra placere potest!
Sed fines ultra solitos discordia tendit,
Cum flores ipsos bilis et ira movent.

Hortus ubi dulces præbet tacitosque recessus,
Se rapit in partes gens animosa duas;
Hic sibi regales Amaryllis candida cultus,
Illic purpureo vindicat ore Rosa.

Ira Rosam et meritis quæsita superbia tangunt,
Multaque ferventi vix cohibenda sinu,
Dum sibi fautorum ciet undique nomina vatum,
Jusque suum, multo carmine fulta, probat.

Altior emicat illa, et celso vertice nutat,
Ceu flores inter non habitura parem,
Fastiditque alios, et nata videtur in usus
Imperii, sceptrum, Flora quod ipsa gerat.

Nec Dea non sensit civilis murmura rixæ,
  Cui curæ est pictas pandere ruris opes,
Deliciasque suas nunquam non prompta tueri,
  Dum licet et locus est, ut tueatur, adest.

Et tibi forma datur procerior omnibus, inquit;
  Et tibi, principibus qui solet esse, color;
Et donec vincat quædam formosior ambas,
  Et tibi reginæ nomen, et esto tibi.

His ubi sedatus furor est, petit utraque nympham,
  Qualem inter Veneres Anglia sola parit;
Hanc penes imperium est, nihil optant amplius, hujus
  Regnant in nitidis, et sine lite, genis.

THE POPLAR FIELD.

The poplars are felled, farewell to the shade,
And the whispering sound of the cool colonnade;
The winds play no longer and sing in the leaves,
Nor Ouse on his bosom their image receives.

Twelve years have elaps'd, since I last took a view
Of my favorite field, and the bank where they grew;
And now in the grass behold they are laid,
And the tree is my seat, that once lent me a shade

The blackbird has fled to another retreat,
Where the hazels afford him a screen from the heat,
And the scene, where his melody charm'd me before,
Resounds with his sweet-flowing ditty no more.

My fugitive years are all hasting away,
And I must ere long lie as lowly as they,
With a turf on my breast, and a stone at my head,
Ere another such grove shall arise in its stead.

'Tis a sight to engage me, if any thing can,
To muse on the perishing pleasures of man;
Though his life be a dream, his enjoyments, I see,
Have a being less durable even than he. *

* Mr. Cowper afterwards altered this last stanza in the following manner:—

The change both my heart and my fancy employs,
I reflect on the frailty of man, and his joys;
Short-lived as we are, yet our pleasures, we see,
Have a still shorter date, and die sooner than we.

IDEM LATINE REDDITUM.

Populeæ cecidit gratissima copia silvæ,
Conticuêre susurri, omnisque evanuit umbra,
Nullæ jam levibus se miscent frondibus auræ,
Et nulla in fluvio ramorum ludit imago.

Hei mihi! bis senos dum luctu torqueor annos,
His cogor silvis suetoque carere recessu,
Cum serò rediens, stratasque in gramine cernens,
Insedi arboribus, sub queîs errare solebam.

Ah ubi nunc merulæ cantus? Felicior illum
Silva tegit, duræ nondum permissa bipenni;
Scilicet exustos colles camposque patentes
Odit, et indignans et non rediturus abivit.

Sed qui succisas doleo succidar et ipse,
Et priùs huic parilis quàm creverit altera silva
Flebor, et, exequiis parvis donatus, habebo
Defixum lapidem tumulique cubantis acervum.

Tam subitò periisse videns tam digna manere,
Agnosco humanas sortes et tristia fata—
Sit licèt ipse brevis, volucrique simillimus umbræ,
Est homini brevior citiùsque obitura voluptas.

VOTUM.

O Matutini rores, auræque salubres,
O nemora, et lætæ rivis felicibus herbæ,
Graminei colles, et amœnæ in vallibus umbræ!
Fata modò dederint quas olim in rure paterno
Delicias, procul arte, procul formidine novi.
Quàm vellem ignotus, quod mens mea semper avebat,
Ante larem proprium placidam expectare senectam,
Tum demùm, exactis non infeliciter annis,
Sortiri tacitum lapidem, aut sub cespite condi!

CICINDELA.

BY VINCENT BOURNE.

Sub sepe exiguum est, nec rarò in margine ripæ,
Reptile, quod lucet nocte, dieque latet.
Vermis habet speciem, sed hăbet de lumine nomen
At priscâ à famâ non liquet, unde micet.
Plerique à caudâ credunt procedere lumen;
Nec desunt, credunt qui rutilare caput.
Nam superas stellas quæ nox accendit, et illi
Parcam eadem lucem dat, moduloque parem.
Forsitan hoc prudens voluit Natura caveri,
Ne pede quis duro reptile contereret:
Exiguam, in tenebris ne gressum offenderet ullus,
Prætendi voluit forsitan illa facem.
Sive usum hunc Natura parens, seu maluit illum,
Haud frustra accensa est lux, radiique dati.
Ponite vos fastus, humiles nec spernite, magni;
Quando habet et minimum reptile, quod niteat.

I. THE GLOWWORM.

TRANSLATION OF THE FOREGOING.

Beneath the hedge, or near the stream,
A worm is known to stray;
That shows by night a lucid beam,
Which disappears by day.

Disputes have been, and still prevail,
From whence his rays proceed;
Some give that honor to his tail,
And others to his head.

But this is sure—the hand of night,
That kindles up the skies,
Gives *him* a modicum of light
Proportion'd to his size.

Perhaps indulgent Nature meant,
By such a lamp bestow'd,
To bid the trav'ller, as he went,
Be careful where he trod:

Nor crush a worm, whose useful light
  Might serve, however small,
To show a stumbling stone by night,
  And save him from a fall.

Whate'er she meant, this truth divine
  Is legible and plain,
'Tis pow'r almighty bids him shine,
  Nor bids him shine in vain.

Ye proud and wealthy, let this theme
  Teach humbler thoughts to you,
Since such a reptile has its gem,
  And boasts its splendor too.

CORNICULA.

BY VINCENT BOURNE.

Nigras inter aves avis est, quæ plurima turres,
  Antiquas ædes, celsaque fana colit.
Nil tam sublime est, quod non audace volatu,
  Aeriis spernens inferiora, petit.
Quo nemo ascendat cui non vertige cerebrum
  Corripiat, certè hunc seligit illa locum.
Quo vix à terra tu suspicis absque tremore,
  Illa metûs expers incolumisque sedet.
Lamina delubri supra fastigia, ventus
  Quâ cœli spiret de regione, docet;
Hanc ea præ reliquis mavult, secura pericli,
  Nec curat, nedum cogitat, unde cadat.
Res inde humanas, sed summa per otia, spectat,
  Et nihil ad sese, quas videt, esse videt.
Concursus spectat, plateâque negotia in omni,
  Omnia pro nugis at sapienter habet.
Clamores, quas infra audit, si forsitan audit,
  Pro rebus nihili negligit, et crocitat.
Ille tibi invideat, felix Cornicula, pennas,
  Qui sic humanis rebus abesse velit.

II. THE JACKDAW.

TRANSLATION OF THE FOREGOING.

There is a bird, who by his coat,
And by the hoarseness of his note,
Might be suppos'd a crow;
A great frequenter of the church,
Where bishop-like he finds a perch,
And dormitory too.

Above the steeple shines a plate,
That turns and turns, to indicate
From what point blows the weather,
Look up—your brains begin to swim,
'Tis in the clouds—that pleases him,
He chooses it the rather.

Fond of the speculative height,
Thither he wings his airy flight,
And then securely sees
The bustle and the raree-show,
That occupy mankind below,
Secure and at his ease.

You think, no doubt, he sits and muses
On future broken bones and bruises,
If he should chance to fall.
No; not a single thought like that
Employs his philosophic pate,
Or troubles it at all.

He sees, that this great roundabout,
The world, with all its motley rout,
Church, army, physic, law,
Its customs, and its bus'nesses,
Is no concern at all of his,
And says—what says he?—Caw.

Thrice happy bird! I too have seen
Much of the vanities of men;
And, sick of having seen 'em,
Would cheerfully these limbs resign
For such a pair of wings as thine,
And such a head between 'em.

AD GRILLUM.

Anacreonticum.

BY VINCENT BOURNE.

O qui meæ culinæ
Argutulus choraules,
Et hospes es canorus,
Quacunque commoreris,
Felicitatis omen;
Jucundiore cantu
Siquando me salutes,
Et ipse te rependam,
Et ipse, quâ valebo,
Remunerabo musâ.

Dicêris innocensque
Et gratus inquilinus;
Nec victitans rapinis,
Ut sorices voraces,
Muresve curiosi,
Furumque delicatum
Vulgus domesticorum;
Sed tutus in camini
Recessibus, quiete
Contentus et calore.

Beatior Cicadâ,
Quæ te referre formâ,
Quæ voce te videtur;
Et saltitans per herbas,
Unius, haud secundæ,
Æstatis est chorista;
Tu carmen integratum
Reponis ad Decembrem,
Lætus per universum
Incontinenter annum.

Te nulla lux relinquit,
Te nulla nox revisit,
Non musicæ vacantem,
Curisve non solutum:
Quin amplies canendo,
Quin amplies fruendo,
Ætatulam, vel omni,
Quam nos homunciones
Absumimus querendo,
Ætate longiorem.

III. THE CRICKET.

TRANSLATION OF THE FOREGOING.

Little inmate, full of mirth,
Chirping on my kitchen hearth,
Wheresoe'er be thine abode,
Always harbinger of good,
Pay me for thy warm retreat
With a song more soft and sweet;
In return thou shalt receive
Such a strain as I can give.

Thus thy praise shall be express'd,
Inoffensive, welcome guest!
While the rat is on the scout,
And the mouse with curious snout,
With what vermin else infest
Ev'ry dish, and spoil the best;
Frisking thus before the fire,
Thou hast all thine heart's desire.

Though in voice and shape they be
Form'd as if akin to thee,
Thou surpassest, happier far,
Happiest grasshoppers that are;
Theirs is but a summer's song,
Thine endures the winter long,
Unimpair'd, and shrill, and clear,
Melody throughout the year.

Neither night, nor dawn of day,
Puts a period to thy play:
Sing then—and extend thy span
Far beyond the date of man.
Wretched man, whose years are spent
In repining discontent,
Lives not, aged though he be,
Half a span, compar'd with thee.

SIMILE AGIT IN SIMILE.

BY VINCENT BOURNE.

Cristatus, pictisque ad Thaida Psittacus alis,
  Missus ab Eoo munus amante venit.
Ancillis mandat primam formare loquelam,
  Archididascaliæ dat sibi Thais opus.
Psittace, ait Thais, fingitque sonantia molle
  Basia, quæ docilis molle refingit avis.
Jam captat, jam dimidiat tyrunculus; et jam
  Integrat auditos articulatque sonos.
Psittace mi pulcher pulchelle, hera dicit alumno;
  Psittace mi pulcher, reddit alumnus heræ.
Jamque canit, ridet, deciesque ægrotat in horâ,
  Et vocat ancillas nomine quamque suo.
Multaque scurratur mendax, et multa jocatur,
  Et lepido populum detinet augurio.
Nunc tremulum illudet fratrem, qui suspicit, et Pol!
  Carnalis, quisquis te docet, inquit, homo est;
Argutæ nunc stridet anûs argutulus instar;
  Respicit, et nebulo es, quisquis es, inquit anus.
Quando fuit melior tyro, meliorve magistra!
  Quando duo ingeniis tam coiêre pares!
Ardua discenti nulla est, res nulla docenti
  Ardua; cum doceat fœmina, discat avis.

IV. THE PARROT.

TRANSLATION OF THE FOREGOING.

In painted plumes superbly dress'd,
A native of the gorgeous east,
  By many a billow toss'd,
Poll gains at length the British shore,
Part of the captain's precious store,
  A present to his toast.

Belinda's maids are soon preferr'd,
To teach him now and then a word,
  As Poll can master it;
But 'tis her own important charge,
To qualify him more at large,
  And make him quite a wit.

Sweet Poll! his doating mistress cries,
Sweet Poll! the mimic bird replies;
And calls aloud for sack.
She next instructs him in the kiss;
'Tis now a little one, like Miss,
And now a hearty smack.

At first he aims at what he hears;
And, list'ning close with both his ears,
Just catches at the sound;
But soon articulates aloud,
Much to the amusement of the crowd,
And stuns the neighbours round.

A querulous old womans' voice
His hum'rous talent next employs;
He scolds, and gives the lie.
And now he sings, and now is sick,
Here Sally, Susan, come, come quick,
Poor Poll is like to die!

Belinda and her bird! 'tis rare,
To meet with such a well-match'd pair,
The language and the tone,
Each character in ev'ry part
Sustain'd with so much grace and art,
And both in unison.

When children first begin to spell,
And stammer out a syllable,
We think them tedious creatures;
But difficulties soon abate,
When birds are to be taught to prate,
And women are the teachers.

TRANSLATION OF PRIOR'S CHLOE AND EUPHELIA.

Mercator, vigiles oculos ut fallere possit,
Nomine sub ficto trans mare mittit opes;
Lené sonat liquidumque meis Euphelia chordis,
Sed solam exoptant te, mea vota, Chlöe.

Ad speculum ornabat nitidos Euphelia crines,
Cum dixit mea lux, Heus, cane, sume lyram.
Namque lyram juxta positam cum carmine vidit,
Suave quidem carmen dulcisonamque lyram.

Fila lyræ vocemque paro, suspiria surgunt,
Et miscent numeris murmura mœsta meis,
Dumque tuæ memoro laudes, Euphelia, formæ,
Tota anima intereà pendet ab ore Chlöes.

Subrubet illa pudore, et contrahit altera frontem
Me torquet mea mens conscia, psallo, tremo;
Atque Cupidineâ dixit Dea cincta coronâ,
Heu! fallendi artem quam didicêre parum.

THE DIVERTING

HISTORY OF JOHN GILPIN:

Showing how he went farther than he intended, and came safe home again.

John Gilpin was a citizen
Of credit and renown,
A train-band captain eke was he
Of famous London town.

John Gilpin's spouse said to her dear,
Though wedded we have been
These twice ten tedious years, yet we
No holiday have seen.

To-morrow is our wedding day,
And we will then repair
Unto the Bell at Edmonton
All in a chaise and pair.

My sister, and my sister's child,
Myself, and children three,
Will fill the chaise; so you must
On horseback after we.

He soon replied, I do admire
Of womankind but one,
And you are she, my dearest dear,
Therefore it shall be done.

I am a linendraper bold,
As all the world doth know,
And my good friend the calend'rer
Will lend his horse to go.

Quoth Mrs. Gilpin, That's well said;
  And for that wine is dear,
We will be furnish'd with our own,
  Which is both bright and clear.

John Gilpin kiss'd his loving wife;
  O'erjoy'd was he to find,
That though on pleasure she was bent,
  She had a frugal mind.

The morning came, the chaise was brought,
  But yet was not allow'd
To drive up to the door, lest all
  Should say that she was proud.

So three doors off the chaise was stay'd,
  Where they did all get in;
Six precious souls, and all agog
  To dash through thick and thin.

Smack went the whip, round went the wheels,
  Were never folk so glad,
The stones did rattle underneath,
  As if Cheapside were mad.

John Gilpin at his horse's side
  Seiz'd fast the flowing mane,
And up he got, in haste to ride,
  But soon came down again;

For saddletree scarce reach'd had he,
  His journey to begin,
When, turning round his head, he saw
  Three customers come in.

So down he came; for loss of time,
  Although it griev'd him sore;
Yet loss of pence, full well he knew,
  Would trouble him much more.

'Twas long before the customers
  Were suited to their mind,
When Betty screaming came down stairs,
  'The wine is left behind!'

Good lack! quoth he—yet bring it me,
  My leathern belt likewise,
In which I bear my trusty sword,
  When I do exercise.

Now mistress Gilpin (careful soul !)
   Had two stone bottles found,
To hold the liquor that she lov'd,
   And keep it safe and sound.

Each bottle had a curling ear,
   Through which the belt he drew,
And hung a bottle on each side,
   To make his balance true.

Then over all, that he might be
   Equipp'd from top to toe,
His long red-cloak, well brush'd and neat,
   He manfully did throw.

Now see him mounted once again
   Upon his nimble steed,
Full slowly pacing o'er the stones,
   With caution and good heed.

But finding soon a smoother road
   Beneath his well-shod feet,
The snorting beast began to trot,
   Which gall'd him in his seat.

So, Fair and softly, John he cried,
   But John he cried in vain ;
That trot became a gallop soon,
   In spite of curb and rein.

So stooping down, as needs he must,
   Who cannot sit upright,
He grasp'd the mane with both his hands,
   And eke with all his might.

His horse, who never in that sort
   Had handled been before,
What thing upon his back had got
   Did wonder more and more.

Away went Gilpin, neck or nought ;
   Away went hat and wig;
He little dreamt, when he set out,
   Of running such a rig.

The wind did blow, the cloak did fly,
   Like streamer long and gay,
Till, loop and button failing both,
   At last it flew away

Then might all people well discern
  The botties he had slung:
A bottle swinging at each side,
  As hath been said or sung.

The dogs did bark, the children scream'd,
  Up flew the windows all;
And ev'ry soul cried out, Well done!
  As loud as he could bawl.

Away went Gilpin—who but he?
  His fame soon spread around,
He carries weight! he rides a race!
  'Tis for a thousand pound!

And still, as fast as he drew near,
  'Twas wonderful to view,
How in a trice the turnpike men
  Their gates wide open threw.

And now, as he went bowing down
  His reeking head full low,
The bottles twain behind his back
  Were shatter'd at a blow.

Down ran the wine into the road,
  Most piteous to be seen,
Which made his horse's flanks to smoke
  As they had basted been.

But still he seem'd to carry weight,
  With leathern girdle brac'd;
For all might see the bottle necks
  Still dangling at his waist.

Thus all through merry Islington
  These gambols he did play,
Until he came unto the Wash
Of Edmonton so gay;

And there he threw the wash about
  On both sides of the way,
Just like unto a trundling mop,
  Or a wild goose at play.

At Edmonton his loving wife
  From the balcony spied
Her tender husband, wond'ring much
  To see how he did ride.

Stop, stop, John Gilpin!—Here's the house—
They all at once did cry;
The dinner waits, and we are tir'd;
Said Gilpin—So am I!

But yet his horse was not a whit
Inclin'd to tarry there;
For why?—his owner had a house
Full ten miles off, at Ware.

So like an arrow swift he flew,
Shot by an archer strong;
So did he fly—which brings me to
The middle of my song.

Away went Gilpin out of breath,
And sore against his will,
Till at his friend the calend'rers,
His horse at last stood still.

The calend'rer, amaz'd to see
His neighbour in such trim,
Laid down his pipe, flew to the gate,
And thus accosted him:

What news? what news? your tidings tell;
Tell me you must and shall—
Say why bareheaded you are come,
Or why you come at all?

Now Gilpin had a pleasant wit,
And lov'd a timely joke;
And thus unto the calend'rer
In merry guise he spoke:

I came because your horse would come;
And, if I well forbode,
My hat and wig will soon be here,
They are upon the road.

The calend'rer, right glad to find
His friend in merry pin,
Return'd him not a single word,
But to the house went in;

Whence straight he came with hat and wig;
A wig that flow'd behind,
A hat not much the worse for wear,
Each comely in its kind.

He held them up, and in his turn
  Thus show'd his ready wit,
My head is twice as big as yours,
  They therefore needs must fit.

But let me scrape the dirt away,
  That hangs upon your face;
And stop and eat, for well you may
  Be in a hungry case.

Said John, It is my wedding-day,
  And all the world would stare,
If wife should dine at Edmonton,
  And I should dine at Ware.

So turning to his horse, he said,
  I am in haste to dine;
'Twas for your pleasure you came here,
  You shall go back for mine.

Ah luckless speech, and bootless boast!
  For which he paid full dear;
For, while he spake, a braying ass
  Did sing most loud and clear;

Whereat his horse did snort, as he
  Had heard a lion roar,
And gallop'd off with all his might,
  As he had done before.

Away went Gilpin, and away
  Went Gilpin's hat and wig:
He lost them sooner than at first,
  For why?—they were too big.

Now mistress Gilpin, when she saw
  Her husband posting down
Into the country far away,
  She pull'd out half a crown;

And thus unto the youth she said
  That drove them to the Bell,
This shall be yours, when you bring back
  My husband safe and well.

The youth did ride, and soon did meet
  John coming back amain;
Whom in a trice he tried to stop,
  By catching at his rein;

But not performing what he meant,
  And gladly would have done,
The frighted steed he frighted more,
  And made him faster run.

Away went Gilpin, and away
  Went postboy at his heels,
The postboy's horse right glad to miss
  The lumb'ring of the wheels.

Six gentlemen upon the road,
  Thus seeing Gilpin fly,
With postboy scamp'ring in the rear,
  They rais'd the hue and cry :—

Stop thief! stop thief!—a highwayman!
  Not one of them was mute;
And all and each that pass'd that way
  Did join in the pursuit.

And now the turnpike-gates again
  Flew open in short space;
The toll-men thinking as before,
  That Gilpin rode a race.

And so he did, and won it too,
  For he got first to town;
Nor stopp'd till where he had got up,
  He did again get down.

Now let us sing, long live the king,
  And Gilpin, long live he:
And, when he next doth ride abroad,
  May I be there to see!

AN EPISTLE

TO

AN AFFLICTED PROTESTANT LADY IN FRANCE.

MADAM,

A stranger's purpose in these lays
Is to congratulate, and not to praise.
To give the creature the Creator's due
Were sin in me, and an offence to you.

From man to man, or e'en to woman paid,
Praise is the medium of a knavish trade,
A coin by craft for folly's use design'd,
Spurious, and only current with the blind.
The path of sorrow, and that path alone,
Leads to the land where sorrow is unknown;
No trav'ller ever reach'd that bless'd abode,
Who found not thorns and briers in his road.
The World may dance along the flow'ry plain,
Cheer'd as they go by many a sprightly strain,
Where Nature has her mossy velvet spread,
With unshod feet they yet securely tread,
Admonish'd, scorn the caution and the friend,
Bent all on pleasure, heedless of its end.
But he, who knew what human hearts would prove
How slow to learn the dictates of his love,
That, hard by nature and of stubborn will,
A life of ease would make them harder still,
In pity to the souls his grace design'd
To rescue from the ruins of mankind,
Call'd for a cloud to darken all their years,
And said, 'Go, spend them in the vale of tears.
O balmy gales of soul-reviving air!
O salutary streams, that murmur there!
These flowing from the fount of grace above,
Those breath'd from lips of everlasting love.
The flinty soil indeed the feet annoys;
Chill blasts of trouble nip their springing joys;
An envious world will interpose its frown,
To mar delights superior to its own;
And many a pang, experienc'd still within,
Reminds them of their hated inmate, Sin:
But ills of ev'ry shape and ev'ry name,
Transform'd to blessings, miss their cruel aim;
And ev'ry moment's calm that soothes the breast,
Is giv'n in earnest of eternal rest.
Ah, be not sad, although thy lot be cast
Far from the flock, and in a boundless waste!
No shepherd's tents within thy view appear,
But the chief Shepherd even there is near;
Thy tender sorrows and thy plaintive strain,
Flow in a foreign land, but not in vain;
Thy tears all issue from a source divine,
And ev'ry drop bespeaks a Saviour thine—
So once in Gideon's fleece the dews were found,
And drought on all the drooping herbs around.

TO THE

REV. W. CAWTHORNE UNWIN.

Unwin, I should but ill repay
  The kindness of a friend,
Whose worth deserves as warm a lay,
  As ever friendship penn'd,
Thy name omitted in a page,
That would reclaim a vicious age.

A union form'd, as mine with thee,
  Not rashly, or in sport,
May be as fervent in degree,
  And faithful in its sort,
And may as rich in comfort prove,
As that of true fraternal love.

The bud inserted in the rind,
  The bud of peach or rose,
Adorns, though diff'ring in its kind,
  The stock whereon it grows,
With flow'r as sweet, or fruit as fair,
As if produc'd by Nature there.

Not rich, I render what I may,
  I seize thy name in haste,
And place it in this first essay,
  Lest this should prove the last.
'Tis where it should be—in a plan,
That holds in view the good of man.

The poet's lyre, to fix his fame,
  Should be the poet's heart;
Affection lights a brighter flame
  Than ever blaz'd by art.
No muses on these lines attend,
I sink the poet in the friend.

THE TASK.

BOOK I.

THE SOFA.

ARGUMENT OF THE FIRST BOOK.

Historical deduction of seats, from the stool to the Sofa.—A Schoolboy's ramble.—A walk in the country.—The scene described.—Rural sounds as well as sights delightful.—Another walk.—Mistake concerning the charms of solitude corrected.—Colonnades commended.—Alcove, and the view from it.—The wilderness.—The grove.—The thresher.—The necessity and the benefits of exercise.—The works of nature superior to, and in some instances inimitable by, art.—The wearisomeness of what is commonly called a life of pleasure.—Change of scene sometimes expedient.—A common described, and the character of crazy Kate introduced.—Gipsies.—The blessings of civilized life.—That state most favorable to virtue.—The South Sea islanders compassionated, but chiefly Omai.—His present state of mind supposed.—Civilized life friendly to virtue, but not great cities.—Great cities, and London in particular, allowed their due praises, but censured.—Fête champêtre.—The book concludes with a reflection on the total effects of dissipation and effeminacy upon our public measures.

I sing the *Sofa*. I, who lately sang
Truth, Hope, and Charity,* and touch'd with awe
The solemn chords, and with a trembling hand,
Escap'd with pain from that advent'rous flight,
Now seek repose upon an humbler theme;
The theme though humble, yet august and
Th'occasion—for the Fair commands the song
Time was, when clothing sumptuous or for use
Save their own painted skins, our sires had none.
As yet black breeches were not; satin smooth,
Or velvet soft, or plush with shaggy pile:
The hardy chief upon the rugged rock
Wash'd by the sea, or on the grav'lly bank
Thrown up by wintry torrents roaring loud,
Fearless of wrong, repos'd his wearied strength.
Those barb'rous ages past, succeeded next
The birth-day of Invention; weak at first,
Dull in design, and clumsy to perform.

* See Poems, pages 38, 74, 94.

Joint-stools were then created; on three legs
Upborne they stood. Three legs upholding firm
A massy slab, in fashion square or round.
On such a stool immortal Alfred sat,
And sway'd the sceptre of his infant realms:
And such in ancient halls and mansions drear
May still be seen; but perforated sore,
And drill'd in holes, the solid oak is found,
By worms voracious eaten through and through.
At length a generation more refin'd
Improv'd the simple plan; made three legs four,
Gave them a twisted form vermicular,
And o'er the seat, with plenteous wadding stuff'd,
Induc'd a splendid cover, green and blue,
Yellow and red, of tapestry richly wrought
And woven close, or needlework sublime.
There might ye see the peony spread wide,
The full-blown rose, the shepherd and his lass,
Lapdog and lambkin with black staring eyes,
And parrots with twin cherries in their beak.
Now came the cane from India, smooth and bright
With Nature's varnish; sever'd into stripes,
That interlac'd each other, these supplied
Of texture firm a lattice-work, that brac'd
The new machine, and it became a chair.
But restless was the chair; the back erect
Distress'd the weary loins, that felt no ease;
The slipp'ry seat betray'd the sliding part,
That press'd it, and the feet hung dangling down,
Anxious in vain to find the distant floor.
These for the rich; the rest, whom Fate had plac'd
In modest mediocrity, content
With base materials, sat on well-tann'd hides,
Obdurate and unyielding, glassy smooth,
With here and there a tuft of crimson yarn,
Or scarlet crewel, in the cushion fix'd,
If cushion might be call'd, what harder seem'd
Than the firm oak, of which the frame was form'd.
No want of timber then was felt or fear'd
In Albion's happy isle. The lumber stood
Pond'rous and fix'd by its own massy weight.
But elbows still were wanting; these, some say,
An alderman of Cripplegate contriv'd;
And some ascribe th'invention to a priest,
Burly, and big, and studious of his ease.
But rude at first, and not with easy slope
Receding wide, they press'd against the ribs,
And bruis'd the side; and, elevated high,
Taught the rais'd shoulders to invade the ears.

Long time elaps'd or e'er our rugged sires
Complain'd, though incommodiously pent in,
And ill at ease behind. The ladies first
'Gan murmur, as became the softer sex.
Ingenious Fancy, never better pleas'd,
Than when employ'd t'accomodate the fair,
Heard the sweet moan with pity, and devis'd
The soft settee; one elbow at each end,
And in the midst an elbow it receiv'd,
United yet divided, twain at once.
So sit two kings of Brentford on one throne;
And so two citizens, who take the air,
Close pack'd, and smiling, in a chaise and one.
But relaxation of the languid frame,
By soft recumbency of outstretch'd limbs,
Was bliss reserv'd for happier days. So slow
The growth of what is excellent; so hard
T'attain perfection in this nether world.
Thus first Necessity invented stools,
Convenience next suggested elbow chairs,
And Luxury th'acomplish'd *Sofa* last.
The nurse sleeps sweetly, hir'd to watch the sick,
Whom snoring she disturbs. As sweetly he,
Who quits the coach-box at the midnight hour
To sleep within the carriage more secure,
His legs depending at the open door.
Sweet sleep enjoys the curate in his desk,
The tedious rector drawling o'er his head;
And sweet the clerk below. But neither sleep
Of lazy nurse, who snores the sick man dead;
Nor his, who quits the box at midnight hour,
To slumber in the carriage more secure;
Nor sleep enjoy'd by curate in his desk;
Nor yet the dozings of the clerk, are sweet,
Compar'd with the repose the *Sofa* yields.
O may I live exempted (while I live
Guiltless of pamper'd appetite obscene)
From pangs arthritic, that infest the toe
Of libertine Excess. The *Sofa* suits
The gouty limb, 'tis true; but gouty limb,
Though on a *Sofa*, may I never feel:
For I have lov'd the rural walk through lanes
Of grassy swarth, close cropp'd by nibbling sheep,
And skirted thick with intertexture firm
Of thorny boughs; have lov'd the rural walk
O'er hills, through valleys, and by rivers' brink,
E'er since a truant boy I pass'd my bounds,
T'enjoy a ramble on the banks of Thames;
And still remember, nor without regret

Of hours, that sorrow since has much endear'd,
How oft, my slice of pocket store consum'd,
Still hung'ring, penniless, and far from home,
I fed on scarlet hips and stony haws,
Or blushing crabs, or berries, that emboss
The bramble, black as jet, or sloes austere.
Hard fare! but such as boyish appetite
Disdains not; nor the palate, undeprav'd
By culinary arts, unsav'ry deems.
No *Sofa* then awaited my return;
Nor *Sofa* then I needed. Youth repairs
His wasted spirits quickly, by long toil
Incurring short fatigue; and, though our years,
As life declines, speed rapidly away,
And not a year but pilfers as he goes
Some youthful grace, that age would gladly keep;
A tooth or auburn lock, and by degrees
Their length and color from the locks they spare;
Th'elastic spring of an unwearied foot,
That mounts the stile with ease, or leaps the fence,
That play of lungs, inhaling and again
Respiring freely the fresh air, that makes
Swift pace or steep ascent no toil to me,
Mine have not pilfer'd yet, nor yet impair'd
My relish of fair prospect; scenes that sooth'd
Or charm'd me young, no longer young, I find
Still soothing, and of pow'r to charm me still.
And witness, dear companion of my walks,
Whose arm this twentieth winter I perceive
Fast lock'd in mine, with pleasure such as love,
Confirm'd by long experience of thy worth
And well-tried virtues, could alone inspire—
Witness a joy that thou hast doubled long.
Thou know'st my praise of nature most sincere,
And that my raptures are not conjur'd up
To serve occasions of poetic pomp,
But genuine, and art partner of them all.
How oft upon yon eminence our pace
Has slacken'd to a pause, and we have borne
The ruffling wind, scarce conscious that it blew,
While Admiration, feeding at the eye,
And still unsated, dwelt upon the scene.
Thence with what pleasure have we just discern'd
The distant plough slow moving, and beside
His lab'ring team, that swerv'd not from the track,
The sturdy swain diminish'd to a boy!
Here Ouse, slow winding through a level plain
Of spacious meads with cattle sprinkled o'er,
Conducts the eye along his sinuous course

Delighted. There, fast rooted in their bank,
Stand, never overlook'd, our fav'rite elms,
That screen the herdsman's solitary hut;
While far beyond, and overthwart the stream,
That, as with molten glass, inlays the vale,
The sloping land recedes into the clouds;
Displaying on its varied side the grace
Of hedge row beauties numberless, square tow'r,
Tall spire, from which the sound of cheerful bells
Just undulates upon the list'ning ear,
Groves, heaths, and smoking villages, remote.
Scenes must be beautiful, which daily view'd
Please daily, and whose novelty survives
Long knowledge and the scrutiny of years:
Praise justly due to those that I describe.
Nor rural sights alone, but rural sounds,
Exhilarate the spirit, and restore
The tone of languid Nature. Mighty winds,
That sweep the skirt of some far-spreading wood
Of ancient growth, make music not unlike
The dash of Ocean on his winding shore,
And lull the spirit while they fill the mind;
Unnumber'd branches waving in the blast,
And all their leaves fast flutt'ring, all at once.
Nor less composure waits upon the roar
Of distant floods, or on the softer voice
Of neighb'ring fountain, or of rills that slip
Through the cleft rock, and, chiming as they fall
Upon loose pebbles, lose themselves at length
In matted grass, that with a livelier green
Betrays the secret of their silent course.
Nature inanimate employs sweet sounds,
But animated Nature sweeter still,
To sooth and satisfy the human ear.
Ten thousand warblers cheer the day, and one
The livelong night: nor these alone, whose notes
Nice-finger'd Art must emulate in vain,
But cawing rooks, and kites that swim sublime
In still repeated circles, screaming loud,
The jay, the pie, and e'en the boding owl,
That hails the rising moon, have charms for me.
Sounds inharmonious in themselves and harsh,
Yet heard in scenes where peace for ever reigns,
And only there, please highly for their sake.
Peace to the artist whose ingenious thought
Devis'd the weather-house, that useful toy!
Fearless of humid air and gath'ring rains,
Forth steps the man—an emblem of myself!
More delicate his tim'rous mate retires.

When Winter soaks the fields, and female feet,
Too weak to struggle with tenacious clay,
Or ford the rivulets, are best at home,
The task of new discov'ries falls on me.
At such a season, and with such a charge,
Once went I forth; and found, till then unknown,
A cottage, whither oft we since repair:
'Tis perch'd upon the green hill top, but close
Environ'd with a ring of branching elms,
That overhang the thatch, itself unseen
Peeps at the vale below; so thick beset
With foliage of such dark redundant growth,
I call'd the low-roof'd lodge the *peasant's nest.*
And, hidden as it is, and far remote
From such unpleasing sounds, as haunt the ear
In village or in town, the bay of curs
Incessant, clinking hammers, grinding wheels,
And infants' clam'rous, whether pleas'd or pain'd,
Oft have I wish'd the peaceful covert mine.
Here, I have said, at least I should possess
The poet's treasure, silence, and indulge
The dreams of fancy, tranquil and secure.
Vain thought! the dweller in that still retreat
Dearly obtains the refuge it affords.
Its elevated site forbids the wretch
To drink sweet waters of the crystal well;
He dips his bowl into the weedy ditch,
And, heavy laden, brings his bev'rage home,
Far fetch'd and little worth; nor seldom waits,
Dependent on the baker's punctual call,
To hear his creaking panniers at the door,
Angry and sad, and his last crust consum'd.
So farewell envy of the *peasant's nest!*
If solitude make scant the means of life,
Society for me!—thou seeming sweet,
Be still a pleasing object in my view;
My visit still, but never mine abode.
  Not distant far, a length of colonnade
Invites us. Monument of ancient taste,
Now scorn'd, but worthy of a better fate.
Our fathers knew the value of a screen
From sultry suns: and, in their shaded walks
And long protracted bow'rs, enjoy'd at noon
The gloom and coolness of declining day.
We bear our shades about us; self-depriv'd
Of other screen, the thin umbrella spread,
And range an Indian waste without a tree.
Thanks to Benevolus*—he spares me yet

John Courtney Throckmorton, Esq. of Weston Underwood.

These chesnuts rang'd in corresponding lines;
And though himself so polish'd, still repreives
The obsolete prolixity of shade.
Descending now (but cautious, lest too fast)
A sudden steep, upon a rustic bridge
We pass a gulf, in which the willows dip
Their pendent boughs, stooping as if to drink.
Hence, ancle deep in moss and flow'ry thyme,
We mount again, and feel at ev'ry step
Our foot half sunk in hillocks green and soft,
Rais'd by the mole, the miner of the soil.
He, not unlike the great ones of mankind,
Disfigures Earth: and, plotting in the dark,
Toils much to earn a monumental pile,
That may record the mischiefs he has done.
  The summit gain'd, behold the proud alcov
That crowns it! yet not all its pride secures
The grand retreat from injuries impress'd
By rural carvers, who with knives deface
The panels, leaving an obscure, rude name,
In characters uncouth, and spelt amiss.
So strong the zeal to immortalize himself
Beats in the breast of man, that e'en a few,
Few transient years, won from th'abyss abhorr'd
Of blank oblivion, seem a glorious prize,
And even to a clown. Now roves the eye;
And, posted on this speculative height,
Exults in its command. The sheepfold here
Pours out its fleecy tenants o'er the glebe.
At first, progressive as a stream, they seek
The middle field; but, scatter'd by degrees,
Each to his choice, soon whiten all the land.
There from the sun-burnt hayfield homeward creeps
The loaded wain; while, lighten'd of its charge,
The wain that meets it passes swiftly by;
The boorish driver leaning o'er his team
Vocif'rous, and impatient of delay.
Nor less attractive is the woodland scene,
Diversified with trees of ev'ry growth,
Alike, yet various. Here the gray smooth trunks
Of ash, or lime, or beech, distinctly shine,
Within the twilight of their distant shades;
There, lost behind a rising ground, the wood
Seems sunk, and shorten'd to its topmost boughs
No tree in all the grove but has its charms,
Though each its hue peculiar; paler some,
And of a wanish gray; the willow such,
And poplar, that with silver lines his leaf,
And ash far-stretching his umbrageous arm;

Of deeper green the elm; and deeper still,
Lord of the woods, the long surviving oak.
Some glossy-leav'd, and shining in the sun,
The maple, and the beach of oily nuts
Prolific, and the lime at dewy eve
Diffusing odors: nor unnoted pass
The sycamore, capricious in attire,
Now green, now tawny, and ere autumn yet
Have chang'd the woods, in scarlet honors bright.
O'er these, but far beyond (a spacious map
Of hill and valley interpos'd between),
The Ouse, dividing the well-water'd land,
Now glitters in the sun, and now retires,
As bashful, yet impatient to be seen.
 Hence the declivity is sharp and short,
And such the re-ascent; between them weeps
A little naiad her impov'rish'd urn
All summer long, which winter fills again.
The folded gates would bar my progress now,
But that the lord* of this enclos'd demesne,
Communicative of the good he owns,
Admits me to a share; the guiltless eye
Commits no wrong, nor wastes what it enjoys.
Refreshing change! where now the blazing sun?
By short transition we have lost his glare,
And stepp'd at once into a cooler clime.
Ye fallen avenues! once more I mourn
Your fate unmerited, once more rejoice
That yet a remnant of your race survives.
How airy and how light the graceful arch,
Yet awful as the consecrated roof
Re-echoing pious anthems! while beneath
The checker'd earth seems restless as a flood
Brush'd by the wind. So sportive is the light
Shot through the boughs, it dances as they dance.
Shadow and sunshine intermingling quick,
And dark'ning and enlightening, as the leaves
Play wanton, ev'ry moment, ev'ry spot.
 And now, with nerves new-brac'd and spirits cheer'd,
We tread the wilderness, whose well-roll'd walks,
With curvature of slow and easy sweep—
Deception innocent—give ample space
To narrow bounds. The grove receives us next;
Between the upright shafts of whose tall elms
We may discern the thresher at his task.
Thump after thump resounds the constant flail,
That seems to swing uncertain, and yet falls

* See the foregoing note.

Full on the destin'd ear. Wide flies the chaff,
The rustling straw sends up a frequent mist
Of atoms, sparkling in the noonday beam.
Come hither, ye that press your beds of down,
And sleep not; see him sweating o'er his bread
Before he eats it. 'Tis the primal curse,
But soften'd into mercy; made the pledge
Of cheerful days, and nights without a groan.
  By ceaseless action all that is subsists.
Constant rotation of th'unwearied wheel,
That Nature rides upon, maintains her health,
Her beauty, her fertility. She dreads
An instant's pause, and lives but while she moves.
Its own revolvency upholds the world.
Winds from all quarters agitate the air,
And fit the limpid element for use,
Else noxious; oceans, rivers, lakes, and streams,
All feel the fresh'ning impulse, and are cleans'd
By restless undulation: e'en the oak
Thrives by the rude concussion of the storm:
He seems indeed indignant, and to feel
Th'impression of the blast with proud disdain,
Frowning, as if in his unconscious arm
He held the thunder: but the monarch owes
His firm stability to what he scorns,
More fix'd below, the more disturb'd above.
The law, by which all creatures else are bound,
Binds man, the lord of all. Himself derives
No mean advantage from a kindred cause,
From strenuous toil his hours of sweetest ease.
The sedentary stretch their lazy length
When Custom bids, but no refreshment find,
For none they need: the languid eye, the cheek
Deserted of its bloom, the flaccid, shrunk,
And wither'd muscle, and the vapid soul,
Reproach their owner with that love of rest,
To which he forfeits e'en the rest he loves.
Not such the alert and active. Measure life
By its true worth, the comfort it affords,
And theirs alone seems worthy of the name.
Good health, and, its associate in the most,
Good temper; spirits prompt to undertake,
And not soon spent, though in an arduous task;
The pow'rs of fancy and strong thought are theirs;
E'en age itself seems privileg'd in them
With clear exemption from its own defects.
A sparkling eye beneath a wrinkled front
The vet'ran shows, and, gracing a gray beard
With youthful smiles, descends toward the grave

Sprightly, and old almost without decay.
Like a coy maiden, Ease, when courted most,
Farthest retires—an idol, at whose shrine
Who oft'nest sacrifice are favor'd least.
The love of Nature, and the scenes she draws,
Is Nature's dictate. Strange! there should be found
Who, self-imprison'd in their proud saloons,
Renounce the odors of the open field
For the unscented fictions of the loom;
Who, satisfied with only pencill'd scenes,
Prefer to the performance of a God
Th'inferior wonders of an artist's hand!
Lovely indeed the mimic works of Art;
But Nature's works far lovelier. I admire,
None more admires, the painter's magic skill,
Who shows me that which I shall never see,
Conveys a distant country into mine,
And throws Italian light on English walls:
But imitative strokes can do no more
Than please the eye—sweet Nature's ev'ry sense.
The air salubrious of her lofty hills,
The cheering fragrance of her dewy vales,
And music of her woods—no works of man
May rival these, these all bespeak a pow'r
Peculiar, and exclusively her own.
Beneath the open sky she spreads the feast
'Tis free to all—'tis ev'ry day renew'd;
Who scorns it starves deservedly at home.
He does not scorn it, who, imprison'd long,
In some unwholesome dungeon, and a prey
To sallow sickness, which the vapors, dank
And clammy, of his dark abode have bred,
Escapes at last to liberty and light:
His cheek recovers soon its healthful hue;
His eye relumines its extinguish'd fires;
He walks, he leaps, he runs—is wing'd with joy,
And riots in the sweets of ev'ry breeze.
He does not scorn it, who has long endur'd
A fever's agonies, and fed on drugs.
Nor yet the mariner, his blood inflam'd
With acrid salts: his very heart athirst,
To gaze at Nature in her green array,
Upon the ship's tall side he stands, possess'd
With visions prompted by intense desire:
Fair fields appear below, such as he left
Far distant, such as he would die to find—
He seeks them headlong, and is seen no more.
The spleen is seldom felt where Flora reigns,
The low'ring eye, the petulance, the frown,

And sullen sadness, that o'ershade, distort,
And mar the face of beauty, when no cause
For such immeasurable woe appears,
These Flora banishes, and gives the fair
Sweet smiles, and bloom less transient than her own.
It is the constant revolution, stale
And tasteless, of the same repeated joys,
That palls and satiates, and makes languid life
A pedlar's pack, that bows the bearer down.
Health suffers, and the spirits ebb, the heart
Recoils from its own choice—at the full feast
Is famish'd—finds no music in the song,
No smartness in the jest; and wonders why.
Yet thousands still desire to journey on,
Though halt, and weary of the path they tread.
The paralytic, who can hold her cards,
But cannot play them, borrows a friend's hand
To deal and shuffle, to divide and sort
Her mingled suits and sequences; and sits,
Spectatress both and spectacle, a sad
And silent cipher, while her proxy plays.
Others are dragg'd into the crowded room
Between supporters; and, once seated, sit,
Through downright inability to rise,
Till the stout bearers lift the corpse again.
These speak a loud memento. Yet e'en these
Themselves love life, and cling to it, as he,
That overhangs a torrent, to a twig.
They love it, and yet loath it; fear to die,
Yet scorn the purposes for which they live.
Then wherefore not renounce them? No—the dread,
The slavish dread of solitude, that breeds
Reflection and remorse, the fear of shame?
And their invet'rate habits, all forbid.
  Whom call we gay? That honor has been long
The boast of mere pretenders to the name.
The innocent are gay—the lark is gay,
That dries his feathers, saturate with dew,
Beneath the rosy cloud, while yet the beams
Of dayspring overshoot his humble nest.
The peasant too, a witness of his song,
Himself a songster, is as gay as he.
But save me from the gaiety of those,
Whose headachs nail them to a noonday bed;
And save me too from theirs, whose haggard eyes
Flash desperation, and betray their pangs
For property stripp'd off by cruel chance;
From gaiety, that fills the bones with pain,

The mouth with blasphemy, the heart with woe.
  The earth was made so various, that the mind
Of desultory man, studious of change,
And pleas'd with novelty, might be indulg'd.
Prospects, however lovely, may be seen
Till half their beauties fade; the weary sight,
Too well acquainted with their smiles, slides off
Fastidious, seeking less familiar scenes.
Then snug enclosures in the shelter'd vale,
Where frequent hedges intercept the eye,
Delight us; happy to renounce a while,
Not senseless of its charms, what still we love,
That such short absence may endear it more.
Then forests, or the savage rock, may please,
That hides the sea-mew in his hollow clefts
Above the reach of man. His hoary head,
Conspicuous many a league, the mariner
Bound homeward, and in hope already there,
Greets with three cheers exulting. At his waist,
A girdle of half wither'd shrubs he shows,
And at his feet the baffled billows die.
The common, overgrown with fern, and rough
With prickly gorse, that, shapeless and deform'd,
And dang'rous to the touch, has yet its bloom
And deck itself with ornaments of gold,
Yields no unpleasing ramble; there the turf
Smells fresh, and, rich in odorif'rous herbs
And fungous fruits of earth, regales the sense
With luxury of unexpected sweets.
  There often wanders one, whom better days
Saw better clad, in cloak of satin trimm'd
With lace, and hat with splendid ribbon bound.
A serving maid was she, and fell in love
With one who left her, went to sea, and died.
Her fancy follow'd him through foaming waves
To distant shores; and she would sit and weep
At what a sailor suffers; fancy too,
Delusive most where warmest wishes are,
Would oft anticipate his glad return,
And dream of transports she was not to know.
She heard the doleful tidings of his death—
And never smil'd again! and now she roams
The dreary waste; there spends the livelong day,
And there, unless when charity forbids,
The livelong night. A tatter'd apron hides,
Worn as a cloak, and hardly hides, a gown
More tatter'd still; and both but ill conceal
A bosom heav'd with never ceasing sighs.
She begs an idle pin of all she meets,

And hoards them in her sleeve; but needful food,
Though press'd with hunger oft, or comelier clothes,
Though pinch'd with cold, asks never.—Kate is craz'd.
I see a column of slow-rising smoke
O'ertop the lofty wood that skirts the wild.
A vagabond and useless tribe there eat
Their miserable meal. A kettle, slung
Between two poles upon a stick transverse,
Receives the morsel—flesh obscene of dog,
Or vermin, or at best of cock purloin'd
From his accustom'd perch. Hard faring race!
They pick their fuel out of ev'ry hedge,
Which, kindled with dry leaves, just saves unquench'd
The spark of life. The sportive wind blows wide
Their flutt'ring rags, and shows a tawny skin,
The vellum of the pedigree they claim
Great skill have they in palmistry, and more
To conjure clean away the gold they touch,
Conveying worthless dross into its place;
Loud when they beg, dumb only when they steal.
Strange! that a creature rational, and cast
In human mould, should brutalize by choice
His nature; and, though capable of arts,
By which the world might profit, and himself,
Self-banish'd from society, prefer
Such squalid sloth to honorable toil!
Yet even these, though feigning sickness oft
They swathe the forehead, drag the limping limb,
And vex their flesh with artificial sores,
Can change their whine into a mirthful note,
When safe occasion offers; and with dance,
And music of the bladder and the bag,
Beguile their woes, and make the woods resound.
Such health and gaiety of heart enjoy
The houseless rovers of the sylvan world;
And, breathing wholesome air, and wand'ring much,
Need other physic none to heal th' effects
Of loathsome diet, penury, and cold.
Blest he, though undistinguish'd from the crowd
By wealth or dignity, who dwells secure,
Where man, by nature fierce, has laid aside
His fierceness, having learnt, though slow to learn,
The manners and the arts of civil life.
His wants indeed are many; but supply
Is obvious, plac'd within the easy reach
Of temperate wishes and industrious hands.
Here virtue thrives as in her proper soil;
Not rude and surly, and beset with thorns,
And terrible to sight, as when she springs

(If e'er she spring spontaneous) in remote
And barbarous climes, where violence prevails,
And strength is lord of all; but gentle, kind,
By culture tam'd, by liberty refresh'd,
And all her fruits by radiant truth matured.
War and the chace engross the savage whole;
War followed for revenge, or to supplant
The envied tenants of some happier spot:
The chace for sustenance, precarious trust!
His hard condition with severe constraint
Binds all his faculties, forbids all growth
Of wisdom, proves a school, in which he learns
Sly circumvention, unrelenting hate,
Mean self-attachment, and scarce aught beside
Thus fares the shiv'ring natives of the north,
And thus the rangers of the western world,
Where it advances far into the deep,
Tow'rds the antartic. E'en the favored isles
So lately found, although the constant sun
Cheer all their seasons with a grateful smile,
Can boast but little virtue; and inert
Through plenty, lose in morals, what they gain
In manners—victims of luxurious ease.
These therefore I can pity, plac'd remote
From all that science traces, art invents,
Or inspiration teaches; and enclos'd
In boundless oceans, never to be pass'd
By navigators uninformed as they,
Or plough'd perhaps by British bark again:
But far beyond the rest, and with most cause,
Thee, gentle savage!* whom no love of thee
Or thine, but curiosity perhaps,
Or else vain glory, prompted us to draw
Forth from thy native bow'rs, to show thee here
With what superior skill we can abuse
The gifts of Providence, and squander life.
The dream is past; and thou hast found again
Thy cocoas and bananas, palms and yams,
And homestall thatch'd with leaves. But hast thou found
Their former charms? And, having seen our state,
Our palaces, our ladies, and our pomp
Of equipage, our gardens, and our sports,
And heard our music; are thy simple friends,
Thy simple fare, and all thy plain delights,
As dear to thee as once? And have thy joys
Lost nothing by comparison with ours?
Rude as thou art (for we returned thee rude

* Omai.

And ignorant except of outward show)
I cannot think thee yet so dull of heart
And spiritless, as never to regret
Sweets tasted here, and left as soon as known.
Methinks I see thee straying on the beach,
And asking of the surge, that bathes thy foot,
If ever it has wash'd our distant shore,
I see thee weep, and thine are honest tears,
A patriot's for his country: thou art sad
At thought of her forlorn and abject state,
From which no pow'r of thine can raise her up.
Thus Fancy paints thee, and, though apt to err,
Perhaps errs little when she paints thee thus.
She tells me too, that duly ev'ry morn
Thou climb'st the mountain top, with eager eye
Exploring far and wide the wat'ry waste
For sight of ship from England. Ev'ry speck
Seen in the dim horizon turns thee pale
With conflict of contending hopes and fears.
But comes at last the dull and dusky eve,
And sends thee to thy cabin, well prepar'd
To dream all night of what the day denied.
Alas! expect it not. We found no bait
To tempt us in thy country. Doing good,
Disinterested good, is not our trade.
We travel far, 'tis true, but not for nought;
And must be bribed to compass Earth again
By other hopes and richer fruits than yours.
  But though true worth and virtue in the mild
And genial soil of cultivated life
Thrive most, and may perhaps thrive only there,
Yet not in cities oft: in proud, and gay,
And gain-devoted cities. Thither flow,
As to a common and most noisome sewer,
The dregs and feculence of ev'ry land.
In cities foul example on most minds
Begets its likeness. Rank abundance breeds,
In gross and pampered cities, sloth, and lust,
And wantonness, and gluttonous excess.
In cities vice is hidden with most ease,
Or seen with least reproach; and virtue, taught
By frequent lapse, can hope no triumph there
Beyond th' achievement of successful flight.
I do confess them nurs'ries of the art
In which they flourish most; where, in the beams
Of warm encouragement, and in the eye
Of public note, they reach their perfect size.
Such London is, by taste and wealth proclaim'd
The fairest capital of all the world,

By riot and incontinence the worst.
There, touch'd by Reynolds, a dull blank becomes
A lucid mirror, in which Nature sees
All her reflected features. Bacon there
Gives more than female beauty to a stone,
And Chatham's eloquence to marble lips.
Nor does the chisel occupy alone
The pow'rs of sculpture, but the style as much;
Each province of her art her equal care.
With nice incision of her guided steel
She ploughs a brazen field, and clothes a soil
So sterile with what charms soe'er she will,
The richest scen'ry and the loveliest forms.
Where finds Philosophy her eagle eye,
With which she gazes at yon burning disk
Undazzled, and detects and counts his spots?
In London. Where her implements exact,
With which she calculates, computes, and scans
All distance, motion, magnitude, and now
Measures an atom, and now girds a world?
In London. Where has commerce such a mart,
So rich, so throng'd, so drain'd, and so supplied,
As London—opulent, enlarg'd, and still
Increasing London? Babylon of old
Not more the glory of the earth than she,
A more accomplish'd world's chief glory now.
  She has her praise. Now mark a spot or two,
That so much beauty would do well to purge;
And show this queen of cities, that so fair
May yet be foul; so witty, yet not wise.
It is not seemly, nor of good report,
That she is slack in discipline; more prompt
T' avenge than to prevent the breach of law·
That she is rigid in denouncing death
On petty robbers, and indulges life
And liberty, and oftimes honor too,
To peculators of the public gold:
That thieves at home must hang, but he, that puts
Into his overgorg'd and bloated purse
The wealth of Indian provinces, escapes.
Nor is it well, nor can it come to good,
That, through profane and infidel contempt
Of holy writ, she has presum'd t'annul
And abrogate, as roundly as she may,
The total ordinance and will of God;
Advancing Fashion to the post of Truth,
And centering all authority in modes
And customs of her own, till sabbath rites
Have dwindled into unrespected forms,

And knees and hassocks are well-nigh divorc'd.
  God made the country, and man made the town.
What wonder then that health and virtue, gifts
That can alone make sweet the bitter draught,
That life holds out to all, should most abound
And least be threaten'd in the fields and groves?
Possess ye therefore, ye who, borne about
In chariots and sedans, know no fatigue
But that of idleness, and taste no scenes
But such as art contrives, possess ye still
Your element; there only can ye shine;
There only minds like yours can do no harm.
Our groves were planted to console at noon
The pensive wand'rer in their shades. At eve
The moon-beam, sliding softly in between
The sleeping leaves, is all the light they wish,
Birds warbling all the music. We can spare
The splendor of your lamps; they but eclipse
Our softer satellite. Your songs confound
Our more harmonious notes: the thrush departs
Scar'd, and th'offended nightingale is mute.
There is a public mischief in your mirth;
It plagues your country. Folly such as yours,
Grac'd with a sword, and worthier of a fan,
Has made, what enemies could ne'er have done,
Our arch of empire, stedfast but for you,
A mutilated structure, soon to fall.

THE TASK.

BOOK II.

THE TIME-PIECE.

ARGUMENT OF THE SECOND BOOK.

Reflections suggested by the conclusion of the former book.—Peace among the nations recommended, on the ground of their common fellowship in sorrow.—Prodigies enumerated.—Sicilian earthquakes.—Man rendered obnoxious to these calamities by sin.—God the agent in them. —The philosophy that stops at secondary causes reproved.—Our own late miscarriages accounted for.—Satirical notice taken of our trips to Fontaine-Bleau.—But the pulpit, not satire, the proper engine of reformation.—The Reverend Advertiser of engraved sermons.—Petit-maître parson.—The good preacher.—Picture of a theatrical clerical coxcomb. —Story-tellers and jesters in the pulpit reproved.—Apostrophe to popular applause.—Retailers of ancient philosophy expostulated with.—Sum of the whole matter.—Effects of sacerdotal mismanagement on the laity. —Their folly and extravagance.—The mischiefs of profusion.—Profusion itself, with all its consequent evils, ascribed, as to its principal cause, to the want of discipline in the universities.

O for a lodge in some vast wilderness,
Some boundless contiguity of shade,
Where rumor of oppression and deceit,
Of unsuccessful or successful war,
Might never reach me more. My ear is pain'd,
My soul is sick with ev'ry days report
Of wrong and outrage with which Earth is fill'd.
There is no flesh in man's obdurate heart,
It does not feel for man; the nat'ral bond
Of brotherhood is sever'd as the flax,
That falls asunder at the touch of fire.
He finds his fellow guilty of a skin
Not color'd like his own; and having pow'r
T'enforce the wrong, for such a worthy cause
Dooms and devotes him as his lawful prey.
Lands intersected by a narrow frith
Abhor each other. Mountains interpos'd
Make enemies of nations, who had else
Like kindred drops been mingled into one.

Thus man devotes his brother, and destroys;
And, worse than all, and most to be deplor'd
As human nature's broadest, foulest blot,
Chains him, and tasks him, and exacts his sweat
With stripes, that mercy with a bleeding heart
Weeps, when she sees inflicted on a beast.
Then what is man? And what man, seeing this,
And having human feelings, does not blush,
And hang his head, to think himself a man?
I would not have a slave to till my ground,
To carry me, to fan me while I sleep,
And tremble when I wake, for all the wealth
That sinews bought and sold have ever earn'd,
No: dear as freedom is, and in my heart's
Just estimation priz'd above all price,
I had much rather be myself the slave,
And wear the bonds, than fasten them on him.
We have no slaves at home—then why abroad?
And they themselves once ferried o'er the wave
That parts us, are emancipate and loos'd.
Slaves cannot breathe in England; if their lungs
Receive our air, that moment they are free;
They touch our country, and their shackles fall.
That's noble, and bespeaks a nation proud
And jealous of the blessing. Spread it then,
And let it circulate through ev'ry vein
Of all your empire; that, where Britain's pow'r
Is felt, mankind may feel her mercy too.
  Sure there is need of social intercourse,
Benevolence, and peace, and mutual aid,
Between the nations in a world, that seems
To toll the death-bell of its own decease,
And by the voice of all its elements
To preach the gen'ral doom.* When were the winds
Let slip with such a warrant to destroy?
When did the waves so haughtily o'erleap
Their ancient barriers, deluging the dry?
Fires from beneath, and meteors † from above,
Portentous, unexampled, unexplain'd,
Have kindled beacons in the skies; and th' old
And crazy Earth has had her shaking fits
More frequent, and foregone her usual rest.
Is it a time to wrangle, when the props
And pillars of our planet seem to fail,
And Nature‡ with a dim and sickly eye

* Alluding to the calamities in Jamaica.

† August 18, 1783.

‡ Alluding to the fog, that covered both Europe and Asia during the whole summer of 1783.

To wait the close of all? But grant her end
More distant, and that prophesy demands
A longer respite, unaccomplish'd yet;
Still they are frowning signals, and bespeak
Displeasure in His breast, who smites the Earth
Or heals it, makes it languish or rejoice.
And 'tis but seemly, that, where all deserve
And stand expos'd by common peccancy
To what no few have felt, there should be peace,
And brethren in calamity should love.
   Alas for Sicily! rude fragments now
Lie scatter'd, where the shapely column stood.
Her palaces are dust. In all her streets
The voice of singing and the sprightly chord
Are silent. Revelry, and dance, and show,
Suffer a syncope and solemn pause;
While God performs upon the trembling stage
Of his own works his dreadful part alone.
How does the Earth receive him?—with what signs
Of gratulation and delight her king?
Pours she not all her choicest fruits abroad,
Her sweetest flow'rs, her aromatic gums,
Disclosing Paradise where'er she treads?
She quakes at his approach. Her hollow womb,
Conceiving thunders, through a thousand deeps
And fiery caverns, roars beneath his foot.
The hills move lightly, and the mountains smoke,
For he has touch'd them. From th'extremest point
Of elevation down into the abyss
His wrath is busy, and his frown is felt.
The rocks fall headlong, and the valleys rise,
The rivers die into offensive pools,
And, charg'd with putrid verdure, breathe a gross
And mortal nuisance into all the air.
What solid was, by transformation strange,
Grows fluid; and the fix'd and rooted earth,
Tormented into billows, heaves and swells,
Or with vortiginous and hideous whirl
Sucks down its prey insatiable. Immense
The tumult and the overthrow, the pangs
And agonies of human and of brute
Multitudes, fugitive on ev'ry side,
And fugitive in vain. The sylvan scene
Migrates uplifted; and, with all its soil
A lighting in far distant fields, finds out
A new possessor, and survives the change
Ocean has caught the frenzy, and, upwrought
To an enormous and o'er bearing height,
Not by a mighty wind, but by that voice,

Which winds and waves obey, invades the shore
Resistless. Never such a sudden flood,
Upridg'd so high, and sent on such a charge,
Possess'd an inland scene. Where now the throng,
That press'd the beach, and, hasty to depart,
Look'd to the sea for safety? They are gone,
Gone with the refluent wave into the deep—
A prince with half his people! Ancient tow'rs,
And roofs embattled high, the gloomy scenes,
Where beauty oft and letter'd worth consume
Life in the unproductive shades of death,
Fall prone: the pale inhabitants come forth,
And, happy in their unforeseen release
From all the rigors of restraint, enjoy
The terrors of the day, that sets them free.
Who then, that has thee, would not hold thee fast,
Freedom? whom they that lose thee so regret,
That e'en a judgment, making way for thee,
Seems in their eyes a mercy for thy sake?
  Such evils Sin hath wrought; and such a flame
Kindled in Heav'n, that it burns down to Earth,
And in the furious inquest, that it makes
On God's behalf, lays waste his fairest works.
The very elements, though each be meant
The minister of man, to serve his wants,
Conspire against him. With his breath he draws
A plague into his blood; and cannot use
Life's necessary means, but he must die.
Storms rise t'o'erwhelm him: or, if stormy winds
Rise not, the waters of the deep shall rise,
And, needing none assistance of the storm,
Shall roll themselves ashore, and reach him there.
The earth shall shake him out of all his holds,
Or make his house his grave: nor so content,
Shall counterfeit the motions of the flood,
And drown him in her dry and dusty gulfs.
What then!—were they the wicked above all,
And we the righteous, whose fast-anchor'd isle
Mov'd not, while theirs was rock'd, like a light skiff,
The sport of ev'ry wave? No: none are clear,
And none than we more guilty. But, where all
Stand chargeable with guilt, and to the shafts
Of wrath obnoxious, God may choose his mark:
May punish, if he please, the less, to warn
The more malignant. If he spar'd not them,
Tremble and be amaz'd at thine escape,
Far guiltier England, lest he spare not thee!
  Happy the man, who sees a God employ'd
In all the good and ill, that checker life!

Resolving all events, with their effects
And manifold results, into the will
And arbitration wise of the Supreme.
Did not his eye rule all things, and intend
The least of our concerns (since from the least
The greatest oft originate); could chance
Find place in his dominion, or dispose
One lawless particle to thwart his plan;
Then God might be surpris'd, and unforeseen
Contingence might alarm him, and disturb
The smooth and equal course of his affairs.
This truth Philosophy, though eagle-ey'd
In nature's tendencies, oft overlooks;
And, having found his instrument, forgets,
Or disregards, or, more presumptuous still,
Denies, the pow'r that wields it. God proclaims
His hot displeasure against foolish men,
That live an atheist life: involves the Heav'n
In tempests; quits his grasp upon the winds,
And gives them all their fury; bids a plague
Kindle a fiery boil upon the skin,
And putrefy the breath of blooming Health.
He calls for Famine, and the meagre fiend
Blows mildew from between his shrivell'd lips,
And taints the golden ear. He springs his mines,
And desolates a nation at a blast.
Forth steps the spruce philosopher, and tells
Of homogeneal and discordant springs
And principles; of causes, how they work
By necessary laws their sure effects;
Of action and reaction: he has found
The source of the disease, that nature feels,
And bids the world take heart and banish fear.
Thou fool! will thy discov'ry of the cause
Suspend th'effect, or heal it? Has not God
Still wrought by means since first he made the world?
And did he not of old employ his means
To drown it? What is his creation less
Than a capacious reservoir of means
Form'd for his use, and ready at his will?
Go, dress thine eyes with eye-salve; ask of him,
Or ask of whomsoever he has taught;
And learn, though late, the genuine cause of all.
  England, with all thy faults, I love thee still—
My country! and, while yet a nook is left,
Where English minds and manners may be found,
Shall be constrain'd to love thee. Though thy clime
Be fickle, and thy year most part deform'd
With dripping rains, or wither'd by a frost,

I would not yet exchange thy sullen skies,
And fields without a flow'r, for warmer France
With all her vines: nor for Ausonia's groves
Of golden fruitage, and her myrtle bow'rs.
To shake thy senate, and from heights sublime
Of patriot eloquence to flash down fire
Upon thy foes, was never meant my task:
But I can feel thy fortunes, and partake
Thy joys and sorrows, with as true a heart
As any thund'rer there. And I can feel
Thy follies too; and with a just disdain
Frown at effeminates, whose very looks
Reflect dishonor on the land I love.
How, in the name of soldiership and sense,
Should England prosper, when such things, as smooth
And tender as a girl, all essenc'd o'er
With odors, and as profligate as sweet;
Who sell their laurel for a myrtle wreath,
And love when they should fight; when such as these
Presume to lay their hands upon the ark
Of her magnificent and awful cause?
Time was when it was praise and boast enough
In ev'ry clime, and travel where we might,
That we were born her children. Praise enough
To fill th'ambition of a private man,
That Chatham's language was his mother tongue,
And Wolfe's great name compatriot with his own.
Farewell those honors, and farewell with them
The hope of such hereafter! They have fall'n
Each in his field of glory; one in arms,
And one in council—Wolfe upon the lap
Of smiling Victory that moment won,
And Chatham heart-sick of his country's shame!
They made us many soldiers. Chatham, still
Consulting England's happiness at home,
Secur'd it by an unforgiving frown,
If any wrong'd her. Wolfe, where'er he fought,
Put so much of his heart into his act,
That his example had a magnet's force,
And all were swift to follow whom all lov'd.
Those suns are set. O rise some other such!
Or all that we have left is empty talk
Of old achievements, and despair of new.
Now hoist the sail, and let the streamers float
Upon the wanton breezes. Strew the deck
With lavender, and sprinkle liquid sweets,
That no rude savor maritime invade
The nose of nice nobility! Breathe soft
Ye clarionets, and softer still ye flutes;

That winds and waters, lull'd by magic sounds,
May bear us smoothly to the Gallic shore!
True, we have lost an empire—let it pass.
True; we may thank the perfidy of France,
That pick'd the jewel out of England's crown,
With all the cunning of an envious shrew.
And let that pass—'twas but a trick of state!
A brave man knows no malice, but at once
Forgets in peace the injuries of war,
And gives his direst foe a friend's embrace.
And, sham'd as we have been, to th'very beard
Brav'd and defied, and in our own sea prov'd
Too weak for those decisive blows, that once
Ensur'd us mast'ry there, we yet retain
Some small pre-eminence; we justly boast
At least superior jockeyship, and claim
The honors of the turf as all our own!
Go then, well worthy of the praise ye seek,
And show the shame, ye might conceal at home,
In foreign eyes!—be grooms and win the plate,
Where once your nobler fathers won a crown!—
'Tis gen'rous to communicate your skill
To those that need it. Folly is soon learn'd:
And under such preceptors who can fail!
There is a pleasure in poetic pains,
Which only poets know. The shifts and turns,
Th'expedients and inventions multiform,
To which the mind resorts, in chase of terms
Though apt, yet coy, and difficult to win—
T'arrest the fleeting images, that fill
The mirror of the mind, and hold them fast,
And force them sit, till he has pencil'd off
A faithful likeness of the forms he views;
Then to dispose his copies with such art,
That each may find its most propitious light,
And shine by situation, hardly less
Than by the labor and the skill it cost;
Are occupations of the poet's mind
So pleasing, and that steal away the thought
With such address from themes of sad import,
That, lost in his own musings, happy man!
He feels th'anxieties of life, denied
Their wonted entertainment, all retire.
Such joys has he that sings. But ah! not such,
Or seldom such, the hearers of his song.
Fastidious, or else listless, or perhaps
Aware of nothing arduous in a task
They never undertook, they little note
His dangers or escapes, and haply find

Their least amusement where he found the most.
But is amusement all? Studious of song,
And yet ambitious not to sing in vain,
I would not trifle merely, though the world
Be loudest in their praise, who do no more.
Yet what can satire, whether grave or gay?
It may correct a foible, may chastise
The freaks of fashion, regulate the dress,
Retrench a sword-blade, or displace a patch;
But where are its sublimer trophies found?
What vice has it subdued? whose heart reclaim'd
By rigor, or whom laugh'd into reform?
Alas! Leviathan is not so tam'd:
Laugh'd at he laughs again; and stricken hard,
Turns to the stroke his adamantine scales,
That fear no discipline of human hands.
The pulpit, therefore (and I name it fill'd
With solemn awe, that bids me well beware
With what intent I touch that holy thing)—
The pulpit (when the sat'rist has at last,
Strutting and vap'ring in an empty school,
Spent all his force, and made no proselyte)—
I say the pulpit (in the sober use
Of its legitimate, peculiar pow'rs)
Must stand acknowledg'd, while the world shall stand,
The most important and effectual guard,
Support, and ornament of Virtue's cause.
There stands the messenger of truth: there stands
The legate of the skies!—His theme divine,
His office sacred, his credentials clear.
By him the violated law speaks out
Its thunders; and by him, in strains as sweet
As angels use, the Gospel whispers peace.
He stablishes the strong, restores the weak,
Reclaims the wand'rer, binds the broken heart,
And, arm'd himself in panoply complete
Of heav'nly temper, furnishes with arms
Bright as his own, and trains, by ev'ry rule
Of holy discipline, to glorious war,
The sacramental host of God's elect!
Are all such teachers?—would to Heav'n all were!
But hark—the doctor's voice!—fast wedg'd between
Two empirics he stands, and with swol'n cheeks
Inspires the news, his trumpet. Keener far
Than all invective is his bold harangue,
While through that public organ of report
He hails the clergy; and, defying shame,
Announces to the world his own and theirs!
He teaches those to read, whom schools dismiss'd,

And colleges, untaught; sells accent, tone,
And emphasis in score, and gives to pray'r
Th' *adagio* and *andante* it demands.
He grinds divinity of other days
Down into modern use; transforms old print
To zigzag manuscript, and cheats the eyes
Of gall'ry critics by a thousand arts.
Are there who purchase of the doctor's ware?
O, name it not in Gath!—it cannot be,
That grave and learned clerks should need such aid.
He doubtless is in sport, and does but droll,
Assuming thus a rank unknown before—
Grand caterer and dry-nurse of the church!
I venerate the man, whose heart is warm,
Whose hands are pure, whose doctrine and whose life
Coincident, exhibit lucid proof
That he is honest in the sacred cause.
To such I render more than mere respect,
Whose actions say, that they respect themselves.
But loose in morals, and in manners vain,
In conversation frivolous, in dress
Extreme, at once rapacious and profuse;
Frequent in park with lady at his side,
Ambling and prattling scandal as he goes;
But rare at home, and never at his books,
Or with his pen, save when he scrawls a card;
Constant at routs, familiar with a round
Of ladyships, a stranger to the poor;
Ambitious of preferment for its gold,
And well-prepar'd, by ignorance and sloth,
By infidelity and love of world,
To make God's work a sinecure; a slave
To his own pleasures and his patron's pride;
From such apostles, O ye mitred heads,
Preserve the church! and lay not careless hands
On sculls, that cannot teach, and will not learn.
Would I describe a preacher, such as Paul,
Were he on earth, would hear, approve, and own,
Paul should himself direct me. I would trace
His master-strokes, and draw from his design.
I would express him simple, grave, sincere;
In doctrine uncorrupt; in language plain,
And plain in manner; decent, solemn, chaste,
And natural in gesture; much impress'd
Himself, as conscious of his awful charge,
And anxious mainly that the flock he feeds
May feel it too; affectionate in look,
And tender in address, as well becomes
A messenger of grace to guilty men.

Behold the picture!—Is it like?—Like whom?
The things that mount the rostrum with a skip.
And then skip down again; pronounce a text;
Cry—hem; and reading what they never wrote
Just fifteen minutes, huddle up their work,
And with a well-bred whisper close the scene!
  In man or woman, but far most in man,
And most of all in man that ministers
And serves the altar, in my soul I loathe
All affectation. 'Tis my perfect scorn;
Object of my implacable disgust.
What!—will a man play tricks, will he indulge
A silly fond conceit of his fair form,
And just proportion, fashionable mien,
And pretty face, in presence of his God?
Or will he seek to dazzle me with tropes,
As with the diamond on his lily hand,
And play his brilliant parts before my eyes,
When I am hungry for the bread of life?
He mocks his Maker, prostitutes and shames
His noble office, and, instead of truth,
Displaying his own beauty, starves his flock.
Therefore avaunt all attitude, and stare,
And start theatric, practis'd at the glass!
I seek divine simplicity in him,
Who handles things divine; and all besides,
Though learn'd with labor, and though much admir'd
By curious eyes and judgments ill inform'd,
To me is odious as the nasal twang
Heard at conventicle, where worthy men,
Misled by custom, strain celestial themes
Through the press'd nostril, spectacle-bestrid.
Some decent in demeanor while they preach,
That task perform'd, relapse into themselves;
And, having spoken wisely, at the close
Grow wanton, and give proof to ev'ry eye,
Whoe'er was edified, themselves were not!
Forth comes the pocket mirror.—First we stroke
An eyebrow; next compose a straggling lock;
Then with an air most gracefully perform'd
Fall back into our seat, extend an arm,
And lay it at its ease with gentle care,
With handkerchief in hand depending low:
The better hand more busy gives the nose
Its bergamot, or aids th' indebted eye
With op'ra glass, to watch the moving scene,
And recognize the slow-retiring fair.—
Now this is fulsome, and offends me more
Than in a churchman slovenly neglect

And rustic coarseness would. A heav'nly mind
May be indiff'rent to her house of clay,
And slight the hovel as beneath her care;
But how a body so fantastic, trim,
And quaint, in its deportment and attire,
Can lodge a heav'nly mind—demands a doubt.
He, that negotiates between God and man,
As God's ambassador, the grand concerns
Of judgment and of mercy, should beware
Of lightness in his speech. 'Tis pitiful
To court a grin, when you should woo a soul;
To break a jest, when pity would inspire
Pathetic exhortation; and t'address
The skittish fancy with facetious tales,
When sent with God's commission to the heart!
So did not Paul. Direct me to a quip
Or merry turn in all he ever wrote,
And I consent you take it for your text,
Your only one, till sides and benches fail.
No: he was serious in a serious cause,
And understood too well the weighty terms,
That he had tak'n in charge. He would not stoop
To conquer those by jocular exploits,
Whom truth and soberness assail'd in vain.
O Popular Applause! what heart of man
Is proof against thy sweet seducing charms?
The wisest and the best feel urgent need
Of all their caution in thy gentlest gales;
But swell'd into a gust—who then, alas!
With all his canvass set, and inexpert,
And therefore heedless, can withstand thy pow'r?
Praise from the shrivell'd lips of toothless, bald
Decrepitude, and in the looks of lean
And craving Poverty, and in the bow
Respectful of the smutch'd artificer,
Is oft too welcome, and may much disturb
The bias of the purpose. How much more,
Pour'd forth by beauty splendid and polite,
In language soft as Adoration breathes?
Ah spare your idol! think him human still.
Charms he may have, but he has frailties too!
Dote not too much, nor spoil what ye admire.
All truth is from the sempiternal source
Of light divine. But Egypt, Greece, and Rome,
Drew from the stream below. More favor'd we
Drink, when we choose it, at the fountain-head.
To them it flow'd much mingled and defil'd
With hurtful error, prejudice, and dreams
Illusive of philosophy, so call'd

But falsely. Sages after sages strove
In vain to filter off a crystal draught
Pure from the lees, which often more enhanc'd
The thirst than slak'd it, and not seldom bred
Intoxication and delirium wild.
In vain they push'd inquiry to the birth
And spring-time of the world; ask'd, Whence is man?
Why form'd at all? and wherefore as he is?
Where must he find his Maker? with what rites
Adore him? Will he hear, accept, and bless?
Or does he sit regardless of his works?
Has man within him an immortal seed?
Or does the tomb take all? If he survive
His ashes, where? and in what weal or woe?
Knots worthy of solution, which alone
A Deity could solve. Their answers, vague
And all at random, fabulous and dark,
Left them as dark themselves. Their rules of life,
Defective and unsanction'd, prov'd too weak
To bind the roving appetite, and lead
Blind nature to a God not yet reveal'd.
'Tis Revelation satisfies all doubts,
Explains all mysteries, except her own,
And so illuminates the path of life,
That fools discover it, and stray no more.
Now tell me, dignified and sapient sir,
My man of morals, nurtur'd in the shades
Of Academus—is this false or true?
Is Christ the abler teacher, or the schools?
If Christ, then why resort at ev'ry turn
To Athens or to Rome, for wisdom short
Of man's occasions, when in him reside
Grace, knowledge, comfort—an unfathom'd store?
How oft, when Paul has serv'd us with a text,
Has Epictetus, Plato, Tully, preach'd!
Men that, if now alive, would sit content
And humble learners of a Saviour's worth,
Preach it who might. Such was their love of truth,
Their thirst of knowledge, and their candor too!
  And thus it is.—The pastor, either vain
By nature, or by flatt'ry made so, taught
To gaze at his own splendor, and t'exalt
Absurdly, not his office, but himself;
Or unenlighten'd, and too proud to learn;
Or vicious, and not therefore apt to teach;
Perverting often by the stress of lewd
And loose example, whom he should instruct;
Exposes, and holds up to broad disgrace,
The noblet function, and discredits much

The brightest truths that man has ever seen.
For ghostly counsel; if it either fall
Below the exigence, or be not back'd
With show of love, at least with hopeful proof
Of some sincerity on the giver's part;
Or be dishonor'd in th'exterior form
And mode of its conveyance by such tricks
As move derision, or by foppish airs
And histrionic mumm'ry, that let down
The pulpit to the level of the stage;
Drops from the lips a disregarded thing.
The weak perhaps are mov'd, but are not taught,
While prejudice in men of stronger minds
Takes deeper root, confirm'd by what they see.
A relaxation of religion's hold
Upon the roving and untutor'd heart
Soon follows, and, the curb of conscience snapp'd,
The laity run wild.—But do they now?
Note their extravagance, and be convinc'd.
  As nations, ignorant of God, contrive
A wooden one; so we, no longer taught
By monitors that mother church supplies,
Now make our own. Posterity will ask
(If e'er posterity see verse of mine)
Some fifty or a hundred lustrums hence,
What was a monitor in George's days?
My very gentle reader, yet unborn,
Of whom I needs must augur better things,
Since Heav'n would sure grow weary of a world
Productive only of a race like ours,
A monitor is wood—plank shaven thin.
We wear it at our backs. There, closely brac'd
And neatly fitted, it compresses hard
The prominent and most unsightly bones,
And binds the shoulders flat. We prove its use
Sov'reign and most effectual to secure
A form, not now gymnastic as of yore,
From rickets and distortion, else our lot.
But thus admonish'd, we can walk erect—
One proof at least of manhood! while the friend
Sticks close, a Mentor worthy of his charge.
Our habits, costlier than Lucullus wore,
And by caprice as multiplied as his,
Just please us while the fashion is at full,
But change with ev'ry moon. The sycophant,
Who waits to dress us, arbitrates their date;
Surveys his fair reversion with keen eye;
Finds one ill made, another obsolete,
This fits not nicely, that is ill conceiv'd;

And, making prize of all that he condemns,
With our expenditure defrays his own.
Variety's the very spice of life,
That gives it all its flavor. We have run
Through ev'ry change, that Fancy, at the loom
Exhausted, has had genius to supply;
And, studious of mutation still, discard
A real elegance, a little us'd,
For monstrous novelty, and strange disguise.
We sacrifice to dress, till household joys
And comforts cease. Dress drains our cellar dry,
And keeps our larder lean; puts out our fires;
And introduces hunger, frost, and woe,
Where peace and hospitality might reign.
What man that lives, and that knows how to live,
Would fail t'exhibit at the public shows
A form as splendid as the proudest there,
Though appetite raise outcries at the cost?
A man o' th' town dines late, but soon enough,
With reasonable forecast and dispatch,
T'ensure a side-box station at half-price.
You think perhaps, so delicate his dress,
His daily fare as delicate. Alas!
He picks clean teeth, and, busy as he seems
With an old tavern quill, is hungry yet!
The rout is Folly's circle, which she draws
With magic wand. So potent is the spell,
That none, decoy'd into that fatal ring,
Unless by Heav'n's peculiar grace, escape.
There we grow early gray, but never wise;
There form connexions, but acquire no friend;
Solicit pleasure hopeless of success;
Waste youth in occupations only fit
For second childhood, and devote old age
To sports, which only childhood could excuse.
There they are happiest, who dissemble best
Their weariness; and they the most polite,
Who squander time and treasure with a smile,
Though at their own destruction. She that asks
Her dear five hundred friends, contemns them all,
And hates their coming. They (what can they less?)
Make just reprisals; and, with cringe and shrug,
And bow obsequious, hide their hate of her.
All catch the frenzy, downward from her grace,
Whose flambeaux flash against the morning skies,
And gild our chamber ceilings as they pass,
To her, who, frugal only that her thrift
May feed excesses she can ill afford,
Is hackney'd home unlackey'd; who, in haste

Alighting, turns the key in her own door,
And, at the watchman's lantern borr'wing light,
Finds a cold bed her only comfort left.
Wives beggar husbands, husbands starve their wives,
On Fortune's velvet altar off'ring up
Their last poor pittance—Fortune, most severe
Of goddesses yet known, and costlier far
Than all, that held their routs in Juno's heav'n.—
So fare we in this prison-house the World;
And 'tis a fearful spectacle to see
So many maniacs dancing in their chains.
They gaze upon the links, that hold them fast,
With eyes of anguish, execrate their lot,
Then shake them in despair, and dance again!
  Now basket up the family of plagues,
That waste our vitals; peculation, sale
Of honor, perjury, corruption, frauds
By forgery, by subterfuge of law,
By tricks and lies as num'rous and as keen
As the necessities their authors feel;
Then cast them, closely bundled, ev'ry brat
At the right door. Profusion is the sire.
Profusion unrestrain'd, with all that's base
In character, has litter'd all the land,
And bred, within the mem'ry of no few,
A priesthood, such as Baal's was of old,
A people, such as never was till now.
It is a hungry vice:—it eats up all
That gives society its beauty, strength,
Convenience, and security, and use:
Makes men mere vermin, worthy to be trapp'd
And gibbeted, as fast as catchpole claws
Can seize the slipp'ry prey: unties the knot
Of union, and converts the sacred band,
That holds mankind together, to a scourge.
Profusion, deluging a state with lusts
Of grossest nature and of worst effects,
Prepares it for its ruin: hardens, blinds,
And warps, the consciences of public men,
Till they can laugh at Virtue; mock the fools,
That trust them; and in th'end disclose a face,
That would have shock'd Credulity herself,
Unmask'd, vouchsafing this their sole excuse—
Since all alike are selfish, why not they?
This does Profusion, and th'accursed cause
Of such deep mischief has itself a cause.
  In colleges and halls in ancient days,
When learning, virtue, piety, and truth,
Were precious, and inculcated with care,

There dwelt a sage call'd Discipline. His head,
Not yet by time completely silver'd o'er,
Bespoke him past the bounds of freakish youth,
But strong for service still, and unimpair'd.
His eye was meek and gentle, and a smile
Play'd on his lips; and in his speech was heard
Paternal sweetness, dignity, and love.
The occupation dearest to his heart
Was to encourage goodness. He would stroke
The head of modest and ingenuous worth,
That blush'd at its own praise; and press the youth
Close to his side, that pleas'd him. Learning grew
Beneath his care a thriving vig'rous plant;
The mind was well inform'd, the passions held
Subordinate, and diligence was choice.
If e'er it chanc'd, as sometimes chance it must,
That one among so many overleap'd
The limits of control, his gentle eye
Grew stern, and darted a severe rebuk.
His frown was full of terror, and his voice
Shook the delinquent with such fits of awe,
As left him not, till penitence had won
Lost favor back again, and clos'd the breach.
But Discipline, a faithful servant long,
Declin'd at length into the vale of years:
A palsy struck his arm; his sparkling eye
Was quench'd in rheums of age; his voice, unstrung,
Grew tremulous, and drew derision more
Than rev'rence in perverse, rebellious youth.
So colleges and halls neglected much
Their good old friend; and Discipline at length,
O'erlook'd and unemploy'd, fell sick and died.
Then Study languish'd, Emulation slept,
And Virtue fled. The schools became a scene
Of solemn farce, where Ignorance in stilts,
His cap well lin'd with logic not his own,
With parrot tongue perform'd the scholar's part,
Proceeding soon a graduated dunce.
Then compromise had place, and scrutiny
Became stone blind; precedence went in truck,
And he was competent whose purse was so.
A dissolution of all bonds ensued;
The curbs invented for the mulish mouth
Of headstrong youth were broken; bars and bolts
Grew rusty by disuse; and massy gates
Forgot their office, op'ning with a touch;
Till gowns at length are found mere masquerade,
The tassel'd cap and the spruce band a jest,
A mock'ry of the world! What need of these

For gamesters, jockeys, brothellers impure,
Spendthrifts, and booted sportsmen, oft'ner seen
With belted waist and pointers at their heels,
Than in the bounds of duty? What was learn'd,
If aught was learn'd in childhood, is forgot;
And such expense, as pinches parents blue,
And mortifies the lib'ral hand of love,
Is squander'd in pursuit of idle sports
And vicious pleasures; buys the boy a name,
That sits a stigma on his father's house,
And cleaves through life inseparably close
To him that wears it. What can after-games
Of riper joys, and commerce with the world,
The lewd vain world, that must receive him soon,
Add to such erudition, thus acquir'd,
Where science and where virtue are profess'd?
They may confirm his habits, rivet fast
His folly, but to spoil him is a task,
That bids defiance to th'united pow'rs
Of fashion, dissipation, taverns, stews.
Now blame we most the nurslings or the nurse?
The children crook'd, and twisted, and deform'd,
Through want of care; or her, whose winking eye
And slumb'ring oscitancy mars the brood?
The nurse no doubt. Regardless of her charge,
She needs herself correction; needs to learn,
That it is dang'rous sporting with the world,
With things so sacred as a nation's trust,
The nurture of her youth, her dearest pledge.
All are not such. I had a brother once—
Peace to the mem'ry of a man of worth,
A man of letters, and of manners too!
Of manners sweet as Virtue always wears,
When gay Good-nature dresses her in smiles.
He grac'd a college,* in which order yet
Was sacred; and was honor'd, lov'd, and wept,
By more than one, themselves conspicuous there.
Some minds are temper'd happily, and mix'd
With such ingredients of good sense, and taste
Of what is excellent in man, they thirst
With such a zeal to be what they approve,
That no restraints can circumscribe them more
Than they themselves by choice, for wisdom's sake.
Nor can example hurt them: what they see
Of vice in others but enhancing more
The charms of virtue in their just esteem.
If such escape contagion, and emerge

* Bene't Coll. Cambridge.

Pure from so foul a pool to shine abroad,
And give the world their talents and themselves,
Small thanks to those whose negligence or sloth
Expos'd their inexperience to the snare,
And left them to an undirected choice.
  See then the quiver broken and decay'd,
In which are kept our arrows! Rusting there
In wild disorder, and unfit for use,
What wonder if, discharg'd into the world,
They shame their shooters with a random flight,
Their points obtuse, and feathers drunk with wine!
Well may the church wage unsuccessful war
With such artill'ry arm'd. Vice parries wide
Th'undreaded volley with a sword of straw,
And stands an impudent and fearless mark.
  Have we not track'd the felon home, and found
His birth-place and his dam? The country mourns,
Mourns because ev'ry plague, that can infest
Society, and that saps and worms the base
Of th'edifice, that Policy has rais'd,
Swarms in all quarters: meets the eye, the ear,
And suffocates the breath at ev'ry turn.
Profusion breeds them; and the cause itself
Of that calamitous mischief has been found:
Found too where most offensive, in the skirts
Of the rob'd pedagogue! Else let th'arraign'd
Stand up unconscious, and refute the charge.
So when the Jewish leader stretch'd his arm,
And wav'd his rod divine, a race obscene,
Spawn'd in the muddy beds of Nile, came forth,
Polluting Egypt: gardens, fields, and plains,
Were cover'd with the pest; the streets were fill'd;
The croaking nuisance lurk'd in every nook;
Nor palaces, nor even chambers, scap'd;
And the land stank—so num'rous was the fry.

THE TASK.

BOOK III.

THE GARDEN.

ARGUMENT OF THE THIRD BOOK.

Self-recollection and reproof.—Address to domestic happiness.—Some account of myself.—The vanity of many of their pursuits who are reputed wise.—Justification of my censures.—Divine illumination necessary to the most expert philosopher.—The question, What is truth? answered by other questions.—Domestic happiness addressed again.—Few lovers of the country.—My tame hare.—Occupations of a retired gentleman in his garden.—Pruning.—Framing.—Green-house—Sowing of flower-seeds.—The country preferable to the town even in winter.—Reasons why it is deserted at that season.—Ruinous effects of gaming, and of expensive improvement.—Book concludes with an apostrophe to the metropolis.

As one, who long in thickets and in brakes
Entangled, winds now this way and now that
His devious course uncertain, seeking home;
Or, having long in miry ways been foil'd
And sore discomfited, from slough to slough
Plunging, and half despairing of escape;
If chance at length he find a greensward smooth
And faithful to the foot, his spirits rise,
He cherubs brisk his ear-erecting steed,
And winds his way with pleasure and with ease;
So I, designing other themes, and call'd
T'adorn the Sofa with eulogium due,
To tell its slumbers, and to paint its dreams,
Have rambled wide: in country, city, seat
Of academic fame (howe'er deserv'd),
Long held, and scarcely disengag'd at last.
But now with pleasant pace a cleanlier road
I mean to tread: I feel myself at large,
Courageous, and refresh'd for future toil,
If toil await me, or if dangers new.
Since pulpits fail, and sounding-boards reflect
Most part an empty, ineffectual sound,

What chance that I, to fame so little known,
Nor conversant with men or manners much,
Should speak to purpose, or with better hope
Crack the satiric thong? 'T were wiser far
For me, enamour'd of sequester'd scenes,
And charm'd with rural beauty, to repose,
Where chance may throw me, beneath elm or vine,
My languid limbs, when summer sears the plains,
Or, when rough winter rages, on the soft
And shelter'd sofa, while the nitrous air
Feeds a blue flame, and makes a cheerful hearth;
There, undisturbed by Folly, and appris'd
How great the danger of disturbing her,
To muse in silence, or, at least, confine
Remarks, that gall so many, to the few
My partners in retreat. Disgust conceal'd
Is oftimes proof of wisdom, when the fault
Is obstinate, and cure beyond our reach.
 Domestic Happiness, thou only bliss
Of Paradise, that hast survived the fall!
Though few now taste thee unimpair'd and pure
Or tasting, long enjoy thee! too infirm,
Or too incautious, to preserve thy sweets
Unmix'd with drops of bitter, which neglect,
Or temper, sheds into thy crystal cup;
Thou art the nurse of Virtue, in thine arms
She smiles, appearing, as in truth she is,
Heav'n-born, and destin'd to the skies again.
Thou art not known where Pleasure is ador'd,
That reeling goddess with the zoneless waist
And wand'ring eyes, still leaning on the arm
Of Novelty, her fickle, frail support;
For thou art meek and constant, hating change,
And finding in the calm of truth-tried love
Joys that her stormy raptures never yield.
Forsaking thee, what shipwreck have we made
Of honor, dignity, and fair renown!
Till prostitution elbows us aside
In all our crowded streets; and senates seem
Conven'd for purposes of empire less,
Than to release th' adultress from her bond.
Th' adultress! what a theme for angry verse!
What provocation to th' indignant heart,
That feels for injur'd love! but I disdain
The nauseous task to paint her as she is,
Cruel, abandon'd, glorying in her shame!
No: let her pass, and charioted along
In guilty splendor, shake the public ways
The frequency of crimes has washed them white,

And verse of mine shall never brand the wretch,
Whom matron's now of character unsmirched,
And chaste themselves, are not ashamed to own.
Virtue and vice had bound'ries in old time,
Not to be passed: and she, that had renounc'd
Her sex's honor, was renounc'd herself
By all that priz'd it; not for prud'ry's sake,
But dignity's, resentful of the wrong.
'T was hard perhaps on here and there a waif,
Desirous to return, and not receiv'd:
But 't was a wholesome rigor in the main,
And taught th' unblemished to preserve with care
That purity, whose loss was loss of all.
Men too were nice in honor in those days,
And judg'd offenders well. Then he that sharped,
And pocketed a prize by fraud obtain'd,
Was mark'd and shunn'd as odious. He that sold
His country, or was slack when she requir'd
His ev'ry nerve in action and at stretch,
Paid with the blood that he had basely spared
The price of his default. But now—yes, now,
We are become so candid and so fair,
So lib'ral in construction, and so rich
In Christian charity, (good-natured age!)
That they are safe, sinners of either sex,
Transgress what laws they may. Well dress'd, well-bred,
Well equipag'd, is ticket good enough
To pass us readily through ev'ry door.
Hypocrisy, detest her as we may,
(And no man's hatred ever wrong'd her yet),
May claim this merit still—that she admits
The worth of what she mimics with such care,
And thus gives virtue indirect applause;
But she has burnt her mask, not needed here,
Where vice has such allowance, that her shifts
And specious semblances have lost their use.
I was a stricken deer, that left the herd
Long since. With many an arrow deep infix'd
My panting side was charg'd, when I withdrew
To seek a tranquil death in distant shades.
There was I found by one who had himself
Been hurt by th' archers. In his side he bore,
And in his hands and feet, the cruel scars.
With gentle force soliciting the darts,
He drew them forth, and heal'd, and bade me live.
Since then, with few associates, in remote
And silent woods I wander, far from those
My former partners of the peopled scene;
With few associates, and not wishing more.
Here much I ruminate, as much I may,

With other views of men and manners now
Than once, and others of a life to come.
I see that all are wand'rers, gone astray
Each in his own delusions; they are lost
In chase of fancied happiness, still woo'd
And never won. Dream after dream ensues;
And still they dream that they shall still succeed,
And still are disappointed. Rings the world
With the vain stir. I sum up half mankind,
And add two-thirds of the remaining half,
And find the total of their hopes and fears
Dreams, empty dreams. The million flit as gay
As if created only like the fly,
That spreads his motley wings in th' eye of noon,
To sport their season, and be seen no more.
The rest are sober dreamers, grave and wise,
And pregnant with discov'ries new and rare.
Some write a narrative of wars, and feats
Of heroes little known; and call the rant
A history: describe the man, of whom
His own coevals took but little note,
And paint his person, character, and views,
As they had known him from his mother's womb.
They disentangle from the puzzled skein,
In which obscurity has wrapped them up,
The threads of politic and shrewd design,
That ran through all his purposes, and charge
His mind with meanings that he never had,
Or, having, kept conceal'd. Some drill and bore
The solid earth, and from the strata there
Extract a register, by which we learn,
That he who made it, and reveal'd its date
To Moses, was mistaken in its age.
Some, more acute, and more industrious still,
Contrive creation; travel Nature up
To the sharp peak of her sublimest height,
And tell us whence the stars, why some are fix'd,
And planetary some; what gave them first
Rotation, from what fountain flow'd their light.
Great contest follows, and much learned dust
Involves the combatants; each claiming truth,
And truth disclaiming both. And thus they spend
The little wick of life's poor shallow lamp
In playing tricks with Nature, giving laws
To distant worlds, and trifling in their own.
Is't not a pity now that tickling rheums
Should ever tease the lungs, and blear the sight
Of oracles like these? Great pity too,
That having wielded th' elements, and built

A thousand systems, each in his own way,
They should go out in fume, and be forgot?
Ah! what is life thus spent? and what are they
But frantic who thus spend it? all for smoke—
Eternity for bubbles proves at last
A senseless bargain. When I see such games
Play'd by the creatures of a Pow'r, who swears
That he will judge the earth, and call the fool
To a sharp reck'ning, that has lived in vain;
And when I weigh this seeming wisdom well,
And prove it in th' infallible result
So hollow and so false—I feel my heart
Dissolve in pity, and account the learn'd,
If this be learning, most of all deceiv'd.
Great crimes alarm the conscience, but it sleeps,
While thoughtful man is plausibly amus'd.
Defend me, therefore, common sense, say I,
From reveries so airy, from the toil
Of dropping buckets into empty wells,
And growing old in drawing nothing up!
 'Twere well, says one sage erudite, profound,
Terribly arch'd, and aquiline his nose,
And overbuilt with most impending brows,
'Twere well, could you permit the world to live
As the world pleases: what's the world to you?
Much. I was born of woman, and drew milk
As sweet as charity, from human breasts.
I think, articulate, I laugh and weep,
And exercise all functions of a man.
How then should I and any man that lives
Be strangers to each other? Pierce my vein,
Take of the crimson stream meand'ring there,
And catechise it well; apply thy glass,
Search it, and prove now if it be not blood
Congenial with thine own: and, if it be,
What edge of subtlety canst thou suppose
Keen enough, wise and skilful as thou art,
To cut the link of brotherhood, by which
One common Maker bound me to the kind?
True; I am no proficient, I confess,
In arts like yours. I cannot call the swift
And perilous light'nings from the angry clouds,
And bid them hide themselves in earth beneath;
I cannot analyse the air, nor catch
The parallax of yonder lum'nous point,
That seems half-quench'd in the immense abyss;
Such powers I boast not—neither can I rest
A silent witness of the headlong rage,
Or heedless folly, by which thousands die,

Bone of my bone, and kindred souls to mine.
  God never meant that man should scale the heav'ns
By strides of human wisdom, in his works,
Though wondrous: he commands us in his word
To seek him rather where his mercy shines.
The mind, indeed, enlighten'd from above,
Views him in all; ascribes to the grand cause
The grand effect; acknowledges with joy
His manner, and with rapture tastes his style.
But never yet did philosophic tube,
That brings the planets home into the eye
Of Observation, and discovers, else
Not visible, his family of worlds,
Discover Him that rules them; such a veil
Hangs over mortal eyes, blind from the birth,
And dark in things divine. Full often, too,
Our wayward intellect, the more we learn
Of nature, overlooks her author more;
From instrumental causes proud to draw
Conclusions retrogade, and mad mistake.
But if his Word once teach us, shoot a ray
Through all the heart's dark chambers, and reveal
Truths undiscern'd but by that holy light,
Then all is plain. Philosophy, baptised
In the pure fountain of eternal love,
Has eyes indeed; and viewing all she sees
As meant to indicate a God to man,
Gives *him* his praise, and forfeits not her own.
Learning has borne such fruit in other days
On all her branches: piety has found
Friends in the friends of science, and true pray'r
Has flow'd from lips wet with Castalian dews.
Such was thy wisdom, Newton, child-like sage!
Sagacious reader of the works of God,
And in his word sagacious. Such too thine,
Milton, whose genius had angelic wings,
And fed on manna! And such thine, in whom
Our British Themis gloried with just cause,
Immortal Hale; for deep discernment prais'd,
And sound integrity, not more than fam'd
For sanctity of manners undefil'd.
  All flesh is grass, and all its glory fades
Like the fair flow'r dishevell'd in the wind;
Riches have wings, and grandeur is a dream.
The man we celebrate must find a tomb,
And we that worship him ignoble graves.
Nothing is proof against the gen'ral curse
Of vanity, that seizes all below.
The only amaranthine flow'r on earth

Is virtue; th' only lasting treasure, truth.
But what is truth? 'Twas Pilate's question put
To truth itself, that deign'd him no reply.
And wherefore? will not God impart his light
To them that ask it?—Freely—'tis his joy,
His glory, and his nature, to impart.
But to the proud, uncandid, insincere,
Or negligent inquirer, not a spark.
What's that, which brings contempt upon a book,
And him who writes it, though the style be neat,
The method clear, and argument exact?
That makes a minister in holy things
The joy of many, and the dread of more,
His name a theme for praise and for reproach?—
That, while it gives us worth in God's account,
Depreciates and undoes us in our own?
What pearl is it, that rich men cannot buy,
That learning is too proud to gather up;
But which the poor, and the despis'd of all,
Seek and obtain, and often find unsought?
Tell me—and I will tell thee what is truth.
O friendly to the best pursuits of man,
Friendly to thought, to virtue, and to peace,
Domestic life in rural pleasure pass'd!
Few know thy value, and few taste thy sweets;
Though many boast thy favors, and affect
To understand and choose thee for their own.
But foolish man forgoes his proper bliss,
E'en as his first progenitor, and quits,
Though plac'd in Paradise (for earth has still
Some traces of her youthful beauty left),
Substantial happiness for transient joy.
Scenes form'd for contemplation, and to nurse
The growing seeds of wisdom; that suggest,
By ev'ry pleasing image they present,
Reflections such as meliorate the heart,
Compose the passions, and exalt the mind;
Scenes such as these 'tis his supreme delight
To fill with riot and defile with blood.
Should some contagion, kind to the poor brutes
We persecute, annihilate the tribes,
That draw the sportsman over hill and dale
Fearless, and rapt away from all his cares;
Should never game-fowl hatch her eggs again,
Nor baited hook deceive the fish's eye;
Could pageantry and dance, and feast and song,
Be quell'd in all our summer-months' retreats;
How many self-deluded nymphs and swains,
Who dream they have a taste for fields and groves,

Would find them hideous nurs'ries of the spleen,
And crowd the roads, impatient for the town!
They love the country, and none else, who seek
For their own sake its silence, and its shade.
Delights which who would leave, that has a heart
Susceptible of pity, or a mind
Cultur'd and capable of sober thought,
For all the savage din of the swift pack,
And clamors of the field?—Detested sport,
That owes its pleasure to another's pain;
That feeds upon the sobs and dying shrieks
Of harmless nature, dumb, but yet endued
With eloquence, that agonies inspire,
Of silent tears and heart-distending sighs?
Vain tears, alas, and sighs that never find
A corresponding tone in jovial souls!
Well—one at least is safe. One shelter'd hare
Has never heard the sanguinary yell
Of cruel man, exulting in her woes.
Innocent partner of my peaceful home,
Whom ten long years' experience of my care
Has made at last familiar; she has lost
Much of her vigilant instinctive dread,
Not needful here, beneath a roof like mine.
Yes—thou mayst eat thy bread, and lick the hand
That feeds thee; thou mayst frolic on the floor
At ev'ning, and at night retire secure
To thy straw couch, and slumber unalarm'd;
For I have gain'd thy confidence, have pledg'd
All that is human in me, to protect
Thine unsuspecting gratitude and love.
If I survive thee, I will dig thy grave;
And, when I place thee in it, sighing say,
I knew at least one hare that had a friend.*
How various his employments, whom the world
Calls idle; and who justly in return
Esteems that busy world an idler too!
Friends, books, a garden, and perhaps his pen,
Delightful industry enjoy'd at home,
And Nature in her cultivated trim
Dress'd to his taste, inviting him abroad—
Can he want occupation, who has these?
Will he be idle, who has much t' enjoy?
Me therefore studious of laborious ease,
Not slothful, happy to deceive the time,
Not waste it, and aware that human life
Is but a loan to be repaid with use,

* See the note at the end of this volume.

When He shall call his debtors to account,
From whom are all our blessings, business finds
E'en here: while sedulous I seek t' improve,
At least neglect not, or leave unemploy'd,
The mind he gave me; driving it, though slack
Too oft, and much impeded in its work
By causes not to be divulg'd in vain,
To its just point—the service of mankind.
He, that attends to his interior self,
That has a heart, and keeps it; has a mind
That hungers, and supplies it; and who seeks
A social not a dissipated life,
Has business; feels himself engaged t' acheive
No unimportant, though a silent, task.
A life all turbulence and noise may seem
To him that leads it wise, and to be praised;
But wisdom is a pearl with most success
Sought in still water, and beneath clear skies.
He that is ever occupied in storms
Or dives not for it, or brings up instead,
Vainly industrious, a disgraceful prize.
The morning finds the self-sequester'd man
Fresh for his task, intend what task he may.
Whether inclement seasons recommend
His warm but simple home, where he enjoys
With her, who shares his pleasures and his heart,
Sweet converse, sipping calm the fragrant lymph,
Which neatly she prepares; then to his book
Well chosen, and not sullenly perus'd
In selfish silence, but imparted oft,
As aught occurs, that she may smile to hear,
Or turn to nourishment, digested well.
Or if the garden with its many cares,
All well repaid, demand him, he attends
The welcome call, conscious how much the hand
Of lubbard Labour needs his watchful eye,
Oft loit'ring lazily, if not o'erseen,
Or misapplying his unskilful strength.
Nor does he govern only or direct,
But much performs himself. No works indeed,
That ask robust, tough sinews, bred to toil,
Servile employ; but such as may amuse,
Not tire, demanding rather skill than force.
Proud of his well-spread walls, he views his trees,
That meet, no barren interval between,
With pleasure more than e'en their fruits afford;
Which, save himself who trains them, none can feel.
These therefore are his own peculiar charge;
No meaner hand may discipline the shoots,

None but his steel approach them. What is weak,
Distemper'd, or has lost prolific pow'rs,
Impair'd by age, his unrelenting hand
Dooms to the knife nor does he spare the soft:
And succulent, that feeds its giant growth,
But barren, at th' expense of neighb'ring twigs
Less ostentatious, and yet studded thick
With hopeful gems. The rest, no portion left
That may disgrace his art, or disappoint
Large expectation, he disposes neat
At measured distances, that air and sun,
Admitted freely, may afford their aid,
And ventilate and warm the swelling buds.
Hence Summer has her riches, Autumn hence,
And hence e'en Winter fills his wither'd hand
With blushing fruits, and plenty not his own.*
Fair recompense of labor well bestow'd,
And wise precaution; which a clime so rude
Makes needful still, whose Spring is but the child
Of churlish Winter, in her froward moods
Discov'ring much the temper of her sire.
For oft, as if in her the stream of mild
Maternal nature had revers'd its course,
She brings her infants forth with many smiles;
But once deliver'd kills them with a frown.
He therefore timely warn'd himself supplies
Her want of care, screening and keeping warm
The plenteous bloom, that no rough blast may sweep
His garlands from the boughs. Again, as oft
As the sun peeps and vernal airs breathe mild,
The fence withdrawn, he gives them ev'ry beam,
And spreads his hopes before the blaze of day.
  To raise the prickly and green-coated gourd,
So grateful to the palate, and when rare
So coveted, else base and disesteemed—
Food for the vulgar merely—is an art
That toiling ages have but just matur'd,
And at this moment unassay'd in song.
Yet gnats have had, and frogs and mice, long since,
Their eulogy; those sang the Mantuan bard,
And these the Grecian, in ennobling strains;
And in thy numbers, Phillips, shines for aye
The solitary shilling. Pardon then,
Ye sage dispensers of poetic fame,
Th' ambition of one meaner far, whose pow'rs,
Presuming an attempt not less sublime,

* 'Miraturque novos fructus et non sua poma.
Virg.

Pant for the praise of dressing to the taste
Of critic appetite, no sordid fare,
A cucumber, while costly yet and scarce.
The stable yields a stercoraceous heap,
Impregnated with quick fermenting salts,
And potent to resist the freezing blast:
For, ere the beech and elm have cast their leaf
Deciduous, when now November dark
Checks vegetation in the torpid plant
Expos'd to his cold breath, the task begins.
Warily therefore, and with prudent heed,
He seeks a favor'd spot; that where he builds
Th' agglomerated pile his frame may front
The sun's meridian disk, and at the back
Enjoy close shelter, wall, or reeds, or hedge
Impervious to the wind. First he bids spread
Dry fern or litter'd hay, that may imbibe
Th' ascending damps; then leisurely impose,
And lightly, shaking it with agile hand
From the full fork, the saturated straw.
What longest binds the closest forms secure,
The shapely side, that as it rises takes,
By just degrees, an overhauging breadth,
Shelt' ring the base with its projected eaves;
Th' uplifted frame, compact at ev'ry joint,
And overlaid with clear translucent glass,
He settles next upon the sloping mount,
Whose sharp declivity shoots off secure
From the dash'd pane the deluge as it falls.
He shuts it close, and the first labour ends
Thrice must the voluble and restless Earth
Spin round upon her axle, ere the warmth,
Slow gath'ring in the midst, through the square mass
Diffus'd, attain the surface: when, behold!
A pestilent and most corrosive steam,
Like a gross fog Bœotian, rising fast,
And fast condens'd upon the dewy sash,
Asks egress; which obtained, the overcharg'd
And drench'd conservatory breathes abroad
In volumes wheeling slow, the vapor dank;
And, purified, rejoices to have lost
Its foul inhabitant. But to assuage
Th' impatient fervor, which it first conceives
Within its reeking bosom, threat'ning death
To his young hopes, requires discreet delay.
Experience, slow preceptress, teaching oft
The way to glory by miscarriage foul,
Must prompt him, and admonish how to catch
Th' auspicious moment, when the temper'd heat

Friendly to vital motion, may afford
Soft fomentation, and invite the seed.
The seed, selected wisely, plump, and smooth,
And glossy, he commits to pots of size
Diminutive, well fill'd with well-prepar'd
And fruitful soil, that has been treasur'd long,
And drank no moisture from the dripping clouds.
These on the warm and genial earth, that hides
The smoking manure, and o'erspreads it all,
He places lightly, and, as time subdues
The rage of fermentation, plunges deep
In the soft medium, till they stand immers'd.
Then rise the tender germs, upstarting quick,
And spreading wide their spongy lobes; at first
Pale, wan, and livid; but assuming soon,
If fann'd by balmy and nutritious air,
Strain'd through the friendly mats, a vivid green.
Two leaves produc'd, two rough indented leaves,
Cautious he pinches from the second stalk
A pimple, that portends a future sprout,
And interdicts its growth. Thence straight succeed
The branches, sturdy to his utmost wish;
Prolific all, and harbingers of more.
The crowded roots demand enlargement now,
And transplantation in an ampler space.
Indulged in what they wish, they soon supply
Large foliage, o'ershadowing golden flowers,
Blown on the summit of th' apparent fruit.
These have their sexes! and, when summer shines,
The bee transports the fertilizing meal
From flow'r to flow'r, and e'en the breathing air
Wafts the rich prize to its appointed use.
Not so when winter scowls. Assistant Art
Then acts in Nature's office, brings to pass
The glad espousals, and ensures the crop.
  Grudge not, ye rich, (since Luxury must have
His dainties, and the World's more num'rous half
Lives by contriving delicates for you,)
Grudge not the cost. Ye little know the cares,
The vigilance, the labor, and the skill,
That day and night are exercis'd, and hang
Upon the ticklish balance of suspense,
That ye may garnish your profuse regales
With summer fruits brought forth by wintry suns.
Ten thousand dangers lie in wait to thwart
The process. Heat and cold, and wind, and steam,
Moisture and drought, mice, worms, and swarming flies
Minute as dust, and numberless, oft work
Dire disappointment, that admits no cure,

And which no care can obviate. It were long,
Too long, to tell th' expedients and the shifts,
Which he that fights a season so severe
Devises, while he guards his tender trust;
And oft at last in vain. The learn'd and wise
Sarcastic would exclaim, and judge the song
Cold as its theme, and like its theme the fruit
Of too much labor, worthless when produc'd.
Who loves a garden loves a greenhouse too.
Unconscious of a less propitious clime,
There blooms exotic beauty, warm and snug,
While the winds whistle, and the snows descend.
The spiry myrtle with unwith'ring leaf
Shines there, and flourishes. The golden boast
Of Portugal and western India there,
The ruddier orange, and the paler lime,
Peep through their polish'd foliage at the storm,
And seem to smile at what they need not fear.
Th' amomum there with intermingling flow'rs
And cherries hangs her twigs. Geranium boasts
Her crimson honors; and the spangled beau,
Ficoides, glitters bright the winter long.
All plants, of ev'ry leaf, that can endure
The winter's frown, if screen'd from his shrewd bite,
Live there, and prosper. Those Ausonia claims,
Levantine regions these; th' Azores send
Their jessamine, her jessamine remote
Caffraia: foreigners from many lands,
They form one social shade, as if conven'd
By magic summons of th' Orphean lyre.
Yet just arrangement, rarely brought to pass
But by a master's hand, disposing well
The gay diversities of leaf and flow'r,
Must lend its aid t' illustrate all their charms,
And dress the regular yet various scene.
Plant behind plant aspiring, in the van
The dwarfish, in the rear retir'd, but still
Sublime abode the rest, the statelier stand.
So once were rang'd the sons of ancient Rome,
A noble show! while Roscius trod the stage,
And so, while Garrick, as renowned as he,
The sons of Albion; fearing each to lose
Some note of Nature's music from his lips,
And covetous of Shakspeare's beauty, seen
In ev'ry flash of his far-beaming eye.
Nor taste alone and well-contriv'd display
Suffice to give the marshall'd ranks the grace
Of their complete effect. Much yet remains
Unsung, and many cares are yet behind,

And more laborious cares on which depends
Their vigor, injur'd soon, not soon restor'd.
The soil must be renew'd, which often wash'd
Loses its treasure of salubrious salts,
And disappoints the roots; the slender roots
Close interwoven, where they meet the vase
Must smooth be shorn away; the sapless branch
Must fly before the knife; the wither'd leaf
Must be detach'd, and where it strews the floor
Swept with a woman's neatness, breeding else
Contagion, and disseminating death.
Discharge but these kind offices, (and who
Would spare, that loves them, offices like these?
Well they reward the toil. The sight is pleas'd,
The scent regal'd, each odorif'rous leaf,
Each op'ning blossom, freely breathes abroad
Its gratitude, and thanks him with its sweets.
So manifold, all pleasing in their kind,
All healthful, are th'employs of rural life,
Reiterated as the wheel of time
Runs round; still ending, and beginning still.
Nor are these all. To deck the shapely knoll,
That softly swell'd and gaily dress'd appears
A flow'ry island, from the dark green lawn
Emerging, must be deem'd a labor due
To no mean hand, and asks the touch of taste.
Here also grateful mixture of well-match'd
And sorted hues (each giving each relief,
And by contrasted beauty shining more)
Is needful. Strength may wield the pond'rous spade
May turn the clod, and wheel the compost home;
But elegance, chief grace the garden shows,
And most attractive, is the fair result
Of thought, the creature of a polish'd mind.
Without it all is gothic as the scene,
To which th'insipid citizen resorts
Near yonder heath; where Industry mispent,
But proud of his uncouth ill-chosen task,
Has made a heav'n on earth; with suns and moons
Of close-ramm'd stones has charg'd th'encumber'd soil,
And fairly laid the zodiac in the dust.
He, therefore, who would see his flow'rs dispos'd
Sightly and in just order, ere he gives
The beds the trusted treasure of their seeds,
Forecasts the future whole; that when the scene
Shall break into its preconceiv'd display,
Each for itself, and all as with one voice
Conspiring, may attest his bright design.
Nor even then, dismissing as perform'd
His pleasant work, may he suppose it done.

Few self-supported flow'rs endure the wind
Uninjur'd, but expect th'upholding aid
Of the smooth-shaven prop, and, neatly tied,
Are wedded thus, like beauty to old age,
For int'rest sake, the living to the dead.
Some clothe the soil that feeds them, far diffus'd
And lowly creeping, modest and yet fair,
Like virtue, thriving most where little seen:
Some more aspiring catch the neighbour shrub
With clasping tendrils, and invest his branch,
Else unadorn'd, with many a gay festoon
And fragrant chaplet, recompensing well
The strength they borrow with the grace they lend.
All hate the rank society of weeds,
Noisome, and ever greedy to exhaust
Th'impov'rish'd earth; an overbearing race,
That, like the multitude made faction-mad,
Disturb good order, and degrade true worth.
O blest seclusion from a jarring world,
Which he, thus occupied, enjoys! Retreat
Cannot indeed to guilty man restore
Lost innocence, or cancel follies past;
But it has peace, and much secures the mind
From all assaults of evil; proving still
A faithful barrier, not o'erleap'd with ease
By vicious Custom, raging uncontroll'd
Abroad, and desolating public life.
When fierce Temptation, seconded within
By traitor Appetite, and arm'd with darts
Temper'd in hell, invades the throbbing breast,
To combat may be glorious, and success
Perhaps may crown us; but to fly is safe.
Had I the choice of sublunary good,
What could I wish, that I possess not here?
Health, leisure, means t'improve it, friendship, peace,
No loose or wanton, though a wand'ring, muse,
And constant occupation without care.
Thus blest I draw a picture of that bliss
Hopeless, indeed, that dissipated minds,
And profligate abusers of a world
Created fair so much in vain for them,
Should seek the guiltless joys, that I describe,
Allur'd by my report: but sure no less,
That self-condemn'd they must neglect the prize,
And what they will not taste must yet approve.
What we admire we praise; and, when we praise,
Advance it into notice, that, its worth
Acknowledg'd, others may admire it too.
I therefore recommend, though at the risk
Of popular disgust, yet boldly still,

The cause of piety, and sacred truth,
And virtue, and those scenes, which God ordain'd
Should best secure them, and promote them most;
Scenes, that I love, and with regret perceive
Forsaken, or through folly not enjoy'd.
Pure is the nymph, though lib'ral of her smiles
And chaste, though unconfin'd, whom I extol
Not as the prince in Shushan, when he call'd,
Vain glorious of her charms, his Vashti forth,
To grace the full pavilion. His design
Was but to boast his own peculiar good,
Which all might view with envy, none partake.
My charmer is not mine alone; my sweets
And she that sweetens all my bitters too,
Nature, enchanting Nature, in whose form
And lineaments divine I trace a hand,
That errs not, and find raptures still renew'd,
Is free to all men—universal prize.
Strange that so fair a creature should yet want
Admirers, and be destin'd to divide
With meaner objects e'en the few she finds!
Stripp'd of her ornaments, her leaves and flow'rs,
She loses all her influence. Cities then
Attract us, and neglected Nature pines
Abandon'd, as unworthy of our love.
But are not wholesome airs, though unperfum'd
By roses; and clear suns, though scarcely felt;
And groves, if unharmonious, yet secure
From clamor, and whose very silence charms;
To be preferr'd to smoke, to the eclipse,
That metropolitan volcanos make,
Whose Stygian throats breathe darkness all day long;
And to the stir of Commerce, driving slow,
And thund'ring loud, with his ten thousand wheels?
They would be, were not madness in the head,
And folly in the heart; were England now,
What England was, plain, hospitable, kind,
And undebauch'd. But we have bid farewell
To all the virtues of those better days,
And all their honest pleasures. Mansions once
Knew their own masters; and laborious hinds,
Who had surviv'd the father, serv'd the son.
Now the legitimate and rightful lord
Is but a transient guest, newly arriv'd,
As soon to be supplanted. He, that saw
His patrimonial timber cast its leaf,
Sells the last scantling, and transfers the price
To some shrewd sharper, ere it buds again.
Estates are landscapes, gaz'd upon a while,

Then advertis'd, and auctioneer'd away.
The country starves, and they, that feed th'o'ercharg'd
And surfeited lewd town with her fair dues,
By a just judgment strip and starve themselves.
The wings, that waft our riches out of sight,
Grow on the gamester's elbows; and th'alert
And nimble motion of those restless joints,
That never tire, soon fans them all away
Improvement too, the idol of the age,
Is fed with many a victim. Lo, he comes!
Th'omnipotent magician, Brown, appears!
Down falls the venerable pile, th'abode
Of our forefathers—a grave whisker'd race,
But tasteless. Springs a palace in its stead,
But in a distant spot; where more expos'd
It may enjoy th'advantage of the north,
And aguish east, till time shall have transform'd
Those naked acres to a shelt'ring grove.
He speaks. The lake in front becomes a lawn;
Woods vanish, hills subside, and valleys rise;
And streams, as if created for his use,
Pursue the track of his directing wand,
Sinuous or straight, now rapid and now slow,—
Now murm'ring soft, now roaring in cascades—
E'en as he bids! Th'enraptur'd owner smiles.
'Tis finish'd, and yet, finish'd as it seems,
Still wants a grace, the loveliest it could show,
A mine to satisfy th'enormous cost.
Drain'd to the last poor item of his wealth,
He sighs, departs, and leaves th'accomplish'd plan,
That he has touch'd, retouch'd, many a long day
Labor'd, and many a night pursu'd in dreams,
Just when it meets his hopes, and proves the heav'n
He wanted, for a wealthier to enjoy!
And now perhaps the glorious hour is come,
When, having no stake left, no pledge t'endear
Her int'rests, or that gives her sacred cause
A moment's operation on his love,
He burns with most intense and flagrant zeal
To serve his country. Ministerial grace
Deals him out money from the public chest;
Or, if that mine be shut, some private purse
Supplies his need with a usurious loan,
To be refunded duly, when his vote
Well-manag'd shall have earn'd its worthy price.
O innocent, compar'd with arts like these,
Crape, and cock'd pistol, and the whistling ball
Sent through the trav'ller's temples! He, that finds
One drop of Heav'n's sweet mercy in his cup,

Can dig, beg, rot, and perish, well content,
So he may wrap himself in honest rags
At his last gasp; but could not for a world
Fish up his dirty and dependent bread
From pools and ditches of the commonwealth,
Sordid and sick'ning at his own succ ss.
Ambition, av'rice, penury incurr'd
By endless riot, vanity, the lust
Of pleasure and variety, dispatch,
As duly as the swallows disappear,
The world of wand'ring knights and squires to town.
London ingulfs them all! The shark is there,
And the shark's prey; the spendthrift, and the leech
That sucks him: there the sycophant, and he
Who, with bareheaded and obsequious bows,
Begs a warm office, doom'd to a cold jail
And groat per diem, if his patron frown.
The levee swarms, as if in golden pomp
Were character'd on ev'ry statesman's door,
'*Batter'd and bankrupt fortunes mended here.*'
These are the charms, that sully and eclipse
The charms of nature. 'Tis the cruel gripe
That lean, hard-handed Poverty inflicts,
The hope of better things, the chance to win,
The wish to shine, the thirst to be amus'd,
That at the sound of Winter's hoary wing
Unpeople all our counties of such herds
Of flutt'ring, loit'ring, cringing, begging, loose,
And wanton vagrants, as make London, vast
And boundless as it is, a crowded coop.
O thou, resort and mart of all the earth,
Checker'd with all complexions of mankind,
And spotted with all crimes; in whom I see
Much that I love, and more that I admire,
And all that I abhor; thou freckled fair,
That pleasest and yet shock'st me, I can laugh,
And I can weep, can hope, and can despond,
Feel wrath and pity, when I think on thee!
Ten righteous would have sav'd a city once,
And thou hast many righteous.—Well for thee—
That salt preserves thee; more corrupted else,
And therefore more obnoxious, at this hour,
Than Sodom in her day had pow'r to be,
For whom God heard his Abr'ham plead in vain.

THE TASK.

BOOK IV.

THE WINTER EVENING.

ARGUMENT OF THE FOURTH BOOK.

The post comes in.—The newspaper is read.—The world contemplated at a distance.—Address to Winter.—The rural amusements of a winter evening compared with the fashionable ones.—Address to Evening.—A brown study.—Fall of snow in the evening.—The waggoner.—A poor family-piece.—The rural thief.—Public houses.—The multitude of them censured.—The farmer's daughter: what she was—what she is.—The simplicity of country manners almost lost.—Causes of the change. Desertion of the country by the rich.—Neglect of magistrates.—The militia principally in fault.—The new recruit and his transformation.—Reflection on bodies corporate.—The love of rural objects natural to all, and never to be totally extinguished.

Hark! 'tis the twanging horn o'er yonder bridge
That with its wearisome but needful length
Bestrides the wintry flood, in which the moon
Sees her unwrinkled face reflected bright;—
He comes, the herald of a noisy world,
With spatter'd boots, strapp'd waist, and frozen locks;
News from all nations lumb'ring at his back.
True to his charge, the close-pack'd load behind,
Yet careless what he brings, his one concern
Is to conduct it to the destin'd inn;
And, having dropp'd th'expected bag, pass on.
He whistles as he goes, light-hearted wretch,
Cold and yet cheerful: messenger of grief
Perhaps to thousands, and of joy to some;
To him indiff'rent whether grief or joy.
Houses in ashes, and the fall of stocks,
Births, deaths, and marriages, epistles wet
With tears, that trickled down the writer's cheeks
Fast as the periods from his fluent quill,
Or charg'd with am'rous sighs of absent swains,
Or nymphs responsive, equally affect
His horse and him, unconscious of them all.

But O th' important budget! usher'd in
With such heart-shaking music, who can say
What are its tidings? have our troops awak'd?
Or do they still, as if with opium drugg'd,
Snore to the murmurs of th'Atlantic wave?
Is India free? and does she wear her plum'd
And jewell'd turban with a smile of peace,
Or do we grind her still? The grand debate,
The popular harangue, the tart reply,
The logic, and the wisdom, and the wit,
And the loud laugh—I long to know them all;
I burn to set th'imprison'd wranglers free,
And give them voice and utt'rance once again.
   Now stir the fire, and close the shutters fast,
Let fall the curtains, wheel the sofa round,
And, while the bubbling and loud hissing urn
Throws up a steamy column, and the cups,
That cheer but not inebriate, wait on each,
So let us welcome peaceful ev'ning in.
Not such his ev'ning, who with shining face
Sweats in the crowded theatre, and, squeez'd
And bor'd with elbow-points through both his sides,
Outscolds the ranting actor on the stage:
Nor his, who patient stands till his feet throb,
And his head thumps, to feed upon the breath
Of patriots, bursting with heroic rage,
Or placemen, all tranquillity and smiles.
This folio of four pages, happy work!
Which not e'en critics criticise; that holds
Inquisitive Attention, while I read,
Fast bound in chains of silence, which the fair,
Though eloquent themselves, yet fear to break;
What is it, but a map of busy life,
Its fluctuations, and its vast concerns?
Here runs the mountainous and craggy ridge,
That tempts Ambition. On the summit see
The seals of office glitter in his eyes;
He climbs, he pants, he grasps them! At his heels,
Close at his heels, a demagogue ascends,
And with a dext'rous jerk soon twists him down,
And wins them, but to lose them in his turn.
Here rills of oily eloquencce in soft
Meanders lubricate the course they take;
The modest speaker is asham'd and griev'd,
T'engross a moment's notice; and yet begs,
Begs a propitious ear for his poor thoughts,
However trivial all that he conceives.
Sweet bashfulness! it claims at least this praise;
The dearth of information and good sense,

That it foretells us, always comes to pass.
Cat'racts of declamation thunder here;
There forests of no meaning spread the page,
In which all comprehension wanders lost;
While fields of pleasantry amuse us there
With merry descants on a nation's woes.
The rest appears a wilderness of strange
But gay confusion; roses for the cheeks,
And lilies for the brows of faded age,
Teeth for the toothless, ringlets for the bald,
Heav'n, earth, and ocean, plunder'd of their sweets,
Nectareous essences, Olympian dews,
Sermons, and city feasts, and fav'rite airs,
Æthereal journeys, submarine exploits,
And Katerfelto, with his hair on-end
At his own wonders, wond'ring for his bread.
'Tis pleasant, through the loopholes of retreat,
To peep at such a world; to see the stir
Of the great Babel, and not feel the crowd;
To hear the roar she sends through all her gates
At a safe distance, where the dying sound
Falls a soft murmur on th'uninjur'd ear.
Thus sitting, and surveying thus at ease
The globe and its concerns, I seem advanc'd
To some secure and more than mortal height,
That lib'rates and exempts me from them all.
It turns submitted to my view, turns round
With all its generations; I behold
The tumult, and am still. The sound of war
Has lost its terrors ere it reaches me;
Grieves, but alarms me not. I mourn the pride
And av'rice, that make man a wolf to man;
Hear the faint echo of those brazen throats,
By which he speaks the language of his heart,
And sigh, but never tremble at the sound.
He travels and expatiates, as the bee
From flow'r to flow'r, so he from land to land;
The manners, customs, policy, of all
Pay contribution to the store he gleans;
He sucks intelligence in ev'ry clime,
And spreads the honey of his deep research
At his return—a rich repast for me.
He travels, and I too. I tread his deck,
Ascend his topmast, through his peering eyes
Discover countries, with a kindred heart
Suffer his woes, and share in his escapes;
While fancy, like the finger of a clock,
Runs the great circuit, and is still at home.
O Winter, ruler of th'inverted year,

Thy scatter'd hair with sleet like ashes fill'd,
Thy breath congeal'd upon thy lips, thy cheeks
Fring'd with a beard made white with other snows
Than those of age, thy forehead wrapp'd in clouds,
A leafless branch thy sceptre, and thy throne
A sliding car, indebted to no wheels,
But urg'd by storms along its slipp'ry way,
I love thee, all unlovely as thou seem'st
And dreaded as thou art! Thou hold'st the sun
A pris'ner in the yet undawning east,
Short'ning his journey between morn and noon,
And hurrying him, impatient of his stay,
Down to the rosy west; but kindly still
Compensating his loss with added hours
Of social converse and instructive ease,
And gath'ring, at short notice, in one group
The family dispers'd, and fixing thought,
Not less dispers'd by daylight and its cares.
I crown thee king of intimate delights,
Fire-side enjoyments, homeborn happiness,
And all the comforts, that the lowly roof
Of undisturb'd Retirement, and the hours
Of long uninterrupted ev'ning, know.
No rattling wheels stop short before these gates;
No powder'd pert proficient in the art
Of sounding an alarm assaults these doors
Till the street rings; no stationary steeds
Cough their own knell, while, heedless of the sound,
The silent circle fan themselves, and quake:
But here the needle plies its busy task,
The pattern grows, the well-depicted flow'r,
Wrought patiently into the snowy lawn,
Unfolds its bosom; buds, and leaves, and sprigs,
And curling tendrils, gracefully dispos'd,
Follow the nimble finger of the fair;
A wreath, that cannot fade, of flow'rs, that blow
With most success when all besides decay.
The poet's or historian's page by one
Made vocal for th'amusement of the rest;
The sprightly lyre, whose treasure of sweet sounds
The touch from many a trembling chord shakes out;
And the clear voice symphonious, yet distinct,
And in the charming strife triumphant still;
Beguile the night, and set a keener edge
On female industry: the threaded steel
Flies swiftly, and unfelt the task proceeds.
The volume clos'd, the customary rites
Of the last meal commence. A Roman meal;
Such as the mistress of the world once found

Delicious, when her patriots of high note,
Perhaps by moonlight, at their humble doors
And under an old oak's domestic shade,
Enjoy'd, spare feast! a radish and an egg.
Discourse ensues, not trivial, yet not dull,
Nor such as with a frown forbids the play
Of fancy, or proscribes the sound of mirth:
Nor do we madly, like an impious world,
Who deem religion frenzy, and the God
That made them, an intruder on their joys,
Start at his awful name, or deem his praise
A jarring note. Themes of a graver tone,
Exciting oft our gratitude and love,
While we retrace with Mem'ry's pointing wand,
That calls the past to our exact review,
The dangers we have 'scap'd, the broken snare,
The disappointed foe, deliv'rance found
Unlook'd for, life preserv'd, and peace restor'd,
Fruits of omnipotent eternal love.
O ev'nings worthy of the gods! exclaim'd
The Sabine bard. O ev'nings, I reply,
More to be priz'd and coveted than yours,
As more illumin'd, and with nobler truths,
That I, and mine, and those we love, enjoy.
Is Winter hideous in a garb like this?
Needs he the tragic fur, the smoke of lamps,
The pent-up breath of an unsav'ry throng,
To thaw him into feeling; or the smart
And snappish dialogue, that flippant wits
Call comedy, to prompt him with a smile?
The self-complacent actor, when he views
(Stealing a sidelong glance at a full house)
The slope of faces from the floor to th'roof
(As if one master-spring controll'd them all)
Relax'd into a universal grin,
Sees not a count'nance there that speaks of joy
Half so refin'd or so sincere as ours.
Cards were superfluous here, with all the tricks,
That idleness has ever yet contriv'd
To fill the void of an unfurnish'd brain,
To palliate dullness, and give time a shove.
Time, as he passes us, has a dove's wing,
Unsoil'd, and swift, and of a silken sound;
But the world's Time is Time in masquerade!
Theirs, should I paint him, has his pinions fledg'd
With motley plumes; and, where the peacock shows
His azure eyes, is tinctur'd black and red
With spots quadrangular of diamond form,
Ensanguin'd hearts, clubs typical of strife,

And spades, the emblem of untimely graves.
What should be, and what was an hourglass once,
Becomes a dice box, and a billiard-mace
Well does the work of his destructive scythe.
Thus deck'd, he charms a world whom fashion blinds
To his true worth, most pleas'd when idle most;
Whose only happy are their wasted hours.
E'en misses, at whose age their mothers wore
The backstring and the bib, assume the dress
Of womanhood, fit pupils in the school
Of card-devoted Time, and night by night
Plac'd at some vacant corner of the board,
Learn ev'ry trick, and soon play all the game.
But truce with censure. Roving as I rove,
Where shall I find an end, or how proceed?
As he that travels far oft turns aside,
To view some rugged rock or mould'ring tow'r,
Which seen delights him not; then coming home
Describes and prints it, that the world may know
How far he went for what was nothing worth;
So I, with brush in hand, and palette spread,
With colors mix'd for a far diff'rent use,
Paint cards, and dolls, and ev'ry idle thing,
That Fancy finds in her excursive flights.
  Come, Ev'ning, once again, season of peace;
Return, sweet Ev'ning, and continue long!
Methinks I see thee in the streaky west,
With matron step slow moving, while the Night
Treads on thy sweeping train; one hand employ'd
In letting fall the curtain of repose
On bird and beast, the other charg'd for man
With sweet oblivion of the cares of day:
Not sumptuously adorn'd, not needing aid,
Like homely-featur'd Night, of clust'ring gems;
A star or two, just twinkling on thy brow,
Suffices thee; save that the moon is thine
No less than hers, not worn indeed on high
With ostentatious pageantry, but set
With modest grandeur in thy purple zone,
Resplendent less, but of an ampler round.
Come then, and thou shalt find thy vot'ry calm,
Or make me so. Composure is thy gift:
And, whether I devote thy gentle hours
To books, to music, or the poet's toil;
To weaving nets for bird-alluring fruit;
Or twining silken threads round iv'ry reels,
When they command whom man was born to please,
I slight thee not, but make thee welcome still.
  Just when our drawing-rooms begin to blaze

With lights, by clear reflection multiplied
From many a mirror, in which he of Gath,
Goliah, might have seen his giant bulk
Whole without stooping, tow'ring crest and all,
My pleasures too begin. But me perhaps
The glowing heart may satisfy a while
With faint illumination, that uplifts
The shadows to the ceiling, there by fits
Dancing uncouthly to the quiv'ring flame.
Not undelightful is an hour to me
So spent in parlor-twilight: such a gloom
Suits well the thoughtful or unthinking mind,
The mind contemplative, with some new theme
Pregnant, or indispos'd alike to all.
Laugh ye, who boast your more mercurial pow'rs,
That never felt a stupor, know no pause,
Nor need one; I am conscious, and confess
Fearless, a soul that does not always think.
Me oft has Fancy ludicrous and wild
Sooth'd with a waking dream of houses, tow'rs,
Trees, churches, and strange visages, express'd
In the red cinders, while with poring eye
I gaz'd, myself creating what I saw.
Nor less amus'd have I quiescent watch'd
The sooty films that play upon the bars
Pendulous, and foreboding in the view
Of superstition, prophesying still,
Though still deceived, some stranger's near approach
'Tis thus the understanding takes repose
In indolent vacuity of thought,
And sleeps and is refresh'd. Meanwhile the face
Conceals the mood lethargic with a mask
Of deep deliberation, as the man
Were task'd to his full strength, absorb'd and lost.
Thus oft, reclined at ease, I lose an hour
At ev'ning, till at length the freezing blast,
That sweeps the bolted shutter, summons home
The recollected pow'rs; and snapping short
The glassy threads, with which the fancy weaves
Her brittle toils, restores me to myself.
How calm is my recess; and how the frost,
Raging abroad, and the rough wind endear
The silence and the warmth enjoy'd within!
I saw the woods and fields at close of day
A variegated show; the meadows green,
Though faded; and the lands, where lately wav'd
The golden harvest, of a mellow brown,
Upturn'd so lately by the forceful share.
I saw far off the weedy fallows smile

With verdure not unprofitable, graz'd
By flocks, fast feeding, and selecting each
His fav'rite herb ; while all the leafless groves
That skirt th'horizon, wore a sable hue,
Scarce notic'd in the kindred dusk of eve.
To-morrow brings a change, a total change !
Which even now, though silently perform'd,
And slowly, and by most unfelt, the face
Of universal nature undergoes.
Fast falls a fleecy show'r : the downy flakes
Descending, and, with never-ceasing lapse,
Softly alighting upon all below,
Assimilate all objects. Earth receives
Gladly the thick'ning mantle ; and the green
And tender blade, that fear'd the chilling blast,
Escapes unhurt beneath so warm a veil.
In such a world, so thorny, and where none
Finds happiness unblighted, or, if found,
Without some thistly sorrow at its side,
It seems the part of wisdom, and no sin
Against the law of love, to measure lots
With less distinguish'd than ourselves ; that thus
We may with patience bear our mod'rate ills,
And sympathize with others suff'ring more.
Ill fares the trav'ller now, and he that stalks
In pond'rous boots beside his reeking team.
The wain goes heavily, impeded sore
By congregated loads adhering close
To the clogg'd wheels ; and in its sluggish pace
Noiseless appears a moving hill of snow.
The toiling steeds expand the nostril wide,
While ev'ry breath, by respiration strong
Forc'd downward, is consolidated soon
Upon their jutting chests. He, form'd to bear
The pelting brunt of the tempestuous night,
With half-shut eyes, and pucker'd cheeks, and teeth
Presented bare against the storm, plods on.
One hand secures his hat, save when with both
He brandishes his pliant length of whip,
Resounding oft, and never heard in vain.
O happy ; and in my account denied
That sensibility of pain, with which
Refinement is endued, thrice happy thou !
Thy frame, robust and hardy, feels indeed
The piercing cold, but feels it unimpair'd.
The learn'd finger never need explore
Thy vig'rous pulse ; and the unhealthful east
That breathes the spleen, and searches ev'ry bone
Of the infirm, is wholesome air to thee.

Thy days roll on exempt from household care;
Thy waggon is thy wife; and the poor beasts,
That drag the dull companion to and fro,
Thine helpless charge, dependent on thy care.
Ah! treat them kindly; rude as thou appear'st,
Yet show that thou hast mercy! which the great,
With needless hurry whirl'd from place to place,
Humane as they would seem, not always show.
  Poor, yet industrious, modest, quiet, neat,
Such claim compassion in a night like this,
And have a friend in ev'ry feeling heart.
Warm'd while it lasts, by labor, all day long
They brave the season, and yet find at eve,
Ill clad and fed but sparely, time to cool.
The frugal housewife trembles when she lights
Her scanty stock of brushwood, blazing clear,
But dying soon, like all terrestrial joys.
The few small embers left she nurses well;
And, while her infant race, with outspread hands,
And crowded knees, sit cow'ring o'er the sparks,
Retires, content to quake, so they be warm'd.
The man feels least, as more inur'd than she
To winter, and the current in his veins
More briskly mov'd by his severer toil;
Yet he too finds his own distress in theirs.
The taper soon extinguish'd, which I saw
Dangled along at the cold finger's end,
Just when the day declin'd; and the brown loaf
Lodg'd on the shelf, half eaten without sauce
Of sav'ry cheese, or butter, costlier still;
Sleep seems their only refuge: for, alas!
Where penury is felt the thought is chain'd,
And sweet colloquial pleasures are but few.
With all this thrift they thrive not. All the care
Ingenious Parsimony takes, but just
Saves the small inventory, bed, and stool,
Skillet, and old carv'd chest, from public sale.
They live, and live without extorted alms
From grudging hands; but other boast have none,
To soothe their honest pride, that scorns to beg,
Nor comfort else, but in their mutual love.
I praise you much, ye meek and patient pair,
For ye are worthy; choosing rather far
A dry but independent crust, hard earn'd,
And eaten with a sigh, than to endure
The rugged frowns, and insolent rebuffs
Of knaves in office, partial in the work
Of distribution: lib'ral of their aid
To clam'rous Importunity in rags,

But ofttimes deaf to suppliants, who would blush
To wear a tattered garb however coarse,
Whom famine cannot reconcile to filth:
These ask with painful shyness, and refus'd
Because deserving, silently retire!
But be ye of good courage! Time itself
Shall much befriend you. Time shall give increase;
And all your num'rous progeny, well-train'd
But helpless, in few years shall find their hands,
And labour too. Meanwhile ye shall not want
What, conscious of your virtues, we can spare,
Nor what a wealthier than ourselves may send.
I mean the man, who, when the distant poor
Need help, denies them nothing but his name.
But poverty with most, who whimper forth
Their long complaints, is self-inflicted woe;
The effect of laziness or sottish waste.
Now goes the nightly thief prowling abroad
For plunder; much solicitous how best
He may compensate for a day of sloth
By works of darkness and nocturnal wrong.
Woe to the gard'ner's pale, the farmer's hedge,
Plash'd neatly, and secur'd with driven stakes
Deep in the loamy bank. Uptorn by strength,
Resistless in so bad a cause, but lame
To better deeds, he bundles up the spoil,
An ass's burthen, and when laden most
And heaviest, light of foot steals fast away.
Nor does the boarded hovel better guard
The well-stack'd pile of riven logs and roots
From his pernicious force. Nor will he leave
Unwrench'd the door, however well secur'd,
Where chanticleer amidst his harem sleeps
In unsuspecting pomp. 'Twitch'd from the perch,
He gives the princely bird, with all his wives,
To his voracious bag, struggling in vain,
And loudly wond'ring at the sudden change.
Nor this to feed his own. 'Twere some excuse,
Did pity of their suff'rings warp aside
His principle, and tempt him into sin
For their support, so destitute. But they
Neglected pine at home; themselves, as more
Expos'd than others, with less scruple made
His victims, robb'd of their defenceless all.
Cruel is all he does. 'Tis quenchless thirst
Of ruinous ebriety, that prompts
His ev'ry action, and imbrutes the man.
O for a law to noose the villain's neck,
Who starves his own; who persecutes the blood

He gave them in his children's veins, and hates
And wrongs the woman he has sworn to love!
  Pass where we may, through city or through town,
Village, or hamlet, of this merry land,
Though lean and beggard, ev'ry twentieth pace
Conducts th'unguarded nose to such a whiff
Of stale debauch, forth issuing from the styes
That Law has licens'd, as makes Temp'rance reel.
There sit, involv'd and lost in curling clouds
Of Indian fume, and guzzling deep, the boor,
The lackey, and the groom: The craftsman there
Takes a Lethean leave of all his toil;
Smith, cobbler, joiner, he that plies the shears,
And he that kneads the dough; all loud alike,
All learned, and all drunk! the fiddle screams
Plaintive and piteous, as it wept and wail'd
Its wasted tones and harmony unheard:
Fierce the dispute whate'er the theme; while she,
Fell Discord, arbitress of such debate,
Perch'd on the signpost, holds with even hand
Her undecisive scales. In this she lays
A weight of ignorance; in that, of pride;
And smiles delighted with th'eternal poise.
Dire is the frequent curse, and its twin sound,
The cheek-distending oath, not to be prais'd
As ornamental, musical, polite,
Like those, which modern senators employ,
Whose oath is rhet'ric, and who swear for fame!
Behold the schools in which plebeian minds
Once simple are initiated in arts,
Which some may practice with politer grace,
But none with readier skill!—'tis here they learn
The road, that leads from competence and peace
To indigence and rapine; till at last
Society, grown weary of the load,
Shakes her encumber'd lap, and casts them out.
But censure profits little: vain th'attempt
To advertise in verse a public pest,
That, like the filth with which the peasant feeds
His hungry acres, stinks, and is of use.
Th'excise is fatten'd with the rich result
Of all this riot; and ten thousand casks,
For ever dribbling out their base contents,
Touch'd by the Midas finger of the state,
Bleed gold for ministers to sport away.
Drink, and be mad then; 'tis your country bids!
Gloriously drunk obey th' important call!
Her cause demands th'assistance of your throats;—
Ye all can swallow, and she asks no more.

Would I had fall'n upon those happier days,
That poets celebrate; those golden times,
And those Arcadian scenes that Maro sings,
And Sidney, warbler of poetic prose.
Nymphs were Dianas then, and swains had hearts,
That felt their virtues: Innocence, it seems,
From courts dismiss'd, found shelter in the groves;
The footsteps of Simplicity, impress'd
Upon the yielding herbage, (so they sing)
Then were not all effac'd: then speech profane,
And manners profligate, were rarely found,
Observ'd as prodigies, and soon reclaim'd.
Vain wish! those days were never: airy dreams
Sat for the picture: and the poet's hand,
Imparting substance to an empty shade,
Impos'd a gay delirium for a truth.
Grant it: I still must envy them an age,
That favor'd such a dream; in days like these
Impossible, when Virtue is so scarce,
That to suppose a scene where she presides,
Is tramontane, and stumbles all belief.
No: we are polish'd now. The rural lass
Whom once her virgin modesty and grace,
Her artless manners, and her neat attire,
So dignified, that she was hardly less
Than the fair shepherdess of old romance,
Is seen no more. The character is lost!
Her head, adorn'd with lappets pinn'd aloft,
And ribands streaming gay, superbly rais'd,
And magnified beyond all human size,
Indebted to some smart wig-weaver's hand
For more than half the tresses it sustains;
Her elbows ruffled, and her tott'ring form
Ill-propp'd upon French heels; she might be deem'd
(But that the basket dangling on her arm
Interprets her more truly) of a rank
Too proud for dairy-work, or sale of eggs.
Expect her soon with footboy at her heels,
No longer blushing for her awkward load,
Her train and her umbrella all her care!
The town has ting'd the country; and the stain
Appears a spot upon a vestal's robe,
The worse for what it soils. The fashion runs
Down into scenes still rural; but, alas,
Scenes rarely grac'd with rural manners now!
Time was when in the pastoral retreat
Th'unguarded door was safe; men did not watch
T'invade another's right, or guard their own.
Then sleep was undisturb'd by fear, unscar'd

By drunken howlings; and the chilling tale
Of midnight murder was a wonder heard
With doubtful credit, told to frighten babes.
But farewell now to unsuspicious nights,
And slumbers unalarm'd! Now, ere you sleep,
See that your polish'd arms be prim'd with care,
And drop the night-bolt; ruffians are abroad;
And the first larum of the cock's shrill throat
May prove a trumpet, summoning your ear,
To horrid sounds of hostile feet within.
E'en daylight has its dangers; and the walk
Through pathless wastes and woods, unconscious once
Of other tenants than melodious birds,
Or harmless flocks, is hazardous and bold.
Lamented change! to which full many a cause
Invet'rate, hopeless of a cure, conspires.
The course of human things from good to ill,
From ill to worse, is fatal, never fails.
Increase of pow'r begets increase of wealth;
Wealth luxury, and luxury excess;
Excess the scrofulous and itchy plague,
That seizes first the opulent, descends
To the next rank contagious, and in time
Taints downward all the graduated scale
Of order, from the chariot to the plough.
The rich, and they that have an arm to check
The licence of the lowest in degree,
Desert their office; and themselves, intent
On pleasure, haunt the capital, and thus
To all the violence of lawless hands
Resign the scenes their presence might protect.
Authority herself not seldom sleeps,
Though resident, and witness of the wrong.
The plump convivial parson often bears
The magisterial sword in vain, and lays
His rev'rence and his worship both to rest
On the same cushion of habitual sloth.
Perhaps timidity restrains his arm;
When he should strike he trembles, and sets free,
Himself enslav'd by terror of the band,
Th' audacious convict whom he dares not bind.
Perhaps, though by profession ghostly pure,
He too may have his vice, and sometimes prove
Less dainty than becomes his grave outside
In lucrative concerns. Examine well
His milk white hand; the palm is hardly clean—
But here and there an ugly smutch appears.
Foh! 'twas a bribe that left it: he has touch'd
Corruption. Whoso seeks an audit here

Propitious, pays his tribute, game or fish,
Wild fowl or ven'son; and his errand speeds.
But faster far, and more than all the rest,
A noble cause, which none, who bears a spark
Of public virtue, ever wish'd remov'd,
Works the deplor'd and mischievous effect.
'T is universal soldiership has stabb'd
The heart of merit in the meaner class.
Arms, through the vanity and brainless rage
Of those that bear them, in whatever cause,
Seem most at variance with all moral good,
And incompatible with serious thought.
The clown, the child of nature, without guile,
Blest with an infant's ignorance of all
But his own simple pleasures; now and then
A wrestling match, a foot-race, or a fair;
Is ballotted, and trembles at the news:
Sheepish he doffs his hat, and mumbling swears
A bible oath to be whate'er they please,
To do he knows not what. The task perform'd,
That instant he becomes the sergeant's care,
His pupil, and his torment and his jest.
His awkward gait, his introverted toes,
Bent knees, round shoulders, and dejected looks,
Procure him many a curse. By slow degrees,
Unapt to learn, and form'd of stubborn stuff,
He yet by slow degrees puts off himself,
Grows conscious of a change, and likes it well:
He stands erect; his slouch becomes a walk;
He steps right onward, martial in his air,
His form, and movement; is as smart above
As meal and larded locks can make him; wears
His hat, or his plum'd helmet, with a grace;
And, his three years of heroship expir'd,
Returns indignant to the slighted plough.
He hates the field, in which no fife or drum
Attends him; drives his cattle to a march;
And sighs for the smart comrades he has left,
'Twere well if his exterior change were all—
But with his clumsy port the wretch has lost
His ignorance and harmless manners too
To swear, to game, to drink; to show at home
By lewdness, idleness, and sabbath-breach,
The great proficiency he made abroad;
T'astonish and to grieve his gazing friends,
To break some maiden's and his mother's heart;
To be a pest where he was useful once;
Are his sole aim, and all his glory, now.
Man in society is like a flow'r

Blown in its native bed; 'tis there alone
His faculties, expanded in full bloom,
Shine out; there only reach their proper use.
But man, associated and leagu'd with man
By regal warrant, or self-join'd by bond
For int'rest-sake, or swarming into clans
Beneath one head, for purposes of war,
Like flow'rs selected from the rest, and bound
And bundled close to fill some crowded vase,
Fades rapidly, and, by compression marr'd,
Contracts defilement not to be endur'd.
Hence charter'd boroughs are such public plagues;
And burghers, men immaculate perhaps
In all their private functions, once combin'd,
Become a loathsome body, only fit
For dissolution, hurtful to the main.
Hence merchants, unimpeachable of sin
Against the charities of domestic life,
Incorporated, seem at once to lose
Their nature; and, disclaiming all regard
For mercy and the common rights of man,
Build factories with blood, conducting trade
At the sword's point, and dyeing the white robe
Of innocent commercial Justice red.
Hence too the field of glory, as the world
Misdeems it, dazzled by its bright array,
With all its majesty of thund'ring pomp,
Enchanting music and immortal wreaths,
Is but a school, where thoughtlessness is taught
On principle, where foppery atones
For folly, gallantry for ev'ry vice.
But slighted as it is, and by the great
Abandon'd, and, which still I more regret,
Infected with the manners and the modes
It knew not once, the country wins me still.
I never fram'd a wish, or form'd a plan,
That flatter'd me with hopes of earthly bliss,
But there I laid the scene. There early stray'd
My fancy, ere yet liberty of choice
Had found me, or the hope of being free.
My very dreams were rural; rural too
The first-born efforts of my youthful muse,
Sportive and jingling her poetic bells,
Ere yet her ear was mistress of their pow'rs.
No bard could please me but whose lyre was tun'd
To Nature's praises. Heroes and their feats
Fatigu'd me, never weary of the pipe
Of Tityrus, assembling, as he sang,
The rustic throng beneath his fav'rite beech.

Then Milton had indeed a poet's charms:
New to my taste his Paradise surpass'd
The struggling efforts of my boyish tongue,
To speak its excellence. I danc'd for joy.
I marvell'd much, that, at so ripe an age
As twice seven years, his beauties had then first
Engag'd my wonder; and admiring still,
And still admiring, with regret suppos'd
The joy half lost, because not sooner found.
There too enamor'd of the life I lov'd,
Pathetic in its praise, in its pursuit
Determin'd, and possessing it at last
With transports, such as favor'd lovers feel,
I studied, priz'd, and wish'd that I had known
Ingenious Cowley! and, though now reclaim'd
By modern lights from an erroneous taste,
I cannot but lament thy splendid wit
Entangled in the cobwebs of the schools.
I still revere thee, courtly though retir'd!
Though stretch'd at ease in Chertsey's silent bow'rs.
Not unemploy'd; and finding rich amends
For a lost world in solitude and verse.
'Tis born with all: the love of Nature's works
Is an ingredient in the compound man
Infus'd at the creation of the kind.
And, though th'Almighty Maker has throughout
Discriminated each from each, by strokes
And touches of his hand, with so much art
Diversified, that two were never found
Twins at all points—yet this obtains in all,
That all discern a beauty in his works,
And all can taste them: minds, that have been form'd
And tutor'd, with a relish more exact,
But none without some relish, none unmov'd.
It is a flame, that dies not even there,
Where nothing feeds it: neither business, crowds,
Nor habits of luxurious city-life,
Whatever else they smother of true worth
In human bosoms, quench it or abate.
The villas with which London stands begirt,
Like a swarth Indian, with his belt of beads,
Prove it. A breath of unadult'rate air,
The glimpse of a green pasture, how they cheer
The citizen, and brace his languid frame!
E'en in the stifling bosom of the town
A garden, in which nothing thrives, has charms,
That soothe the rich possessor; much consol'd,
That here and there some sprigs of mournful mint,
Of nightshade, or valerian, grace the well

He cultivates. These serve him with a hint,
That Nature lives; that sight-refreshing green
Is still the liv'ry she delights to wear,
Though sickly samples of th'exub'rant whole.
What are the casements lin'd with creeping herbs,
The prouder sashes fronted with a range
Of orange, myrtle, or the fragrant weed,
The Frenchman's darling? are they not all proofs,
That man, immur'd in cities, still retains
His inborn inextinguishable thirst
Of rural scenes, compensating his loss
By supplemental shifts, the best he may?
The most unfurnish'd with the means of life,
And they, that never pass their brick-wall bounds,
To range the fields, and treat their lungs with air,
Yet feel the burning instinct: over head
Suspend their crazy boxes, planted thick
And water'd duly. There the pitcher stands
A fragment, and the spoutless tea-pot there;
Sad witnesses how close-pent man regrets
The country, with what ardor he contrives
A peep at Nature, when he can no more.
Hail, therefore, patroness of health and ease,
And contemplation, heart-consoling joys,
And harmless pleasures, in the throng'd abode
Of multitudes unknown; hail, rural life!
Address himself who will to the pursuit
Of honors, or emolument, or fame;
I shall not add myself to such a chase,
Thwart his attempts, or envy his success.
Some must be great. Great offices will have
Great talents. And God gives to ev'ry man
The virtue, temper, understanding, taste,
That lifts him into life, and lets him fall
Just in the niche he was ordain'd to fill.
To the deliv'rer of an injur'd land
He gives a tongue t' enlarge upon, a heart
To feel, and courage to redress her wrongs;
To monarchs dignity; to judges sense;
To artists ingenuity and skill;
To me, an unambitious mind, content
In the low vale of life, that early felt
A wish for ease and leisure, and ere long
Found here that leisure, and that ease I wish'd.

* Mignonnette.

THE TASK.

BOOK V.

THE WINTER MORNING WALK.

ARGUMENT OF THE FIFTH BOOK.

A frosty morning.—The foddering of cattle.—The woodman and his dog.—The poultry.—Whimsical effects of frost at a waterfall.—The Empress of Russia's palace of ice.—Amusements of monarchs.—War, one of them.—Wars, whence;—And whence monarchy.—The evils of it.—English and French loyalty contrasted.—The Bastile, and a prisoner there.—Liberty the chief recommendation of this country.—Modern patriotism questionable, and why.—The perishable nature of the best human institutions.—Spiritual liberty not perishable.—The slavish state of man by nature.—Deliver him, Deist, if you can.—Grace must do it.—The respective merits of patriots and martyrs stated.—Their different treatment.—Happy freedom of the man whom grace makes free.—His relish of the works of God.—Address to the Creator.

'T is morning; and the sun, with ruddy orb
Ascending, fires th' horison; while the clouds,
That crowd away before the driving wind,
More ardent as the disk emerges more,
Resemble most some city in a blaze,
Seen through the leafless wood. His slanting ray
Slides ineffectual down the snowy vale,
And, tingeing all with his own rosy hue,
From ev'ry herb and ev'ry spiry blade
Stretches a length of shadow o'er the field.
Mine, spindling into longitude immense,
In spite of gravity, and sage remark
That I myself am but a fleeting shade,
Provokes me to a smile. With eye askance
I view the muscular proportion'd limb
Transform'd to a lean shank. The shapeless pair,
As they design'd to mock me, at my side
Take step for step; and, as I near approach
The cottage, walk along the plaster'd wall,
Prepost'rous sight! the legs without the man.

The verdure of the plain lies buried deep
Beneath the dazzling deluge; and the bents,
And coarser grass, upspearing o'er the rest,
Of late unsightly and unseen, now shine
Conspicuous, and in bright apparel clad,
And, fledg'd with icy feathers, nod superb.
The cattle mourn in corners, where the fence
Screens them, and seem half petrified to sleep
In unrecumbent sadness. There they wait
Their wonted fodder; not like hung'ring man,
Fretful if unsupplied; but silent, meek,
And patient of the slow-pac'd swain's delay.
He from the stack carves out th' accustom'd load,
Deep-plunging, and again deep-plunging oft,
His broad keen knife into the solid mass:
Smooth as a wall the upright remnant stands,
With such undeviating and even force
He severs it away: no needless care,
Lest storms should overset the leaning pile
Deciduous, or its own unbalanc'd weight.
Forth goes the woodman, leaving unconcern'd
The cheerful haunts of man; to wield the axe,
And drive the wedge, in yonder forest drear,
From morn to eve his solitary task.
Shaggy, and lean, and shrewd, with pointed ears
And tail cropp'd short, half lurcher and half cur,
His dog attends him. Close behind his heel
Now creeps he slow; and now, with many a frisk
Wide-scamp'ring, snatches up the drifted snow
With iv'ry teeth, or ploughs it with his snout;
Then shakes his powder'd coat, and barks for joy.
Heedless of all his pranks, the sturdy churl
Moves right toward the mark; nor stops for aught,
But now and then with pressure of his thumb
T' adjust the fragrant charge of a short tube,
That fumes beneath his nose: the trailing cloud
Streams far behind him, scenting all the air.
Now from the roost, or from the neighb'ring pale,
Where, diligent to catch the first faint gleam
Of smiling day, they gossip'd side by side,
Come trooping at the housewife's well-known call
The feather'd tribes domestic. Half on wing,
And half on foot, they brush the fleecy flood,
Conscious and fearful of too deep a plunge.
The sparrows peep, and quit the shelt'ring eaves,
To seize the fair occasion; well they eye
The scatter'd grain, and thievishly resolv'd
T' escape th' impending famine, often scar'd
As oft return, a pert voracious kind.

Clean riddance quickly made, one only care
Remains to each, the search of sunny nook,
Or shed impervious to the blast. Resign'd
To sad necessity, the cock forgoes
His wonted strut; and, wading at their head
With well consider'd steps, seems to resent
His alter'd gait and stateliness retrench'd.
How find the myriads, that in summer cheer
The hills and valleys with their ceaseless songs,
Due sustenance, or where subsist they now?
Earth yields them nought; th' imprison'd worm is safe
Beneath the frozen clod; all seeds of herbs
Lie cover'd close; and berry-bearing thorns,
That feed the thrush, (whatever some suppose)
Afford the smaller minstrels no supply.
The long protracted rigor of the year
Thins all their num'rous flocks. In chinks and holes
Ten thousand seek an unmolested end,
As instinct prompts; self-buried ere they die.
The very rooks and daws forsake the fields,
Where neither grub, nor root, nor earth-nut, now
Repays their labor more; and perch'd aloft
By the wayside, or stalking in the path,
Lean pensioners upon the trav'llers track,
Pick up their nauseous dole, though sweet to them,
Of voided pulse or half-digested grain.
The streams are lost amid the splendid blank,
O'erwhelming all distinction. On the flood,
Indurated and fix'd, the snowy weight
Lies undissolv'd; while silently beneath,
And unperceiv'd, the current steals away.
Not so where, scornful of a check, it leaps
The milldam, dashes on the restless wheel,
And wantons in the pebbly gulf below:
No frost can bind it there; its utmost force
Can but arrest the light and smoky mist,
That in its fall the liquid sheet throws wide.
And see where it has hung th' embroider'd banks
With forms so various, that no pow'rs of art,
The pencil or the pen, may trace the scene!
Here glitt'ring turrets rise, upbearing high
(Fantastic misarrangements!) on the roof
Large growth of what may seem the sparkling trees
And shrubs of fairy land. The crystal drops,
That trickle down the branches, fast congeal'd,
Shoot into pillars of pellucid length,
And prop the pile they but adorn'd before.
Here grotto within grotto safe defies
The sunbeam; there, emboss'd and fretted wild,

The growing wonder takes a thousand shapes
Capricious, in which fancy seeks in vain
The likeness of some object seen before.
Thus Nature works as if to mock at Art,
And in defiance of her rival pow'rs;
By these fortuitous and random strokes
Performing such inimitable feats,
As she with all her rules can never reach.
Less worthy of applause, though more admir'd,
Because a novelty, the work of man,
Imperial mistress of the fur-clad Russ,
Thy most magnificent and mighty freak,
The wonder of the North. No forest fell,
When thou would'st build; no quarry sent its stores
T' enrich thy walls: but thou didst hew the floods,
And make thy marble of the glassy wave.
In such a palace Aristæus found
Cyrene, when he bore the plaintive tale
Of his lost bees to her maternal ear:
In such a palace Poetry might place
The armory of Winter; where his troops,
The gloomy clouds, find weapons, arrowy sleet,
Skin-piercing volley, blossom-bruising hail,
And snow, that often blinds the trav'llers course,
And wraps him in an unexpected tomb.
Silently as a dream the fabric rose;
No sound of hammer or of saw was there:
Ice upon ice, the well-adjusted parts
Were soon conjoined, nor other cement ask'd
Than water interfus'd to make them one.
Lamps gracefully dispos'd, and of all hues,
Illumin'd ev'ry side: a wat'ry light
Gleam'd through the clear transparency, that seem'd
Another moon new-risen, or meteor fall'n
From Heav'n to Earth, of lambent flame serene.
So stood the brittle prodigy; though smooth
And slipp'ry the materials, yet frostbound
Firm as a rock. Nor wanted aught within,
Their royal residence might well befit,
For grandeur or for use. Long wavy wreaths
Of flow'rs, that fear'd no enemy but warmth,
Blush'd on the panels. Mirror needed none
Where all was vitreous; but in order due
Convivial table and commodious seat
(What seem'd at least commodious seat) were there;
Sofa, and couch, and high-built throne august.
The same lubricity was found in all,
And all was moist to the warm touch; a scene
Of evanescent glory, once a stream,

And soon to slide into a stream again.
Alas! 't was but a mortifying stroke
Of undesign'd severity, that glanc'd
(Made by a monarch) on her own estate,
On human grandeur and the courts of kings.
'T was transient in its nature, as in show
'T was durable ; as worthless, as it seem'd
Intrinsically precious ; to the foot
Treach'rous and false ; it smil'd, and it was cold.
Great princes have great playthings. Some have play'd
At hewing mountains into men, and some
At building human wonders mountain-high.
Some have amus'd the dull, sad years of life,
(Life spent in indolence, and therefore sad)
With schemes of monumental fame ; and sought
By pyramids and mausolean pomp,
Short-liv'd themselves, t' immortalize their bones.
Some seek diversion in the tented field,
And make the sorrows of mankind their sport.
But war's a game, which, were their subjects wise,
Kings would not play at. Nations would do well
T' extort their truncheons from the puny hands
Of heroes, whose infirm and baby minds
Are gratified with mischief ; and who spoil,
Because men suffer it, their toy the World.
When Babel was confounded, and the great
Confed'racy of projectors wild and vain
Was split into diversity of tongues,
Then, as a shepherd separates his flock,
These to the upland, to the valley those,
God drave asunder, and assign'd their lot
To all the nations. Ample was the boon
He gave them, in its distribution fair
And equal ; and he bade them dwell in peace.
Peace was a while their care ; they plough'd and sow'd,
And reap'd their plenty without grudge or strife.
But violence can never longer sleep,
Than human passions please. In ev'ry heart
Are sown the sparks, that kindle fiery war ;
Occasion needs but fan them, and they blaze.
Cain had already shed a brother's blood :
The deluge wash'd it out ; but left unquench'd
The seeds of murder in the breast of man.
Soon by a righteous judgment in the line
Of his descending progeny was found
The first artificer of death ; the shrewd
Contriver, who first sweated at the forge,
And forc'd the blunt and yet unbloodied steel
To a keen edge, and made it bright for war.

Him, Tubal nam'd, the Vulcan of old times,
The sword and falchion their inventor claim;
And the first smith was the first murd'rer's son.
His art surviv'd the waters; and ere long,
When man was multiplied and spread abroad
In tribes and clans, and had begun to call
These meadows and that range of hills his own,
The tasted sweets of property begat
Desire of more, and industry in some,
T' improve and cultivate their just demesne,
Made others covet what they saw so fair.
Thus war began on earth: these fought for spoil,
And those in self-defence. Savage at first
The onset, and irregular. At length
One eminent above the rest for strength,
For stratagem, for courage, or for all,
Was chos'n leader; him they serv'd in war,
And him in peace, for sake of warlike deeds
Reverenc'd no less. Who could with him compare?
Or who so worthy to control themselves,
As he, whose prowess had subdu'd their foes?
Thus war, affording field for the display
Of virtue, made one chief, whom times of peace,
Which have their exigencies too, and call
For skill in government, at length made king.
King was a name too proud for man to wear
With modesty and meekness; and the crown,
So dazzling in their eyes, who set it on,
Was sure t' intoxicate the brows it bound.
It is the abject property of most,
That, being parcel of the common mass,
And destitute of means to raise themselves,
They sink, and settle lower than they need.
They know not what it is to feel within
A comprehensive faculty, that grasps
Great purposes with ease, that turns and wields,
Almost without an effort, plans too vast
For their conception, which they cannot move
Conscious of impotence they soon grow drunk
With gazing, when they see an able man
Step forth to notice: and, besotted thus,
Build him a pedestal, and say, 'Stand there,
And be our admiration and our praise.'
They roll themselves before him in the dust,
Then most deserving in their own account,
When most extravagant in his applause,
As if exalting him they rais'd themselves.
Thus by degrees, self-cheated of their sound
And sober judgment, that he is but man,

They demideify and fume him so,
That in due season he forgets it too.
Inflated and astrut with self-conceit,
He gulps the windy diet; and ere long,
Adopting their mistake, profoundly thinks
The World was made in vain, if not for him.
Thenceforth they are his cattle: drudges, born
To bear his burthens, drawing in his gears,
And sweating in his service, his caprice
Becomes the soul, that animates them all.
He deems a thousand, or ten thousand lives,
Spent in the purchase of renown for him,
An easy reck'ning; and they think the same.
Thus kings were first invented and thus kings
Were burnish'd into heroes, and became
The arbiters of this terraqueous swamp;
Storks among frogs, that have but croak'd and died.
Strange, that such folly, as lifts bloated man
To eminence fit only for a god,
Should ever drivel out of human lips,
E'en in the cradled weakness of the World!
Still stranger much, that when at length mankind
Had reach'd the sinewy firmness of their youth,
And could discriminate and argue well
On subjects more mysterious, they were yet
Babes in the cause of freedom, and should fear
And quake before the gods themselves had made:
But above measure strange, that neither proof
Of sad experience, nor examples set
By some, whose patriot virtue has prevail'd,
Can even now, when they are grown mature
In wisdom, and with philosophic deeds
Familiar, serve t'emancipate the rest!
Such dupes are men to custom, and so prone
To rev'rence what is ancient, and can plead
A course of long observance for its use,
That even servitude, the worst of ills,
Because deliver'd down from sire to son,
Is kept and guarded as a sacred thing.
But is it fit, or can it bear the shock
Of rational discussion, that a man,
Compounded and made up like other men
Of elements tumultuous, in whom lust
And folly in as ample measure meet,
As in the bosoms of the slaves he rules,
Should be a despot absolute, and boast
Himself the only freeman of his land?
Should, when he pleases, and on whom he will,
Wage war, with any or with no pretence

Of provocation giv'n, or wrong sustain'd,
And force the beggarly last doit by means,
That his own humor dictates, from the clutch
Of Poverty, that thus he may procure
His thousands, weary of penurious life
A splendid opportunity to die?
Say ye, who (with less prudence than of old
Jotham ascrib'd to his assembled trees
In politic convention) put your trust
I'th'shadow of a bramble, and reclin'd
In fancied peace beneath his dang'rous branch,
Rejoice in him, and celebrate his sway,
Where find ye passive fortitude? Whence springs
Your self-denying zeal, that holds it good,
To stroke the prickly grievance, and to hang
His thorns with streamers of continual praise?
We too are friends to loyalty. We love
The king, who loves the law, respects his bounds,
And reigns content within them: him we serve
Freely and with delight, who leaves us free:
But recollecting still, that he is man,
We trust him not too far. King though he be,
And king in England too, he may be weak,
And vain enough to be ambitious still;
May exercise amiss his proper pow'rs,
Or covet more than freemen choose to grant:
Beyond that mark is treason. He is ours,
'administer, to guard, t'adorn, the state,
But not to warp or change it. We are his,
To serve him nobly in the common cause,
True to the death, but not to be his slaves.
Mark now the diff'rence, ye that boast your love
Of kings, between your loyalty and ours.
We love the man, the paltry pageant you:
We the chief patron of the commonwealth,
You the regardless author of its woes:
We for the sake of liberty a king,
You chains and bondage for a tyrant's sake.
Our love is principle, and has its root
In reason, is judicious, manly, free;
Yours, a blind instinct, crouches to the rod,
And licks the foot that treads it in the dust.
Were kingship as true treasure as it seems,
Sterling, and worthy of a wise man's wish,
I would not be a king to be belov'd
Causeless, and daub'd with undiscerning praise
Where love is mere attachment to the throne,
Not to the man, who fills it as he ought.
Whose freedom is by suff'rance, and at will

Of a superior, he is never free.
Who lives, and is not weary of a life
Expos'd to manacles, deserves them well.
The state, that strives for liberty, though foil'd,
And forc'd to abandon what she bravely sought,
Deserves at least applause for her attempt,
And pity for her loss. But that's a cause
Not often unsuccessful: pow'r usurp'd
Is weakness when oppos'd; conscious of wrong,
'Tis pusillanimous and prone to flight.
But slaves, that once conceive the glowing thought
Of freedom, in that hope itself possess
All that the contest calls for; spirit, strength,
The scorn of danger, and united hearts;
The surest presage of the good they seek.*
Then shame to manhood, and opprobrious more
To France than all her losses and defeats,
Old or of later date, by sea or land,
Her house of bondage, worse than that of old
Which God aveng'd on Pharaoh—the Bastile.
Ye horrid tow'rs, th'abode of broken hearts
Ye dungeons and ye cages of despair,
That monarchs have supplied from age to age
With music, such as suits their sov'reign ears,
The sighs and groans of miserable men!
There's not an English heart that would not leap
To hear that ye were fall'n at last; to know
That e'en our enemies, so oft employ'd
In forging chains for us, themselves were free.
For he, who values Liberty, confines
His zeal for her predominance within
No narrow bounds; her cause engages him
Wherever pleaded. 'Tis the cause of man.
There dwell the most forlorn of humankind,
Immur'd though unaccus'd, condemn'd untried,
Cruelly spar'd, and hopeless of escape.
There, like the visionary emblem seen
By him of Babylon, life stands a stump,
And, filletted about with hoops of brass,
Still lives, though all his pleasant boughs are gone.
To count the hour-bell and expect no change;
And ever, as the sullen sound is heard,
Still to reflect, that, though a joyless note
To him, whose moments all have one dull pace,
Ten thousand rovers in the world at large

* The author hopes, that he shall not be censured for unnecessary warmth upon so interesting a subject. He is aware, that it is become almost fashionable to stigmatize such sentiments as no better than empty declamation; but it is an ill symptom, and peculiar to modern times.

Account it music; that it summons some
To theatre, or jocund feast, or ball;
The wearied hireling finds it a release
From labor; and the lover, who has chid
Its long delay, feels ev'ry welcome stroke
Upon his heart-strings, trembling with delight—
To fly for refuge from distracting thought
To such amusements as ingenious woe
Contrives, hard-shifting, and without her tools—
To read engraven on the mouldy walls,
In stagg'ring types, his predecessor's tale,
A sad memorial, and subjoin his own—
To turn purveyor to an overgorg'd
And bloated spider, till the pamper'd pest
Is made familiar, watches his approach,
Comes at his call, and serves him for a friend—
To wear out time in numb'ring to an fro
The studs, that thick emboss his iron door;
Then downward and then upward, then aslant
And then alternate; with a sickly hope
By dint of change to give his tasteless task
Some relish; till the sum, exactly found
In all directions, he begins again—
Oh comfortless existence! hemm'd around
With woes, which who that suffers would not knee
And beg for exile, or the pangs of death?
That man should thus encroach on fellow man,
Abridge him of his just and native rights,
Eradicate him, tear him from his hold
Upon th'endearments of domestic life
And social, nip his fruitfulness and use,
And doom him for perhaps a heedless word
To barrenness, and solitude, and tears,
Moves indignation, makes the name of king
(Of king whom such prerogative can please)
As dreadful as the Manichean god.
Ador'd through fear, strong only to destroy.
'Tis liberty alone that gives the flow'r
Of fleeting life its lustre and perfume;
And we are weeds without it. All constraint,
Except what wisdom lays on evil men,
Is evil: hurts the faculties, impedes
Their progress in the road of science; blinds
The eyesight of Discovery; and begets,
In those that suffer it, a sordid mind,
Bestial, a meagre intellect, unfit
To be the tenant of man's noble form.
Thee therefore still, blameworthy as thou art,
With all thy loss of empire, and though squeez'd

By public exigence, till annual food
Fails for the craving hunger of the state,
Thee I account still happy, and the chief
Among the nations, seeing thou art free;
My native nook of earth! Thy clime is rude,
Replete with vapors, and disposes much
All hearts to sadness, and none more than mine:
Thine unadult'rate manners are less soft
And plausible than social life requires,
And thou hast need of discipline and art,
To give thee what politer France receives
From nature's bounty—that humane address
And sweetness, without which no pleasure is
In converse, either starv'd by cold resolve,
Or flush'd with fierce dispute, a senseless brawl.
Yet being free I love thee: for the sake
Of that one feature can be well content,
Disgrac'd as thou hast been, poor as thou art,
To seek no sublunary rest beside.
But, once enslav'd, farewell! I could endure
Chains no where patiently; and chains at home,
Where I am free by birthright, not at all.
Then what were left of roughness in the grain
Of British natures, wanting its excuse
That it belongs to freemen, would disgust
And shock me. I should then with double pain
Feel all the rigor of thy fickle clime;
And, if I must bewail the blessing lost,
For which our Hampdens and our Sidneys bled,
I would at least bewail it under skies
Milder, among a people less austere;
In scenes, which, having never known me free,
Would not reproach me with the loss I felt.
Do I forebode impossible events,
And tremble at vain dreams? Heav'n grant I may!
But th'age of virtuous politics is past,
And we are deep in that of cold pretence.
Patriots are grown too shrewd to be sincere,
And we too wise to trust them. He that takes
Deep in his soft credulity the stamp
Design'd by loud declaimers on the part
Of liberty, themselves the slaves of lust,
Incurs derision for his easy faith,
And lack of knowledge, and with cause enough:
For when was public virtue to be found,
Where private was not? Can he love the whole,
Who loves no part? He be a nation's friend,
Who is in truth the friend of no man there?
Can he be strenuous in his country's cause,

Who slights the charities, for whose dear sake
That country, if at all, must be belov'd?
'Tis therefore sober and good men are sad
For England's glory, seeing it wax pale
And sickly, while her champions wear their hearts
So loose to private duty, that no brain,
Healthful and undisturb'd by factious fumes,
Can dream them trusty to the gen'ral weal.
Such were not they of old, whose temper'd blades
Dispers'd the shackles of usurp'd control,
And hew'd them link from link; then Albion's sons
Were sons indeed; they felt a filial heart
Beat high within them at a mother's wrongs;
And, shining each in his domestic sphere,
Shone brighter still, once call'd to public view.
'Tis therefore many, whose sequester'd lot
Forbids their interference, looking on,
Anticipate perforce some dire event;
And, seeing the old castle of the state,
That promis'd once more firmness, so assail'd,
That all its tempest-beaten turrets shake,
Stand motionless expectants of its fall.
All has its date below; the fatal hour
Was register'd in Heav'n ere time began.
We turn to dust, and all our mightiest works
Die too: the deep foundations that we lay,
Time ploughs them up, and not a trace remains
We build with what we deem eternal rock:
A distant age asks where the fabric stood;
And in the dust, sifted and search'd in vain,
The undiscoverable secret sleeps.
But there is yet a liberty, unsung
By poets, and by senators unprais'd,
Which monarchs cannot grant, nor all the pow'rs
Of earth and hell confed'rate take away:
A liberty, which persecution, fraud,
Oppression, prisons, have no pow'r to bind;
Which whoso tastes can be enslav'd no more.
'Tis liberty of heart deriv'd from Heav'n,
Bought with *His* blood, who gave it to mankind,
And seal'd with the same token. It is held
By charter, and that charter sanction'd sure
By th'unimpeachable and awful oath
And promise of a God. His other gifts
All bear the royal stamp, that speaks them his,
And are august; but this transcends them all.
His other works, the visible display
Of all-creating energy and might,
Are grand no doubt, and worthy of the word,

That, finding an interminable space
Unoccupied, has fill'd the void so well,
And made so sparkling what was dark before.
But these are not his glory. Man, 'tis true,
Smit with the beauty of so fair a scene,
Might well suppose th'artificer divine
Meant it eternal, had he not himself
Pronounc'd it transient, glorious as it is,
And, still designing a more glorious far,
Doom'd it as insufficient for his praise.
These therefore are occasional, and pass;
Form'd for the confutation of the fool,
Whose lying heart disputes against a God;
That office serv'd, they must be swept away.
Not so the labours of his love; they shine
In other heav'ns than these that we behold,
And fade not. There is Paradise that fears
No forfeiture, and of its fruits he sends
Large prelibation oft to saints below.
Of these the first in order, and the pledge,
And confident assurance of the rest,
Is liberty; a flight into his arms,
Ere yet mortality's fine threads give way,
A clear escape from tyrannizing lust,
And full immunity from penal woe.
  Chains are the portion of revolted man,
Stripes, and a dungeon; and his body serves
The triple purpose. In that sickly, foul,
Opprobrious residence he finds them all.
Propense his heart to idols, he is held
In silly dotage on created things,
Careless of their Creator. And that low
And sordid gravitation of his pow'rs
To a vile clod so draws him, with such force
Resistless from the centre he should seek,
That he at last forgets it. All his hopes
Tend downward; his ambition is to sink,
To reach a depth profounder still, and still
Profounder, in the fathomless abyss
Of folly, plunging in pursuit of death.
But ere he gain the comfortless repose
He seeks, and acquiescence of his soul
In Heav'n-renouncing exile, he endures—
What does he not, from lusts oppos'd in vain,
And self-reproaching conscience? He foresees
The fatal issue to his health, fame, peace,
Fortune, and dignity; the loss of all
That can ennoble man, and make frail life,
Short as it is, supportable. Still worse,

Far worse than all the plagues, with which his sins
Infect his happiest moments, he forebodes
Ages of hopeless mis'ry. Future death,
And death still future. Not a hasty stroke,
Like that which sends him to the dusty grave;
But unrepealable enduring death.
Scripture is still a trumpet to his fears:
What none can prove a forg'ry may be true;
What none but bad men wish exploded must.
That scruple checks him. Riot is not loud
Nor drunk enough, to drown it. In the midst
Of laughter his compunctions are sincere;
And he abhors the jest by which he shines.
Remorse begets reform. His master-lust
Falls first before his resolute rebuke,
And seems dethron'd and vanquish'd. Peace ensues,
But spurious and short-liv'd; the puny child
Of self congratulating Pride, begot
On fancied Innocence. Again he falls,
And fights again; but finds his best essay
A presage ominous, portending still
Its own dishonor by a worse relapse
Till Nature, unavailing Nature, foil'd
So oft, and wearied in the vain attempt,
Scoffs at her own performance. Reason now
Takes part with appetite, and pleads the cause
Perversely, which of late she so condemn'd;
With shallow shifts and old devices, worn
And tatter'd in the service of debauch,
Cov'ring his shame from his offended sight.
    Hath God indeed giv'n appetites to man,
And stor'd the earth so plenteously with means,
To gratify the hunger of his wish;
"And doth he reprobate, and will he damn
The use of his own bounty? making first
So frail a kind, and then enacting laws
So strict, that less than perfect must despair?
Falsehood! which whoso but suspects of truth
Dishonors God, and makes a slave of man.
Do they themselves, who undertake for hire
The teacher's office, and dispense at large
Their weekly dole of edifying strains,
Attend to their own music? have they faith
In what with such solemnity of tone
And gesture they propound to our belief?
Nay—conduct hath the loudest tongue. The voice
Is but an instrument, on which the priest
May play what tune he pleases. In the deed,
The unequivocal, authentic deed,

We find sound argument, we read the heart."
  Such reas'nings (if that name must needs belong
T'excuses in which reason has no part)
Serve to compose a spirit well inclin'd,
To live on terms of amity with vice,
And sin without disturbance. Often urg'd,
(As often as libidinous discourse
Exhausted, he resorts to solemn themes
Of theological and grave import)
They gain at last his unreserv'd assent;
Till, harden'd his heart's temper in the forge
Of lust, and on the anvil of despair,
He slights the strokes of conscience. Nothing moves,
Or nothing much, his constancy in ill;
Vain tamp'ring has but foster'd his disease;
'Tis desp'rate, and he sleeps the sleep of death.
Haste now, philosopher, and set him free.
Charm the deaf serpent wisely. Make him hear
Of rectitude and fitness, moral truth
How lovely, and the moral sense how sure,
Consulted and obey'd, to guide his steps
Directly to the *first and only fair.*
Spare not in such a cause. Spend all the pow'rs
Of rant and rhapsody in virtue's praise:
Be most sublimely good, verbosely grand,
And with poetic trappings grace thy prose,
Till it outmantle all the pride of verse.—
Ah, tinkling cymbal, and high-sounding brass,
Smitten in vain! such music cannot charm
The eclipse, that intercepts truth's heav'nly beam,
And chills and darkens a wide-wand'ring soul.
The *still small voice* is wanted. He must speak,
Whose word leaps forth at once to its effect;
Who calls for things that are not, and they come.
  Grace makes the slave a freeman. 'Tis a change,
That turns to ridicule the turgid speech
And stately tone of moralists, who boast,
As if, like him of fabulous renown
They had indeed ability to smooth
The shag of savage nature, and were each
An Orpheus, and omnipotent in song:
But transformation of apostate man
From fool to wise, from earthly to divine,
Is work for Him that made him. He alone,
And he by means in philosophic eyes
Trivial and worthy of disdain, achieves
The wonder; humanizing what is brute
In the lost kind, extracting from the lips
Of asps their venom, overpow'ring strength

By weakness, and hostility by love.
  Patriots have toil'd, and in their country's cause
Bled nobly; and their deeds, as they deserve,
Receive proud recompense. We give in charge
Their names to the sweet lyre. Th'historic muse,
Proud of the treasure, marches with it down
To latest times; and Sculpture, in her turn,
Gives bond in stone and ever-during brass
To guard them, and t'immortalize her trust:
But fairer wreaths are due, though never paid,
To those, who, posted at the shrine of Truth,
Have fall'n in her defence. A patriot's blood,
Well spent in such a strife, may earn indeed,
And for a time ensure, to his lov'd land
The sweets of liberty and equal laws;
But martyrs struggle for a brighter prize,
And win it with more pain. Their blood is shed
In confirmation of the noblest claim,
Our claim to feed upon immortal truth,
To walk with God, to be divinely free,
To soar, and to anticipate the skies.
Yet few remember them. They liv'd unknown,
Till persecution dragg'd them into fame,
And chas'd them up to Heav'n. Their ashes flew
—No marble tells us whither. With their names
No bard embalms and sanctifies his song:
And history, so warm on meaner themes,
Is cold on this. She execrates indeed
The tyranny, that doom'd them to the fire,
But gives the glorious suff'rers little praise.*
  He is the freeman, whom the truth makes free,
And all are slaves besides. There's not a chain,
That hellish foes, confed'rate for his harm,
Can wind around him, but he casts it off,
With as much ease as Samson his green withes.
He looks abroad into the varied field
Of nature, and though poor perhaps, compar'd
With those whose mansions glitter in his sight,
Calls the delightful scen'ry all his own.
His are the mountains, and the valleys his,
And the resplendent rivers: his t'enjoy
With a propriety that none can feel,
But who, with filial confidence inspir'd,
Can lift to Heav'n an unpresumptuous eye,
And smiling say—"My Father made them all!"
Are they not his by a peculiar right,
And by an emphasis of int'rest his,

* See Hume.

Whose eye they fill with tears of holy joy,
Whose heart with praise, and whose exalted mind
With worthy thoughts of that unwearied love,
That plann'd, and built, and still upholds, a world
So cloth'd with beauty for rebellious man?
Yes—ye may fill your garners, ye that reap
The loaded soil, and ye may waste much good
In senselss riot; but ye will not find
In feast, or in the chase, in song or dance,
A liberty like his, who, unimpeach'd
Of usurpation, and to no man's wrong,
Appropriates nature as his Father's work,
And has a richer use of yours than you.
He is indeed a freeman. Free by birth
Of no mean city; plann'd or ere the hills
Were built, the fountains open'd, or the sea
With all his roaring multitude of waves.
His freedom is the same in ev'ry state;
And no condition of this changeful life,
So manifold in cares, whose ev'ry day
Brings its own evil with it, makes it less:
For he has wings, that neither sickness, pain,
Nor penury, can cripple or confine.
No nook so narrow but he spreads them there
With ease, and is at large. Th'oppressor holds
His body bound, but knows not what a range
His spirit takes unconscious of a chain;
And that to bind him is a vain attempt,
Whom God delights in, and in whom he dwells.
  Acquaint thyself with God, if thou wouldst taste
His works. Admitted once to his embrace,
Thou shalt perceive that thou wast blind before:
Thine eye shall be instructed; and thine heart
Made pure shall relish, with divine delight
'Till then unfelt, what hands divine have wrought.
Brutes graze the mountain-top, with faces prone,
And eyes intent upon the scanty herb
It yields them; or, recumbent on its brow,
Ruminate heedless of the scene outspread
Beneath, beyond, and stretching far away
From inland regions to the distant main.
Man views it, and admires; but rests content
With what he views. The landscape has his praise
But not its Author. Unconcern'd who form'd
The Paradise he sees, he finds it such,
And, such well-pleas'd to find it, asks no more.
Not so the mind, that has been touch'd from Heav'n,
And in the school of sacred wisdom taught,
To read his wonders, in whose thought the World,

Fair as it is, existed ere it was.
Not for its own sake merely, but for his
Much more, who fashion'd it, he gives it praise;
Praise that from Earth resulting, as it ought,
To Earth's acknowledg'd Sov'reign, finds at once
Its only just proprietor in Him.
The soul that sees him, or receives sublim'd
New faculties, or learns at least t'employ
More worthily the pow'rs she own'd before,
Discerns in all things what, with stupid gaze
Of ignorance, till then she overlook'd,
A ray of heavn'ly light, gilding all forms
Terrestial in the vast and the minute;
The unambiguous footsteps of the God,
Who gives its lustre to an insect's wing,
And wheels his throne upon the rolling worlds.
Much conversant with Heav'n, she often holds
With those fair ministers of light to man,
That fill the skies nightly with silent pomp,
Sweet conference. Inquires what strains were they
With which Heav'n rang, when ev'ry star, in haste
To gratulate the new-created Earth,
Sent forth a voice, and all the sons of God
Shouted for joy.—"Tell me, ye shining hosts,
That navigate a sea that knows no storms,
Beneath a vault unsullied with a cloud,
If from your elevation, whence ye view
Distinctly scenes invisible to man,
And systems, of whose birth no tidings yet
Have reach'd this nether world, ye spy a race
Favor'd as ours; transgressors from the womb,
And hasting to a grave, yet doom'd to rise,
And to possess a brighter heav'n than yours?
As one, who, long detain'd on foreign shores,
Pants to return, and when he sees afar
His country's weather-bleach'd and batter'd rocks,
From the green wave emerging, darts an eye
Radiant with joy towards the happy land;
So I with animated hopes behold,
And many an aching wish, your beamy fires,
That show like beacons in the blue abyss,
Ordain'd to guide th'embodied spirit home
From toilsome life to never-ending rest.
Loves kindles as I gaze. I feel desires,
That give assurance of their own success,
And that, infus'd from Heav'n, must thither tend."
So reads he nature, whom the lamp of truth
Illuminates. Thy lamp, mysterious Word!
Which whoso sees no longer wanders lost,

With intellects bemaz'd in endless doubt,
But runs the road of wisdom. Thou hast built
With means, that were not till by thee employ'd,
Worlds, that had never been hadst thou in strength
Been less or less benevolent than strong.
They are thy witnesses, who speak thy pow'r
And goodness infinite, but speak in ears,
That hear not, or receive not their report.
In vain thy creatures testify of thee,
Till thou proclaim thyself. Theirs is indeed
A teaching voice; but 'tis the praise of thine,
That whom it teaches it makes prompt to learn,
And with the boon gives talents for its use.
Till thou art heard, imaginations vain
Possess the heart, and fables false as Hell;
Yet, deem'd oracular, lure down to death
The uninform'd and heedless souls of men.
We give to chance, blind chance, ourselves as blind,
The glory of thy work; which yet appears
Perfect and unimpeachable of blame,
Challenging human scrutiny, and prov'd
Then skilful most when most severely judg'd.
But chance is not; or is not where thou reign'st:
Thy providence forbids that fickle pow'r
(If pow'r she be, that works but to confound)
To mix her wild vagaries with thy laws.
Yet thus we dote, refusing while we can
Instructions, and inventing to ourselves
Gods such as guilt makes welcome; gods that sleep,
Or disregard our follies, or that sit
Amus'd spectators of this bustling stage.
Thee we reject, unable to abide
Thy purity, till pure as thou art pure,
Made such by thee, we love thee for that cause,
For which we shunn'd and hated thee before.
Then we are free. Then liberty, like day,
Breaks on the soul, and by a flash from Heav'n
Fires all the faculties with glorious joy.
A voice is heard, that mortal ears hear not,
Till thou hast touch'd them; 'tis the voice of song,
A loud Hosanna sent from all thy works;
Which he that hears it with a shout repeats,
And adds his rapture to the gen'ral praise.
In that blest moment Nature, throwing wide
Her veil opaque, discloses with a smile
The author of her beauties, who, retir'd
Behind his own creation, works unseen
By the impure, and hears his pow'r denied.
Thou art the source and centre of all minds,

Their only point of rest, eternal Word!
From thee departing they are lost, and rove
At random without honor, hope, or peace.
From thee is all, that soothes the life of man,
His high endeavor, and his glad success,
His strength to suffer, and his will to serve.
But O thou bounteous Giver of all good,
Thou art of all thy gifts thyself the crown!
Give what thou canst, without thee we are poor;
And with thee rich, take what thou wilt away

THE TASK.

BOOK VI.

THE WINTER WALK AT NOON.

ARGUMENT OF THE SIXTH BOOK.

Bells at a distance.—Their effect.—A fine noon in winter.—A sheltered walk.—Meditation better than books.—Our familiarity with the course of nature makes it appear less wonderful than it is.—The transformation that spring effects in a shrubbery described.—A mistake concerning the course of nature corrected.—God maintains it by an unremitted act.—The amusements fashionable at this hour of the day reproved.—Animals happy, a delightful sight.—Origin of cruelty to animals.—That it is a great crime proved from Scripture.—That proof illustrated by a tale.—A line drawn between the lawful and unlawful destruction of them.—Their good and useful properties insisted on.—Apology for the enconiums bestowed by the author on animals.—Instances of man's extravagant praise of man.—The groans of the creation shall have an end.—A view taken of the restoration of all things.—An invocation and an invitation of Him, who shall bring it to pass.—The retired man vindicated from the charge of uselessness.—Conclusion.

There is in souls a sympathy with sounds,
And as the mind is pitch'd, the ear is pleas'd
With melting airs or martial, brisk or grave;
Some chord in unison with what we hear
Is touch'd within us, and the heart replies.
How soft the music of those village bells,
Falling at intervals upon the ear
In cadence sweet, now dying all away,
Now pealing loud again, and louder still,
Clear and sonorous, as the gale comes on!
With easy force it opens all the cells
Where Mem'ry slept. Wherever I have heard
A kindred melody, the scene recurs,
And with it all its pleasures and its pains.
Such comprehensive views the spirit takes,
That in a few short moments I retrace,
(As in a map the voyager his course)
The windings of my way through many years.
Short as in retrospect the journey seems,
It seem'd not always short; the rugged path,

And prospect oft so dreary and forlorn,
Mov'd many a sigh at its disheartening length.
Yet feeling present evils, while the past
Faintly impress the mind, or not at all,
How readily we wish time spent revok'd,
That we might try the ground again where once
(Through inexperience, as we now perceive)
We miss'd that happiness we might have found!
Some friend is gone, perhaps his son's best friend,
A father, whose authority, in show
When most severe, and must'ring all its force,
Was but the graver countenance of love;
Whose favor, like the clouds of spring, might low'r,
And utter now and then an awful voice,
But had a blessing in its darkest frown,
Threat'ning at once and nourishing the plant.
We lov'd but not enough, the gentle hand
That rear'd us. At a thoughtless age, allur'd
By ev'ry gilded folly, we renounc'd
His shelt'ring side, and wilfully forewent
That converse, which we now in vain regret.
How gladly would the man recall to life
The boy's neglected sire! a mother too,
That softer friend, perhaps more gladly still,
Might he demand them at the gates of death.
Sorrow has, since they went, subdu'd and tam'd
The playful humor; he could now endure,
(Himself grown sober in the vale of tears)
And feel a parent's presence no restraint.
But not to understand a treasure's worth,
Till time has stol'n away the slighted good,
Is cause of half the poverty we feel.
And makes the world the wilderness it is.
The few that pray at all, pray oft amiss,
And, seeking grace t' improve the prize they hold,
Would urge a wiser suit than asking more.
The night was winter in his roughest mood;
The morning sharp and clear. But now at noon
Upon the southern side of the slant hills,
And where the woods fence off the northern blast,
The season smiles, resigning all its rage,
And has the warmth of May. The vault is blue
Without a cloud, and white without a spe
The dazzling splendor of the scene below.
Again the harmony comes o'er the vale;
And through the trees I view th' embattled tow'r,
Whence all the music. I again perceive
The soothing influence of the wafted strains,
And settled in soft musings as I tread

The walk, still verdant, under oaks and elms
Whose outspread branches overarch the glade.
The roof, though moveable through all its length
As the wind sways it, has yet well suffic'd,
And, intercepting in their silent fall
The frequent flakes, has kept a path for me.
No noise is here, or none that hinders thought.
The redbreast warbles still, but is content
With slender notes, and more than half-suppress'd;
Pleas'd with his solitude, and flitting light
From spray to spray, where'er he rests he shakes
From many a twig the pendent drops of ice,
That tinkle in the wither'd leaves below.
Stillness, accompanied with sounds so soft,
Charms more than silence. Meditation here
May think down hours to moments. Here the heart
May give a useful lesson to the head,
And Learning wiser grow without his books.
Knowledge and wisdom, far from being one,
Have ofttimes no connexion. Knowledge dwells
In heads replete with thoughts of other men;
Wisdom in minds attentive to their own.
Knowledge, a rude unprofitable mass,
The mere materials with which Wisdom builds,
Till smooth'd and squar'd, and fitted to its place,
Does but encumber whom it seems t' enrich.
Knowledge is proud that he has learn'd so much;
Wisdom is humble that he knows no more.
Books are not seldom talismans and spells,
By which the magic art of shrewder wits
Holds an unthinking multitude enthrall'd.
Some to the fascination of a name
Surrender judgment, hoodwink'd. Some the style
Infatuates, and through labyrinths and wilds
Of error leads them, by a tune entranc'd.
While sloth seduces more, too weak to bear
The insupportable fatigue of thought,
And swallowing therefore without pause or choice
The total grist unsifted, husks and all.
But trees and rivulets, whose rapid course
Defies the check of winter, haunts of deer,
And sheep-walks populous with bleating lambs,
And lanes in which the primrose ere her time
Peeps through the moss, that clothes the hawthorn root,
Deceive no student. Wisdom there, and truth,
Not shy, as in the world, and to be won
By slow solicitation, seize at once
The roving thought, and fix it on themselves
 What prodigies can pow'r divine perform

More grand than it produces year by year
And all in sight of inattentive man?
Familiar with the effect we slight the cause,
And in the constancy of nature's course,
The regular return of genial months,
And renovation of a faded world,
See nought to wonder at. Should God again,
As once in Gibeon, interrupt the race
Of the undeviating and punctual sun,
How would the world admire! but speaks it less
An agency divine, to make him know
His moment when to sink and when to rise,
Age after age, than to arrest his course?
All we behold is miracle; but seen
So duly, all is miracle in vain.
Where now the vital energy, that mov'd,
While summer was, the pure and subtle lymph
Through th' imperceptible meand'ring veins
Of leaf and flow'r? It sleeps; and th' icy touch
Of unprolific winter has impress'd
A cold stagnation on th' intestine tide.
But let the months go round, a few short months,
And all shall be restor'd. These naked shoots,
Barren as lances, among which the wind
Makes wintry music, sighing as it goes,
Shall put their graceful foliage on again,
And more aspiring, and with ampler spread,
Shall boast new charms, and more than they have lost.
Then each, in its peculiar honors clad,
Shall publish even to the distant eye
Its family and tribe. Laburnum, rich
In streaming gold; syringa, iv'ry pure;
The scentless and scented rose; this red,
And of an humbler growth, the other* tall,
And throwing up into the darkest gloom
Of neighb'ring cypress, or more sable yew,
Her silver globes, light as the foamy surf
That the wind severs from the broken wave;
The lilac, various in array, now white,
Now sanguine, and her beauteous head now set
With purple spikes pyramidal, as if
Studious of ornament, yet unresolv'd
Which hue she most approv'd, she chose them all;
Copious of flow'rs the woodbine, pale and wan,
But well compensating her sickly looks
With never-cloying odours, early and late;
Hypericum all bloom, so thick a swarm

* The Guelder-rose.

Of flow'rs, like flies clothing her slender rods,
That scarce a leaf appears; mezereon too,
Though leafless, well attired, and thick beset
With blushing wreaths, investing every spray;
Althæa with the purple eye; the broom,
Yellow and bright, as bullion unalloy'd,
Her blossoms; and luxuriant above all
The jasmine, throwing wide her elegant sweets,
The deep dark green of whose unvarnish'd leaf
Makes more conspicuous, and illumines more,
The bright profusion of her scatter'd stars.—
These have been, and these shall be in their day;
And all this uniform uncolor'd scene
Shall be dismantled of its fleecy load,
And flush into variety again.
From dearth to plenty, and from death to life,
Is Nature's progress, when she lectures man
In heavenly truth; evincing, as she makes
The grand transition, that there lives and works
A soul in all things, and that soul is God.
The beauties of the wilderness are his,
That makes so gay the solitary place,
Where no eye sees them. And the fairer forms,
That cultivation glories in, are his.
He sets the bright procession on its way,
And marshals all the order of the year;
He marks the bounds, which Winter may not pass,
And blunts his pointed fury; in its case,
Russet and rude, folds up the tender germ,
Uninjur'd, with inimitable art;
And, ere one flow'ry season fades and dies,
Designs the blooming wonders of the next.
Some say that in the origin of things,
When all creation started into birth,
The infant elements received a law,
From which they swerve not since. That under force
Of that controlling ordinance they move,
And need not his immediate hand, who first
Prescrib'd their course, to regulate it now.
Thus dream they, and contrive to save a God
Th' encumbrance of his own concerns, and spare
The great artificer of all that moves
The stress of a continual act, the pain
Of unremitted vigilance and care,
As too laborious and severe a task.
So man, the moth, is not afraid, it seems,
To span omnipotence, and measure might,
That knows no measure, by the scanty rule
And standard of his own, that is to-day,

And is not ere to-morrow's sun go down.
But how should matter occupy a charge,
Dull as it is, and satisfy a law
So fast in its demands, unless impell'd
To ceaseless service by a ceaseless force,
And under pressure of some conscious cause?
The Lord of all, himself through all diffus'd,
Sustains, and is the life of all that lives.
Nature is but a name for an effect,
Whose cause is God. He feeds the sacred fire
By which the mighty process is maintain'd,
Who sleeps not, is not weary; in whose sight
Slow circling ages are as transient days;
Whose work is without labour; whose designs
No flaw deforms, no difficulty thwarts;
And whose beneficence no charge exhausts.
Him blind antiquity profan'd, not serv'd,
With self-taught rites, and under various names,
Female and male, Pomona, Pales, Pan,
And Flora, and Vertumnus; peopling earth
With tutelary goddesses and gods,
That were not; and commending as they would
To each some province, garden, field, or grove.
But all are under one. One spirit—His,
Who wore the platted thorns with bleeding brows,
Rules universal nature. Not a flow'r
But shows some touch, in freckle, streak, or stain,
Of his unrivall'd pencil. He inspires
Their balmy odors, and imparts their hues,
And bathes their eyes with nectar, and includes,
In grains as countless as the seaside sands,
The forms with which he sprinkles all the earth.
Happy who walks with him! whom what he finds
Of flavor or of scent in fruit or flow'r,
Or what he views of beautiful or grand
In nature, from the broad majestic oak
To the green blade that twinkles in the sun,
Prompts with remembrance of a present God.
His presence, who made all so fair, perceiv'd,
Makes all still fairer. As with him no scene
Is dreary, so with him all seasons please.
Though winter had been none, had man been true,
And earth be punish'd for its tenant's sake,
Yet not in vengeance; as this smiling sky,
So soon succeeding such an angry night,
And these dissolving snows, and this clear stream
Recov'ring fast its liquid music, prove.
  Who then, that has a mind well strung and tun'd
To contemplation, and within his reach

A scene so friendly to his fav'rite task,
Would waste attention at the checker'd board,
His host of wooden warriors to and fro
Marching and countermarching, with an eye
As fix'd as marble, with a forehead ridg'd
And furrow'd into storms, and with a hand
Trembling, as if eternity were hung
In balance on his conduct of a pin?
Nor envies he aught more their idle sport,
Who pant with application misapplied
To trivial toys, and, pushing iv'ry balls
Across a velvet level, feel a joy
Akin to rapture, when the bauble finds
Its destin'd goal, of difficult access.
Nor deems he wiser him, who gives his noon
To Miss, the mercer's plague, from shop to shop
Wand'ring, and litt'ring with unfolded silks
The polish'd counter, and approving none,
Or promising with smiles to call again.
Nor him, who by his vanity seduc'd,
And sooth'd into a dream that he discerns
The diff'rence of a Guido from a daub,
Frequents the crowded auction: station'd there
As duly as the Langford of the show,
With glass at eye, and catalogue in hand,
And tongue accomplish'd in the fulsome cant
And pedantry, that coxcombs learn with ease;
Oft as the price-deciding hammer falls,
He notes it in his book, then raps his box,
Swears 'tis a bargain, rails at his hard fate,
That he has let it pass—but never bids.
Here unmolested, through whatever sign
The sun proceeds, I wander. Neither mist,
Nor freezing sky, nor sultry, checking me,
Nor stranger, intermeddling with my joy.
E'en in the spring and playtime of the year,
That calls th'unwonted villager abroad
With all her little ones, a sportive train,
To gather kingcups in the yellow mead,
And prink their hair with daisies, or to pick
A cheap but wholesome salad from the brook,
These shades are all my own. The tim'rous hare,
Grown so familiar with her frequent guest,
Scarce shuns me; and the stockdove unalarm'd
Sits cooing in the pine-tree, nor suspends
His long love-ditty for my near approach.
Drawn from his refuge in some lonely elm,
That age or injury has hollow'd deep,
Where, on his bed of wool and matted leaves,

He has outslept the winter, ventures forth
To frisk a while, and bask in the warm sun,
The squirrel, flippant, pert, and full of play;
He sees me, and at once, swift as a bird,
Ascends the neighb'ring beech; there whisks his brush,
And perks his ears, and stamps, and cries aloud,
With all the prettiness of feign'd alarm,
And anger insignificantly fierce.
  The heart is hard in nature, and unfit
For human fellowship, as being void
Of sympathy, and therefore dead alike
To love and friendship both, that is not pleas'd
With sight of animals enjoying life,
Nor feels their happiness augment his own.
The bounding fawn that darts across the glade
When one pursues, through mere delight of heart,
And spirits buoyant with excess of glee;
The horse as wanton, and almost as fleet,
That skims the spacious meadow at full speed,
Then stops, and snorts, and, throwing high his heels,
Starts to the voluntary race again;
The very kine, that gambol at high noon,
The total herd receiving first from one,
That leads the dance, a summons to be gay,
Though wild their strange vagaries, and uncouth
Their efforts, yet resolv'd with one consent
To give such act and utt'rance, as they may
To ecstasy too big to be suppress'd—
These, and a thousand images of bliss,
With which kind Nature graces ev'ry scene,
Where cruel man defeats not her design,
Impart to the benevolent, who wish
All that are capable of pleasure pleas'd,
A far superior happiness to theirs,
The comfort of a reasonable joy.
  Man scarce had ris'n, obedient to his call
Who form'd him from the dust, his future grave,
When he was crown'd as never king was since.
God set the diadem upon his head,
And angel choirs attended. Wond'ring stood
The new-made monarch, while before him pass'd,
All happy, and all perfect in their kind,
The creatures, summon'd from their various haunts,
To see their sov'reign, and confess his sway.
Vast was his empire, absolute his pow'r,
Or bounded only by a law, whose force
'Twas his sublimest privilege to feel
And own, the law of universal love.
He rul'd with meekness, they obey'd with joy;

No cruel purpose lurk'd within his heart,
And no distrust of his intent in theirs.
So Eden was a scene of harmless sport,
Where kindness on his part, who rul'd the whole,
Begat a tranquil confidence in all,
And fear as yet was not, nor cause for fear.
But sin marr'd all; and the revolt of man,
That source of evils not exhausted yet,
Was punished with revolt of his from him.
Garden of God, how terrible the change
Thy groves and lawns then witness'd! Ev'ry heart,
Each animal, of ev'ry name, conceiv'd
A jealousy, and an instinctive fear,
And, conscious of some danger, either fled
Precipitate the loath'd abode of man,
Or growl'd defiance in such angry sort,
As taught him too to tremble in his turn.
Thus harmony and family accord
Were driv'n from Paradise; and in that hour
The seeds of cruelty, that since have swell'd
To such gigantic and enormous growth,
Were sown in human nature's fruitful soil.
Hence date the persecution and the pain,
That man inflicts on all inferior kinds,
Regardless of their plaints. To make him sport,
To gratify the frenzy of his wrath,
Or his base gluttony, are causes good
And just in his account, why bird and beast
Should suffer torture, and the streams be dyed
With blood of their inhabitants impal'd.
Earth groans beneath the burden of a war
Wag'd with defenceless innocence, while he,
Not satisfied to prey on all around,
Adds tenfold bitterness to death by pangs
Needless, and first torments ere he devours.
Now happiest they, that occupy the scenes
The most remote from his abhorr'd resort,
Whom once, as delegate of God on earth,
They fear'd, and as his perfect image lov'd.
The wilderness is theirs, with all its caves,
Its hollow glens, its thickets, and its plains,
Unvisited by man. There they are free,
And howl and roar as likes them, uncontroll'd;
Nor ask his leave to slumber or to play.
Wo to the tyrant, if he dare intrude
Within the confines of their wild domain:
The lion tells him—I am monarch here—
And, if he spare him, spares him on the terms
Of royal mercy, and through gen'rous scorn

To rend a victim trembling at his foot.
In measure, as by force of instinct drawn,
Or by necessity constrain'd, they live
Dependent upon man; those in his fields,
These at his crib, and some beneath his roof.
They prove too often at how dear a rate
He sells protection—Witness at his foot
The spaniel dying for some venial fault.
Under dissection of the knotted scourge;
Witness the patient ox, with stripes and yells
Driv'n to the slaughter, goaded, as he runs,
To madness; while the savage at his heels
Laughs at the frantic suff'rer's fury, spent
Upon the guiltless passenger o'erthrown.
He too is witness, noblest of the train
That wait on man, the flight-performing horse;
With unsuspecting readiness he takes
His murd'rer on his back, and push'd all day
With bleeding sides and flanks, that heave for life,
To the far distant goal, arrives and dies.
So little mercy shows who needs so much!
Does law, so jealous in the cause of man,
Denounce no doom on the delinquent? None.
He lives, and o'er his brimming beaker boasts
(As if barbarity were high desert)
Th'inglorious feat, and clamorous in praise
Of the poor brute, seems wisely to suppose
The honors of his matchless horse his own.
But many a crime, deem'd innocent on earth,
Is register'd in heav'n; and these no doubt
Have each their record, with a curse annex'd
Man may dismiss compassion from his heart,
But God will never. When he charg'd the Jew
T'assist his foe's down-fallen beast to rise;
And when the bush-exploring boy, that seiz'd
The young, to let the parent bird go free;
Prov'd he not plainly, that his meaner works
Are yet his care, and have an int'rest all,
All, in the universal Father's love?
On Noah, and in him on all mankind,
The charter was conferr'd, by which we hold
The flesh of animals in fee, and claim
O'er all we feed on pow'r of life and death.
But read the instrument, and mark it well:
Th'oppression of a tyrannous control
Can find no warrant there. Feed then, and yield
Thanks for thy food. Carnivorous, through sin,
Feed on the slain, but spare the living brute!
The Governor of all, himself to all

So bountiful, in whose attentive ear
The unfledg'd raven and the lion's whelp
Plead not in vain for pity on the pangs
Of hunger unassuag'd, has interpos'd,
Not seldom, his avenging arm, to smite
Th'injurious trampler upon nature's law,
That claims forbearance even for a brute.
He hates the hardness of a Balaam's heart;
And, prophet as he was, he might not strike
The blameless animal, without rebuke,
On which he rode. Her opportune offence
Sav'd him, or th'unrelenting seer had died.
He sees that human equity is slack
To interfere, though in so just a cause;
And makes the task his own. Inspiring dumb
And helpless victims with a sense so keen
Of injury, with such knowledge of their strength,
And such sagacity to take revenge,
That oft the beast has seem'd to judge the man.
An ancient, not a legendary tale,
By one of sound intelligence rehears'd,
(If such who plead for Providence may seem
In modern eyes,) shall make the doctrine clear.
Where England, stretch'd towards the setting sun,
Narrow and long, o'erlooks the western wave,
Dwelt young Misagathus; a scorner he
Of God and goodness, atheist in ostent,
Vicious in act, in temper savage-fierce.
He journey'd; and his chance was, as he went
To join a trav'ller, of far diff'rent note,
Evander, fam'd for piety, for years
Deserving honor, but for wisdom more.
Fame had not left the venerable man
A stranger to the manners of the youth,
Whose face too was familiar to his view.
Their way was on the margin of the land,
O'er the green summit of the rocks, whose base
Beats back the roaring surge, scarce heard so high.
The charity, that warm'd his heart, was mov'd
At sight of the man-monster. With a smile
Gentle, and affable, and full of grace,
As fearful of offending whom he wish'd
Much to persuade, he plied his ear with truths
Not harshly thunder'd forth, or rudely press'd,
But, like his purpose, gracious, kind, and sweet.
"And dost thou dream," th'impenetrable man
Exclaim'd, "that me the lullabies of age,
And fantasies of dotards such as thou,
Can cheat, or move a moment's fear in me?

Mark now the proof I give thee, that the brave
Need no such aids, as superstition lends
To steel their hearts against the dread of death."
He spoke, and to the precipice at hand
Push'd with a madman's fury. Fancy shrinks
And the blood thrills and curdles, at the thought
Of such a gulf as he design'd his grave.
But, though the felon on his back could dare
The dreadful leap, more rational, his steed
Declin'd the death, and wheeling swiftly round,
Or e'er his hoof had press'd the crumbling verge,
Baffled his rider, sav'd against his will.
The frenzy of the brain may be redress'd
By med'cine well applied, but without grace
The heart's insanity admits no cure.
Enrag'd the more, by what might have reform'd
His horrible intent, again he sought
Destruction, with a zeal to be destroy'd,
With sounding whip, and rowels dyed in blood.
But still in vain. The Providence, that meant
A longer date to the far nobler beast,
Spar'd yet again th'ignoble for his sake.
And now, his prowess prov'd, and his sincere
Incurable obduracy evinc'd,
His rage grew cool; and, pleas'd perhaps t'have earn'd
So cheaply the renown of that attempt,
With looks of some complacence he resum'd
His road, deriding much the blank amaze
Of good Evander, still where he was left
Fix'd motionless, and petrified with dread.
So on they far'd. Discouse on other themes
Ensuing seem'd t'obliterate the past;
And tamer far for so much fury shown,
(As is the course of rash and fiery men)
The rude companion smil'd, as if transform'd.
But 'twas a transient calm. A storm was near,
An unsuspected storm. His hour was come.
The impious challenger of Pow'r divine
Was now to learn, that Heav'n, though slow to wrath,
Is never with impunity defied.
His horse, as he had caught his master's mood,
Snorting, and starting into sudden rage,
Unbidden, and not now to be controll'd,
Rush'd to the cliff, and, having reach'd it, stood.
At once the shock unseated him: he flew
Sheer o'er the craggy barrier; and, immers'd
Deep in the flood, found, when he sought it not,
The death he had deserv'd, and died alone.
So God wrought double justice; made the fool

The victim of his own tremendous choice,
And taught a brute the way to safe revenge.
I would not enter on my list of friends
(Though grac'd with polish'd manners and fine sense,
Yet wanting sensibility) the man
Who needlessly sets foot upon a worm.
An inadvertent step may crush the snail,
That crawls at ev'ning in the public path;
But he that has humanity, forewarn'd,
Will tread aside, and let the reptile live.
The creeping vermin, loathsome to the sight,
And charg'd perhaps with venom, that intrudes,
A visitor unwelcome, into scenes
Sacred to neatness and repose, th'alcove,
The chamber, or refectory, may die:
A necessary act incurs no blame.
Not so when, held within their proper bounds,
And guiltless of offence, they range the air,
Or take their pastime in the spacious field;
There they are privileg'd; and he that hunts
Or harms them there is guilty of a wrong,
Disturbs th'economy of Nature's realm,
Who, when she form'd, design'd them an abode.
The sum is this. If man's convenience, health,
Or safety, interfere, his rights and claims
Are paramount, and must extinguish theirs.
Else they are all—the meanest things that are,
As free to live, and to enjoy that life,
As God was free to form them at the first,
Who in his sov'reign wisdom made them all.
Ye, therefore, who love mercy, teach your sons
To love it too. The springtime of our years
Is soon dishonor'd and defil'd in most
By budding ills, that ask a prudent hand,
To check them. But alas! none sooner shoots,
If unrestrain'd, into luxuriant growth,
Than cruelty, most dev'lish of them all.
Mercy to him, that shows it, is the rule
And righteous limitation of its act,
By which Heav'n moves in pard'ning guilty man
And he that shows none, being ripe in years,
And conscious of the outrage he commits,
Shall seek it, and not find it, in his turn.
Distinguish'd much by reason, and still more
By our capacity of Grace divine,
From creatures, that exist but for our sake,
Which, having serv'd us, perish, we are held
Accountable; and God some future day
Will reckon with us roundly for th'abuse

Of what he deems no mean or trivial trust.
Superior as we are, they yet depend
Not more on human help than we on theirs.
Their strength, or speed, or vigilance, were giv'n
In aid of our defects. In some are found
Such teachable and apprehensive parts,
That man's attainments in his own concerns,
Match'd with th' expertness of the brutes in theirs,
Are ofttimes vanquish'd, and thrown far behind.
Some show that nice sagacity of smell,
And read with such discernment, in the port
And figure of the man, his secret aim,
That oft we owe our safety to a skill
We could not teach, and must despair to learn.
But learn we might, if not too proud to stoop
To quadruped instructors, many a good
And useful quality, and virtue too,
Rarely exemplified among ourselves;
Attachment never to be wean'd, or chang'd
By any change of fortune; proof alike
Against unkindness, absence, and neglect;
Fidelity, that neither bribe nor threat
Can move or warp; and gratitude for small
And trivial favors, lasting as the life,
And glist'ning even in the dying eye.
    Man praises man. Desert in arts or arms
Wins public honor; and ten thousand sit
Patiently present at a sacred song,
Commemoration-mad; content to hear
(O wonderful effect of music's pow'r!)
Messiah's eulogy for Handel's sake.
But less, methinks, than sacrilege might serve—
(For, was it less, what heathen would have dar'd
To strip Jove's statue of his oaken wreath,
And hang it up in honor of a man?)
Much less might serve, when all that we design
Is but to gratify an itching ear,
And give the day to a musician's praise.
Remember Handel? Who, that was not born
Deaf as the dead to harmony, forgets,
Or can, the more than Homer of his age?
Yes—we remember him; and, while we praise
A talent so divine, remember too
That His most holy book, from whom it came,
Was never meant, was never us'd before,
To buckram out the mem'ry of a man.
But hush!—the muse perhaps is too severe;
And with a gravity beyond the size
And measure of th'offence, rebukes a deed

Less impious than absurd, and owing more
To want of judgment than to wrong design.
So in the chapel of old Ely House,
When wand'ring Charles, who meant to be the third,
Had fled from William, and the news was fresh,
The simple clerk, but loyal, did announce,
And eke did rear right merrily, two staves,
Sung to the praise and glory of King George!
—Man praises man; and Garrick's mem'ry next,
When time had somewhat mellow'd it, and made
The idol of our worship while he liv'd
The God of our idolatry once more,
Shall have its altar; and the world shall go
In pilgrimage to bow before his shrine.
The theatre too small shall suffocate
Its squeez'd contents, and more than it admits
Shall sigh at their exclusion, and return
Ungratified: for there some noble lord
Shall stuff his shoulders with king Richard's hunch,
Or wrap himself in Hamlet's inky cloak,
And strut, and storm, and straddle, stamp and stare,
To show the world how Garrick did not act.
For Garrick was a worshipper himself;
He drew the liturgy, and fram'd the rites
And solemn ceremonial of the day,
And call'd the world to worship on the banks
Of Avon, fam'd in song. Ah, pleasant proof
That piety has still in human hearts
Some place, a spark or two not yet extinct.
The mulb'rry-tree was hung with blooming wreaths;
The mulb'rry-tree stood centre of the dance;
The mulb'rry-tree was hymn'd with dulcet airs;
And from his touchwood trunk the mulb'rry-tree
Supplied such relics as devotion holds
Still sacred, and preserves with pious care.
So 'twas a hallow'd time: decorum reign'd,
And mirth without offence. No few return'd,
Doubtless, much edified, and all refresh'd.—
Man praises man. The rabble all alive
From tippling benches, cellars, stalls and sties,
Swarm in the streets. The statesman of the day,
A pompous and slow-moving pageant, comes.
Some shout him, and some hang upon his car,
To gaze in's eyes, and bless him. Maidens wave
Their kerchiefs, and old women weep for joy:
While others, not so satisfied, unhorse
The gilded equipage, and, turning loose
His steeds, usurp a place they well deserve.
Why? what has charm'd them? Hath he sav'd the state?

No. Doth he purpose its salvation? No.
Enchanting novelty, that moon at full,
That finds out ev'ry crevice of the head
That is not sound and perfect, hath in theirs
Wrought this disturbance. But the wane is near,
And his own cattle must suffice him soon.
Thus idly do we waste the breath of praise,
And dedicate a tribute, in its use
And just direction sacred, to a thing
Doom'd to the dust, or lodg'd already there.
Encomium in old time was poets' work;
But poets, having lavishly long since
Exhausted all materials of the art,
The task now falls into the public hand;
And I, contented with an humbler theme,
Have pour'd my stream of panegyric down
The vale of Nature, where it creeps, and winds
Among her lovely works with a secure
And unambitious course, reflecting clear,
If not the virtues, yet the worth, of brutes.
And I am recompens'd, and deem the toils
Of poetry not lost, if verse of mine
May stand between an animal and wo,
And teach one tyrant pity for his drudge.
The groans of Nature in this nether world,
Which Heav'n has heard for ages, have an end.
Foretold by prophets, and by poets sung,
Whose fire was kindled at the prophets' lamp,
The time of rest, the promis'd sabbath, comes.
Six thousand years of sorrow have well-nigh
Fullfill'd their tardy and disastrous course
Over a sinful world; and what remains
Of this tempestuous state of human things
Is merely as the working of a sea
Before a calm, that rocks itself to rest:
For He, whose car the winds are and the clouds
The dust that waits upon his sultry march,
When sin hath mov'd him, and his wrath is hot,
Shall visit earth in mercy; shall descend
Propitious in his chariot pav'd with love;
And what his storms have blasted and defac'd
For man's revolt shall with a smile repair.
Sweet is the harp of prophecy; too sweet
Not to be wrong'd by a mere mortal touch:
Nor can the wonders it records be sung
To meaner music, and not suffer loss.
But when a poet, or when one like me,
Happy to rove among poetic flow'rs,
Though poor in skill to rear them, lights at last

On some fair theme, some theme divinely fair,
Such is the impulse and the spur he feels,
To give it praise proportion'd to its worth,
That not t'attempt it, arduous as he deems
The labour, were a task more arduous still.
O scenes surpassing fable, and yet true,
Scenes of accomplish'd bliss! which who can see,
Though but in distant prospect, and not feel
His soul refresh'd with foretaste of the joy?
Rivers of gladness water all the earth,
And clothe all climes with beauty; the reproach
Of barrenness is past. The fruitful field
Laughs with abundance; and the land, once lean,
Or fertile only in its own disgrace,
Exults to see its thistly curse repeal'd.
The various seasons woven into one,
And that one season an eternal spring,
The garden fears no blight, and needs no fence,
For there is none to covet, all are full.
The lion, and the libbard, and the bear,
Graze with the fearless flocks; all bask at noon,
Together, or all gambol in the shade,
Of the same grove, and drink one common stream.
Antipathies are none. No foe to man
Lurks in the serpent now: the mother sees,
And smiles to see, her infant's playful hand
Stretch'd forth to dally with the crested worm,
He stroke his azure neck, or to receive
The lambent homage of his arrowy tongue.
All creatures worship man, and all mankind
One Lord, one father. Error has no place:
That creeping pestilence is driv'n away;
The breath of Heav'n has chas'd it. In the heart
No passion touches a discordant string,
But all is harmony and love. Disease
Is not: the pure and uncontaminate blood
Holds its due course, nor fears the frost of age,
One song employs all nations; and all cry
"Worthy the Lamb, for he was slain for us!"
The dwellers in the vales and on the rocks
Shout to each other, and the mountain-tops
From distant mountains catch the flying joy;
Till, nation after nation taught the strain,
Earth rolls the rapturous Hosanna round.
Behold the measure of the promise fill'd;
See Salem built, the labour of a God!
Bright as a sun the sacred city shines;
All kingdoms and all princes of the earth
Flock to that light; the glory of all lands

Flows into her; unbounded is her joy,
And endless her increase. Thy rams are there,
Nebaioth, and the flocks of Kedar there: *
The looms of Ormus, and the mines of Ind,
And Saba's spicy groves, pay tribute there.
Praise is in all her gates: upon her walls,
And in her streets, and in her spacious courts
Is heard salvation. Eastern Java there
Kneels with the native of the farthest west;
And Æthiopia spreads abroad the hand,
And worships. Her report has travell'd forth
Into all lands. From ev'ry clime they come
To see thy beauty, and to share thy joy,
O Sion! an assembly such as earth
Saw never, such as heav'n stoops down to see.
Thus heav'nward all things tend. For all were once
Perfect, and all must be at length restor'd.
So God has greatly purpos'd; who would else
In his dishonor'd works himself endure
Dishonor, and be wrong'd without redress.
Haste then, and wheel away a shatter'd world,
Ye slow-revolving seasons! we would see
(A sight to which our eyes are strangers yet)
A world, that does not dread and hate his laws,
And suffer for its crime; would learn how fair
The creature is that God pronounces good,
How pleasant in itself what pleases him.
Here ev'ry drop of honey hides a sting:
Worms wind themselves into our sweetest flow'rs
And e'en the joy, that haply some poor heart
Derives from Heav'n, pure as the fountain is,
Is sullied in the stream, taking a taint
From touch of human lips, at best impure.
O for a world in principle as chaste
As this is gross and selfish! over which
Custom and prejudice shall bear no sway
That govern all things here, should'ring aside
The meek and modest Truth, and forcing her
To seek a refuge from the tongue of Strife
In nooks obscure, far from the ways of men:
Where Violence shall never lift the sword,
Nor Cunning justify the proud man's wrong,
Leaving the poor no remedy but tears:
Where he, that fills an office, shall esteem
Th'occasion it presents of doing good

* Nebaioth and Kedar, the sons of Ishmael, and progenitors of the Arabs, in the prophetic scripture here alluded to, may be reasonably considered as representatives of the Gentiles at large.

More than the perquisite: where Law shall speak
Seldom, and never but as Wisdom prompts
And equity; not jealous more to guard
A worthless form, than to decide aright:
Where Fashion shall not sanctify abuse,
Nor smooth Good-breeding (supplemental grace)
With lean performance ape the work of Love!
  Come then, and, added to thy many crowns,
Receive yet one, the crown of all the earth,
Thou who alone art worthy! It was thine
By ancient covenant, ere Nature's birth;
And thou hast made it thine by purchase since,
And overpaid its value with thy blood.
Thy saints proclaim thee king; and in their hearts
Thy title is engraven with a pen
Dipp'd in the fountain of eternal love.
Thy saints proclaim thee king; and thy delay
Gives courage to their foes, who, could they see
The dawn of thy last advent, long-desir'd,
Would creep into the bowels of the hills,
And flee for safety to the falling rocks.
The very spirit of the world is tir'd
Of its own taunting question, ask'd so long,
"Where is the promise of your Lord's approach?"
The infidel has shot his bolts away,
Till, his exhausted quiver yielding none,
He gleans the blunted shafts, that have recoil'd,
And aims them at the shield of Truth again.
The veil is rent, rent too by priestly hands,
That hides divinity from mortal eyes;
And all the mysteries to faith propos'd,
Insulted and traduc'd, are cast aside,
As useless, to the moles and to the bats
They now are deem'd the faithful, and are prais'd,
Who, constant only in rejecting thee,
Deny thy Godhead with a martyr's zeal,
And quit their office for their error's sake.
Blind, and in love with darkness! yet, e'en these
Worthy, compar'd with sycophants, who kneel
Thy name adoring, and then preach thee man!
So fares thy church. But how thy church may fare
The world takes little thought. Who will may preach,
And what they will. All pastors are alike
To wand'ring sheep, resolv'd to follow none.
Two gods divide them all—Pleasure and Gain:
For these they live, they sacrifice to these,
And in their service wage perpetual war
With Conscience and with thee. Lust in their hearts,
And mischief in their hands, they roam the earth,

To prey upon each other: stubborn, fierce,
High-minded, foaming out their own disgrace.
Thy prophets speak of such; and, noting down
The features of the last degen'rate times,
Exhibit ev'ry lineament of these.
Come then, and, added to thy many crowns,
Receive yet one, as radiant as the rest,
Due to thy last and most effectual work,
Thy word fulfill'd, the conquest of a world!
He is the happy man, whose life e'en now
Shows somewhat of that happier life to come;
Who, doom'd to an obscure but tranquil state,
Is pleas'd with it, and, were he free to choose,
Would make his fate his choice; whom peace, the fruit
Of virtue, and whom virtue, fruit of faith,
Prepare for happiness; bespeak him one
Content indeed to sojourn while he must
Below the skies, but having there his home.
The world o'erlooks him in her busy search
Of objects, more illustrious in her view;
And, occupied as earnestly as she,
Though more sublimely, he o'erlooks the world.
She scorns his pleasures, for she knows them not;
He seeks not hers, for he has prov'd them vain.
He cannot skim the ground like summer birds
Pursuing gilded flies; and such he deems
Her honors, her emoluments, her joys.
Therefore in contemplation is his bliss,
Whose pow'r is such, that whom she lifts from earth
She makes familiar with a heav'n unseen,
And shows him glories yet to be reveal'd.
Not slothful he, though seeming unemploy'd,
And censur'd oft as useless. Stillest streams
Oft water fairest meadows, and the bird,
That flutters least, is longest on the wing.
Ask him, indeed, what trophies he has rais'd,
Or what achievements of immortal fame
He purposes, and he shall answer—None.
His warfare is within. There unfatigu'd
His fervent spirit labours. There he fights,
And there obtains fresh triumphs o'er himself,
And never with'ring wreaths, compar'd with which,
The laurels that a Cæsar reaps are weeds.
Perhaps the self-approving haughty world,
That as she sweeps him with her whistling silks
Scarce deigns to notice him, or, if she see,
Deems him a cypher in the works of God,
Receives advantage from his noiseless hours,
Of which she little dreams. Perhaps she owes

Her sunshine and her rain, her blooming spring
And plenteous harvest, to the pray'r he makes,
When, Isaac-like, the solitary saint
Walks forth to meditate at eventide,
And think on her, who thinks not for herself.
Forgive him then, thou bustler in concerns
Of little worth, an idler in the best,
If, author of no mischief and some good,
He seek his proper happiness by means
That may advance, but cannot hinder, thine.
Nor, though he tread the secret path of life,
Engage no notice, and enjoy much ease,
Account him an encumbrance on the state,
Receiving benefits, and rend'ring none.
His sphere though humble, if that humble sphere
Shine with his fair example, and though small
His influence, if that influence all be spent
In soothing sorrow, and in quenching strife,
In aiding helpless indigence, in works,
From which at least a grateful few derive
Some taste of comfort in a world of woe;
Then let the supercilious great confess
He serves his country, recompenses well
The state, beneath the shadow of whose vine
He sits secure, and in the scale of life
Holds no ignoble, though a slighted, place.
The man, whose virtues are more felt than seen,
Must drop indeed the hope of public praise;
But he may boast, what few that win it can,
That, if his country stand not by his skill,
At least his follies have not wrought her fall.
Polite Refinement offers him in vain
Her golden tube, through which a sensual world
Draws gross impurity, and likes it well,
The neat conveyance hiding all th' offence.
Not that he peevishly rejects a mode
Because that world adopts it. If it bear
The stamp and clear impression of good sense,
And be not costly more than of true worth,
He puts it on, and for decorum sake
Can wear it e'en as gracefully as she.
She judges of refinement by the eye,
He by the test of conscience, and a heart
Not soon deceiv'd; aware that what is base
No polish can make sterling; and that vice,
Though well perfum'd and elegantly dress'd,
Like an unburied carcass trick'd with flow'rs,
Is but a garnish'd nuisance, fitter far
For cleanly riddance, than for fair attire.

So life glides smoothly and by stealth away,
More golden than that age of fabled gold
Renown'd in ancient song; not vex'd with care
Or stain'd with guilt, beneficent, approv'd
Of God and man, and peaceful in its end.
So glide my life away, and so at last,
My share of duties decently fulfill'd,
May some disease, not tardy to perform
Its destin'd office, yet with gentle stroke,
Dismiss me weary to a safe retreat,
Beneath the turf, that I have often trod.
It shall not grieve me then, that once, when call'd
To dress a Sofa with the flow'rs of verse,
I play'd a while, obedient to the fair,
With that light task; but soon, to please her more,
Whom flow'rs alone I knew would little please,
Let fall th' unfinish'd wreath, and rov'd for fruit;
Roved far, and gathered much: some harsh, 'tis true,
Picked from the thorns and briers of reproof,
But wholesome, well digested; grateful some
To palates that can taste immortal truth;
Insipid else, and sure to be despis'd.
But all is in His hand, whose praise I seek.
In vain the poet sings, and the world hears,
If he regard not, though divine the theme.
'Tis not in artful measures, in the chime
And idle tinkling of a minstrel's lyre,
To charm his ear, whose eye is on the heart;
Whose frown can disappoint the proudest strain,
Whose approbation—prosper even mine.

AN EPISTLE

TO JOSEPH HILL ESQ.

Dear Joseph—five and twenty years ago—
Alas how time escapes!—'tis even so—
With frequent intercourse, and always sweet,
And alway friendly, we were wont to cheat
A tedious hour—and now we never meet!
As some grave gentleman in Terence says,
('T was therefore much the same in ancient days)
Good lack, we know not what to-morrow brings—
Strange fluctation of all human things!
True. Changes will befall, and friends may part,
But distance only cannot change the heart;
And were I call'd to prove th' assertion true,
One proof should serve—a reference to you.
Whence comes it then, that in the wane of life,
Though nothing have occurr'd to kindle strife,
We find the friends we fancied we had won,
Though num'rous once, reduc'd to few or none?
Can gold grow worthless, that has stood the touch?
No; gold they seem'd, but they were never such.
Horatio's servant once, with bow and cringe,
Swinging the parlor-door upon its hinge,
Dreading a negative, and overaw'd
Lest he should trespass, begg'd to go abroad.
Go, fellow!—whither?—turning short about—
Nay. Stay at home—you 're always going out.
'Tis but a step, sir, just at the street's end.—
For what?—An please you, sir, to see a friend—
A friend! Horatio cried, and seem'd to start—
Yea marry shalt thou, and with all my heart.—
And fetch my cloak; for, though the night be raw,
I'll see him too—the first I ever saw.

I knew the man, and knew his nature mild,
And was his plaything often when a child;
But somewhat at that moment pinch'd him close,
Else he was seldom bitter or morose.
Perhaps his confidence just then betray'd,
His grief might prompt him with the speech he made;
Perhaps, 'twas mere good-humour gave it birth,
The harmless play of pleasantry and mirth.
Howe'er it was, his language, in my mind,
Bespoke at least a man that knew mankind.
But not to moralize too much, and strain
To prove an evil, of which all complain,
(I hate long arguments verbosely spun)
One story more, dear Hill, and I have done.
Once on a time an emp'ror, a wise man,
No matter where, in China or Japan,
Decreed, that whomsoever should offend
Against the well-known duties of a friend
Convicted once should ever after wear
But half a coat, and show his bosom bare.
The punishment importing this, no doubt,
That all was naught within, and all found out.
O happy Britain! we have not to fear
Such hard and arbitrary measure here;
Else, could a law, like that which I relate,
Once have the sanction of our triple state,
Some few, that I have known in days of old,
Would run most dreadful risk of catching cold
While you, my friend, whatever wind should blow,
Might traverse England safely to and fro,
An honest man, close-button'd to the chin,
Broad-cloth without, and a warm heart within.

TIROCINIUM:

OR,

A REVIEW OF SCHOOLS:

Κεφαλαιον δη παιδειας ορθη τροφη. *Plato.*
Αρχη πολιτειας απασης νεων τροφα *Diog. Laert.*

It is not from his form, in which we trace
Strength join'd with beauty, dignity with grace,
That man, the master of this globe, derives
His right of empire over all that lives.
That form indeed, th'associate of a mind
Vast in its pow'rs, ethereal in its kind,
That form, the labour of almighty skill,
Fram'd for the service of a freeborn will,
Asserts precedence, and bespeaks control,
But borrows all its grandeur from the soul.
Hers is the state, the splendor, and the throne,
An intellectual kingdom, all her own.
For her the Mem'ry fills her ample page
With truths pour'd down from ev'ry distant age;
For her amasses an unbounded store,
The wisdom of great nations, now no more;
Though laden, not encumber'd with her spoil;
Laborious, yet unconscious of her toil;
When copiously supplied, then most enlarg'd;
Still to be fed and not to be surcharg'd.
For her the Fancy, roving unconfin'd,
The present muse of ev'ry pensive mind,
Works magic wonders, adds a brighter hue
To Nature's scenes than Nature ever knew.
At her command winds rise, and waters roar,
Again she lays them slumb'ring on the shore;
With flow'r and fruit the wilderness supplies,
Or bids the rocks in ruder pomp arise.
For her the Judgment, umpire in the strife,
That Grace and Nature have to wage through life,
Quick-sighted arbiter of good and ill,
Appointed sage preceptor to the Will,
Condemns, approves, and with a faithful voice,

Guides the decision of a doubtful choice
  Why did the fiat of a God give birth
To yon fair Sun, and his attendant Earth?
And, when descending he resigns the skies,
Why takes the gentler Moon her turn to rise,
Whom Ocean feels through all his countless waves,
And owns her pow'r on ev'ry shore he laves?
Why do the seasons still enrich the year,
Fruitful and young as in their first career?
Spring hangs her infant blossoms on the trees,
Rock'd in the cradle of the western breeze;
Summer in haste the thriving charge receives
Beneath the shade of her expanded leaves,
Till Autumn's fiercer heats and plenteous dews
Dye them at last in all their glowing hues.—
'Twere wild profusion all, and bootless waste,
Pow'r misemploy'd, munificence misplac'd,
Had not its author dignified the plan,
And crown'd it with the majesty of man.
Thus form'd, thus plac'd, intelligent, and taught,
Look where he will, the wonders God has wrought,
The wildest scorner of his Maker's laws
Finds in a sober moment time to pause,
To press th'important question on his heart,
"Why form'd at all, and wherefore as thou art?"
If man be what he seems, this hour a slave,
The next mere dust and ashes in the grave;
Endu'd with reason only to descry
His crimes and follies with an aching eye;
With passions, just that he may prove, with pain,
The force he spends against their fury vain;
And if, soon after having burnt, by turns,
With ev'ry lust, with which frail Nature burns,
His being end, where death dissolves the bond,
The tomb take all, and all be blank beyond;
Then he, of all that Nature has brought forth,
Stands self-impeach'd the creature of least worth,
And useless while he lives and when he dies,
Brings into doubt the wisdom of the skies.
  Truths, that the learn'd pursue with eager thought,
Are not important always as dear-bought,
Proving at last, though told in pompous strains,
A childish waste of philosophic pains;
But truths, on which depends our main concern,
That 'tis our shame and mis'ry not to learn,
Shine by the side of ev'ry path we tread
With such a lustre, he that runs may read.
'Tis true that, if to trifle life away
Down to the sunset of their latest day,

Then perish on futurity's wide shore
Like fleeting exhalations, found no more,
Were all that Heav'n requir'd of humankind,
And all the plan their destiny design'd,
What none could rev'rence all might justly blame,
And man would breathe but for his Maker's shame.
But reason heard, and nature well perus'd,
At once the dreaming mind is disabus'd.
If all we find possessing earth, sea, air,
Reflect his attributes, who plac'd them there,
Fulfil the purpose, and appear design'd
Proofs of the wisdom of th'all-seeing mind,
'Tis plain the creature, whom he chose t'invest
With kingship and dominion o'er the rest,
Receiv'd his nobler nature, and was made
Fit for the pow'r, in which he stands array'd;
That first, or last, hereafter, if not here,
He too might make his author's wisdom clear,
Praise him on Earth, or, obstinately dumb,
Suffer his justice in a world to come.
This once believ'd, 'twere logic misapplied,
To prove a consequence by none denied,
That we are bound to cast the minds of youth
Betimes into the mould of heav'nly truth,
That taught of God they may indeed be wise,
Nor ignorantly wand'ring miss the skies.
In early days the conscience has in most
A quickness, which in later life is lost:
Preserv'd from guilt by salutary fears,
Or guilty soon relenting into tears.
Too careless often, as our years proceed,
What friends we sort with, or what books we read,
Our parents yet exert a prudent care,
To feed our infant minds with proper fare;
And wisely store the nurs'ry by degrees
With wholesome learning, yet acquir'd with ease.
Neatly secur'd from being soil'd or torn
Beneath a pane of thin translucent horn,
A book (to please us at a tender age
'Tis call'd a book, though but a single page)
Presents the pray'r the Saviour deign'd to teach,
Which children use, and parsons—when they preach.
Lisping our syllables, we scramble next
Through moral narrative, or sacred text;
And learn with wonder how this world began,
Who made, who marr'd, and who has ransom'd, man.
Points, which, unless the Scripture made them plain,
The wisest heads might agitate in vain.
O thou, whom, borne on fancy's eager wing

Back to the season of life's happy spring,
I pleas'd remember, and, while mem'ry yet
Holds fast her office here, can ne'er forget;
Ingenious dreamer, in whose well-told tale
Sweet fiction and sweet truth alike prevail;
Whose hum'rous vein, strong sense, and simple style,
May teach the gayest, make the gravest smile;
Witty, and well employ'd, and, like thy Lord,
Speaking in parables his slighted word;
I name thee not, lest so despis'd a name
Should move a sneer at thy deserved fame;
Yet e'en in transitory life's late day,
That mingles all my brown with sober gray,
Revere the man, whose *pilgrim* marks the road,
And guides the *progress* of the soul to God.
'Twere well with most, if books, that could engage
Their childhood, pleas'd them at a riper age;
The man, approving what had charm'd the boy,
Would die at last in comfort, peace, and joy;
And not with curses on his heart, who stole
The gem of truth from his unguarded soul.
The stamp of artless piety impress'd
By kind tuition on his yielding breast,
The youth now bearded, and yet pert and raw,
Regards with scorn, though once receiv'd with awe;
And, warp'd into the labyrinth of lies,
That babblers, call'd philosophers, devise,
Blasphemes his creed, as founded on a plan
Replete with dreams, unworthy of a man.
Touch but his nature in its ailing part,
Assert the native evil of his heart,
His pride resents the charge, although the proof *
Rise in his forehead, and seem rank enough:
Point to the cure, describe a Saviour's cross
As God's expedient to retrieve his loss,
The young apostate sickens at the view,
And hates it with the malice of a Jew.
How weak the barrier of mere Nature proves,
Oppos'd against the pleasures Nature loves!
While self-betray'd, and wilfully undone,
She longs to yield, no sooner woo'd than won.
Try now the merits of this blest exchange
Of modest truth for wit's eccentric range.
Time was, he clos'd as he began the day
With decent duty, not asham'd to pray:
The practice was a bond upon his heart,
A pledge he gave for a consistent part;

* See 2 Chron. ch. XXVI, ver. 19.

Nor could he dare presumptuously displease
A pow'r, confess'd so lately on his knees.
But now farewell all legendary tales,
The shadows fly, philosophy prevails;
Pray'r to the winds, and caution to the waves;
Religion makes the free by nature slaves.
Priests have invented, and the world admir'd
What knavish priests promulgate as inspir'd;
Till Reason, now no longer overaw'd,
Resumes her pow'rs, and spurns the clumsy fraud;
And, common-sense diffusing real day,
The meteor of the Gospel dies away.
Such rhapsodies our shrewd discerning youth
Learn from expert inquiries after truth;
Whose only care, might truth presume to speak,
Is not to find what they profess to seek.
And thus, well-tutor'd only while we share
A mother's lectures and a nurse's care;
And taught at schools much mythologic stuff,*
But sound religion sparingly enough;
Our early notices of truth, disgrac'd,
Soon lose their credit, and are all effac'd.
Would you your son should be a sot or dunce,
Lascivious, headstrong, or all these at once;
That in good time the stripling's finish'd taste
For loose expense, and fashionable waste,
Should prove your ruin, and his own at last;
Train him in public with a mob of boys,
Childish in mischief only and in noise,
Else of a mannish growth, and five in ten
In infidelity and lewdness men.
There shall he learn, ere sixteen winters old,
That authors are most useful pawn'd or sold;
That pedantry is all that schools impart,
But taverns teach the knowledge of the heart;
There waiter Dick, with Bacchanalian lays,
Shall win his heart, and have his drunken praise,
His counsellor and bosom friend shall prove,
And some street-pacing harlot his first love.
Schools, unless discipline were doubly strong,
Detain their adolescent charge too long;
The management of tiroes of eighteen
Is difficult; their punishment obscene.

* The author begs leave to explain.—Sensible that, without such knowledge, neither the ancient poets nor historians can be tasted, or indeed understood, he does not mean to censure the pains that are taken to instruct a schoolboy in the religion of the Heathen, but merely that neglect of Christian culture which leaves him shamefully ignorant of his own.

The stout tall captain, whose superior size
The minor heroes view with envious eyes,
Becomes their pattern, upon whom they fix
Their whole attention, and ape all his tricks.
His pride, that scorns t'obey or to submit,
With them is courage; his effront'ry wit.
His wild excursions, window-breaking feats,
Robb'ry of gardens, quarrels in the streets,
His hairbreadth 'scapes, and all his daring schemes,
Transport them, and are made their fav'rite themes.
In little bosoms such achievements strike
A kindred spark: they burn to do the like.
Thus, half-accomplish'd ere he yet begin
To show the peeping down upon his chin;
And, as maturity of years comes on,
Made just th'adept that you design'd your son;
T'ensure the perseverance of his course,
And give your monstrous project all its force,
Send him to college. If he there be tam'd,
Or in one article of vice reclaim'd,
Where no regard of ord'nances is shown
Or look'd for now, the fault must be his own.
Some sneaking virtue lurks in him, no doubt,
Where neither strumpets' charms nor drinking-bout,
Nor gambling practices, can find it out.
Such youths of spirit, and that spirit too,
Ye nurs'ries of our boys, we owe to you:
Though from ourselves the mischief more proceeds.
For public schools 'tis public folly feeds.
The slaves of custom and establish'd mode,
With packhorse constancy we keep the road,
Crooked or straight, through quags or thorny dells,
True to the jingling of our leader's bells.
To follow foolish precedents, and wink
With both our eyes, is easier than to think:
And such an age as ours baulks no expense,
Except of caution, and of common-sense;
Else sure notorious fact, and proof so plain,
Would turn our steps into a wiser train.
I blame not those, who with what care they can
O'erwatch the num'rous and unruly clan;
Or, if I blame, 'tis only that they dare
Promise a work, of which they must despair.
Have ye, ye sage intendants of the whole,
A ubiquarian presence and control,
Elisha's eye, that, when Gehazi stray'd,
Went with him, and saw all the game he play'd?
Yes—ye are conscious; and on all the shelves
Your pupils strike upon have struck yourselves.

Or if, by nature sober, ye had then,
Boys as ye were, the gravity of men;
Ye knew at least, by constant proofs address'd
To ears and eyes, the vices of the rest.
But ye connive at what ye cannot cure,
And evils, not to be endur'd, endure,
Lest pow'r exerted, but without success,
Should make the little ye retain still less.
Ye once were justly fam'd for bringing forth
Undoubted scholarship and genuine worth;
And in the firmament of fame still shines
A glory, bright as that of all the signs,
Of poets rais'd by you, and statesmen, and divines
Peace to them all! those brilliant times are fled,
And no such lights are kindling in their stead.
Our striplings shine indeed, but with such rays,
As set the midnight riot in a blaze;
And seem, if judg'd by their expressive looks,
Deeper in none than in their surgeon's books
  Say muse, (for, education made the song,
No muse can hesitate, or linger long)
What causes move us, knowing as we must,
That these *menageries* all fail their trust,
To send our sons to scout and scamper there,
While colts and puppies cost us so much care?
  Be it a weakness, it deserves some praise,
We love the playplace of our early days;
The scene is touching, and the heart is stone,
That feels not at that sight, and feels at none.
The wall on which we tried our graving skill,
The very name we carv'd subsisting still;
The bench on which we sat while deep employ'd.
Tho' mangled, hack'd, and hew'd not yet destroy'd;
The little ones, unbutton'd, glowing hot,
Playing our games, and on the very spot;
As happy as we once, to kneel and draw
The chalky ring, and knuckle down at taw;
To pitch the ball into the grounded hat,
Or drive it devious with a dext'rous pat;
The pleasing spectacle at once excites
Such recollection of our own delights,
That, viewing it, we seem almost t'obtain
Our innocent sweet simple years again.
This fond attachment to the well-known place,
Whence first we started into life's long race,
Maintains its hold with such unfailing sway,
We feel it e'en in age, and at our latest day.
Hark! how the sire of chits, whose future share
Of classic food begins to be his care,

With his own likeness plac'd on either knee,
Indulges all a father's heart-felt glee;
And tells them, as he strokes their silver locks,
That they must soon learn Latin, and to box;
Then turning he regales his list'ning wife
With all th'adventures of his early life;
His skill in coachmanship, or driving chaise,
In bilking tavern bills, and spouting plays;
What shifts he us'd, detected in a scrape,
How he was flogg'd, or had the luck t'escape;
What sums he lost at play, and how he sold
Watch, seals, and all—till all his pranks are told.
Retracing thus his frolics, ('tis a name
That palliates deeds of folly and of shame)
He gives the local bias all its sway;
Resolves that where he play'd his sons shall play,
And destines their bright genius to be shown
Just in the scene where he display'd his own.
The meek and bashful boy will soon be taught,
To be as bold and forward as he ought;
The rude will scuffle through with ease enough,
Great schools suit best the sturdy and the rough.
Ah happy designation, prudent choice,
Th'event is sure; expect it; and rejoice!
Soon see your wish fulfill'd in either child,
The pert made perter, and the tame made wild.
The great indeed, by titles, riches, birth,
Excus'd th'encumbrance of more solid worth,
Are best dispos'd of where with most success
They may acquire that confident address,
Those habits of profuse and lewd expense,
That scorn of all delights but those of sense,
Which, though in plain plebeians we condemn,
With so much reason all expect from them.
But families of less illustrious fame,
Whose chief distinction is their spotless name,
Whose heirs, their honors none, their income small,
Must shine by true descent, or not at all,
What dream they of, that with so little care
They risk their hopes, their dearest treasure, there?
They dream of little Charles or William grac'd
With wig prolix, down flowing to his waist;
They see th'attentive crowds his talents draw,
They hear him speak—the oracle of law.
The father, who designs his babe a priest,
Dreams him episcopally such at least;
And, while the playful jockey scours the room
Briskly, astride upon the parlor broom,
In fancy sees him more superbly ride

In coach with purple lin'd, and mitres on its side.
Events improbable and strange as these,
Which only a parental eye foresees,
A public school shall bring to pass with ease.
But how? resides such virtue in that air,
As must create an appetite for pray'r?
And will it breathe into him all the zeal,
That candidates for such a prize should feel,
To take the lead and be the foremost still
In all true worth and literary skill?
"Ah blind to bright futurity, untaught
The knowledge of the world, and dull of thought!
Church-ladders are not always mounted best
By learned clerks, and Latinists profess'd.
Th'exalted prize demands an upward look,
Not to be found by poring on a book.
Small skill in Latin, and still less in Greek,
Is more than adequate to all I seek.
Let erudition grace him, or not grace,
I give the bauble but the second place;
His wealth, fame, honors, all that I intend,
Subsist and centre in one point—a friend.
A friend, whate'er he studies or neglects,
Shall give him consequence, heal all defects.
His intercourse with peers and sons of peers—
There dawns the splendor of his future years:
In that bright quarter his propitious skies
Shall blush betimes, and there his glory rise.
Your Lordship, and *Your Grace*! what school can teach
A rhet'ric equal to those parts of speech?
What need of Homer's verse, or Tully's prose,
Sweet interjections! if he learn but those?
Let rev'rend churls his ignorance rebuke,
Who starve upon a dog's-ear'd Pentateuch,
The parson knows enough, who knows a duke"
Egregious purpose! worthily begun
In barb'rous prostitution of your son;
Press'd on *his* part by means, that would disgrace
A scriv'ner's clerk, or footman out of place,
And ending, if at last its end be gain'd,
In sacrilege, in God's own house profan'd.
It may succeed; and, if his sins should call,
For more than common punishment, it shall;
The wretch shall rise, and be the thing on Earth
Least qualified in honor, learning, worth,
To occupy a sacred, awful post,
In which the best and worthiest tremble most.
The *royal letters* are a thing of course,
A king, that would, might recommend his horse;

And deans, no doubt, and chapters, with one voice,
As bound in duty, would confirm the choice.
Behold your bishop! well he plays his part,
Christian in name, and infidel in heart,
Ghostly in office, earthly in his plan,
A slave at court, elsewhere a lady's man.
Dumb as a senator, and as a priest
A piece of mere church-furniture at best;
To live estrang'd from God his total scope,
And his end sure, without one glimpse of hope.
But fair although and feasible it seem,
Depend not much upon your golden dream;
For Providence, that seems concern'd t' exempt
The hallow'd bench from absolute contempt,
In spite of all the wrigglers into place,
Still keeps a seat or two for worth and grace;
And therefore 'tis, that, though the sight be rare,
We sometimes see a Lowth or Bagot there.
Besides, school-friendships are not always found,
Though fair in promise, permanent and sound;
The most disint'rested and virtuous minds,
In early years connected, time unbinds;
New situations give a diff'rent cast
Of habit, inclination, temper, taste;
And he, that seem'd our counterpart at first,
Soon shows the strong similitude revers'd.
Young heads are giddy, and young hearts are warm,
And make mistakes for manhood to reform.
Boys are at best but pretty buds unblown,
Whose scent and hues are rather guess'd than known;
Each dreams that each is just what he appears,
But learns his error in maturer years,
When disposition, like a sail unfurl'd,
Shows all its rents and patches to the world.
If, therefore, e'en when honest in design,
A boyish friendship may so soon decline,
'Twere wiser sure t' inspire a little heart
With just abhorrence of so mean a part,
Than set your son to work at a vile trade
For wages so unlikely to be paid.
Our public hives of puerile resort,
That are of chief and most approv'd report,
To such base hopes, in many a sordid soul,
Owe their repute in part, but not the whole.
A principle, whose proud pretensions pass
Unquestion'd, though the jewel be but glass—
That with a world, not often over-nice,
Ranks as a virtue, and is yet a vice;
Or rather a gross compound, justly tried,

Of envy, hatred, jealousy, and pride—
Contributes most perhaps t'enhance their fame;
And emulation is its specious name.
Boys, once on fire with that contentious zeal,
Feel all the rage, that female rivals feel;
The prize of beauty in a woman's eyes
Not brighter than in theirs the scholar's prize.
The spirit of that competition burns
With all varities of ills by turns;
Each vainly magnifies his own success,
Resents his fellow's, wishes it were less;
Exults in his miscarriage, if he fail;
Deems his reward too great, if he prevail;
And labours to surpass him day and night,
Less for improvement than to tickle spite.
The spur is pow'rful, and I grant its force;
It pricks the genius forward in its course,
Allows short time for play, and none for sloth;
And, felt alike by each, advances both;
But judge, where so much evil intervenes,
The end, though plausible, not worth the means.
Weigh, for a moment, classical desert
Against a heart deprav'd and temper hurt;
Hurt too perhaps for life; for early wrong,
Done to the nobler part, affects it long;
And you are staunch indeed in learning's cause,
If you can crown a discipline, that draws
Such mischiefs after it, with much applause.
  Connection form'd for int'rest, and endear'd
By selfish views, thus censur'd and cashier'd;
And emulation, as engend'ring hate,
Doom'd to a no less ignominious fate:
The props of such proud seminaries fall,
The Jachin and the Boaz of them all.
Great schools rejected then, as those that swell
Beyond a size that can be manag'd well,
Shall royal institutions miss the bays,
And small academies win all the praise?
Force not my drift beyond its just intent,
I praise a school as Pope a government;
So take my judgment in his language dress'd,
" Whate'er is best administer'd is best."
Few boys are born with talents that excel,
But all are capable of living well;
Then ask not, Whether limited or large?
But, Watch they strictly, or neglect their charge?
If anxious only, that their boys may *learn*,
While *morals* languish, a despis'd concern,
The great and small deserve one common blame,

Diff'rent in size, but in effect the same.
Much zeal in virtue's cause all teachers boast,
Though motives of mere lucre sway the most;
Therefore in towns and cities they abound,
For there the game they seek is easiest found;
Though there, in spite of all that care can do,
Traps to catch youth are most abundant too.
If shrewd, and of a well constructed brain,
Keen in pursuit, and vig'rous to retain,
Your son come forth a prodigy of skill;
As, wheresoever taught, so form'd, he will;
The pedagogue, with self-complacent air,
Claims more than half the praise as his due share.
But if, with all his genius, he betray,
Not more intelligent than loose and gay,
Such vicious habits as disgrace his name,
Threaten his health, his fortune, and his fame;
Though want of due restraint alone have bred
The symptoms that you see with so much dread;
Unenvied there, he may sustain alone
The whole reproach, the fault was all his own.
O 'tis a sight to be with joy perus'd,
By all whom sentiment has not abus'd;
New-fangled sentiment, the boasted grace
Of those who never feel in the right place;
A sight surpass'd by none that we can show,
'Though Vestris on one leg still shine below;
A father blest with an ingenuous son,
Father, and friend, and tutor, all in one.
How!—turn again to tales long since forgot,
Æsop, and Phædrus, and the rest?—Why not?
He will not blush, that has a father's heart,
To take in childish plays a childish part;
But bends his sturdy back to any toy,
That youth takes pleasure in, to please his boy;
Then why resign into a stranger's hand
A task as much within your own command,
That God and nature, and your int'rest too,
Seem with one voice to delegate to you?
Why hire a lodging in a house unknown
For one whose tend'rest thoughts all hover round your own?
This second weaning, needless as it is,
How does it lac'rate both your heart and his!
Th' indented stick, that loses day by day
Notch after notch, till all are smooth'd away,
Bears witness, long ere his dismission come,
With what intense desire he wants his home.
But though the joys he hopes beneath your roof
Bid fair enough to answer in the proof,

Harmless, and safe, and nat'ral, as they are,
A dissappointment waits him even there:
Arriv'd, he feels an unexpected change,
He blushes, hangs his head, is shy and strange,
No longer takes, as once, with fearless ease,
His fav'rite stand between his father's knees,
But seeks the corner of some distant seat,
And eyes the door and watches a retreat,
And, least familiar where he should be most,
Feels all his happiest privileges lost
Alas, poor boy!—the natural effect
Of love by absence chill'd into respect,
Say, what accomplishments, at school acquir'd,
Brings he, to sweeten fruits so undesir'd?
Thou well deserv'st an alienated son,
Unless thy conscious heart acknowledge—none;
None that, in thy domestic snug recess,
He had not made his own with more address,
Though some perhaps, that shock thy feeling mind,
And better never learn'd, or left behind.
Add too, that, thus estrang'd, thou canst obtain
By no kind arts his confidence again;
That here begins with most that long complaint
Of filial frankness lost, and love grown faint,
Which, oft neglected, in life's waning years
A parent pours into regardless ears.
Like caterpillars, dangling under trees
By slender threads, and swinging in the breeze,
Which filthily bewray and sore disgrace
The boughs in which are bred th'unseemly race;
While ev'ry worm industriously weaves
And winds his web about the rivell'd leaves;
So num'rous are the follies, that annoy
The mind and heart of ev'ry sprightly boy;
Imaginations noxious and perverse,
Which admonition can alone disperse.
Th'encroaching nuisance asks a faithful hand,
Patient, affectionate, of high command,
To check the procreation of a breed
Sure to exhaust the plant on which they feed,
'Tis not enough, that Greek or Roman page,
At stated hours, his freakish thoughts engage;
E'en in his pastimes he requires a friend,
To warn, and teach him safely to unbend;
O'er all his pleasures gently to preside,
Watch his emotions, and control their tide;
And levying thus, and with an easy sway,
A tax of profit from his very play,
T'impress a value, not to be eras'd,

On moments squander'd else, and running all to wast
And seems it nothing in a father's eye,
That unimprov'd those many moments fly?
And is he well content his son should find
No nourishment to feed his growing mind
But conjugated verbs, and nouns declin'd?
For such is all the mental food purvey'd
By public hackneys in the schooling trade;
Who feed a pupil's intellect with store
Of syntax, truly, but with little more;
Dismiss their cares, when they dismiss their flock,
Machines themselves, and govern'd by a clock.
Perhaps a father, blest with any brains,
Would deem it no abuse, or waste of pains,
T'improve this diet, at no great expense,
With sav'ry truth and wholesome common sense;
To lead his son, for prospects of delight,
To some not steep, though philosophic, height,
Thence to exhibit to his wond'ring eyes
Yon circling worlds, their distance, and their size;
The moons of Jove, and Saturn's belted ball,
And the harmonious order of them all;
To show him in an insect or a flow'r
Such microscopic proof of skill and pow'r,
As, hid from ages past, God now displays,
To combat atheists with in modern days;
To spread the earth before him, and commend,
With designation of the finger's end,
Its various parts to his attentive note,
Thus bringing home to him the most remote;
To teach his heart to glow with gen'rous flame,
Caught from the deeds of men of ancient fame:
And, more than all, with commendation due,
To set some living worthy in his view,
Whose fair example may at once inspire
A wish to copy what he must admire.
Such knowledge gain'd betimes, and which appears,
Though solid, not too weighty for his years,
Sweet in itself, and not forbidding sport,
When health demands it, of athletic sort,
Would make him—what some lovely boys have been,
And more than one perhaps that I have seen—
An evidence and reprehension both
Of the mere schoolboy's lean and tardy growth.
  Art thou a man professionally tied,
With all thy faculties elsewhere applied,
Too busy to intend a meaner care,
Than how t'enrich thyself, and next thine heir;

Or art thou (as though rich, perhaps thou art)
But poor in knowledge, having none t'impart:—
Behold that figure, neat, though plainly clad;
His sprightly mingled with a shade of sad;
Not of a nimble tongue, though now and then
Heard to articulate like other men;
No jester, and yet lively in discourse,
His phrase well chosen, clear, and full of force;
And his address, if not quite French in ease,
Not English stiff, but frank, and form'd to please;
Low in the world, because he scorns its arts;
A man of letters, manners, morals, parts;
Unpatroniz'd, and therefore little known;
Wise for himself and his few friends alone—
In him thy well-appointed proxy see,
Arm'd for a work too difficult for thee;
Prepar'd by taste, by learning, and true worth,
To form thy son, to strike his genius forth;
Beneath thy roof, beneath thine eye, to prove
The force of discipline, when back'd by love;
To double all thy pleasure in thy child,
His mind inform'd, his morals undefil'd.
Safe under such a wing, the boy shall show
No spots contracted among grooms below,
Nor taint his speech with meannesses, design'd
By footman Tom for witty and refin'd.
There, in his commerce with the liv'ried herd,
Lurks the contagion chiefly to be fear'd;
For since (so fashion dictates) all, who claim
A higher than a mere plebeian fame,
Find it expedient, come what mischief may,
To entertain a thief or two in pay,
(And they that can afford th'expense of more,
Some half a dozen, and some half a score,)
Great cause occurs, to save him from a band
So sure to spoil him, and so near at hand;
A point secur'd, if once he be supplied
With some such Mentor always at his side.
Are such men rare? perhaps they would abound,
Were occupation easier to be found,
Were education, else so sure to fail,
Conducted on a manageable scale,
And schools, that have outliv'd all just esteem,
Exchang'd for the secure domestic scheme.—
But, having found him, be thou duke or earl,
Show thou hast sense enough to prize the pearl,
And, as thou wouldst th'advancement of thine heir
In all good faculties beneath his care,
Respect, as is but rational and just,

A man deem'd worthy of so dear a trust.
Despis'd by thee, what more can he expect
From youthful folly than the same neglect;
A flat and fatal negative obtains
That instant upon all his future pains;
His lessons tire, his mild rebukes offend,
And all th'instructions of thy son's best friend
Are a stream chok'd, or trickling to no end.
Doom him not then to solitary meals;
But recollect that he has sense, and feels;
And that, possessor of a soul refin'd,
An upright heart, and cultivated mind,
His post not mean, his talents not unknown,
He deems it hard to vegetate alone.
And, if admitted at thy board he sit,
Account him no just mark for idle wit;
Offend not him, whom modesty restrains
From repartee, with jokes that he disdains;
Much less transfix his feelings with an oath;
Nor frown, unless he vanish with the cloth.—
And, trust me, his utility may reach
To more than he is hir'd or bound to teach;
Much trash unutter'd, and some ills undone,
Through rev'rence of the censor of thy son.
   But, if thy table be indeed unclean,
Foul with excess, and with discourse obscene,
And thou a wretch, whom, foll'wing her old plan
The world accounts an honorable man,
Because forsooth thy courage has been tried,
And stood the test perhaps on the wrong side;
Though thou hadst never grace enough to prove
That any thing but vice could win thy love;—
Or hast thou a polite, card-playing wife,
Chain'd to the routs that she frequents for life;
Who, just when industry begins to snore,
Flies, wing'd with joy, to some coach-crowded door;
And thrice in ev'ry winter throngs thine own
With half the chariots and sedans in town,
Thyself meanwhile e'en shifting as thou mayst;
Not very sober though, nor very chaste;
Or is thine house, though less superb thy rank,
If not a scene of pleasure, a mere blank,
And thou at best, and in thy sob'rest mood,
A trifler vain, and empty of all good;
Though mercy for thyself thou canst have none,
Hear nature plead, show mercy to thy son.
Sav'd from his home, where ev'ry day brings forth
Some mischief fatal to his future worth,
Find him a better in a distant spot,

Within some pious pastor's humble cot,
Where vile example (yours I chiefly mean,
The most seducing, and the oft'nest seen)
May never more be stamp'd upon his breast,
Not yet perhaps incurably impress'd.
Where early rest makes early rising sure,
Disease or comes not, or finds easy cure,
Prevented much by diet neat and plain;
Or, if it enter, soon starv'd out again:
Where all th'attention of his faithful host,
Discreetly limited to two at most,
May raise such fruits as shall reward his care,
And not at last evaporate in air:
Where, stillness aiding study, and his mind
Serene, and to his duties much inclin'd,
Not occupied in day-dreams, as at home,
Of pleasures past, or follies yet to come,
His virtuous toil may terminate at last
In settled habit and decided taste—
But whom do I advise? the fashion-led,
Th'incorrigibly young, the deaf, the dead,
Whom care and cool deliberation suit
Not better much than spectacles a brute;
Who, if their sons some slight tuition share,
Deem it of no great moment whose, or where;
Too proud t'adopt the thoughts of one unknown,
And much too gay t'have any of their own.
But courage, man! methought the muse replied,
Mankind are various, and the world is wide:
The ostrich, silliest of the feather'd kind,
And form'd of God without a parent's mind,
Commits her eggs incautious to the dust,
Forgetful that the foot may crush the trust;
And, while on public nurs'ries they rely,
Not knowing, and too oft not caring, why,
Irrational in what they thus prefer,
No few, that would seem wise, resemble her.
But all are not alike. Thy warning voice
May here and there prevent erroneous choice;
And some perhaps, who, busy as they are,
Yet make their progeny their dearest care,
(Whose hearts will ache, once told what ills may reach
Their offspring, left upon so wild a beach,)
Will need no stress of argument t'enforce
Th'expedience of a less advent'rous course:
The rest will slight thy counsel, or condemn;
But *they* have human feelings, turn to *them*.
To you then, tenants of life's middle state,
Securely plac'd between the small and great,

Whose character, yet undebauch'd, retains
Two thirds of all the virtue that remains,
Who, wise yourselves, desire your son should learn
Your wisdom and your ways—to you I turn.
Look round you on a world perversely blind;
See what contempt is fall'n on humankind;
See wealth abus'd, and dignities misplac'd,
Great titles, offices, and trusts disgrac'd,
Long lines of ancestry, renown'd of old,
Their noble qualities all quench'd and cold;
See Bedlam's closetted and hand-cuff'd charge
Surpass'd in frenzy by the mad at large;
See great commanders making war a trade,
Great lawyers, lawyers without study made;
Churchmen, in whose esteem their best employ
Is odious, and their wages all their joy,
Who, far enough from furnishing their shelves
With Gospel lore, turn infidels themselves;
See womanhood despis'd, and manhood sham'd
With infamy too nauseous to be nam'd,
Fops at all corners, lady-like in mien,
Civetted fellows, smelt ere they are seen,
Else coarse and rude in manners, and their tongue
On fire with curses, and with nonsense hung,
Now flush'd with drunk'nness, now with whoredom pale,
Their breath a sample of last night's regale;
See volunteers in all the vilest arts,
Men well endow'd, of honorable parts,
Design'd by Nature wise, but self-made fools;
All these, and more like these, were bred at schools.
And if it chance, as sometimes chance it will,
That though school-bred, the boy be virtuous still;
Such rare exceptions, shining in the dark,
Prove, rather than impeach, the just remark:
As here and there a twinkling star descried
Serves but to show how black is all beside.
Now look on him, whose very voice in tone
Just echoes thine, whose features are thine own,
And stroke his polish'd cheek of purest red,
And lay thine hand upon his flaxen head,
And say, My boy, th'unwelcome hour is come,
When thou, transplanted from thy genial home,
Must find a colder soil and bleaker air,
And trust for safety to a stranger's care;
What character, what turn thou wilt assume
From constant converse with I know not whom;
Who there will court thy friendship, with what views,
And, artless as thou art, whom thou wilt choose
Though much depends on what thy choice shall be,

Is all chance-medley, and unknown to me.
Canst thou, the tear just trembling on thy lids,
And while the dreadful risk foreseen forbids,
Free too, and under no constraining force,
Unless the sway of custom warp thy course;
Lay such a stake upon the losing side,
Merely to gratify so blind a guide?
Thou canst not! Nature, pulling at thine heart
Condemns th'unfatherly, th'imprudent part.
Thou wouldst not, deaf to Nature's tend'rest plea,
Turn him adrift upon a rolling sea,
Nor say, *Go thither*, conscious that there lay
A brood of asps, or quicksands in his way;
Then, only govern'd by the self-same rule
Of nat'ral pity, send him not to school.
No—guard him better. Is he not thine own,
Thyself in miniature, thy flesh, thy bone?
And hop'st thou not ('tis ev'ry father's hope)
That, since thy strength must with thy years elope,
And thou wilt need some comfort, to assuage
Health's last farewell, a staff of thine old age,
That then, in recompense of all thy cares,
Thy child shall show respect to thy gray hairs,
Befriend thee, of all other friends bereft,
And give thy life its only cordial left?
Aware then how much danger intervenes,
To compass that good end, forecast the means.
His heart, now passive, yields to thy command;
Secure it thine, its key is in thine hand.
If thou desert thy charge, and throw it wide,
Nor heed what guests there enter and abide,
Complain not if attachments lewd and base
Supplant thee in it, and usurp thy place.
But, if thou guard its sacred chambers sure
From vicious inmates, and delights impure,
Either his gratitude shall hold him fast,
And keep him warm and filial to the last;
Or, if he prove unkind (as who can say
But, being man, and therefore frail, he may?),
One comfort yet shall cheer thine aged heart,
Howe'er he slight thee, thou hast done thy part.
  Oh, barb'rous! wouldst thou with a Gothic hand
Pull down the schools—what!—all the schools i'th'land;
Or throw them up to liv'ry-nags and grooms,
Or turn them into shops and auction rooms?—
A captious question, sir (and yours is one),
Deserves an answer similar, or none.
Wouldst thou, possessor of a flock, employ
(Appris'd that he is such) a careless boy,

And feed him well, and give him handsome pay,
Merely to sleep, and let them run astray?
Survey our schools and colleges, and see
A sight not much unlike my simile.
From education, as the leading cause,
The public character its color draws;
Thence the prevailing manners take their cast,
Extravagant or sober, loose or chaste.
And, though I would not advertise them yet,
Nor write on each—*This building to be let*,
Unless the world were all prepar'd t'embrace
A plan well worthy to supply their place;
Yet, backward as they are, and long have been,
To cultivate and keep the *morals* clean,
(Forgive the crime) I wish them, I confess,
Or better manag'd, or encourag'd less.

TO THE REVEREND MR. NEWTON.

AN INVITATION INTO THE COUNTRY.

The swallows in their torpid state
  Compose their useless wing,
And bees in hives as idly wait
  The call of early Spring.

The keenest frost that binds the stream,
  The wildest wind that blows,
Are neither felt nor fear'd by them,
  Secure of their repose.

But man, all feeling and awake,
  The gloomy scene surveys;
With present ills his heart must ache,
  And pant for brighter days.

Old Winter, halting o'er the mead,
  Bids me and Mary mourn;
But lovely Spring peeps o'er his head,
  And whispers your return.

Then April, with her sister May,
  Shall chase him from the bow'rs,
And weave fresh garlands ev'ry day,
  To crown the smiling hours.

And if a tear, that speaks regret
  Of happier times, appear,
A glimpse of joy, that we have met,
  Shall shine and dry the tear.

CATHARINA.

ADDRESSED TO MISS STAPLETON,

(NOW MRS. COURTNEY.)

She came—she is gone—we have met—
 And meet perhaps never again;
The sun of that moment is set,
 And seems to have risen in vain.
Catharina has fled like a dream—
 (So vanishes pleasure, alas!)
But has left a regret and esteem,
 That will not so suddenly pass.

The last evening ramble we made,
 Catharina, Maria, and I,
Our progress was often delay'd
 By the nightingale warbling nigh.
We paus'd under many a tree,
 And much she was charm'd with a tone
Less sweet to Maria and me,
 Who so lately had witness'd her own.

My numbers that day she had sung,
 And gave them a grace so divine,
As only her musical tongue
 Could infuse into numbers of mine.
The longer I heard, I esteem'd
 The work of my fancy the more,
And e'en to myself never seem'd
 So tuneful a poet before.

Though the pleasures of London exceed
 In number the days of the year,
Catharina, did nothing impede,
 Would feel herself happier here;
For the close-woven arches of limes
 On the banks of our river, I know,
Are sweeter to her many times
 Than aught that the city can show.

So it is, when the mind is endu'd
With a well-judging taste from above;
Then, whether embellish'd or rude,
'Tis nature alone that we love.
The achievements of art may amuse,
May even our wonder excite,
But groves, hills, and valleys, diffuse
A lasting, a sacred delight.

Since then in the rural recess
Catharina alone can rejoice,
May it still be her lot to possess
The scene of her sensible choice!
To inhabit a mansion remote
From the clatter of street-pacing steeds,
And by Philomel's annual note
To measure the life that she leads.

With her book, and her voice, and her lyre,
To wing all her moments at home;
And with scenes that new rapture inspire,
As oft as it suits her to roam;
She will have just the life she prefers,
With little to hope or to fear,
And ours would be pleasant as hers,
Might we view her enjoying it here.

THE MORALIZER CORRECTED

A TALE.

A hermit, (or if 'chance you hold
That title now too trite and old)
A man, once young, who liv'd retir'd
As hermit could have well desir'd,
His hours of study clos'd at last,
And finish'd his concise repast,
Stoppled his cruise, replac'd his book
Within its customary nook,
And, staff in hand, set forth to share
The sober cordial of sweet air,
Like Isaac, with a mind applied
To serious thought at ev'ningtide.

Autumnal rains had made it chill,
And from the trees, that fring'd his hill,
Shades slanting at the close of day
Chill'd more his else delightful way.
Distant a little mile he spied
A western bank's still sunny side,
And right toward the favor'd place
Proceeding with his nimblest pace,
In hope to bask a little yet,
Just reach'd it when the sun was set.
Your hermit, young and jovial sirs!
Learns something from whate'er occurs—
And hence, he said, my mind computes
The real worth of man's pursuits.
His object chosen, wealth or fame,
Or other sublunary game
Imagination to his view
Presents it deck'd with ev'ry hue,
That can seduce him not to spare
His pow'rs of best exertion there,
But youth, health, vigor to expend
On so desirable an end.
Ere long approach life's ev'ning shades,
The glow, that fancy gave it, fades;
And, earn'd too late, it wants the grace
That first engag'd him in the chase.
True, answer'd an angelic guide,
Attendant at the senior's side—
But whether all the time it cost,
To urge the fruitless chase be lost,
Must be decided by the worth
Of that, which call'd his ardor forth.
Trifles pursu'd, whate'er th' event,
Must cause him shame or discontent;
A vicious object still is worse,
Successful there he wins a curse;
But he, whom e'en in life's last stage
Endeavors laudable engage,
Is paid, at least in peace of mind,
And sense of having well design'd;
And if, ere he attain his end,
His sun precipitate descend,
A brighter prize than that he meant
Shall recompense his mere intent.
No virtuous wish can bear a date
Either too early or too late.

THE FAITHFUL BIRD.

The greenhouse is my summer seat;
My shrubs displac'd from that retreat
Enjoy'd the open air;
Two goldfinches, whose sprightly song
Had been their mutual solace long,
Liv'd happy pris'ners there.

They sang, as blythe as finches sing,
That flutter loose on golden wing,
And frolic where they list;
Strangers to liberty, 'tis true,
But that delight they never knew
And therefore never miss'd.

But nature works in ev'ry breast,
With force not easily suppress'd;
And Dick felt some desires,
That, after many an effort vain,
Instructed him at length to gain
A pass between his wires.

The open widows seem'd t' invite
The freeman to a farewell flight;
But Tom was still confin'd;
And Dick, although his way was clear
Was much too gen'rous and sincere,
To leave his friend behind.

So settling on his cage, by play,
And chirp, and kiss, he seem'd to say,
You must not live alone—
Nor would he quit that chosen stand
Till I, with slow and cautious hand,
Return'd him to his own.

O ye, who never taste the joys
Of Friendship, satisfied with noise,
Fandango, ball, and rout!
Blush, when I tell you how a bird,
A prison with a friend preferr'd
To liberty without.

THE NEEDLESS ALARM.

A TALE.

There is a field, through which I often pass,
Thick overspread with moss and silky grass,
Adjoining close to Kilwick's echoing wood,
Where oft the bitch-fox hides her hapless brood,
Reserv'd to solace many a neighb'ring squire,
That he may follow them through brake and brier
Contusion hazarding of neck, or spine,
Which rural gentlemen call sport divine.
A narrow brook, by rushy banks conceal'd,
Runs in a bottom, and divides the field;
Oaks insterperse it, that had once a head,
But now wear crests of oven-wood instead;
And where the land slopes to its wat'ry bourn,
Wide yawns a gulf beside a ragged thorn;
Bricks line the sides, but shiver'd long ago,
And horrid brambles intertwine below;
A hollow scoop'd, I judge, in ancient time,
For baking earth, or burning rock to lime.
Not yet the hawthorn bore her berries red,
With which the fieldfare, wintry guest, is fed;
Nor Autumn yet had brush'd from ev'ry spray,
With her chill hand, the mellow leaves away;
But corn was hous'd, and beans were in the stack,
Now therefore issu'd forth the spotted pack,
With tails high mounted, ears hung low, and throats,
With a whole gamut fill'd of heavenly notes,
For which, alas! my destiny severe,
Though ears she gave me two, gave me no ear
The Sun, accomplishing his early march,
His lamp now planted on Heav'ns topmost arch,
When, exercise and air my only aim,
And heedless whither, to that field I came
Ere yet with ruthless joy the happy hound
Told hill and dale that Reynard's track was found,
Or with the high-rais'd horn's melodious clang
All Kilwick and all Dinglederry* rang.
Sheep graz'd the field; some with soft bosom press'd
The herb as soft, while nibbling stray'd the rest;
Nor noise was heard but of the hasty brook,

* Two woods belonging to John Throckmorton, Esq.

Struggling, detain'd in many a petty nook.
All seem'd so peaceful, that, from them convey'd,
To me their peace by kind contagion spread.
 But when the huntsman, with distended cheek,
'Gan make his instrument of music speak,
And from within the wood that crash was heard,
Though not a hound from whom it burst appear'd,
The sheep recumbent, and the sheep that graz'd,
All huddling into phalanx, stood and gaz'd,
Admiring, terrified, the novel strain,
Then cours'd the field around, and cours'd it round again;
But, recollecting with a sudden thought,
That flight in circles urg'd, advanc'd them nought,
They gather'd close around the old pit's brink,
And thought again—but knew not what to think.
 The man to solitude accustom'd long
Perceives in ev'ry thing that lives a tongue;
Not animals alone, but shrubs and trees
Have speech for him, and understood with ease;
After long drought, when rains abundant fall,
He hears the herbs and flow'rs rejoicing all;
Knows what the freshness of their hue implies,
How glad they catch the largess of the skies;
But, with precision nicer still, the mind
He scans of ev'ry locomotive kind;
Birds of all feather, beasts of ev'ry name,
That serve mankind, or shun them, wild or tame;
The looks and gestures of their griefs and fears
Have all articulation in his ears;
He spells them true by intuition's light,
And needs no glossary to set him right.
 This truth premis'd was needful as a text,
To win due credence to what follows next.
 A while they mus'd; surveying ev'ry face,
Thou hadst suppos'd them of superior race;
Their periwigs of wool, and fears combin'd,
Stamp'd on each countenance such marks of mind,
That sage they seem'd, as lawyer's o'er a doubt,
Which, puzzling long, at last they puzzle out;
Or academic tutors, teaching youths,
Sure ne'er to want them, mathematic truths;
When thus a mutton, statelier than the rest,
A ram, the ewes and wethers sad address'd.
 Friends! we have liv'd too long. I never heard
Sounds such as these, so worthy to be fear'd.
Could I believe, that winds for ages pent
In earth's dark womb have found at last a vent,
And from their prison-house below arise,

With all these hideous howlings to the skies,
I could be much compos'd nor should appear,
For such a cause, to feel the slightest fear.
Yourselves have seen, what time the thunders roll'd
All night, me resting quiet in the fold.
Or heard we that tremendous bray alone,
I could expound the melancholy tone;
Should deem it by our old companion made,
The ass; for he, we know, has lately stray'd,
And being lost perhaps, and wand'ring wide,
Might be suppos'd to clamour for a guide.
But ah! those dreadful yells what soul can hear
That owns a carcass, and not quake for fear?
Demons produce them doubtless, brazen-claw'd
And fang'd with brass the demons are abroad;
I hold it therefore wisest and most fit,
That, life to save, we leap into the pit.
Him answer'd then his loving mate and true,
But more discreet than he, a Cambrian ewe.
How? leap into the pit our life to save?
To save our life leap all into the grave?
For can we find it less? Contemplate first,
The depth how awful! falling there, we burst:
Or should the brambles, interpos'd, our fall
In part abate, that happiness were small;
For with a race like theirs no chance I see
Of peace or ease to creatures clad as we.
Meantime, noise kills not. Be it Dapple's bray,
Or be it not, or be it whose it may,
And rush those other sounds, that seem by tongues
Of demons utter'd, from whatever lungs,
Sounds are but sounds; and, till the cause appear,
We have at least commodious standing here.
Come fiend, come fury, giant, monster, blast
From earth or hell, we can but plunge at last.
While thus she spake, I fainter heard the peals,
For Reynard, close attended at his heels
By panting dog, tir'd man, and spatter'd horse,
Through mere good fortune, took a diff'rent course.
The flock grew calm again; and I, the road
Foll'wing, that led me to my own abode,
Much wonder'd, that the silly sheep had found
Such cause of terror in an empty sound,
So sweet to huntsman, gentleman, and hound.

MORAL.

Beware of desp'rate steps. The darkest day,
Live till to-morrow, will have pass'd away.

BOADICEA.

AN ODE.

When the British warrior queen,
Bleeding from the Roman rods,
Sought, with an indignant mien,
Counsel of her country's gods,

Sage, beneath the spreading oak
Sat the Druid, hoary chief;
Ev'ry burning word he spoke
Full of rage, and full of grief.

Princess! if our aged eyes
Weep upon thy matchless wrongs,
'Tis because resentment ties
All the terrors of our tongues.

Rome shall perish—write that word
In the blood that she has spilt;
Perish, hopeless and abhorr'd,
Deep in ruin as in guilt.

Rome, for empire far renown'd,
Tramples on a thousand states;
Soon her pride shall kiss the ground—
Hark! the Gaul is at her gates!

Other Romans shall arise,
Heedless of a soldier's name;
Sounds, not arms, shall win the prize,
Harmony the path to fame.

Then the progeny that springs
From the forests of our land,
Arm'd with thunder, clad with wings,
Shall a wider world command.

Regions Cæsar never knew
  Thy posterity shall sway;
Where his eagles never flew,
  None invincible as they.

Such the bard's prophetic words,
  Pregnant with celestial fire,
Bending as he swept the chords
  Of his sweet but awful lyre.

She, with all a monarch's pride,
  Felt them in her bosom glow:
Rush'd to battle, fought and died
  Dying hurl'd them at the foe.

Ruffians, pitiless as proud,
  Heav'n awards the vengeance due;
Empire is on us bestow'd,
  Shame and ruin wait for you.

HEROISM.

ere was a time when Etna's silent fire
unperceiv'd, the mountain yet entire;
n, conscious of no danger from below,
ower'd a cloud-capt pyramid of snow.
No thunders shook with deep intestine sound
The blooming groves, that girdled her around.
Her unctuous olives, and her purple vines
(Unfelt the fury of those bursting mines)
The peasant's hopes, and not in vain, assur'd,
In peace upon her sloping sides matur'd.
When on a day, like that of the last doom,
A conflagration lab'ring in her womb,
She teem'd and heav'd with an infernal birth,
That shook the circling seas and solid earth.
Dark and voluminous the vapours rise,
And hang their horrors in the neighb'ring skies,
While through the Stygian veil, that blots the day,
In dazzling streaks the vivid lightnings play.

But oh! what muse, and in what pow'rs of song,
Can trace the torrent as it burns along;
Havoc and devastation in the van,
It marches o'er the prostrate works of man;
Vines, olives, herbage, forests disappear,
And all the charms of a Sicilian year.
Revolving seasons, fruitless as they pass,
See it an uninform'd and idle mass;
Without a soil t'invite the tiller's care,
Or blade, that might redeem it from despair.
Yet time at length (what will not time achieve?)
Clothes it with earth, and bids the produce live.
Once more the spiry myrtle crowns the glade,
And ruminating flocks enjoy the shade.
O bliss precarious, and unsafe retreats,
O charming Paradise of short-liv'd sweets!
The self-same gale, that wafts the fragrance round,
Brings to the distant ear a sullen sound:
Again the mountain feels th'imprison'd foe,
Again pours ruin on the vale below.
Ten thousand swains the wasted scene deplore,
That only future ages can restore.
Ye monarchs, whom the lure of honor draws,
Who write in blood the merits of your cause,
Who strike the blow, then plead your own defence,
Glory your aim, but justice your pretence;
Behold in Etna's emblematic fires,
The mischief your ambitious pride inspires!
Fast by the stream, that bounds your just domain,
And tells you where ye have a right to reign,
A nation dwells not envious of your throne,
Studious of peace, their neighbours' and their own.
Ill-fated race! how deeply must they rue
Their only crime, vicinity to you!
The trumpet sounds, your legions swarm abroad,
Through the ripe harvest lies their destin'd road;
At ev'ry step beneath their feet they tread
The life of multitudes, a nation's bread!
Earth seems a garden in its loveliest dress
Before them, and behind a wilderness.
Famine, and Pestilence, her first-born son,
Attend to finish what the sword begun;
And echoing praises, such as fiends might earn,
And Folly pays, resound at your return.
A calm succeeds—but Plenty, with her train
Of heartfelt joys, succeeds not soon again,
And years of pining indigence must show
What scourges are the gods that rule below.
Yet man, laborious man, by slow degrees,

(Such is his thirst of opulence and ease)
Plies all the sinews of industrious toil,
Gleans up the refuse of the gen'ral spoil,
Rebuilds the tow'rs, that smok'd upon the plain,
And the sun gilds the shining spires again
  Increasing commerce and reviving art
Renew the quarrel on the conqu'ror's part;
And the sad lesson must be learnt once more,
That wealth within is ruin at the door.
What are ye, monarchs, laurell'd heroes, say,
But Etnas of the suff'ring world ye sway?
Sweet Nature, stripp'd of her embroider'd robe,
Deplores the wasted regions of her globe;
And stands a witness at Truth's awful bar,
To prove you there destroyers as ye are.
  O place me in some Heav'n-protected isle,
Where Peace, and Equity, and Freedom smile;
Where no volcano pours his fiery flood,
No crested warrior dips his plume in blood;
Where Pow'r secures what Industry has won;
Where to succeed is not to be undone;
A land, that distant tyrants hate in vain,
In Britain's isle, beneath a George's reign!

ON THE RECEIPT OF
MY MOTHER'S PICTURE.

OUT OF NORFOLK;

The gift of my cousin, Ann Bodham.

  O that those lips had language! Life has pass'd
With me but roughly since I heard thee last.
Those lips are thine—thy own sweet smile I see,
The same, that oft in childhood solac'd me;
Voice only fails, else how distinct they say,
"Grieve not, my child, chase all thy fears away!"
The meek intelligence of those dear eyes
(Blest be the art that can immortalize,
The art that baffles Time's tyrannic claim
To quench it) here shines on me still the same.
  Faithful remembrancer of one so dear,
O welcome guest, though unexpected here!

Who bidd'st me honor with an artless song,
Affectionate, a mother lost so long.
I will obey, not willingly alone,
But gladly, as the precept were her own;
And, while that face renews my filial grief,
Fancy shall weave a charm for my relief,
Shall steep me in Elysian reverie,
A momentary dream, that thou art she.
My mother! when I learn'd that thou wast dead,
Say, wast thou conscious of the tears I shed?
Hover'd thy spirit o'er thy sorr'wing son,
Wretch even then, life's journey just begun?
Perhaps thou gav'st me, though unfelt, a kiss;
Perhaps a tear, if souls can weep in bliss—
Ah that maternal smile! it answers—Yes.
I heard the bell toll'd on thy burial day,
I saw the hearse that bore thee slow away,
And, turning from my nurs'ry window, drew
A long, long sigh, and wept a last adieu!
But was it such?—It was.—Where thou art gone,
Adieus and farewells are a sound unknown.
May I but meet thee on that peaceful shore,
The parting word shall pass my lips no more!
Thy maidens, griev'd themselves at my concern,
Oft gave me promise of thy quick return.
What ardently I wish'd, I long believ'd,
And, disappointed still, was still deceiv'd.
By expectation ev'ry day beguil'd,
Dupe of *to-morrow* even from a child.
Thus many a sad to-morrow came and went,
Till, all my stock of infant sorrow spent,
I learn'd at last submission to my lot,
But, though I less deplor'd thee, ne'er forgot.
Where once we dwelt our name is heard no more,
Children not thine have trod my nurs'ry floor;
And where the gard'ner Robin, day by day,
Drew me to school along the public way,
Delighted with my bauble coach and wrapp'd
In scarlet mantle warm, and velvet cap,
'Tis now become a hist'ry little known,
That once we call'd the past'ral house our own.
Short-liv'd possession! but the record fair,
That mem'ry keeps of all thy kindness there,
Still outlives many a storm, that has effac'd
A thousand other themes less deeply trac'd.
Thy nightly visits to my chamber made,
That thou might'st know me safe and warmly laid;
Thy morning bounties ere I left my home,
The biscuit; or confectionary plum;

The fragrant waters on my cheeks bestow'd
By thy own hand, till fresh they shone and glow'd:
All this, and more endearing still than all,
Thy constant flow of love, that knew no fall,
Ne'er roughen'd by those cataracts and breaks,
That humor interpos'd too often makes;
All this still legible in mem'ry's page,
And still to be so to my latest age,
Adds joy to duty, makes me glad to pay
Such honors to thee as my numbers may;
Perhaps a frail memorial, but sincere,
Not scorn'd in Heav'n, though little notic'd here.
  Could Time, his flight revers'd, restore the hours,
When, playing with thy vesture's tissu'd flow'rs,
The violet, the pink, and jessamine,
I prick'd them into paper with a pin
(And thou wast happier than myself the while,
Wouldst softly speak, and stroke my head, and smile
Could those few pleasant days again appear,
Might one wish bring them, would I wish them here?
I would not trust my heart—the dear delight
Seems so to be desir'd, perhaps I might.—
But no—what here we call our life is such,
So little to be lov'd, and thou so much,
That I should ill requite thee to constrain
Thy unbound spirit into bonds again.
  Thou, as a gallant bark from Albion's coast
(The storms all weather'd and the ocean cross'd),
Shoots into port at some well-haven'd isle,
Where spices breathe, and brighter seasons smile,
There sits quiescent on the floods, that show
Her beauteous form reflected clear below,
While airs impregnated with incense play
Around her, fanning light her streamers gay;
So thou, with sails how swift! hast reach'd the shore,
"Where tempests never beat nor billows roar,"*
And thy lov'd consort on the dang'rous tide
Of life long since has anchor'd by thy side.
But me, scarce hoping to attain that rest,
Always from port withheld, always distress'd—
Me howling blasts drive devious, tempest-toss'd,
Sails ripp'd, seams op'ning wide, and compass lost,
And day by day some current's thwarting force
Sets me more distant from a prosp'rous course.
Yet O the thought, that thou art safe, and he!
That thought is joy, arrive what may to me.
My boast is not, that I deduce my birth

* Garth.

From loins enthron'd, and rulers of the earth;
But higher far my proud pretensions rise—
The son of parents pass'd into the skies.
And now, farewell—Time unrevok'd has run
His wonted course, yet what I wish'd is done.
By contemplation's help, not sought in vain,
I seem'd t'have liv'd my childhood o'er again;
To have renew'd the joys that once were mine,
Without the sin of violating thine;
And, while the wings of Fancy still are free,
And I can view this mimic show of thee,
Time has but half succeeded in his theft—
Thyself remov'd, thy pow'r to soothe me left.

FRIENDSHIP.

WHAT virtue, or what mental grace,
But men unqualified and base
  Will boast it their possession?
Profusion apes the noble part
Of liberality of heart,
  And dulness of discretion.

If every polish'd gem we find,
Illuminating heart or mind,
  Provoke to imitation;
No wonder friendship does the same,
That jewel of the purest flame,
  Or rather constellation.

No knave but boldly will pretend
The requisites that form a friend,
  A real and a sound one;
Nor any fool, he would deceive,
But prove as ready to believe,
  And dream that he had found one.

Candid, and generous, and just,
Boys care but little whom they trust,
  An error soon corrected—
For who but learns in riper years,
That man, when smoothest he appears
  Is most to be suspected?

But here again a danger lies,
Lest, having misapplied our eyes,
  And taken trash for treasure,
We should unwarily conclude
Friendship a false ideal good,
  A mere Utopian pleasure.

An acquisition rather rare
Is yet no subject of despair;
Nor is it wise complaining,
If either on forbidden ground,
Or where it was not to be found,
We sought without attaining.

No friendship will abide the test,
That stands on sordid interest,
Or mean self-love erected;
Nor such as may a while subsist,
Between the sot and sensualist,
For vicious ends connected.

Who seek a friend should come dispos'd,
T' exhibit in full bloom disclos'd
The graces and the beauties,
That form the character he seeks,
For 'tis a union, that bespeaks
Reciprocated duties.

Mutual attention is implied,
And equal truth on either side,
And constantly supported;
'Tis senseless arrogance t' accuse
Another of sinister views,
Our own as much distorted.

But will sincerity suffice?
It is indeed above all price,
And must be made the basis;
But ev'ry virtue of the soul
Must constitute the charming whole,
All shining in their places.

A fretful temper will divide
The closest knot that may be tied,
By ceaseless sharp corrosion;
A temper passionate and fierce
May suddenly your joys disperse
At one immense explosion.

In vain the talkative unite
In hopes of permanent delight—
The secret just committed,
Forgetting its important weight,
They drop through mere desire to prate,
And by themselves outwitted.

How bright soe'er the prospect seems,
All thoughts of friendship are but dreams,
If envy chance to creep in ;
An envious man, if you succeed,
May prove a dang'rous foe indeed,
But not a friend worth keeping.

As envy pines at good possess'd,
So jealousy looks forth distress'd
On good, that seems approaching ;
And, if success his steps attend,
Discerns a rival in a friend,
And hates him for enroaching.

Hence authors of illustrious name,
Unless belied by common fame,
Are sadly prone to quarrel,
To deem the wit a friend displays
A tax upon their own just praise,
And pluck each other's laurel.

A man renown'd for repartee
Will seldom scruple to make free
With friendship's finest feeling,
Will thrust a dagger at your breast,
And say he wounded you in jest,
By way of balm for healing.

Whoever keeps an open ear
For tattlers will be sure to hear
The trumpet of contention ;
Aspersion is the babbler's trade,
To listen is to lend him aid,
And rush into dissension.

A friendship, that in frequent fits
Of controversial rage emits
The sparks of disputation,
Like hand in hand insurance plates,
Most unavoidably creates
The thought of conflagration.

Some fickle creatures boast a soul
True as a needle to the pole,
Their humor yet so various—
They manifest their whole life through
The needle's deviations too,
Their love is so precarious.

The great and small but rarely meet
On terms of amity complete;
  Plebeians must surrender
And yield so much to noble folk,
It is combining fire with smoke,
  Obscurity with splendor.

Some are so placid and serene
(As Irish bogs are always green)
  They sleep secure from waking;
And are indeed a bog, that bears
Your unparticipated cares
  Unmov'd and without quaking.

Courtier and patriot cannot mix
Their het'rogeneous politics
  Without an effervescence,
Like that of salts with lemon juice,
Which does not yet like that produce
  A friendly coalescence.

Religion should extinguish strife,
And make a calm of human life;
  But friends that chance to differ
On points, which God has left at large,
How freely will they meet and charge!
  No combatants are stiffer.

To prove at last my main intent
Needs no expense of argument,
  No cutting and contriving—
Seeking a real friend we seem
T'adopt the chymist's golden dream,
  With still less hope of thriving.

Sometimes the fault is all our own,
Some blemish in due time made known
  By trespass or omission;
Sometimes occasion brings to light
Our friend's defect long hid from sight,
  And even from suspicion.

Then judge yourself, and prove your man
As circumspectly as you can,
  And, having made election,
Beware no negligence of yours,
Such as a friend but ill endures,
  Enfeeble his affection.

That secrets are a sacred trust,
That friends should be sincere and just,
  That constancy befits them,
Are observations on the case,
That savor much of common-place,
  And all the world admits them.

But 'tis not timber, lead, and stone,
An architect requires alone,
  To finish a fine building—
The palace were but half complete,
If he could possibly forget
  The carving and the gilding.

The man that hails you Tom or Jack,
And proves by thumps upon your back
  How he esteems your merit,
Is such a friend, that one had need
Be very much his friend indeed,
  To pardon or to bear it.

As similarity of mind,
Or something not to be defin'd,
  First fixes our attention;
So manners decent and polite,
The same we practis'd at first sight,
  Must save it from declension.

Some act upon this prudent plan,
"Say little, and hear all you can."
  Safe policy, but hateful—
So barren sands imbibe the show'r,
But render neither fruit nor flow'r,
  Unpleasant and ungrateful.

The man I trust, if shy to me,
Shall find me as reserv'd as he:
  No subterfuge or pleading
Shall win my confidence again;
I will by no means entertain
  A spy on my proceeding.

These samples—for alas! at last
These are but samples, and a taste
  Of evils yet unmention'd—
May prove the task a task indeed,
In which 'tis much if we succeed
  However well-intention'd.

Pursue the search, and you will find
Good sense and knowledge of mankind
To be at least expedient,
And, after summing all the rest,
Religion ruling in the breast
A principal ingredient.

The noblest Friendship ever shown
The Saviour's history makes known,
Though some have turn'd and turn'd it;
And, whether being craz'd or blind,
Or seeking with a biass'd mind,
Have not, it seems, discern'd it.

O Friendship, if my soul forego
Thy dear delights while here below;
To mortify and grieve me,
May I myself at last appear
Unworthy, base, and insincere,
Or may my friend deceive me!

ON A MISCHIEVOUS BULL,

WHICH THE OWNER OF HIM SOLD AT THE AUTHOR'S INSTANCE.

Go—Thou art all unfit to share
The pleasures of this place
With such as its old tenants are,
Creatures of gentler race

The squirrel here his hoard provides,
Aware of wintry storms,
And woodpeckers explore the sides
Of rugged oaks for worms.

The sheep here smooths the knotted thorn
With frictions of her fleece;
And here I wander eve and morn,
Like her, a friend to peace.

Ah!—I could Pity thee exil'd
From this secure retreat—
I would not lose it to be styl'd
The happiest of the great.

But thou canst taste no calm delight;
Thy pleasure is to show
Thy magnanimity in fight,
Thy prowess—therefore go—

I care not whether east or north,
So I no more may find thee;
The angry muse thus sings thee forth,
And claps the gate behind thee.

ANNUS MEMORABILIS, 1789.

WRITTEN IN COMMEMORATION OF HIS MAJESTY'S HAPPY RECOVERY.

I Ransack'd, for a theme of song,
Much ancient chronicle, and long;
I read of bright embattled fields,
Of trophied helmets, spears, and shields.
Of chiefs, whose single arm could boast
Prowess to dissipate a host;
Through tomes of fable and of dream
I sought an eligible theme,
But none I found, or found them shar'd
Already by some happier bard.
To modern times, with Truth to guide
My busy search, I next applied;
Here cities won, and fleets dispers'd,
Urg'd loud a claim to be rehears'd,
Deeds of unperishing renown,
Our fathers' triumphs and our own.
Thus, as the bee, from bank to bow'r,
Assiduous sips at ev'ry flow'r,
But rests on none, till that be found,
Where most nectareous sweets abound,
So I, from theme to theme display'd
In many a page historic stray'd,
Siege after siege, fight after fight,
Contemplating with small delight
(For feats of sanguinary hue
Not always glitter in my view;)
Till, settling on the current year,
I found the far-sought treasure near
A theme for poetry divine,

A theme t'ennoble even mine,
In memorable eighty-nine.
The spring of eighty-nine shall be
An era cherish'd long by me,
Which joyful I will oft record,
And thankful at my frugal board;
For then the clouds of eighty-eight,
That threaten'd England's trembling state
With loss of what she least could spare,
Her sov'reign's tutelary care,
One breath of Heav'n, that cried—Restore!
Chas'd, never to assemble more:
And for the richest crown on Earth,
If valu'd by its wearer's worth,
The symbol of a righteous reign
Sat fast on George's brows again.
Then peace and joy again possess'd
Our Queen's long-agitated breast;
Such joy and peace as can be known
By suff'rers like herself alone,
Who losing, or supposing lost,
The good on Earth they valu'd most,
For that dear sorrow's sake forego
All hope of happiness below,
Then suddenly regain the prize,
And flash thanksgivings to the skies!
O Queen of Albion, queen of isles!
Since all thy tears were chang'd to smiles,
The eyes, that never saw thee, shine
With joy not unallied to thine,
Transports not chargeable with art
Illume the land's remotest part,
And strangers to the air of courts,
Both in their toils and at their sports,
The happiness of answer'd pray'rs,
That gilds thy features, show in theirs
If they, who on thy state attend,
Awe-struck, before thy presence bend,
'Tis but the natural effect,
Of grandeur that ensures respect;
But she is something more than Queen,
Who is belov'd where never seen.

HYMN,

FOR THE USE OF THE SUNDAY SCHOOL AT OLNEY.

Hear, Lord, the song of praise and pray'r,
  In Heav'n thy dwelling-place,
From infants made the public care,
  And taught to seek thy face,

Thanks for thy word, and for thy day,
  And grant us, we implore,
Never to waste in sinful play
  Thy holy sabbaths more.

Thanks that we hear,—but O impart
  To each desires sincere,
That we may listen with our heart,
  And léarn as well as hear.

For if vain thoughts the minds engage
  Of older far than we,
What hope, that, at our heedless age
  Our minds should e'er be free?

Much hope, if thou our spirits take
  Under thy gracious sway,
Who canst the wisest wiser make,
  And babes as wise as they.

Wisdom and bliss thy word bestows,
  A sun that ne'er declines,
And be thy mercies show'r'd on *those*,
  Who plac'd us where it shines

STANZAS

SUBJOINED TO THE YEARLY BILL OF MORTALITY OF THE PARISH OF ALL-SAINTS, NORTHAMPTON, ANNO DOMINI 1787.*

Pallida Mors æquo pulsat pede pauperum tabernas,
Regumque turres. HOR.

Pale death with equal foot strikes wide the door
Of royal halls, and hovels of the poor.

While thirteen moons saw smoothly run
The Nen's barge-laden wave,
All these, life's rambling journey done,
Have found their home, the grave.

Was man (frail always) made more frail
Than in foregoing years?
Did Famine or did plague prevail,
That so much death appears?

No; these were vig'rous as their sires,
Nor plague nor famine came;
This annual tribute Death requires,
And never waves his claim.

Like crowded forest-trees we stand,
And some are mark'd to fall;
The axe will smite at God's command,
And soon shall smite us all.

* Composed for John Cox, parish clerk of Northampton.

Green as the bay-tree, ever green,
With its new foliage on,
The gay, the thoughtless, have I seen
I pass'd—and they were gone.

Read, ye that run, the awful truth,
With which I charge my page;
A worm is in the bud of youth,
And at the root of age.

No present health can health ensure
For yet an hour to come;
No med'cine, though it oft can cure
Can always baulk the tomb.

And O! that humble as my lot,
And scorn'd as is my strain,
These truths, though known, too much forgot,
I may not teach in vain.

So prays your clerk with all his heart,
And ere he quits the pen,
Begs you for once to take his part,
And answer all—Amen!

ON A SIMILAR OCCASION,

FOR THE YEAR 1788.

Quod adest, memento
Componere æquus. Cætera fluminis
Ritu feruntur. Hor.

Improve the present hour, for all beside
Is a mere feather on a torrent's tide.

Could I, from Heav'n inspir'd, as sure presage
To whom the rising year shall prove his last,
As I can number in my punctual page,
And item down the victims of the past;

How each would trembling wait the mournful sheet,
On which the press might stamp him next to die;
And, reading here his sentence, how replete
With anxious meaning, Heav'nward turn his eye!

Time then would seem more precious than the joys,
In which he sports away the treasure now;
And pray'r more seasonable than the noise
Of drunkards, or the music-drawing bow.

Then doubtless many a trifler, on the brink
Of this world's hazardous and headlong shore,
Forc'd to a pause, would feel it good to think,
Told that his setting sun must rise no more.

Ah self-deceived! Could I prophetic say
Who next is fated, and who next to fall,
The rest might then seem privileg'd to play;
But, naming *none*, the Voice now speaks to ALL.

Observe the dappled foresters, how light
They bound and airy o'er the sunny glade—
One falls—the rest, wide-scatter'd with affright,
Vanish at once into the darkest shade.

Had we their wisdom, should we, often warn'd,
Still need repeated warnings, and at last,
A thousand awful admonitions scorn'd,
Die self-accus'd of life run all to waste?

Sad waste! for which no after-thrift atones.
The grave admits no cure for guilt or sin;
Dew-drops may deck the turf that hides the bones,
But tears of godly grief ne'er flow within.

Learn then, ye living! by the mouths be taught
Of all these sepulchres, instructors true,
That, soon or late, death also is your lot,
And the next op'ning grave may yawn for you.

ON A SIMILAR OCCASION,

FOR THE YEAR 1789.

—*Placidaque ibi demum morte quievit.* VIRG.
There calm at length he breath'd his soul away.

"O Most delightful hour by man
Experienc'd here below,
The hour that terminates
His folly, and his woe!

"Worlds should not bribe me back to tread
Again life's dreary waste,
To see again my day o'erspread
With all the gloomy past.

"My home henceforth is in the skies,
  Earth, seas. and sun adieu
All heav'n unfolded to mine eyes,
  I have no sight for you."

So spake Aspasio, firm possess'd
  Of faith's supporting rod,
Then breathed his soul into its rest,
  The bosom of his God.

He was a man among the few
  Sincere on virtue's side ;
And all his strength from scripture drew,
  To hourly use applied.

That rule he priz'd, by that he fear'd,
  He hated, hop'd, and lov'd;
Nor ever frown'd, or sad appear'd,
  But when his heart had rov'd.

For he was frail, as thou or I,
  And evil felt within:
But, when he felt it, heav'd a sigh,
  And loath'd the thought of sin.

Such liv'd Aspasio ; and at last
  Call'd up from Earth to Heav'n,
The gulf of death triumphant pass'd,
  By gales of blessing driv'n.

His joys be *mine*, each reader cries,
  When my last hour arrives ;
They shall be yours, my verse replies,
  Such only be your lives.

ON A SIMILAR OCCASION,

FOR THE YEAR 1790.

Ne commanentem recta sperne. BUCHANAN.
Despise not my good counsel.

He who sits from day to day,
  Where the prison'd lark is hung,
Heedless of his loudest lay,
  Hardly knows that he has sung.

Where the watchman in his round
  Nightly lifts his voice on high
None, accustom'd to the sound,
  Wakes the sooner for his cry.

So your verse-man I, and clerk,
  Yearly in my song proclaim
Death at hand— yourselves his mark—
  And the foe's unerring aim.

Duly at my time I come,
  Publishing to all aloud—
Soon the grave must be your home,
  And your only suit a shroud

But the monitory strain,
  Oft repeated in your ears,
Seems to sound too much in vain,
  Wins no notice, wakes no fears.

Can a truth, by all confess'd
  Of such magnitude and weight,
Grow, by being oft impress'd,
  Trivial as a parrot's prate?

Pleasure's call attention wins,
  Hear it often as we may;
New as ever seen our sins,
  Though committed ev'ry day.

Death and Judgment, Heav'n and Hell—
  These alone, so often heard,
No more move us than the bell,
  When some stranger is interr'd.

O then, ere the turf or tomb
  Cover us from ev'ry eye,
Spirit of instruction come,
  Make us learn, that we must die.

ON A SIMILAR OCCASION.

FOR THE YEAR 1792.

Felix, qui potuit rerum cognoscere causas,
Atque metus omnes et inexorabile fatum
Subjecit pedibus, strepitumque Acherontis avari!

VIRG.

Happy the mortal, who has trac'd effects
To their first cause, cast fear beneath his feet,
And Death and roaring Hell's voracious fires!

Thankless for favors from on high,
  Man thinks he fades too soon;
Though 'tis his privilege to die,
  Would he improve the boon.

But he, not wise enough to scan
  His blest concerns aright,
Would gladly stretch life's little span
  To ages, if he might.

To ages in a world of pain,
  To ages, where he goes
Gall'd by affliction's heavy chain,
  And hopeless of repose.

Strange fondness of the human heart,
  Enamour'd of its harm!
Strange world, that costs it so much smart,
  And still has pow'r to charm.

Whence has the world her magic pow'r?
  Why deem we death a foe?
Recoil from weary life's best hour,
  And covet longer woe?

The cause is Conscience—Conscience oft
  Her tale of guilt renews:
Her voice is terrible though soft,
  And dread of death ensues.

Then anxious to be longer spar'd
  Man mourns his fleeting breath:
All evils then seem light, compar'd
  With the approach of Death.

'Tis judgment shakes him; there's the fear
  That prompts the wish to stay;
He has incurr'd a long arrear,
  And must despair to pay.

Pay!—follow Christ, and all is paid;
  His death your peace ensures;
Think on the grave where *he* was laid,
  And calm descend to *yours*.

ON A SIMILAR OCCASION,

FOR THE YEAR 1793.

De sacris autem hæc sit una sententia, ut conserventur.—Cic. de Leg.

But let us all concur in this one sentiment, that things sacred be inviolate.

He lives, who lives to God alone,
And all are dead beside;
For other source than God is none
Whence life can be supplied.

To live to God is to requite
His love as best we may;
To make his precepts our delight,
His promises our stay.

But life, within a narrow ring,
Of giddy joys compris'd,
Is falsely nam'd, and no such thing,
But rather death disguis'd.

Can life in them deserve the name,
Who only live to prove
For what poor toys they can disclaim
An endless life above?

Who, much diseas'd, yet nothing feel;
Much menac'd, nothing dread;
Have wounds, which only God can heal,
Yet never ask his aid?

Who deem his house a useless place,
  Faith, want of common sense;
And ardor in the Christian race,
  A hypocrite's pretence?

Who trample order; and the day
  Which God asserts his own,
Dishonor with unhallow'd play,
  And worship chance alone?

If scorn of God's commands, impress'd
  On word and deed, imply
The better part of man unbless'd
  With life that cannot die:

Such want it, and that want, uncur'd
  Till man resigns his breath,
Speaks him a criminal, assur'd
  Of everlasting death.

Saa period to a pleasant course!
  Yet so will God repay
Sabbaths profan'd without remorse,
  And mercy cast away.

INSCRIPTION

FOR THE TOMB OF MR. HAMILTON

Pause here, and think: a monitory rhyme
Demands one moment of thy fleeting time.
  Consult life's silent clock, thy bounding vien;
Seems it to say—'Health here has long to reign?'
Hast thou the vigor of thy youth? an eye
That beams delight? a heart untaught to sigh?
Yet fear. Youth, ofttimes healthful and at ease,
Anticipates a day it never sees;
And many a tomb, like *Hamilton's*, aloud
Exclaims, 'Prepare thee for an early shroud.'

THE ENCHANTMENT DISSOLVED.

Blinded in youth by Satan's arts,
The world to our unpractis'd hearts
  A flattering prospect shows ;
Our Fancy forms a thousand schemes ;
Of gay delights and golden dreams,
  And undisturb'd repose.

So in the desert's dreary waste
By magic power produced in haste,
  (As ancient fables say),
Castles, and groves, and music sweet,
The senses of the traveller meet,
  And stop him in his way.

But while he listens with surprise,
The charm dissolves, the vision dies,
  'Twas but enchanted ground;
Thus if the Lord our spirit touch,
The world, which promised us so much,
  A wilderness is found.

At first we start and feel distress'd
Convinced we never can have rest
  In such a wretched place ;
But He whose mercy breaks the charm,
Reveals his own Almighty arm,
  And bids us seek his face.

Then we begin to live indeed
When from our sin and bondage freed
  By his beloved Friend;
We follow him from day to day,
Assured of grace through all the way,
  And glory at the end.

LIGHT SHINING OUT OF DARKNESS.

God moves in a mysterious way,
His wonders to perform;
He plants his footsteps in the sea,
And rides upon the storm.

Deep in unfathomable mines
Of never-failing skill,
He treasures up his bright designs,
And works his sovereign will.

Ye fearful saints, fresh courage take,
The clouds ye so much dread
Are big with mercy, and shall break
In blessings on your head.

Judge not the Lord by feeble sense,
But trust him for his grace;
Behind a frowning Providence
He hides a smiling face.

His purposes will ripen fast,
Unfolding every hour;
The bud may have a bitter taste,
But sweet will be the flower.

Blind unbelief is sure to err*
And scan his work in vain;
God is his own interpreter,
And he will make it plain.

* John xiii. 7.

TEMPTATION.

The billows swell, the winds are high,
Clouds overcast my wintry sky;
Out of the depths to thee I call,
My fears are great, my strength is small.

O Lord, the pilot's part perform,
And guide and guard me through the storm,
Defend me from each threat'ning ill,
Control the waves, say, 'Peace, be still.'

Amidst the roaring of the sea,
My soul still hangs her hope on thee;
Thy constant love, thy faithful care,
Is all that saves me from despair.

Dangers of every shape and name
Attend the followers of the Lamb,
Who leave the world's deceitful shore,
And leave it to return no more.

Though tempest-toss'd and half a wreck,
My Saviour through the floods I seek;
Let neither winds nor stormy main
Force back my shatter'd bark again.

SUBMISSION.

O Lord, my best desire fulfil,
And help me to resign
Life, health, and comfort, to thy will
And make thy pleasure mine.

Why should I shrink at thy command,
  Whose love forbids my fears?
Or tremble at the gracious hand
  That wipes away my tears?

No, let me rather freely yield
  What most I prize to Thee;
Who never hast a good withheld,
  Or wilt withhold from me.

Thy favor, all my journey through,
  Thou art engaged to grant;
What else I want, or think I do,
  'Tis better still to want.

Wisdom and mercy guide my way,
  Shall I resist them both?
A poor blind creature of a day,
  And crush'd before the moth!

But ah! my inward spirit cries,
  Still bind me to thy sway;
Else the next cloud that veils my skies,
  Drives all these thoughts away.

TO WARREN HASTINGS, Esq.

BY AN OLD SCHOOLFELLOW OF HIS AT WESTMINSTER.

May, 1792.

Hastings! I knew thee young, and of a mind
While young, humane, conversable, and kind:
Nor can I well believe thee, gentle *then*,
Now grown a villian, and the *worst* of men;
But rather some suspect, who have oppress'd
And worried thee, as not themselves the best.

TO MARY. 1793.

The twentieth year is well nigh past,
Since first our sky was overcast,
Ah would that this might be the last!
My Mary!

Thy spirits have a fainter flow,
I see thee daily weaker grow——
'Twas my distress that brought thee low,
My Mary!

Thy needles, once a shining store,
For my sake restless heretofore,
Now rust disused, and shine no more;
My Mary!

For though thou gladly wouldst fulfil
The same kind office for me still,
Thy sight now seconds not thy will,
My Mary!

But well thou play'dst the housewife's part.
And all thy threads with magic art
Have wound themselves about this heart,
My Mary!

Thy indistinct expressions seem
Like language utter'd in a dream;
Yet me they charm, whate'er the theme
My Mary!

Thy silver locks, once auburn bright,
Are still more lovely in my sight
Than golden beams of orient light,
My Mary!

For could I view nor them nor thee,
What sight worth seeing could I see?
The sun would rise in vain for me,
My Mary!

Partakers of thy sad decline,
Thy hands their little force resign;
Ye—gently press'd, press gently mine,
My Mary!

Such feebleness of limbs thou prov'st,
That now at every step thou mov'st
Upheld by two, yet still thou lov'st,
My Mary!

And still to love, though press'd with ill,
In wintry age to feel no chill,
With me is to be lovely still,
My Mary!

But ah! by constant heed I know,
How oft the sadness that I show,
Transforms thy smiles to looks of woe,
My Mary!

And should my future lot be cast
With much resemblance of the past,
Thy worn-out heart will break at last,
My Mary!

ON THE ICE ISLANDS,

SEEN FLOATING IN THE GERMAN OCEAN.

What portents, from what distant region, ride,
Unseen till now in ours, th'astonish'd tide?
In ages past, old Proteus, with his droves
Of sea-calves, sought the mountains and the groves,
But now, descending whence of late they stood,
Themselves the mountains seem to rove the flood.
Dire times were they, full-charged with human woes;
And these, scarce less calamitous than those.
What view we now? More wondrous still! Behold!
Like burnish'd brass they shine, or beaten gold;
And all around the pearl's pure splend r show,
And all around the ruby's fiery glow.
Come they from India, where the burning Earth,
All bounteous, gives her richest treasures birth;
And where the costly gems, that beam around
The brows of mightiest potentates, are found?

No. Never such a countless dazzling store
Had left, unseen, the Ganges' peopled shore.
Rapacious hands, and ever-watchful eyes,
Should sooner far have mark'd and seized the prize.
Whence sprang they then? Ejected have they come
From Ves'vius', or from Etna's burning womb?
Thus shine they self-illumined, or but display
The borrow'd splendors of a cloudless day? [breathe
With borrow'd beams they shine. The gales, that
Now landward, and the current's force beneath,
Have borne them nearer: and the nearer sight,
Advantaged more, contemplates them aright.
Their lofty summits crested high, they show,
With mingled sleet, and long-incumbent snow.
The rest is ice. Far hence, where, most severe,
Bleak winter well-nigh saddens all the year,
Their infant growth began. He bade arise
Their uncouth forms, portentous in our eyes.
Oft as dissolved by transient suns, the snow
Left the tall cliff, to join the flood below;
He caught, and curdled with a freezing blast,
The current, ere it reach'd the boundless waste.
By slow degrees uprose the wondrous pile,
And long successive ages roll'd the while;
Till, ceaseless in its growth, it claim'd to stand,
Tall as its rival mountains on the land.
Thus stood, and, unremovable by skill,
Or force of man, had stood the structure still;
But that, though firmly fix'd, supplanted yet
By pressure of its own enormous weight,
It left the shelving beach—and, with a sound,
That shook the bellowing waves and rocks around,
Self-launch'd, and swiftly, to the briny wave,
As if instinct, with strong desire to lave,
Down went the pond'rous mass. So bards of old,
How Delos swam th' Ægean deep have told.
But not of ice was Delos. Delos bore
Herb, fruit, and flower. She, crown'd with laurel, wore,
Even under wintry skies, a summer smile;
And Delos was Apollo's fav'rite isle.
But, horrid wand'rers of the deep, to you
He deems Cimmerian darkness only due.
Your hated birth he deign'd not to survey,
But, scornful, turn'd his glorious eyes away.
Hence! Seek your home, nor longer rashly dare
The darts of Phoebus, and a softer air;
Lest ye regret, too late, your native coast,
In no congenial gulph for ever lost!

THE CAST-AWAY.

Obscurest night involved the sky;
  Th'Atlantic billows roar'd,
When such a destined wretch as I,
  Wash'd headlong from on board,
Of friends, of hope, of all bereft,
His floating home for ever left.

No braver chief could Albion boast,
  Than he, with whom he went,
Nor ever ship left Albion's coast,
  With warmer wishes sent.
He lov'd them both, but both in vain,
Nor him beheld, nor her again.

Not long beneath the whelming brine,
  Expert to swim, he lay;
Nor soon he felt his strength decline,
  Or courage die away;
But waged with death a lasting strife
Supported by despair of life.

He shouted; nor his friends had fail'd
  To check the vessel's course,
But so the furious blast prevail'd,
  That, pitiless perforce,
They left their outcast mate behind,
And scudded still before the wind.

Some succour yet they could afford;
  And, such as storms allow,
The cask, the coop, the floated cord,
  Delay'd not to bestow,
But he (they knew) nor ship nor shore,
Whate'er they gave, should visit more.

Nor, cruel as it seem'd, could he
  Their haste himself condemn,
Aware that flight, in such a sea,
  Alone could rescue them;
Yet bitter felt it still to die
Deserted, and his friends so nigh.

He long survives, who lives an hour
  In ocean, self-upheld :
And so long he, with unspent power
  His destiny repell'd :
And ever, as the minutes flew,
Entreated help, or cried—"Adieu!"

At length, his transient respite past,
  His comrades, who before
Had heard his voice in every blast,
  Could catch the sound no more.
For then, by toil subdued, he drank
The stifling wave, and then he sank.

No poet wept him ; but the page
  Of narrative sincere,
That tells his name, his worth, his age,
  Is wet with Anson's tear.
And tears by bards or heroes shed,
Alike immortalize the dead.

I therefore purpose not, or dream,
  Descanting on his fate,
To give the melancholy theme
  A more enduring date.
But misery still delights to trace
Its semblance in another's case.

No voice divine the storm allay'd,
  No light propitious shone ;
When, snatch'd from all effectual aid,
  We perish'd, each alone :
But I beneath a rougher sea,
And whelm'd in deeper gulfs than he.

ON THE LOSS OF THE ROYAL GEORGE.

WRITTEN WHEN THE NEWS ARRIVED, 1782.

Toll for the brave!
  The brave that are no more!
All sunk beneath the wave,
  Fast by their native shore!

Eight hundred of the brave,
  Whose courage well was tried,
Had made the vessel heel,*
  And laid her on her side.

A land breeze shook the shrouds,
  And she was overset;
Down went the Royal George,
  With all her crew complete.

Toll for the brave!
  Brave Kempenfelt is gone;
His last sea-fight is fought;
  His work of glory done.

It was not in the battle;
  No tempest gave the shock:
She sprang no fatal leak,
  She ran upon no rock.

His sword was in its sheath,
  His fingers held the pen,
When Kempenfelt went down,
  With twice four hundred men.

Weigh the vessel up
  Once dreaded by our foes!
And mingle with our cup,
  The tear that England owes

Her timbers yet are sound,
And she may float again,
Full-charged with England's thunder,
And plough the distant main.

But Kempenfelt is gone,
His victories are o'er;
And he and his eight hundred,
Shall plough the wave no more.

SONNET TO MRS. UNWIN. 1793.

Mary! I want a lyre with other strings;
Such aid from heaven as some have feign'd they drew!
An eloquence scarce given to mortals, new,
And undebased by praise of meaner things,
That, ere through age or woe I shed my wings
I may record thy worth, with honor due,
In verse as musical as thou art true,—
Verse that immortalizes whom it sings.
But thou hast little need; there is a book
By seraphs writ, with beams of heavenly light,
On which the eyes of God not rarely look;
A chronicle of actions, just and bright;
There all thy deeds, my faithful Mary, shine,
And since thou own'st that praise, I spare thee mine.

GRATITUDE.

ADDRESSED TO LADY HESKETH. 1786.

This cap that so stately appears,
With ribbon-bound tassel on high,
Which seems by the crest that it rears,
Ambitious of brushing the sky:
This cap to my cousin I owe;
She gave it, and gave me beside,
Wreathed into an elegant bow,
The ribbon with which it is tied.

This wheel-footed studying chair,
Contrived both for toil and repose,
Wide elbow'd and wadded with hair,
In which I both scribble and dose,
Bright studded, to dazzle the eyes,
And rival in lustre of that
In which, or astronomy lies,
Fair Cassiopeia sat.

These carpets so soft to the foot,
Caledonia's traffic and pride!
Oh spare them, ye knights of the boot,
Escaped from a cross-country ride!
This table and mirror within,
Secure from collision and dust,
At which I oft shave cheek and chin,
And periwig nicely adjust.

This moveable structure of shelves,
For its beauty admired and its use,
And charged with octavos and twelves,
The gayest I had to produce;
Where, flaming in scarlet and gold,
My poems enchanted I view,
And hope in due time to behold
My Iliad and Odyssey too.

This china that decks the alcove,
Which here people call a buffet,
But what the gods call it above,
Has ne'er been revealed to us yet.
These curtains that keep the room warm
Or cool, as the season demands;
Those stoves, that for pattern and form,
Seem the labor of Mulciber's hands.

All these are not half what I owe
To One, from our earliest youth
To me ever ready to show
Benignity, friendship, and truth;
For Time, the destroyer declared
And foe of our perishing kind,
If even her face he has spared
Much less could he alter her mind.

Thus compass'd about with the goods
And chattels of leisure and ease,

I indulge my poetical moods
In many such fancies as these:
And fancies I fear they will seem—
Poets' goods are not often so fine;
The poets will swear that I dream,
When I sing of the splendor of mine

THE RETIRED CAT. 1791.

A Poet's cat, sedate and grave
As poet well could wish to have,
Was much addicted to inquire
For nooks to, which she might retire,
And where secure as mouse in chink,
She might repose or sit and think.
I know not where she caught the trick,
Nature perhaps herself had cast her
In such a mould *philosophique*,
Or else she learn'd it of her master.
Sometimes ascending, debonnair,
An apple tree, or lofty pear,
Lodged with convenience in the fork,
She watch'd the gard'ner at his work;
Sometimes her ease and solace sought
In an old empty watering pot.
There, wanting nothing save a fan,
To seem some nymph in her sedan,
Apparell'd in exactest sort,
And ready to be borne to court.
But love of change, it seems, has place
Not only in our wiser race;
Cats also feel, as well as we,
That passion's force, and so did she.
Her climbing, she began to find,
Exposed her too much to the wind,
And the old utensil of tin,
Was cold and comfortless within;
She therefore wish'd instead of those
Some place of more serene repose,
Where neither cold might come, nor air,
Too rudely wanton with her hair,
And sought it in the likeliest mode,
Within her master's snug abode.

A drawer it chanced at bottom lined
With linen of the softest kind,
With such as merchants introduce
From India, for the ladies' use.
A drawer impending o'er the rest,
Half open in the topmost chest,
Of depth enough and none to spare,
Invited hei to slumber there:
Puss, with delight beyond expression,
Survey'd the scene, and took possesion.
Recumbent at her ease, ere long,
And lull'd by her own humdrum song,
She left the cares of life behind,
   And slept as she would sleep her last,
When in came, housewifely inclined,
   The chamber maid, and shut it fast;
By no malignity impell'd,
But all unconcious whom it held,
Awaken'd by the shock (cried puss),
'Was ever cat attended thus?
The open drawer was left, I see,
Merely to prove a nest for me.
For soon as I was well composed,
Then came the maid, and it was closed.
How smooth these kerchiefs and how sweet,
Oh what a delicate retreat!
I will resign myself to rest
Till sol, declining in the west,
Shall call to supper, when, no doubt,
Susan will come and let me out.'
The evening came, the sun descended,
And puss remain'd still unattended.
The night roll'd tardily away,
With her indeed 'twas never day,
The sprightly morn her course renew'd,
The evening grey again ensued,
And puss came into mind no more
Than if entomb'd the day before.
With hunger pinch'd and pinch'd for room,
She now presaged approaching doom,
Nor slept a single wink or purr'd,
Conscious of jeopardy incurr'd.
That night by chance, the poet watching,
Heard an inexplicable scratching;
His noble heart went pit-a-pat,
And to himself he said—"what's that?"
He drew the curtain at his side,
And forth he peep'd, but nothing spied,
Yet, by his ear directed, guess'd

Something imprison'd in the chest,
And, doubtful what, with prudent care
Resolv'd it should continue there.
At length a voice which he well knew,
A long and melancholy mew,
Saluting his poetic ears,
Consoled him and dispell'd his fears;
He left his bed, he trod the floor,
He 'gan in haste the drawers explore,
The lowest first, and without stop,
The rest in order to the top.
For 'tis a truth well known to most,
That whatsoever thing is lost,
We seek it ere it come to light,
In every cranny but the right.
Forth skipp'd the cat, not now replete
As erst with airy self-conceit;
Nor in her own fond apprehension
A theme for all the world's attention;
But modest, sober, cured of all
Her notions hyperbolical,
And wishing for a place of rest
Any thing rather than a chest,
Then stepp'd the poet into bed
With this reflection in his head.

MORAL.

Beware of too sublime a sense
Of your own worth and consequence;
The man who dreams himself so great,
And his importance of such weight,
That all around, in all that's done,
Must move and act for him alone,
Will learn in school of tribulation,
The folly of his expectation.

ON THE SHORTNESS OF HUMAN LIFE.

Suns that set, and moons that wane,
Rise, and are restored again;
Stars that orient day subdues,
Night at her return renews.
Herbs and flowers, the beauteous birth
Of the genial womb of earth,
Suffer but a transient death,
From the winter's cruel breath,
Zephyr speaks; serener skies
Warm the glebe, and they arise.
We, alas! earth's haughty kings,
We, that promise mighty things,
Losing soon life's happy prime,
Droop, and fade in little time.
Spring returns, but not our bloom,
Still 'tis winter in the tomb.

ON THE LATE INDECENT LIBERTIES TAKEN WITH THE REMAINS OF MILTON. 1790.

"Me too, perchance, in future days,
The sculptured stone shall show,
With Paphian myrtle or with bays
Parnassian on my brow.

"But I, or ere that season come,
Escaped from every care,
Shall reach my refuge in the tomb,
And sleep securely there."

So sang, in Roman tone and style,
The youthful bard, ere long
Ordain'd to grace his native isle
With her sublimest song.

Who then, but must conceive disdain,
Hearing the deed unblest,
Of wretches who have dared profane
His dread sepulchral rest?

Ill fare the hands that heaved the stones
Where Milton's ashes lay,
That trembled not to grasp his bones
And steal his dust away!

O ill-requited bard! neglect
Thy living worth repaid,
And blind idolatrous respect
As much affronts thee dead.

SONNET TO DIODATI, FROM THE ITALIAN.

Charles—and I say it wond'ring—thou must know
That I, who once assumed a scornful air,
And scoff'd at Love, am fallen in his snare.
(Full many an upright man has fallen so)
Yet think me not thus dazzled by the flow
Of golden locks, or damask cheek; more rare
The heart-felt beauties of my foreign fair;
A mien majestic, with dark brows, that show
The tranquil lustre of a lofty mind;
Words exquisite, of idioms more than one,
And song, whose fascinating power might bind,
And from her sphere draw down the lab'ring moon;
With such fire-darting eyes, that should I fill
My ears with wax, she would enchant me still.

SONNET TO A LADY, FROM THE ITALIAN.

Enamour'd, artless, young, on foreign ground,
Uncertain whither from myself to fly,
To thee, dear lady, with an humble sigh,
Let me devote my heart, which I have found,
By certain proofs, not few, intrepid, sound,
Good, and addicted to conceptions high:
When tempests shake the world, and fire the sky,
It rests in adamant self-wrapt around,
As safe from envy, and from outrage rude,
From hopes and fears that vulgar minds abuse,
As fond of genius and fix'd fortitude,
Of the resounding lyre, and every Muse,
Weak you will find it only in one part,
Now pierced with love's immedicable dart.

TO THE NIGHTINGALE.

WHICH THE AUTHOR HEARD SING ON NEW YEAR'S DAY, 1792.

Whence is it, that amazed I hear
  From yonder wither'd spray,
This foremost morn of all the year,
  The melody of May.

And why, since thousands would be proud
  Of such a favor shown,
And I selected from the crowd,
  To witness it alone?

Sing'st thou, sweet Philomel, to me,
  For that I also long
Have practised in the groves, like thee,
  Though not like thee in song?

Or sing'st thou rather under force
  Of some divine command,
Commision'd to presage a course
  Of happier days at hand?

Thrice welcome, then! for many a long
  And joyless year have I,
As thou to-day, put forth my song,
  Beneath a wintry sky.

But thee no wintry skies can harm,
  Who only need'st to sing,
To make e'en January charm,
  And every season spring.

TO WILLIAM WILBERFORCE. 1792.

Thy country, Wilberforce, with just disdain,
Hears thee by cruel men and impious, called
Fanatic, for thy zeal to loose th'enthrall'd
From exile, public sale, and slavery's chain.
Friend of the poor, the wronged, the fetter-gall'd,
Fear not, lest labour such as thine be vain.
Thou hast achieved a part; hast gain'd the ear
Of Britain's senate to thy glorious cause;
Hope smiles, joy springs, and though cold caution pause
And weave delay, the better hour is near
That shall remunerate thy toils severe,
By peace for Afric, fenced with British laws.
Enjoy what thou hast won, esteeem and love
From all the just on earth, and all the bless'd above.

TO WILLIAM HAYLEY, ESQ. 1793.

Dear architect of fine CHATEAUX in air,
Worthier to stand for ever, if they could,
Than any built of stone, or yet of wood,
For back of royal elephant to bear!
O for permission from the skies to share,
Much to my own, though little to thy good,
With thee (not subject to the jealous mood!)
A partnership of literary ware!
But I am bankrupt now; and doom'd henceforth
To drudge, in descant dry, on others' lays:
Bards, I acknowledge, of unequall'd worth!
But what is commentator's happiest praise?
That he has furnish'd lights for other eyes,
Which they, who need them, use, and then despise.

VERSES

SENT TO LADY AUSTEN, DURING THE TIME OF A FLOOD, AUGUST, 1782.

To watch the storms, and hear the sky
Give all our almanacs the lie;
To shake with cold, and see the plains
In autumn drown'd with wintry rains;
'Tis thus I spend my moments here,
And wish myself a Dutch mynheer;
I then should have no need of wit:
For lumpish Hollander unfit!
Nor should I then repine at mud,
Or meadows deluged with a flood;
But in a bog live well content,
And find it just my element:
Should be a clod, and not a man;
Nor wish in vain for sister Ann,
With charitable aid to drag
My mind out of its proper quag;
Should have the genius of a boor,
And no ambition to have more.

SONG ON PEACE.

WRITTEN AT THE REQUEST OF LADY AUSTEN, 1783.

No longer I follow a sound;
  No longer a dream I pursue:
O happiness! not to be found.
  Unattainable treasure, adieu!

I have sought thee in splendor and dress,
  In the regions of pleasure and taste;
I have sought thee, and seem'd to possess,
  But have proved thee a vision at last.

An humble ambition and hope
  The voice of true wisdom inspires;
'Tis sufficient, if Peace be the scope,
  And the summit of all our desires.

Peace may be the lot of the mind
  That seeks it in meekness and love
But rapture and bliss are confined
  To the glorified spirits above.

SONG,

WRITTEN AT THE REQUEST OF LADY AUSTEN.

When all within is peace,
  How nature seems to smile!
Delights that never cease,
  The livelong day beguile.
From morn to dewy eve,
  With open hands she showers
Fresh blessings to deceive
  And soothe the silent hours.

It is content of heart
  Gives nature power to please;
The mind that feels no smart,
  Enlivens all it sees;
Can make a wintry sky
  Seem bright as smiling May,
And evening's closing eye
  As peep of early day.

The vast majestic globe,
  So beauteously array'd
In nature's various robe,
  With wondrous skill display'd,
Is to a mourner's heart
  A dreary wild at best;
It flutters to depart,
  And longs to be at rest.

TO GEORGE ROMNEY, Esq.

ON HIS PICTURE OF ME IN CRAYONS, DRAWN AT EARTHAM. 1792.

Romney, expert infallibly to trace
On chart or canvass, not the form alone,
And semblance, but however faintly shown,
The mind's impression too on every face—
With strokes that time ought never to erase,
Thou hast so pencill'd mine, that though I own
The subject worthless, I have never known
The artist shining with superior grace.
But this I mark—that symptoms none of woe
In thy incomparable work appear,
Well—I am satisfied it should be so,
Since, on maturer thought, the cause is clear;
For in my looks what sorrow couldst thou see
When I was Hayley's guest, and sat to thee?

TO MY COUSIN ANNE BODHAM, ON RECEIVING HER A PURSE. 1793.

My gentle Anne, whom heretofore,
When I was young, and thou no more
Than plaything for a nurse,
I danced and fondled on my knee,
A kitten both in size and glee,
I thank thee for my purse.

Gold pays the worth of all things here;
But not of love;—that gem's too dear
For richest rogues to win it;
I therefore, as a proof of love,
Esteem thy present far above
The best things kept within it.

EPITAPH ON JOHNSON.

JANUARY, 1785.

Here Johnson lies—a sage by all allow'd,
Whom to have bred, may well make England proud,

Whose prose was eloquence, by wisdom taught,
The graceful vehicle of virtuous thought;
Whose verse may claim—grave, masculine, and stron
Superior praise to the mere poet's song;
Who many a noble gift from heaven possess'd,
And faith at last, alone worth all the rest.
O man, immortal by a double prize,
By fame on earth,—by glory in the skies!

THE BIRD'S NEST, A TALE. 1793.

This Tale is founded on an anecdote which the Author found in the Buckinghamshire Herald, for Saturday, June 1st, 1793, in the following words:

***Glasgow, May* 23.—In a block or pulley, near the head of the mast of a gabert, now lying at the Broomielaw, there is a Chaffinch's nest and four eggs. The nest was built while the vessel lay at Greenock, and was followed hither by both birds. Though the block is occasionally lowered for the inspection of the curious, the birds have not forsaken the nest. The cock, however, visits the nest but seldom, while the hen never leaves it, but when she descends to the hull for food.**

In Scotland's realm, where trees are few,
Nor even shrubs abound;
But where, however bleak the view,
Some better things are found!

For husband there and wife may boast
Their union undefiled,
And false ones are as rare almost,
As hedge-rows in the wild.

In Scotland's realm forlorn and bare,
The history chanced of late—
This history of a wedded pair,
A chaffinch and his mate.

The spring drew near, each felt a breast
With genial instinct fill'd:
They paired and would have built a nest,
But found not where to build.

The heaths uncovered and the moors,
Except with snow and sleet,
Sea-beaten rocks and naked shores
Could yield them no retreat.

Long time a breeding-place they sought,
Till both grew vex'd and tired;
At length a ship arriving, brought
The good so long desired.

A ship!—could such a restless thing
Afford them place of rest?
Or was the merchant charged to bring
The homeless birds a nest?

Hush!—silent hearers profit most—
This racer of the sea
Proved kinder to them than the coast,
It served them with a tree.

But such a tree! 'twas shaven deal,
The tree they call a mast,
And had a hollow, with a wheel
Through which the tackle pass'd.

Within that cavity aloft,
Their roofless home they fix'd;
Formed with materials neat and soft,
Bents, wool, and feathers mixed.

Four ivory eggs soon pave its floor,
With russet specks bedight,
The vessel weighs, forsakes the shore,
And lessens to the sight.

The mother bird is gone to sea,
As she had changed her kind;
But goes the male? Far wiser he,
Is doubtless left behind!

No!—soon as from the shore he saw
The winged mansion move,
He flew to reach it, by a law
Of never-failing love.

Then perching at his consort's side,
Was briskly borne along,
The billows and the blast defied,
And cheered her with a song.

The seaman with sincere delight,
His feathered shipmates eyes,

Scarce less exulting in the sight
  Than when he tows a prize.

For seamen much believe in signs,
  And from a chance so new,
Each some approaching good divines,
  And may his hopes be true!

Hail, honored land! a desert where
  Not even birds can hide,
Yet parent of this loving pair
  Whom nothing could divide.

And ye who rather than resign
  Your matrimonial plan,
Where not afraid to plough the brine
  In company with man.

To whose lean country much disdain
  We English often show,
Yet from a richer nothing gain
  But wantonness and woe.

Be it your fortune year by year,
  The same resource to prove,
And may ye sometimes, landing here,
  Instruct us how to love.

FIFTH SATIRE OF THE FIRST BOOK OF HORACE. 1759.

A HUMOROUS DESCRIPTION OF THE AUTHOR'S JOURNEY FROM ROME TO BRUNDUSIUM.

'Twas a long journey lay before us,
When I, and honest Heliodorus,
Who far in point of rhetoric
Surpasses ev'ry living Greek,
Each leaving our respective home
Together sallied forth from Rome.

First at Aricia we alight,
And there refresh, and pass the night,
Our entertainment rather coarse
Than sumptuous, but I've met with worse.
Thence o'er the causeway soft and fair
To Appii Forum we repair.
But as this road is well supplied
(Temptation strong!) on either side
With inns commodious, snug, and warm,
We split the journey, and perform
In two days' time what's often done
By brisker travellers in one.
Here, rather choosing not to sup
Than with bad water mix my cup,
After a warm debate, in spite
Of a provoking appetite,
I sturdily resolved at last
To baulk it, and pronounce a fast,
And in a moody humour wait,
While my less dainty comrades bait
Now o'er the spangled hemisphere
Diffused the starry train appear,
When there arose a desp'rate brawl:
The slaves and bargemen, one and all,
Rending their throats (have mercy on us!)
As if they were resolved to stun us,
"Steer the barge this way to the shore;
I tell you we'll admit no more;
Plague! will you never be content?"
Thus a whole hour at least is spent,
While they receive the sev'ral fares,
And kick the mule into his gears.
Happy, these difficulties past,
Could we have fall'n asleep at last!
But, what with humming, croaking, biting,
Gnats, frogs, and all their plagues uniting,
These tuneful natives of the lake
Conspired to keep us broad awake.
Besides, to make the concert full,
Two maudlin wights, exceeding dull,
The bargeman and a passenger,
Each in his turn, essay'd an air,
In honor of his absent fair.
At length the passenger, opprest
With wine, left off, and snored the rest.
The weary bargeman too gave o'er,
And hearing his companions snore,
Seized the occasion, fix'd the barge,
Turn'd out his mule to graze at large,

And slept forgetful of his charge.
And now the sun o'er eastern hill,
Discover'd that our barge stood still;
When one, whose anger vex'd him sore,
With malice fraught, leaps quick on shore;
Plucks up a stake, with many a thwack
Assails the mule and driver's back.
Then slowly moving on with pain,
At ten Feronia's stream we gain,
And in her pure and glassy wave
Our hands and faces gladly lave.
Climbing three miles, fair Anxur's height
We reach, with stony quarries white.
While here, as was agreed, we wait,
Till, charged with business of the state,
Mæcenas and Cocceius come,
The messengers of peace from Rome.
My eyes, by wat'ry humours blear
And sore, I with black balsam smear.
At length they join us, and with them
Our worthy friend Fonteius came;
A man of such complete desert,
Antony loved him at his heart.
At Fundi we refused to bait,
And laugh'd at vain Aufidius' state,
A prætor now, a scribe before,
The purple-border'd robe he wore,
His slave the smoking censer bore.
Tired, at Muræenas we repose,
At Formia sup at Capito's.
With smiles the rising morn we greet,
At Sinuessa pleased to meet
With Plotius, Varius, and the bard,
Whom Mantua first with wonder heard.
The world no purer spirits knows;
For none my heart more warmly glows.
O! what embraces we bestowed,
And with what joy our hearts o'erflow'd!
Sure, while my sense is sound and clear,
Long as I live, I shall prefer
A gay, good natured, easy friend,
To ev'ry blessing Heav'n can send.
At a small village the next night
Near the Vulturnous we alight;
Where, as employ'd on state affairs,
We were supplied by the purvey'rs
Frankly at once, and without hire,
With food for man and horse, and fire.
Capua next day betimes we reach,

Where Virgil and myself, who each
Labour'd with different maladies,
His such a stomach, mine such eyes,
As would not bear strong exercise,
In drowsy mood to sleep resort;
Mæcenas to the tennis-court.
Next at Cocceius's farm we're treated,
Above the Caudian tavern seated;
His kind and hospitable board
With choice of wholesome food was stored.
Now, O ye Nine, inspire my lays!
To nobler themes my fancy raise!
Two combatants, who scorn to yield
The noisy, tongue-disputed field,
Sarmentus and Cicirrus, claim
A poet's tribute to their fame;
Cicirrus of true Oscian breed,
Sarmentus, who was never freed,
But ran away. We don't defame him;
His lady lives, and still may claim him.
Thus dignified, in harder fray
These champions their keen wit display,
And first Sarmentus led the way.
"Thy locks (quoth he), so rough and coarse,
Look like the mane of some wild horse."
We laugh: Cicirrus undismay'd—
"Have at you!"—cries, and shakes his head.
"'Tis well (Sarmenus says) you've lost
That horn your forehead once could boast;
Since, maim'd and mangled as you are,
You seem to butt." A hideous scar
Improved ('tis true) with double grace
The native horrors of his face.
Well. After much jocosely said
Of his grim front, so fiery red
(For carbuncles had blotch'd it o'er,
As usual on Campania's shore),
"Give us (he cried), since you're so big,
A sample of the Cyclops' jig!
Your shanks methinks no buskins ask,
Nor does your phiz require a mask."
To this Cicirrus. "In return
Of you, Sir, now I fain would learn,
When 'twas, no longer deem'd a slave,
Your chains you to the Lares gave.
For tho' a scriv'ner's right your claim,
Your ladys' title is the same.
But what could make you run away,
Since, pigmy as you are, each day

A single pound of bread would quite
O'erpow'r your puny appetite?"
Thus joked the champions, while we laugh'd,
And many a cheerful bumper quaff'd.
To Beneventum next we steer;
Where our good host by over care,
In roasting thrushes lean as mice,
Had almost fall'n a sacrifice.
The kitchen soon was all on fire,
And to the roof the flames aspire.
There might you see each man and master
Striving, amidst the sad disaster,
To save the supper. Then they came
With speed enough to quench the flame.
From hence we first at distance see
Th'Apulian hills, well known to me,
Parch'd by the sultry western blast;
And which we never should have past,
Had not Trivicius by the way
Received us at the close of day.
But each was forced at ent'ring here
To pay the tribute of a tear,
For more of smoke than fire was seen—
The earth was piled with logs so green.
From hence in chaises we were carried
Miles twenty-four, and gladly tarried
At a small town, whose name my verse
(So barb'rous is it) can't rehearse.
Know it you may by many a sign,
Water is dearer far than wine.
There bread is deem'd such dainty fare,
That ev'ry prudent traveller
His wallet loads with many a crust;
For at Canusium you might just
As well attempt to gnaw a stone
As think to get a morsel down:
That too with scanty streams is fed;
Its founder was brave Diomed.
Good Varius (ah, that friends must part!)
Here left us all with aching heart.
At Rubi we arrived that day,
Well jaded by the length of way,
And sure poor mortals ne'er were wetter:
Next day no weather could be better;
No roads so bad; we scarce could crawl
Along to fishy Barium's wall.
Th'Egnatians next, who by the rules
Of common sense are knaves or fools,
Made all our sides with laughter heave

Since we with them must needs believe,
That incense in their temples burns,
And without fire to ashes turns.
To circumcision's bigots tell
Such tales! for me, I know full well
That in high Heav'n, unmoved by care,
The Gods eternal quiet share;
Nor can I deem their spleen the cause,
Why fickle nature breaks her laws.
Brundusium last we reach: and there
Stop short the muse and traveller.

NINTH SATIRE OF THE FIRST BOOK OF HORACE.

THE DESCRIPTION OF AN IMPERTINENT.

(Adapted to the present times, 1759.*)*

Saunt'ring along the street one day,
On trifles musing by the way—
Up steps a free familiar wight,
(I scarcely knew the man by sight),
"Carlos (he cried), your hand, my dear!
Gad, I rejoice to meet you here!
Pray Heav'n I see you well?" "So so;
Ev'n well enough as times now go.
The same good wishes, Sir, to you."
Finding he still pursued me close—
"Sir, you have business, I suppose."
"My business, Sir, is quickly done,
'Tis but to make my merit known.
Sir, I have read"—"O learned Sir,
You and your learning I revere."
Then sweating with anxiety,
And sadly longing to get free,
Gods, how I scamper'd, scuffled for't,
Ran, halted, ran again, stopp'd short,
Beckon'd my boy, and pull'd him near,
And whisper'd nothing in his ear.
Teased with his loose unjointed chat—
"What street is this? What house is that?"
O Harlow, how I envied thee
Thy unabash'd effrontery,

Who dar'st a foe with freedom blame,
And call a coxcomb by his name!
When I return'd him answer none,
Obligingly the fool ran on:
"I see you're dismally distress'd,
Would give the world to be released,
But, by your leave, Sir, I shall still
Stick to your skirts, do what you will;
Pray which way does your journey tend?"
"O, 'tis a tedious way, my friend;
Across the Thames, the Lord knows where;
I would not trouble you so far."
"Well, I'm at leisure to attend you."
"Are you? (thought I) the De'il befriend you!"
No ass with double panniers rack'd,
Oppress'd, o'erladen, broken-back'd,
E'er look'd a thousandth part so dull
As I, nor half so like a fool.
"Sir, I know little of myself,
(Proceeds the pert, conceited elf)
If Gray or Mason you will deem
Than me more worthy your esteem
Poems I write by folios
As fast as other men write prose;
Then I can sing so loud so clear,
That Beard cannot with me compare.
In dancing, too, I all surpass,
Not Cooke can move with such a grace."
Here I made shift with much ado,
To interpose a word or two—
"Have you no parents, Sir, no friends,
Whose welfare on your own depends?"
"Parents, relations, say you? No.
They're all disposed of long ago."—
"Happy to be no more perplex'd!
My fate too threatens, I go next.
Dispatch me, Sir, 'tis now too late,
Alas! to struggle with my fate!
Well I'm convinced my time is come—
When young, a gipsy told my doom.
The beldame shook her palsied head,
As she perused my palm, and said:
Of poison, pestilence, or war,
Gout, stone, defluxion, or catarrh,
You have no reason to beware.
Beware the coxcomb's idle prate;
Chiefly, my son, beware of that.
Be sure, when you behold him, fly
Out of all earshot, or you die."

To Rufus' Hall we now draw near;
Where he was summon'd to appear,
Refute the charge the plaintiff brought,
Or suffer judgment by default.
"For Heav'n's sake, if you love me, wait
One moment! I'll be with you straight."
Glad of a plausible pretence—
"Sir, I must beg you to dispense
With my attendance in the court,
My legs will surely suffer for't."
"Nay, pr'ythee, Carlos, stop awhile!"
"Faith, Sir, in law I have no skill.
Besides, I have no time to spare;
I must be going, you know where."
"Well, I protest I'm doubtful now,
Whether to leave my suit or you!"
"Me, without scruple! (I reply)
Me, by all means, Sir!"—"No, not I.
Allons, Monsieur!" 'Twere vain (you know)
To strive with a victorious foe.
So I reluctantly obey,
And follow, where he leads the way.
"You and Newcastle are so close,
Still hand and glove, Sir—I suppose."
"Newcastle (let me tell you, Sir)
Has not his equal every where."
"Well. There, indeed, your fortune's made.
Faith, Sir, you understand your trade.
Would you but give me your good word,
Just introduce me to my lord.
I should serve charmingly by way
Of second fiddle, as they say;
What think you, Sir? 'twere a good jest.
'Slife, we should quickly scout the rest."—
"Sir, you mistake the matter far,
We have no second fiddles there.—
Richer than I some folks may be;
More learned, but it hurts not me.
Friends though he has of diff'rent kind,
Each has his proper place assign'd."
"Strange matters these alleged by you!"
"Strange they may be, but they are true.'
"Well then, I vow 'tis mighty clever,
Now I long ten times more than ever
To be advanced extremely near
One of his shining character.
Have but the will—there wants no more,
'Tis plain enough you have the power.
His easy temper (that's the worst)

He knows, and is so shy at first.—
But such a cavalier as you—
Lord, Sir, you'll quickly bring him to!—
Well; if I fail in my design,
Sir, it shall be no fault of mine.
If by the saucy servile tribe
Denied, what think you of a bribe?
Shut out to-day, not die with sorrow,
But try my luck again to-morrow.
Never attempt to visit him
But at the most convenient time,
Attend him on each levee day
And there my humble duty pay:
Labour, like this, our want supplies;
And they must stoop, who mean to rise."
While thus he wittingly harangued,
For which you'll guess I wish'd him hang'd,
Campley, a friend of mine, came by,
Who knew his humour more than I.
We stop, salute, and—"Why so fast,
Friend Carlos? Whither all this haste?"
Fired at the thoughts of a reprieve,
I pinch him, pull him, twitch his sleeve,
Nod, beckon, bite my lips, wink, pout,
Do ev'ry thing but speak plain out:
While he, sad dog, from the beginning
Determined to mistake my meaning;
Instead of pitying my curse,
By jeering made it ten times worse.
"Campley, what secret (pray!) was that
You wanted to communicate?"
"I recollect. But 'tis no matter.
Carlos, we'll talk of that hereafter.
E'en let the secret rest. 'Twill tell
Another time, Sir, just as well."
Was ever such a dismal day?
Unlucky cur, he steals away,
And leaves me, half bereft of life,
At mercy of the butcher's knife;
When sudden shouting from afar,
See his antagonist appear!
The bailiff seized him quick as thought,
"Ho, Mr. Scoundrel! Are you caught?
Sir, you are witness to th'arrest."
"Aye, marry, Sir, I'll do my best."
The mob huzzas. Away they trudge,
Culprit and all, before the judge.
Meanwhile I luckily enough
(Thanks to Apollo,) got clear off.

TRANSLATIONS

OF THE

LATIN AND ITALIAN POEMS OF MILTON.

[BEGUN SEPTEMBER 1791; FINISHED MARCH 1792.]

ELEGIES.

ELEGY I.

TO CHARLES DEODATI.

At length, my friend, the far-sent letters come,
Charged with thy kindness, to their destined home:
They come, at length, from Deva's western side,
Where prone she seeks the salt Vergivian tide.
Trust me, my joy is great, that thou shouldst be
Though born of foreign race, yet born for me,
And that my sprightly friend, now free to roam,
Must seek again so soon his wonted home.
I, well content, where Thames with influent tide
My native city laves, meantime reside;
Nor zeal nor duty, now, my steps impel
To reedy Cam, and my forbidden cell.
Nor aught of pleasure in those fields have I,
That, to the musing bard, all shade deny.
'Tis time that I a pedant's threats disdain,
And fly from wrongs my soul will ne'er sustain.
If peaceful days, in letter'd leisure spent
Beneath my father's roof, be banishment,
Then call me banish'd; I will ne'er refuse
A name expressive of the lot I choose.
I would that, exiled to the Pontic shore,
Rome's hapless bard had suffer'd nothing more.
He then had equall'd even Homer's lays,
And, Virgil! thou hadst won but second praise:
For here I woo the muse with no control:
And here my books—my life—absorb me whole.

Here too I visit, or to smile, or weep,
The winding theatre's majestic sweep;
The grave or gay colloquial scene recruits
My spirits, spent in learning's long pursuits;
Whether some senior shrewd, or spendthrift heir,
Suitor or soldier, now unarm'd, be there,
Or some coif'd brooder o'er a ten years' cause,
Thunder the Norman gibb'rish of the laws.
The lacquey, there, oft dupes the wary sire,
And artful, speeds th' enamour'd son's desire.
There, virgins oft, unconscious what they prove,
What love is, known not, yet unknowing love.
Or if impassion'd Tragedy wield high
The bloody sceptre, give her locks to fly
Wild as the winds, and roll her haggard eye,
I gaze, and grieve, still cherishing my grief,
At times, e'en bitter tears! yield sweet relief.
As when from bliss untasted torn away,
Some youth dies, hapless, on his bridal day,
Or when the ghost sent back from shades below,
Fills the assassin's heart with vengeful woe.
When Troy or Argos, the dire scene affords,
Or Creon's hall laments its guilty lords.
Nor always city-pent, or pent at home,
I dwell; but when spring calls me forth to roam,
Expatiate in our proud suburban shades
Of branching elm, that never sun prevades.
Here many a virgin troop I may descry,
Like stars of mildest influence, gliding by.
Oh forms divine! Oh looks that might inspire
E'en Jove himself, grown old, with young desire,
Oft have I gazed on gem-surpassing eyes,
Out-sparkling ev'ry star that gilds the skies.
Necks whiter than the ivory arm bestow'd
By Jove on Pelops, or the milky road!
Bright locks, Love's golden snare! these falling low,
Those playing wanton o'er the graceful brow!
Cheeks too, more winning sweet than after show'r
Adonis turn'd to Flora's fav'rite flower!
Yield, heroines, yield, and he who shared th' embrace
Of Jupiter in ancient times, give place!
Give place, ye turban'd fair of Persia's coast!
And ye, not less renown'd, Assyria's boast!
Submit, ye nymphs of Greece! ye, once the bloom
Of Ilion! and all ye, of haughty Rome,
Who swept, of old, her theatres with trains
Redundant, and still live in classic strains!
To British damsels beauty's palm is due,
Aliens! to follow them is fame for you.

Oh city, founded by Dardanian hands,
Whose tow'ring front the circling realms commands,
Too blest abode! no loveliness we see
In all the earth, but it abounds in thee.
The virgin multitude that daily meets,
Radiant with gold and beauty, in thy streets,
Out-numbers all her train of starry fires,
With which Diana gilds thy lofty spires.
Fame says, that wafted hither by her doves,
With all her host of quiver-bearing loves,
Venus, preferring Paphian scenes no more,
Has fix'd her empire on thy nobler shore,
But lest the sightless boy enforce my stay,
I leave these happy walls, while yet I may.
Immortal Moly shall secure my heart
From all the sorc'ry of Cicæan art,
And I will e'en repass Cam's reedy pools
To face one more the warfare of the schools.
Meantime accept this trifle! rhymes though few,
Yet such, as prove thy friend's remembrance true!

ELEGY II.

ON THE DEATH OF THE UNIVERSITY BEADLE AT CAMBRIDGE.

Composed by Milton, in the 17th year of his age.

Thee, whose refulgent staff, and summons clear,
  Minerva's flock long time was wont t' obey,
Although thyself an herald, famous here,
  The last of heralds, Death, has snatch'd away.
He calls on all alike, nor even deigns
  To spare the office, that himself sustains.

Thy locks were whiter than the plumes display'd
  By Leda's paramour in ancient time,
But thou wast worthy ne'er to have decay'd,
  Or Æson-like to know a second prime,
Worthy, for whom some goddess should have won
New life, oft kneeling to Apollo's son.

Commission'd to convene, with hasty call,
  The gowned tribes, how graceful wouldst thou stand!
So stood Cyllenius erst in Priam's hall,
  Wing-footed messenger of Jove's command!
And so Eurybates, when he address'd
To Peleus' son, Atrides' proud behest.

Dread queen of sepulchres! whose rig'rous laws
  And watchful eyes, run through the realms below,
Oh, oft too adverse to Minerva's cause!
  Too often to the muse not less a foe!
Choose meaner marks, and with more equal aim
Pierce useless drones, earth's burden, and its shame!

Flow, therefore, tears for him, from ev'ry eye,
  All ye disciples of the muses, weep!
Assembling, all, in robes of sable dye,
  Around his bier, lament his endless sleep!
And let complaining elegy rehearse,
In ev'ry school, her sweetest, saddest verse.

ELEGY III.

ON THE DEATH OF THE BISHOP OF WINCHESTER.

Composed in the Author's 17*th year.*

  Silent I sat, dejected, and alone,
Making, in thought, the public woes my own,
When, first, arose the image in my breast
Of England's suffering by that scourge, the Pest!
How death, his fun'ral torch and scythe in hand,
Entering the lordliest mansions of the land,
Has laid the gem-illumined palace low,
And levell'd tribes of nobles at a blow.
I next deplored the famed paternal pair,
Too soon to ashes turn'd, and empty air!
The heroes next, whom snatch'd into the skies,
All Belgia saw, and follow'd with her sighs,
But thee far most I mourned, regretted most,
Wint'ons chief shepherd, and her worthiest boast;
Pour'd out in tears I thus complaining said:
" Death, next in pow'r to him who rules the dead!

Is't not enough that all the woodlands yield
To thy fell force, and ev'ry verdant field;
That lilies, at one noisome blast of thine,
And e'en the Cyprian queen's own roses, pine;
That oaks themselves, although the running rill
Suckle their roots, must wither at thy will
That all the winged nations, even those
Whose heav'n-directed flight the future shows,
And all the beasts, that in dark forests stray,
And all the herds of Proteus are thy prey.
Ah envious! arm'd with pow'rs so unconfined!
Why stain thy hands with blood of human kind?
Why take delight, with darts, that never roam
To chase a heav'n-born spirit from her home?"
While thus I mourn'd, the star of evening stood
Now newly ris'n above the western flood,
And Phœbus from his morning-goal again
Had reach'd the gulfs of the Iberian main.
I wish'd repose, and on my couch reclined
Took early rest, to night and sleep resign'd:
When—Oh for words to paint what I beheld!
I seem'd to wander in a spacious field,
Where all the champaign glow'd with purple light,
Like that of sun-rise on the mountain height;
Flow'rs over all the field, of ev'ry hue
That ever Iris wore, luxuriant grew.
Nor Chloris, with whom am'rous Zephyrs play,
E'er dress'd Alcinous' garden half so gay,
A silver current, like the Tagus, roll'd
O'er golden sands, but sands of purer gold;
With dewy airs Favonius fann'd the flow'rs,
With airs awaken'd under rosy bow'rs.
Such, poets feign, irradiated all o'er
The sun's abode on India's utmost shore.
While I, that splendor, and the mingled shade
Of fruitful vines, with wonder fix'd survey'd,
At once, with looks that beam'd celestial grace,
The seer of Winton stood before my face.
His snowy vesture's hem descending low,
His golden sandals swept, and pure as snow
New-fallen shone the mitre on his brow.
Where'er he trod a tremulous sweet sound
Of gladness shook the flow'ry scene around:
Attendant angels clap their starry wings,
The trumpet shakes the sky, all æther rings,
Each chaunts his welcome, folds him to his breast,
And thus a sweeter voice than all the rest:
"Ascend, my son! thy father's kingdom share!
My son! henceforth be freed from ev'ry care!"

So spake the voice, and at its tender close
With psaltry's sound th' angelic band arose,
Then night retired, and chased by dawning day
The visionary bliss pass'd all away.
I mourn'd my banish'd sleep, with fond concern;
Frequent to me may dreams like this return!

ELEGY IV.

TO HIS TUTOR, THOS. YOUNG, CHAPLAIN TO THE ENGLISH FACTORY AT HAMBURGH.

Written in the Author's 18*th year.*

Hence my epistle—skim the deep—fly o'er
Yon smooth expanse to the Teutonic shore!
Haste—lest a friend should grieve for thy delay—
And the gods grant, that nothing thwart thy way!
I will myself invoke the king, who binds,
In his Sicanian echoing vault, the winds,
With Doris and her nymphs, and all the throng
Of azure gods, to speed thee safe along.
But rather to ensure thy happier haste,
Ascend Medea's chariot if thou may'st:
Or that, whence young Triptolemus of yore
Descended, welcome on the Scythian shore.
The sands, that line the German coast, descried,
To opulent Humburga turn aside!
So called, if legendary fame be true,
From Hama whom a club-arm'd Cymbrian slew!
Their lives, deep-learn'd and primitively just,
A faithful steward of his Christian trust,
My friend, and favorite inmate of my heart,
That now is forced to want its better part!
What mountains now, and seas, alas! how wide!
From me this other, dearer self divide,
Dear, as the sage renown'd for moral truth
To the prime spirit of the Attic youth!
Dear, as the Stagyrite to Ammon's son,
His pupil, who disdain'd the world he won
Nor so did Chiron, or so Phœnix shine
In young Achilles' eyes as he in mine.
First led by him thro' sweet Aonian shade,
Each sacred haunt of Pindus I survey'd

And favor'd by the muse, whom I implored,
Thrice on my lip the hallow'd stream I pour'd
But thrice the sun's resplendent chariot roll'd
To Aries, has new tinged his fleece with gold,
And Chloris twice has dress'd the meadows gay,
And twice has summer parch'd their bloom away,
Since last delighted on his looks I hung,
Or my ear drank the music of his tongue:
Fly, therefore, and surpass the tempests speed:
Aware thyself, that there is urgent need;
Him, entering, thou shalt haply seated see
Beside his spouse, his infants on his knee.
Or turning, page by page, with studious look,
Some bulky father, or God's holy book.
Or minist'ring (which is his weightiest care)
To Christ's assembled flock their heavenly fare,
Give him, whatever his employment be,
Such gratulation, as he claims, from me!
And, with a down-cast eye, and carriage meek,
Addressing him, forget not thus to speak:
"If compass'd round with arms thou canst attend
To verse, verse greets thee from a distant friend,
Long due, and late, I left the English shore;
But make me welcome for that cause the more!
Such from Ulysses, his chaste wife to cheer,
The slow epistle came, tho' late, sincere.
But wherefore this? why palliate I the deed,
For which the culprit's self could hardly plead?
Self-charged, and self-condemned, his proper part
He feels neglected, with an aching heart?
But thou forgive—delinquents, who confess,
And pray forgiveness, merit anger less;
From timid foes the lion turns away,
Nor yawns upon or rends a crouching prey;
Even pike-wielding Thracians learn to spare,
Won by soft influence of a suppliant prayer;
And Heav'n's dread thunderbolt arrested stands
By a cheap victim, and uplifted hands.
Long had he wish'd to write, but was withheld,
And, writes at last, by love alone compell'd;
For fame, too often true, when she alarms,
Reports thy neighbouring fields a scene of arms;
Thy city against fierce besiegers barr'd,
And all the Saxon chiefs for fight prepared.
Enyo wastes thy country wide around,
And saturates with blood the tainted ground;
Mars rests contented in his Thrace no more,
But goads his steeds to fields of German gore;
The ever-verdant olive fades and dies

And Peace, the trumpet-hating goddess, flies,
Flies from that earth which justice long had left
And leaves the world of its last guard bereft.
Thus horror girds thee round. Meantime alone
Thou dwell'st, and helpless in a soil unknown;
Poor, and receiving from a foreign hand
The aid denied thee in thy native land.
Oh, ruthless country, and unfeeling more
Than thy own billow-beaten chalky shore!
Leav'st thou to foreign care the worthies, given
By Providence, to guide thy steps to heav'n?
His ministers, commission'd to proclaim
Eternal blessings in a Saviour's name?
Ah then most worthy, with a soul unfed,
In Stygian night to lie for ever dead!
So once the venerable Tishbite stray'd
An exiled fugitive from shade to shade,
When, flying Ahab, and his fury wife,
In lone Arabian wilds, he shelter'd life;
So, from Philippi, wander'd forth forlorn
Cicilian Paul, with sounding scourges torn;
And Christ himself, so left, and trod no more,
The thankless Gergesene's forbidden shore.
But thou take courage! strive against despair!
Quake not with dread, nor nourish anxious care,
Grim war indeed on ev'ry side appears,
And thou art menaced by a thousand spears;
Yet none shall drink thy blood, or shall offend
E'en the defenceless bosom of my friend.
For thee the Ægis of thy God shall hide,
Jehovah's self shall combat on thy side.
The same, who vanquish'd under Sion's tow'rs
At silent midnight, all Assyria's pow'rs;
The same, who overthrew in ages past,
Damascus' sons that laid Samaria waste!
Their king he fill'd and them with fatal fears
By mimic sound of clarions in their ears,
Of hoofs, and wheels, and neighings from afar,
Of clashing armour, and the din of war.
Thou, therefore (as the most afflicted may),
Still hope, and triumph, o'er thy evil day!
Look forth, expecting happier times to come
And to enjoy, once more, thy native home!

ELEGY V.

ON THE APPROACH OF SPRING.

Written in the Author's Twentieth year.

Time, never wand'ring from his annual round,
Bids Zephyr breathe the spring, and thaw the ground;
Bleak winter flies, new verdure clothes the plain,
And earth assumes her transient youth again.
Dream I, or also to the spring belong
Increase of genius, and new pow'rs of song?
Spring gives them, and, how strange so'er it seems,
Impels me now to some harmonious themes.
Castalia's fountain, and the forked hill
By day, by night, my raptured fancy fill;
My bosom burns and heaves, I hear within
A sacred sound, that prompts me to begin.
Lo! Phœbus comes, with his bright hair he blends
The radiant laurel-wreath; Phœbus descends;
I mount, and, undepress'd by cumbrous clay,
Through cloudy regions win my easy way;
Rapt through poetic shadowy haunts I fly:
The shrines all open to my dauntless eye.
My spirit searches all the realms of light,
And no Tartarean gulfs elude my sight.
But this ecstatic trance—this glorious storm
Of inspiration—what will it perform?
Spring claims the verse, that with his influence glows,
And shall be paid with what himself bestows.
Thou, veil'd with op'ning foliage, lead'st the throng
Of feather'd minstrels, Philomel! in song;
Let us, in concert, to the season sing,
Civic and sylvan heralds of the spring!
With notes triumphant spring's approach declare;
To spring, ye Muses, annual tribute bear!
The Orient left, and Æthiopia's plains,
The Sun now northward turns his golden reins:
Night creeps not now; yet rules with gentle sway;
And drives her dusky horrors swift away;
Now less fatigued, on this æthereal plain
Boötes follows his celestial wain;

And now the radiant sentinels above,
Less num'rous, watch around the courts of Jove,
For with the night, force, ambush, slaughter fly,
And no gigantic guilt alarms the sky.
Now haply says some shepherd, while he views,
Recumbent on a rock, the redd'ning dews,
This night, this surely, Phœbus miss'd the fair,
Who stops his chariot by her am'rous care.
Cynthia, delighted by the morning's glow,
Speeds to the woodland, and resumes her bow;
Resigns her beams, and, glad to disappear,
Blesses his aid, who shortens her career.
Come—Phœbus cries—Aurora come—too late
Thou ling'rest, slumb'ring, with thy wither'd mate!
Leave him, and to Hymettus' top repair!
Thy darling Cephalus expects thee there.
The goddess, with a blush, her love betrays,
But mounts, and driving rapidly, obeys.
Earth now desires thee, Phœbus! and t'engage
Thy warm embrace casts off the guise of age;
Desires thee, and deserves; for who so sweet,
When her rich bosom courts thy genial heat?
Her breath imparts to ev'ry breeze that blows
Arabia's harvest, and the Paphian rose.
Her lofty front she diadems around
With sacred pines, like Ops on Ida crown'd;
His dewy locks, with various flow'rs new-blown,
She interweaves, various, and all her own,
For Proserpine, in such a wreath attired,
Tænarian Dis himself with love inspired.
Fear not, lest, cold and coy, the nymph refuse
Herself, with all her sighing Zephyrs, sues;
Each courts thee, fanning soft his scented wing,
And all her groves with warbled wishes ring,
Nor, unendow'd and indigent, aspires
The am'rous Earth t' engage thy warm desires.
But, rich in balmy drugs, assists thy claim,
Divine Physician! to that glorious name.
If splendid recompense, if gifts can move
Desire in thee (gifts often purchase love),
She offers all the wealth her mountains hide,
And all that rests beneath the boundless tide.
How oft, when headlong from the heav'nly steep,
She sees thee playing in the western deep,
How oft she cries—"Ah Phœbus! why repair
Thy wasted force, why seek refreshment there?
Can Thetis win thee? wherefore shouldst thou lave
A face so fair in her unpleasant wave?
Come, seek my green retreats, and rather choose

To cool thy tresses in my crystal dews,
The grassy turf shall yield thee sweeter rest
Come, lay thy ev'ning glories on my breast,
And breathing fresh, through many a humid rose,
Soft whispering airs shall lull thee to repose!
No fears I feel, like Semele, to die,
Nor let thy burning wheels approach too nigh,
For thou canst govern them—here therefore rest,
And lay thy ev'ning glories on my breast!"
Thus breathes the wanton Earth her am'rous flame
And all her countless offspring feel the same
For Cupid now through every region strays,
Bright'ning his faded fires with solar rays:
His new-strung bow sends forth a deadlier sound,
And his new-pointed shafts more deeply wound;
Nor Dian's self escapes him now untried,
Nor even Vesta at her altar-side;
His mother too repairs her beauty's wane,
And seems sprung newly from the deep again.
Exulting youths the Hymeneal sing,
With Hymen's name roofs, rocks, and valleys ring
He, new-attired, and by the season drest,
Proceeds, all fragrant, in his saffron vest.
Now, many a golden-cinctured virgin roves
To taste the pleasures of the fields and groves;
All wish, and each alike; some fav'rite youth
Hers, in the bonds of Hymeneal truth.
Now pipes the shepherd through his reeds again,
Nor Phillis wants a song, that suits the strain;
With songs the seaman hails the starry sphere,
And dolphins rise from the abyss to hear!
Jove feels himself the season, sports again
With his fair spouse, and banquets all his train
Now too the Satyrs, in the dusk of eve,
Their mazy dance through flow'ry meadows weave;
And neither god nor goat, but both in kind,
Sylvanus, wreath'd with cypress, skips behind.
The Dryads leave their hollow sylvan cells,
To roam the banks and solitary dells;
Pan riots now; and from his am'rous chafe
Geres and Cybele seem hardly safe.
And Faunus, all on fire to reach the prize,
In chase of some enticing Oread flies;
She bounds before, but fears too swift a bound
And hidden lies, but wishes to be found.
Our shades entice th' Immortals from above,
And some kind power presides o'er ev'ry grove!
And long, ye pow'rs, o'er ev'ry grove preside,
For all is safe, and blest, where ye abide!

Return, O Jove! the age of gold restore—
Why choose to dwell where storms and thunders roar?
At least thou, Phœbus! moderate thy speed!
Let not the vernal hours too swift proceed,
Command rough Winter back, nor yield the pole
Too soon to Night's encroaching long control!

ELEGY VI.

TO CHARLES DEODATI.

Who while he spent his Christmas in the country, sent the Author a poetical Epistle, in which he requested that his verses, if not so good as usual, might be excused on account of the many feasts to which his friends invited him, and which would not allow him leisure to finish them as he wished.

With no rich viands overcharged, I send [friend;
Health, which perchance you want, my pamper'd
But wherefore should thy muse tempt mine away
From what she loves, from darkness into day?
Art thou desirous to be told how well
I love thee, and in verse? verse cannot tell.
For verse has bounds, and must in measure move;
But neither bounds nor measure knows my love.
How pleasant, in thy lines described, appear
December's harmless sports, and rural cheer!
French spirits kindling with cærulean fires,
And all such gambols, as the time inspires!
Think not that wine against good verse offends;
The muse and Bacchus have been always friends,
Nor Phœbus blushes sometimes to be found
With ivy, rather than with laurel crown'd.
The Nine themselves oft-times have join'd the song,
And revels of the Bacchanalian throng;
Not even Ovid could in Scythian air
Sing sweetly—why? no vine would flourish there.
What in brief numbers sung Anacreon's muse?
Wine, and the rose, that sparkling wine bedews.

Pindar with Bacchus glows—his ev'ry line
Breathes the rich fragrance of inspiring wine,
While, with loud crash o'erturn'd the chariot lies,
And brown with dust the fiery courser flies.
The Roman lyrist steep'd in wine his lays
So sweet in Glycera's, and Chloe's praise.
Now too the plenteous feast and mantling bowl
Nourish the vigour of thy sprightly soul;
The flowing goblet makes thy numbers flow,
And casks not wine alone, but verse, bestow.
Thus Phœbus favors, and the arts attend,
Whom Bacchus, and whom Ceres, both befriend.
What wonder then thy verses are so sweet,
In which these triple powers so kindly meet!
The lute now also sounds, with gold in-wrought,
And touch'd with flying fingers nicely taught,
In tap'stried halls, high roof'd, the sprightly lyre
Directs the dancers of the virgin choir.
If dull repletion fright the Muse away,
Sights, gay as these, may more invite her stay;
And trust me, while the iv'ry keys resound,
Fair damsels sport, and perfumes steam around,
Apollo's influence, like æthereal flame,
Shall animate at once thy glowing flame,
And all the Muse shall rush into thy breast,
By love and music's blended pow'rs possest.
For num'rous pow'rs light Elegy befriend,
Hear her sweet voice, and at her call attend;
Her, Bacchus, Ceres, Venus, all approve,
And with his blushing mother gentle Love.
Hence to such bards we grant the copious use
Of banquets, and the vine's delicious juice.
But they, who demi-gods and heroes praise,
And feats perform'd in Jove's more youthful days,
Who now the counsels of high heav'n explore,
Now shades, that echo the Cerberean roar,
Simply let these, like him of Samos live,
Let herbs to them a bloodless banquet give;
In beechen goblets let their bev'rage shine,
Cool from the crystal spring, their sober wine!
Their youth should pass, in innocence, secure
From stain licentious, and in manners pure,
Pure as the priest, when robed in white he stands,
The fresh lustration ready in his hands.
Thus Linus lived, and thus, as poets write,
Tiresias, wiser for his loss of sight!
Thus exiled Chalcas, thus the bard of Thrace,
Melodious tamer of the savage race!
Thus train'd by temp'rance, Homer led, of yore,

His chief of Ithaca from shore to shore,
Through magic Circe's monster-peopled reign,
And shoals insidious with the siren train;
And through the realms, where grizly spectres dwell,
Whose tribes he fetter'd in a gory spell;
For these are sacred bards, and, from above,
Drink large infusions from the mind of Jove!
Would'st thou (perhaps 'tis hardly worth thine ear),
Would'st thou be told my occupation here?
The promised King of peace employs my pen,
Th' eternal cov'nant made for guilty men,
The new-born Deity with infant cries
Filling the sordid hovel where he lies;
The hymning angels, and the herald star,
That led the wise, who sought him from afar,
And idols on their own unallow'd shore
Dash'd, at his birth, to be revered no more!
This theme on reeds of Albion I rehearse:
The dawn of that blest day inspired the verse;
Verse, that, reserved in secret, shall attend
Thy candid voice, my critic, and my friend!

ELEGY VII.

Composed in the Author's 19th year.

As yet a stranger to the gentle fires,
That Amathusia's smiling queen inspires,
Not seldom I derided Cupid's darts,
And scorn'd his claim to rule all human hearts.
"Go, child," I said, "transfix the tim'rous dove!
An easy conquest suits an infant love;
Enslave the sparrow, for such prize shall be
Sufficient triumph to a chief like thee!
Why aim thy idle arms at human kind?
Thy shafts prevail not 'gainst the noble mind."
The Cyprian heard, and kindling into ire
(None kindles sooner), burn'd with double fire.
It was the spring, and newly risen day
Peep'd o'er the hamlets on the first of May;
My eyes too tender for the blaze of light,
Still sought the shelter of retiring night,
When Love approach'd in painted plumes array'd,
Th' insidious god his rattling darts betray'd,

Nor less his infant features, and the sly,
Sweet intimations of his threat'ning eye.
 Such the Sigeian boy is seen above,
Filling the goblet for imperial Jove;
Such he, on whom the nymphs bestow'd their charms,
Hylas, who perish'd in a Naiad's arms.
Angry he seem'd, yet graceful in his ire,
And added threats, not destitute of fire.
"My power," he said, "by others' pain alone,
'Twere best to learn; now learn it by thy own!
With those who feel my power, that pow'r attest!
And in thy anguish be my sway confest!
I vanquish'd Phœbus, though returning vain
From his new triumph o'er the Python slain,
And, when he thinks on Daphne, even he
Will yield the prize of archery to me.
A dart less true the Parthian horseman sped,
Behind him killed, and conquer'd as he fled:
Less true th' expert Cydonian, and less true
The youth, whose shaft his latent Procris slew.
Vanquish'd by me, see huge Orion bend,
By me Alcides, and Alcides' friend.
At me should Jove himself a bolt design,
His bosom first should bleed, transfixt by mine.
But all thy doubts this shaft will best explain,
Nor shall it reach thee with a trivial pain.
Thy Muse, vain youth! shall not thy peace ensure,
Nor Phœbus' serpent yield thy wound a cure."
 He spoke, and, waving a bright shaft in air,
Sought the warm bosom of the Cyprian fair.
 That thus a child should bluster in my ear,
Provoked my laughter, more than moved my fear.
I shunn'd not, therefore, public haunts, but stray'd
Careless in city or suburban shade;
And passing, and repassing, nymphs, that mov'd
With grace divine, beheld where'er I roved.
Bright shone the vernal day with double blaze,
As beauty gave new force to Phœbus' rays.
By no grave scruples checked, I freely eyed
The dang'rous show, rash youth my only guide,
And many a look of many a fair unknown
Met full, unable to control my own.
But one I mark'd (then peace forsook my breast)
One—oh how far superior to the rest!
What lovely features! such the Cyprian queen
Herself might wish, and Juno wish her mien.
The very nymph was she, whom when I dared
His arrows, Love had even then prepared!
Nor was himself remote, nor unsupplied

With torch well trimm'd, and quiver at his side;
Now to her lips he clung, her eyelids now,
Then settled on her cheeks, or on her brow;
And with a thousand wounds from ev'ry part,
Pierced, and transpierced, my undefended heart.
A fever, new to me, of fierce desire,
Now seized my soul, and I was all on fire;
But she, the while, whom only I adore,
Was gone, and vanish'd, to appear no more.
In silent sadness I pursue my way;
I pause, I turn, proceed, yet wish to stay;
And while I follow her in thought, bemoan
With tears, my souls delight so quickly flown.
When Jove had hurl'd him to the Lemnian coast,
So Vulcan sorrow'd for Olympus lost;
And so Oeclides, sinking into night,
From the deep gulf look'd up to distant light.
Wretch that I am, what hopes for me remain,
Who cannot cease to love, yet love in vain?
O could I once, once more behold the fair,
Speak to her, tell her, of the pangs I bear;
Perhaps she is not adamant, would show
Perhaps some pity at my tale of woe.
Oh inauspicious flame—'tis mine to prove
A matchless instance of disastrous love.
Ah spare me, gentle power!—if such thou be,
Let not thy deeds and nature disagree.
Spare me, and I will worship at no shrine
With vow and sacrifice, save only thine.
Now I revere thy fires, thy bow, thy darts;
Now own thee sov'reign of all human hearts.
Remove! no—grant me still this raging woe!
Sweet is the wretchedness that lovers know;
But pierce hereafter (should I chance to see
One destin'd mine) at once both her and me.
Such were the trophies that, in earlier days,
By vanity seduc'd, I toil'd to raise;
Studious, yet indolent, and urg'd by youth,
That worst of teachers! from the ways of truth;
Till Learning taught me, in his shady bower,
To quit Love's servile yoke, and spurn his power.
Then, on a sudden, the fierce flame suppress,
A frost continual settled on my breast,
Whence Cupid fears his flames extinct to see,
And Venus dreads a Diomede in me.

EPIGRAMS.

ON THE INVENTOR OF GUNS.

Praise in old times the sage Prometheus won,
Who stole ætherial radiance from the sun;
But greater he, whose bold invention strove
To emulate the fiery bolts of Jove.

[The Poems on the subject of the Gunpowder Treason I have not translated, both because the matter of them is unpleasant, and because they are written with an asperity, which, however it might be warranted in Milton's day, would be extremely unseasonable now.]

TO LEONORA SINGING AT ROME. *

Another Leonora once inspired
Tasso, with fatal love to frenzy fired;
But how much happier lived he now, were he
Pierced with whatever pangs for love of thee!
Since, could he hear that heavenly voice of thine,
With Adriana's lute of sound divine,
Fiercer than Pentneus' though his eye might roll,
Or idiot apathy benumb his soul,
You still, with medicinal sounds might cheer
His senses, wand'ring in a blind career;
And sweetly breathing through his wounded breas
Charm, with soul-soothing song, his thoughts to rest.

* I have translated only two of the three poetical compliments addressed to Leonora, as they appear to me far superior to what I have omitted.

TO THE SAME.

Naples, too credulous, ah! boast no more
The sweet-voiced Syren buried on thy shore,
That, when Parthenope deceased, she gave
Her sacred dust to a Chalcidic grave;
For still she lives, but has exchanged the hoarse
Pausilipo for Tiber's placid course,
Where, idol of all Rome she now in chains
Of magic song both gods and men detains.

THE COTTAGER AND HIS LANDLORD.

A FABLE.

A peasant to his lord paid yearly court,
Presenting pippins of so rich a sort,
That he, displeased to have a part alone,
Removed the tree, that all might be his own.
The tree, too old to travel, though before
So fruitful, wither'd, and would yield no more.
The squire, perceiving all his labour void,
Cursed his own pains so foolishly employ'd;
And "Oh," he cried, "that I had lived content
With tribute, small indeed, but kindly meant!
My avarice has expensive prov'd to me,
Has cost me both my pippins and my tree."

TO CHRISTINA QUEEN OF SWEDEN, WITH CROMWELL'S PICTURE.

Christina, maiden of heroic mien,
Star of the North! of northern stars the queen!
Behold what wrinkles I have earn'd, and how
The iron casque still chafes my vet'ran brow,

While following fate's dark footsteps, I fulfil
The dictates of a hardy people's will.
But soften'd, in thy sight, my looks appear
Not to all Queens or Kings alike severe.

MISCELLANEOUS POEMS.

ON THE DEATH OF THE VICE-CHANCELLOR,

A PHYSICIAN.

Learn, ye nations of the earth,
The condition of your birth,
Now be taught your feeble state!
Know, that all must yield to fate!

If the mournful rover, Death,
Say but once—"Resign your breath!"
Vainly of escape you dream,
You must pass the Stygian stream.

Could the stoutest overcome
Death's assault, and baffle doom,
Hercules had both withstood,
Undiseas'd by Nessus' blood.

Ne'er had Hector press'd the plain
By a trick of Pallas slain,
Nor the chief to Jove allied
By Achilles' phantom died.

Could enchantments life prolong,
Circe saved by magic song,
Still had lived, and equal skill
Had preserved Medea still.

Dwelt in herbs and drugs a pow'r
To avert man's destined hour,
Learn'd Machaon should have known
Doubtless to avert his own.

Chiron had survived the smart
Of the Hydra-tainted dart,
And Jove's bolt had been, with ease,
Foil'd by Asclepiades.

Thou too, sage! of whom forlorn
Helicon and Cirrha mourn,
Still hadst fill'd thy princely place,
Regent of the gowned race;

Hadst advanced to higher fame
Still thy much ennobled name,
Nor in Charon's skiff explored
The tartarean gulf abhorr'd.

But resentful Proserpine,
Jealous of thy skill divine,
Snapping short thy vital thread,
Thee too number'd with the dead.

Wise and good! untroubled be
The green turf that covers thee!
Thence, in gay profusion grow
All the sweetest flow'rs that blow.

Pluto's consort bid thee rest!
Æacus pronounce thee blest!
To her home thy shade consign!
Make Elysium ever thine!

ON THE DEATH OF THE BISHOP OF ELY.

Written in the Author's 17th year.

My lids with grief were tumid yet
And still my sullied cheek was wet
With briny tears, profusely shed
For venerable Winton dead;
When Fame, whose tales of saddest sound,
Alas! are ever truest found,
The news through all our cities spread
Of yet another mitred head
By ruthless fate to death consign'd,
Ely! the honor of his kind!

At once, a storm of passion heaved
My boiling bosom, much I grieved,
But more I raged, at ev'ry breath
Devoting Death himself to death.
With less revenge did Naso teem,
When hated Ibis was his theme;
With less, Archilochus, denied
The lovely Greek, his promised bride.
But lo! while thus I execrate,
Incensed, the minister of fate,
Wondrous accents, soft, yet clear,
Wafted on the gale I hear.
"Ah, much deluded! lay aside
Thy threats and anger misapplied!
Art not afraid with sound like these
T'offend, where thou canst not appease?
Death is not (wherefore dream'st thou thus?)
The son of Night and Erebus;
Nor was of fell Erynnis born
On gulfs, where Chaos rules forlorn:
But, sent from God, his presence leaves
To gather home his ripen'd sheaves,
To call encumber'd souls away
From fleshly bonds to boundless day,
(As when the winged hours excite,
And summon forth the morning-light)
And each to convoy to her place
Before th'Eternal Father's face.
But not the wicked—them, severe
Yet just, from all their pleasures here
He hurries to the realms below,
Terrific realms of penal woe!
Myself no sooner heard his call,
Than, 'scaping through my prison-wall,
I bade adieu to bolts and bars,
And soar'd, with angels, to the stars,
Like him of old, to whom 'twas giv'n
To mount, on fiery wheels to heav'n.
Boötes' waggon, slow with cold,
Appall'd me not; nor to behold
The sword, that vast Orion draws,
Or e'en the Scorpion's horrid claws.
Beyond the Sun's bright orb I fly,
And, far beneath my feet descry
Night's dread goddess, seen with awe,
Whom her winged dragons draw.
Thus ever wond'ring at my speed,
Augmented still as I proceed,
I pass the planetary sphere,

The milky Way—and now appear
Heav'n's crystal battlements, her door
Of massy pearl and em'rald floor.
" But here I cease. For never can
The tongue of once a mortal man
In suitable description trace
The pleasures of that happy place;
Suffice it, that those joys divine
Are all, and all for ever, mine!"

NATURE UNIMPAIRED BY TIME.

Ah, how the human mind wearies itself
With her own wand'rings, and involved in gloom
Impenetrable, speculates amiss!
Measuring, in her folly, things divine
By human; laws inscribed on adamant
By laws of man's device, and counsels fix'd
For ever, by the hours, that pass and die.
How?—shall the face of nature then be plough'd
Into deep wrinkles, and shall years at last
On the great Parent fix a sterile curse?
Shall even she confess old age and halt,
And, palsy-smitten, shake her starry brows?
Shall foul Antiquity with rust and drought,
And Famine, vex the radiant worlds above?
Shall Time's unsated maw crave and ingulf
The very heav'ns, that regulate his flight?
And was the Sire of all able to fence
His works, and to uphold the circling worlds,
But, through improvident and heedless haste,
Let slip th'occasion?—so then—all is lost—
And in some future evil hour, yon arch
Shall crumble, and come thund'ring down the poles.
Jar in collision, the Olympian king
Fall with his throne, and Pallas, holding forth
The terrors of the Gorgon shield in vain,
Shall rush to the abyss like Vulcan hurl'd
Down into Lemnos, through the gate of heav'n.
Thou also, with precipitated wheels,
Phoebus! thine own son's fall shalt imitate,
With hideous ruin shalt impress the deep
Suddenly, and the flood shall reek, and hiss,

At the extinction of the lamp of day.
Then too shall Hemus, cloven to his base,
Be shatter'd, and the huge Ceraunian hills,
Once weapons of Tartarean Dis, immersed
In Erebus, shall fill himself with fear.
No. The Almighty Father surer laid
His deep foundations, and providing well
For the event of all, the scales of Fate
Suspended in just equipoise, and bade
His universal works, from age to age,
One tenor hold, perpetual, undisturb'd.
Hence the prime mover wheels itself about
Continual, day by day, and with it bears
In social measure swift the heav'ns around.
Not tardier now is Saturn than of old,
Nor radiant less the burning casque of Mars.
Phœbus, his vigor unimpair'd still shows
Th'effulgence of his youth, nor needs the god
A downward course, that he may warm the vales,
But, ever rich in influence, runs his road,
Sign after sign, through all the heav'nly zone.
Beautiful, as at first, ascends the star
For odorif'rous Ind, whose office is
To gather home betimes th'ethereal flock,
To pour them o'er the skies again at eve,
And to discriminate the night and day
Still Cynthia's changeful horn waxes, and wanes,
Alternate, and with arms extended still,
She welcomes to her breast her brother's beams.
Nor have the elements deserted yet
Their functions; thunder, with as loud a stroke
As erst, smites thro' the rocks, and scatters them.
The east still howls, still the relentless north
Invades the shudd'ring Scythian, still he breathes
The winter, and still rolls the storms along.
The king of ocean, with his wonted force
Beats on Pelorus, o'er the deep is heard
The hoarse alarm of Triton's sounding shell,
Nor swim the monsters of the Ægean sea
In shallows, or beneath diminish'd waves.
Thou too, thy ancient vegetative pow'r
Enjoy'st, O earth! Narcissus still is sweet,
And, Phœbus! still thy favorite, and still
Thy fav'rite Cytherea! both retain
Their beauty, nor the mountains, ore-enrich'd
For punishment of man, with purer gold
Teem'd ever, or with brighter gems the Deep.
Thus, in unbroken series, all proceeds,
And shall, till wide involving either pole,

And the immensity of yonder heav'n,
The final flames of destiny absorb
The world, consumed in one enormous pyre!

ON THE PLATONIC IDEA.

AS IT WAS UNDERSTOOD BY ARISTOTLE.

Ye sister pow'rs who o'er the sacred grove
Preside, and thou, fair mother of them all,
Mnemosyne! and thou, who in thy grot
Immense, reclined at leisure, hast in charge
The archives, and the ord'nances of Jove,
And dost record the festivals of heav'n,
Eternity!—Inform us who is He,
That great original by nature chos'n
To be the archetype of human kind,
Unchangeable, immortal, with the poles
Themselves coeval, one, yet ev'ry where,
An image of the god who gave him being?
Twin-brother of the goddess born from Jove,
He dwells not in his father's mind, but though
Of common nature with ourselves, exists
Apart, and occupies a local home.
Whether, companion of the stars, he spend
Eternal ages, roaming at his will
From sphere to sphere the tenfold heav'ns, or dwell
On the moon's side, that nearest neighbours earth,
Or torpid on the banks of Lethe sit
Among the multitude of souls ordain'd
To flesh and blood, or whether (as may chance)
That vast and giant model of our kind
In some far distant region of this globe
Sequester'd stalk, with lifted head on high
O'ertow'ring Atlas, on whose shoulders rest
The stars, terrific even to the gods.
Never the Theban seer, whose blindness proved
His best illumination, him beheld
In secret vision; never him the son
Of Pleione, amid the noiseless night
Descending, to the prophet-choir reveal'd:
Him never knew th'Assyrian priest, who yet
The ancestry of Ninus chronicles,

And Belus, and Osiris, far renown'd ;
Nor even thrice great Hermes, although skill'd
So deep in myst'ry to the worshippers
Of Isis show'd a prodigy like him.
  And thou, who hast immortalized the shades
Of Academus, if the schools received
This monster of the fancy first from thee,
Either recall at once the banish'd bards
To thy republic, or thyself evinced
A wilder fabulist, go also forth.

TO HIS FATHER.

  Oh that Pieria's spring would through my breast
Pour its inspiring influence, and rush
No rill, but rather an o'erflowing flood !
That, for my venerable Father's sake,
All meaner themes renounced, my muse, on wings
Of duty borne, might reach a loftier strain.
For thee, my Father! howsoe'er it please,
She frames this slender work, nor know I aught
That may thy gifts more suitably requite;
Though, to requite them suitably, would ask
Returns much nobler, and surpassing far
The meagre stores of verbal gratitude:
But, such as I possess, I send thee all.
This page presents thee, in their full amount,
With thy son's treasures, and the sum is nought;
Nought, save the riches that from airy dream
In secret grottos, and in laurel bow'rs,
I have, by Clio's golden gift, acquired.
  Verse is a work divine; despise not thou
Verse, therefore, which evinces (nothing more)
Man's heavenly source, and which, retaining still
Some scintillations of Promethean fire,
Bespeaks him animated from above.
The Gods love verse; the infernal Pow'rs themselves
Confess the influence of verse, which stirs
The lowest deep, and binds in triple chains
Of adamant both Pluto and the Shades.
In verse the Delphic priestess, and the pale
Tremulous Sybil, make the future known,
And he who sacrifices, on the shrine

Hangs verse, both when he smites the threat'ning bull,
And when he spreads his reeking entrails wide,
To scrutinize the Fates enveloped there.
We too, ourselves, what time we seek again
Our native skies, and one eternal now
Shall be the only measure of our being,
Crown'd all with gold, and chanting to the lyre
Harmonious verse, shall range the courts above,
And make the starry firmament resound.
And, even now, the fiery spirit pure
That wheels yon circling orbs, directs, himself,
Their mazy dance with melody of verse
Unutt'rable, immortal, hearing which
Huge Ophiuchus holds his hiss suppress'd,
Orion soften'd, drops his ardent blade,
And Atlas stands unconscious of his load.
Verse graced of old the feasts of kings, ere yet
Luxurious dainties, destined to the gulf
Immense of gluttony, were known, and ere
Lyæus deluged yet the temp'rate board.
Then sat the bard a customary guest
To share the banquet, and, his length of locks
With beechen honors bound, proposed in verse
The characters of heroes, and their deeds,
To imitation, sang of Chaos old,
Of nature's birth, of gods that crept in search
Of acorns fall'n, and of the thunderbolt
Not yet produced from Ætna's fiery cave.
And what avails, at last, tune without voice,
Devoid of matter? Such may suit perhaps
The rural dance; but such was ne'er the song
Of Orpheus, whom the streams stood still to hear,
And the oaks followed. Not by chords alone
Well touched, but by resistless accents more
To sympathetic tears the ghosts themselves
He moved: these praises to his verse he owes
  Nor thou persist, I pray thee, still to slight
The sacred Nine, and to imagine vain
And useless, powers, by whom inspired, thyself
Art skilful to associate verse with airs
Harmonious, and to give the human voice
A thousand modulations, heir by right
Indisputable of Arion's fame.
Now say what wonder is it, if a son
Of thine delight in verse, if so conjoin'd
In close affinity, we sympathize
In social arts, and kindred studies sweet?
Such distribution of himself to us
Was Phoebus' choice; thou hast thy gift, and I

Mine also, and between us we receive,
Father and Son, the whole inspiring God.
No! howso'er the semblance thou assume
Of hate, thou hatest not the gentle Muse,
My Father! for thou never bad'st me tread
The beaten path, and broad, that leads right on
To opulence, nor didst condemn thy son
To the insipid clamors of the bar,
To laws voluminous, and ill observed;
But, wishing to enrich me more, to fill
My mind with treasure, led'st me far awa
From city din to deep retreats, to banks
And streams Aonian, and, with free consent,
Didst place me happy at Apollo's side.
I speak not now, on more important themes
Intent, of common benefits, and such
As nature bids, but of thy larger gifts,
My Father! who, when I had open'd once
The stores of Roman rhetoric, and learn'd
The full-toned language of the eloquent Greeks,
Whose lofty music graced the lips of Jove,
Thyself didst counsel me to add the flowers
That Gallia boasts: those too with which the smooth
Italian his degen'rate speech adorns,
That witnesses his mixture with the Goth;
And Palestine's prophetic songs divine,
To sum the whole, whate'er the heaven contains,
The earth beneath it, and the air between,
The rivers and the restless deep, may all
Prove intellectual gain to me, my wish
Concurring with thy will; Science herself,
All cloud removed, inclines her beauteous head,
And offers me the lip, if, dull of heart,
I shrink not, and decline her gracious boon.
Go now, and gather dross, ye sordid minds
That covet it; what could my Father more?
What more could Jove himself, unless he gave
His own abode the heaven in which he reigns?
More eligible gifts than these were not
Apollo's to his son, had they been safe,
As they were insecure, who made the boy
The world's vice luminary, bade him rule
The radiant chariot of the day, and bind
To his young brows his own all-dazzling wreath.
I therefore, although last and least, my place
Among the learned in the laurel grove
Will hold, and where the conqu'ror's ivy twines,
Henceforth exempt from the unletter'd throng
Profane, nor even to be seen bv such

Away then, sleepless Care, Complaint, away,
And, Envy, with thy "jealous leer malign!"
Nor let the monster Calumny shoot forth
Her venom'd tongue at me. Detested foes!
Ye all are impotent againt my peace,
For I am privileged, and bear my breast
Safe, and too high, for your viperian wound.
But thou, my Father! since to render thanks
Equivalent, and to requite by deeds
Thy liberality, exceeds my power,
Suffice it, that I thus record thy gifts,
And bear them treasured in a grateful mind!
Ye too, the fav'rite pastime of my youth,
My voluntary numbers, if ye dare
To hope longevity, and to survive
Your master's funeral, not soon absorbed
In the oblivious Lethæan gulf,
Shall to futurity perhaps convey
This theme, and by these praises of my sire
Improve the Fathers of a distant age.

TO SALSILLUS, A ROMAN POET, MUCH INDISPOSED.

original is written in a measure called *Scazon*, which signifies 7; and the measure is so denominated, because, though in other re- Iambic, it terminates with a Spondee, and has consequently a more tardy movement.

The reader will immediately see that this property of the Latin verse cannot be imitated in English.

My halting Muse, that dragg'st by choice along
Thy slow, slow step, in melancholy song,
And lik'st that pace, expressive of thy cares,
Not less than Diopeia's sprightlier airs,
When in the dance, she beats, with measured tread,
Heaven's floor, in front of Juno's golden bed;
Salute Salsillus, who to verse divine
Prefers, with partial love, such lays as mine.
Thus writes that Milton then, who wafted o'er
From his own nest, on Albion's stormy shore,
Where Eurus, fiercest of the Æolian band,
Sweeps, with ungovern'd rage, the blasted land,

Of late to more serene Ausonia came
To view her cities of illustrious name,
To prove, himself a witness of the truth,
How wise her elders, and how learn'd her youth.
Much good, Salsillus! and a body free
From all disease, that Milton asks for thee,
Who now endur'st the languor, and the pains,
That bile inflicts, diffused through all thy veins,
Relentless malady! not moved to spare
By thy sweet Roman voice, and Lesbian air?
  Health, Hebe's sister, sent us from the skies,
And thou, Apollo, whom all sickness flies,
Pythius, or Pæan, or what name divine
Soe'er thou choose, haste, heal a priest of thine!
Ye groves of Faunus, and ye hills, that melt
With vinous dews, where meek Evander dwelt!
If aught salubrious in your confines grow,
Strive which shall soonest heal your poet's woe,
That, render'd to the Muse he loves, again
He may enchant the meadows with his strain.
Numa reclined in everlasting ease,
Amid the shade of dark embow'ring trees,
Viewing with eyes of unabated fire
His loved Ægeria, shall that strain admire:
So soothed, the tumid Tiber shall revere
The tombs of kings, nor desolate the year,
Shall curb his waters with a friendly rein,
And guide them harmless, till they meet the main.

TO

GIOVANNI BATTISTA MANSO,

MARQUIS OF VILLA.

MILTON'S ACCOUNT OF MANSO.

Giovanni Battista Manso, Marquis of Villa, is an Italian nobleman of the highest estimation among his countrymen, for genius, literature, and military accomplishments. To him Torquato Tasso addressed his dialogues on Friendship, for he was much the friend of Tasso, who has also celebrated him among the other princes of his country, in his poem entitled Gerusalemme Conquistata, book xx.

Fra cavalier magnanimi, e cortesi,
Risplende il Manso.

During the Author's stay at Naples, he received at the hands of the Marquis a thousand kind offices and civilities, and desirous not to appear ungrateful, sent him this poem a short time before his departure from that city.

These verses also to thy praise the Nine,
Oh Manso! happy in that theme design,
For, Gallus, and Mæcenas gone, they see,
None such besides, or whom they love as thee,
And, if my verse may give the meed of fame,
Thine too shall prove an everlasting name.
Already such, it shines in Tasso's page
(For thou wast Tasso's friend) from age to age,
And, next, the Muse consign'd (not unaware
How high the charge) Marino to thy care,
Who, singing to the nymphs, Adonis' praise,
Boasts thee the patron of his copious lays.
To thee alone the poet would entrust
His latest vows, to thee alone his dust;
And thou with punctual piety hast paid,
In labor'd brass, thy tribute to his shade.
Nor this contented thee—but lest the grave
Should aught absorb of theirs, which thou couldst save,
All future ages thou hast deign'd to teach
The life, lot, genius, character of each,

Eloquent as the Carian sage, who true
To his great theme, the life of Homer drew,
I, therefore, though a stranger youth, who come
Chill'd by rude blasts, that freeze my northern home,
Thee dear to Clio, confident proclaim,
And thine, for Phœbus' sake, a deathless name.
Nor thou, so kind, wilt view with scornful eye
A muse scarce rear'd beneath our sullen sky,
Who fears not, indiscreet as she is young,
To seek in Latium hearers of her song.
We too, where Thames with his unsullied waves
The tresses of the blue-hair'd Ocean laves,
Hear oft by night, or, slumb'ring, seem to hear,
O'er his wide stream, the swan's voice warbling clear,
And we could boast a Tityrus of yore,
Who trod, a welcome guest, your happy shore.
Yes—dreary as we own our northern clime,
E'en we to Phœbus raise the polish'd rhyme.
We too serve Phœbus; Phœbus has received
(If legends old may claim to be believed)
No sordid gifts from us, the golden ear,
The burnish'd apple, ruddiest of the year,
The fragrant crocus, and to grace his fane,
Fair damsels chosen from the Druid train:
Druids, our native bards in ancient time,
Who gods and heroes praised in hallow'd rhyme:
Hence, often as the maids of Greece surround
Appollo's shrine with hymns of festive sound,
They name the virgins, who arrived of yore,
With British off'rings, on the Delian shore;
Loxo, from giant Corineus sprung,
Upis, on whose blest lips the future hung,
And Hecaerge, with the golden hair,
All deck'd with Pictish hues, and all with bosoms bare.
Thou, therefore, happy sage, whatever clime
Shall ring with Tasso's praise in after-time,
Or with Marino's, shalt be known their friend,
And with an equal flight to fame ascend.
The world shall hear how Phœbus, and the Nine,
Were inmates once, and willing guests of thine.
Yet Phœbus, when of old constrain'd to roam
The earth, an exile from his heavenly home,
Enter'd, no willing guest, Admetus' door,
Though Hercules had ventured there before.
But gentle Chiron's cave was near, a scene
Of rural peace, clothed with perpetual green.
And thither, oft as respite he required
From rustic clamors loud, the god retired.
There, many a time, on Peneus' bank reclined

At some oak's root, with ivy thick entwined,
Won by his hospitable friend's desire,
He soothed his pains of exile with the lyre.
Then shook the hills, then trembled Peneus' shore,
Nor Oeta felt his load of forests more ;
The upland elms descended to the plain,
And softened lynxes wonder'd at the strain.
Well may we think, O dear to all above!
Thy birth distinguish'd by the smile of Jove,
And that Apollo shed his kindliest pow'r,
And Maia's son, on that propitious hour,
Since only minds so born can comprehend
A poet's worth, or yield that worth a friend.
Hence, on thy yet unfaded cheek appears
The ling'ring freshness of thy greener years;
Hence, in thy front, and features, we admire
Nature unwither'd and a mind entire.
Oh might so true a friend to me belong,
So skill'd to grace the votaries of song,
Should I recall hereafter into rhyme
The kings, and heroes of the native clime,
Arthur the chief, who even now prepares,
In subterraneous being, future wars,
With all his martial knights, to be restored,
Each to his seat, around the fed'ral board,
And oh, if spirt fail me not, disperse
Our Saxon plund'rers, in triumphant verse!
Then, after all, when, with the past content,
A life I finish, not in silence spent,
Should he, kind mourner, o'er my death-bed bend,
I shall but need to say—" Be yet my friend:"
He, too, perhaps, shall bid the marble breathe
To honor me, and with the graceful wreathe,
Or of Parnassus, or the Paphian isle,
Shall bind my brows—but I shall rest the while;
Then also, if the fruits of Faith endure,
And virtue's promised recompense be sure,
Borne to those seats, to which the blest aspire
By purity of soul, and virtuous fire,
These rites, as Fate permits, I shall survey
With eyes illumined by celestial day,
And, ev'ry cloud from my poor spirit driv'n,
Joy in the bright beatitude of Heav'n!

ON THE DEATH OF DAMON.

THE ARGUMENT.

Thyrsis and Damon, shepherds and neighbours, had always pursued the same studies, and had, from their earliest days, been united in the closest friendship. Thyrsis, while travelling for improvement, received intelligence of the death of Damon, and after a time, returning and finding it true, deplores himself, and his solitary condition, in this poem.

By Damon is to be understood Charles Deodati, connected with the Italian city of Lucca, by his father's side, in other respects an Englishman; a youth of uncommon genius, erudition, and virtue.

Ye nymphs of Himera (for ye have shed
Erewhile for Daphnis, and for Hylas dead,
And over Dion's long lamented bier,
The fruitless mead of many a sacred tear),
Now through the villas laved by Thames, rehearse
The woes of Thyrsis in Sicilian verse,
What sighs he heaved, and how with groans profound
He made the woods, and hollow rocks resound,
Young Damon dead; nor even ceased to pour
His lonely sorrows, at the midnight hour.
The green wheat twice had nodded in the ear,
And golden harvest twice enriched the year,
Since Damon's lips had gasp'd for vital air
The last, last time, nor Thyrsis yet was there;
For he, enamoured of the muse, remained
In Tuscan Fiorenza long detained,
But, stored at length with all he wish'd to learn,
For his flock's sake now hasted to return;
And when the shepherd had resumed his seat
At the elm's root, within his old retreat,
Then 'twas his lot, then, all his loss to know,
And, from his burthen'd heart, he vented thus his woe.
"Go, seek your home, my lambs; my thoughts are due
To other cares, than those of feeding you.
Alas! what deities shall I suppose
In heav'n, or earth, concern'd for human woes,
Since, oh my Damon! their severe decree
So soon condemns me to regret of thee!
Depart'st thou thus, thy virtues unrepaid
With fame and honor, like a vulgar shade?
Let him forbid it, whose bright rod controls,

And sep'rates sordid from illustrious souls,
Drive far the rabble, and to thee assign
A happier lot, with spirits worthy thine!
"Go, seek your home, my lambs; my thoughts are due
To other cares, than those of feeding you.
Whate'er befal, unless by cruel chance
The wolf first give me a forbidding glance,
Thou shalt not moulder undeplor'd, but long
Thy praise shall dwell on ev'ry shepherd's tongue;
To Daphnis first they shall delight to pay,
And, after him, to thee the votive lay,
While Pales shall the flocks, and pastures, love,
Or Faunus to frequent the field, or grove,
At least, if ancient piety and truth,
With all the learned labours of thy youth,
May serve thee aught, or to have left behind
A sorrowing friend, and of the tuneful kind.
"Go, seek your home, my lambs; my thoughts are due
To other cares, than those of feeding you.
Yes, Damon! such thy sure reward shall be;
But ah! what doom awaits unhappy me?
Who, now, my pains and perils shall divide,
As thou wast wont, for ever at my side,
Both when the rugged frost annoy'd our feet,
And when the herbage all was parch'd with heat!
Whether the grim wolf's ravage to prevent,
Or the huge lions', arm'd with darts we went?
Whose converse now shall calm my stormy day
With charming song, who now beguile my way?
"Go, seek your homes, my lambs; my thoughts are due
To other cares, than those of feeding you.
In whom shall I confide? whose counsel find
A balmy med'cine for my troubled mind?
Or whose discourse, with innocent delight,
Shall fill me now, and cheat the wint'ry night,
While hisses on my hearth the pulpy pear,
And black'ning chesnuts start and crackle there;
While storms abroad the dreary meadows whelm,
And the wind thunders through the neighb'ring elm?
"Go, seek your home, my lambs; my thoughts are due
To other cares, than those of feeding you.
Or who, when summer suns their summit reach,
And Pan sleeps hidden by the shelt'ring beech,
When shepherds disappear, nymphs seek the sedge,
And the stretch'd rustic snores beneath the hedge,
Who then shall render me thy pleasant vein
Of Attic wit, thy jests, thy smiles again?
"Go, seek your home, my lambs; my thoughts are due
To other cares, than those of feeding you.

Where glens and vales are thickest overgrown
With tangled boughs, I wander now alone,
Till night descend, while blust'ring wind and show'r
Beat on my temples through the shatter'd bow'r.
"Go, seek your home, my lambs; my thoughts are d[illegible]
To other cares, than those of feeding you.
Alas! what rampant weeds now shame my fields,
And what a mildew'd crop the furrow yields!
My rambling vines, unwedded to the trees,
Bear shrivell'd grapes, my myrtles fail to please,
Nor please me more my flocks; they, slighted, turn
Their unavailing looks on me, and mourn. [due
"Go, seek your home, my lambs; my thoughts are
To other cares, than those of feeding you.
Ægon invites me to the hazer grove,
Amyntas, on the river's bank to rove,
And young Alphesibœus to a seat
Where branching elms exclude the mid-day heat.
"Here fountains spring—here mossy hillocks rise;"
"Here Zephyr whispers, and the stream replies."
Thus each persuades, but, deaf to ev'ry call,
I gain the thickets, and escape them all. [due
"Go, seek your home, my lambs; my thoughts are
To other cares, than those of feeding you.
Then Mopsus said (the same who reads so well
The voice of birds, and what the stars foretell,
For he by chance had notic'd my return),
'What means thy sullen mood, this deep concern?
Ah, Thyrsis! thou art either crazed with love,
Or some sinister influence from above;
Dull Saturn's influence oft the shepherds rue;
His leaden shaft oblique has pierced thee through.'
"Go, go, my lambs, unpastured as ye are;
My thoughts are all now due to other care.
The nymphs amazed, my melancholy see,
And 'Thyrsis,' cry—'what will become of thee!
What would'st thou, Thyrsis? such should not appear
The brow of youth, stern, gloomy, and severe;
Brisk youth should laugh, and love—ah shun the fate
Of those, twice wretched mopes! who love too late!'
"Go, go, my lambs, unpastured as ye are;
My thoughts are all now due to other care.
Ægle with Hyas came, to soothe my pain,
And Baucis' daughter, Dryope, the vain,
Fair Dryope, for voice and finger neat
Known far and near, and for her self-conceit;
Chloris too came whose cottage on the lands,
That skirt the Idumanian current, stands;
But all in vain they came, and but to see

Kind words, and comfortable, lost on me.
"Go, go, my lambs, unpastured as ye are
My thoughts are all now due to other care.
Ah, blest indiff'rence of the playful herd,
None by his fellow chosen, or preferr'd!
No bonds of amity the flocks enthrall,
But each associates, and is pleased with all;
So graze the dappled deer in num'rous droves,
And all his kind alike the zebra loves;
The same law governs, where the billows roar,
And Proteus' shoals o'erspread the desert shore;
The sparrow, meanest of the feather'd race,
His fit companion finds in ev'ry place,
With whom he picks the grain that suits him best,
Flirts here and there, and late returns to rest,
And whom if chance the falcon makes his prey
Or hedger with his well-aim'd arrow slay,
For no such loss the gay survivor grieves:
New love he seeks, and new delight receives,
We only, an obdurate kind, rejoice,
Scorning all others, in a single choice.
We scarce in thousands meet one kindred mind,
And if the long-sought good at last we find,
When least we fear it, Death our treasure steals,
And gives our heart a wound, that nothing heals
"Go, go, my lambs, unpastured as ye are;
My thoughts are all now due to other care.
Ah, what delusion lured me from my flocks,
To traverse Alpine snows, and rugged rocks
What need so great had I to visit Rome,
Now sunk in ruins, and herself a tomb?
Or, had she flourished still as when of old,
For her sake Tityrus forsook his fold,
What need had I so great t' incur a pause
Of thy sweet intercourse for such a cause,
For such a cause to place the roaring sea,
Rocks, mountains, woods, between my friend and me
Else, had I grasp'd thy feeble hand, composed
Thy decent limbs, thy drooping eyelids closed,
And at the last, had said—'Farewell—ascend—
Nor even in the skies forget thy friend!'
"Go, go, my lambs, untended homeward fare;
My thoughts are all now due to other care.
Although well-pleased, ye tuneful Tuscan swains!
My mind the mem'ry of your worth retains,
Yet not your worth can teach me less to mourn
My Damon lost—He too was Tuscan born,
Born in Lucca, city of renown!
And wit possess'd, and genius, like your own.

Oh how elate was I, when stretch'd beside
The murm'ring course of Arno's breezy tide,
Beneath the poplar grove I pass'd my hours,
Now cropping myrtles, and now vernal flow'rs,
And hearing, as I lay at ease along,
Your swains contending for the prize of song!
I also dared attempt (and, as it seems,
Not much displeased attempting) various themes,
For even I can presents boast from you,
The shepherd's pipe, and ozier basket too,
And Dati, and Francin both have made
My name familiar to the beechen shade,
And they are learn'd, and each in ev'ry place
Renown'd the song, and both of Lydian race.
"Go, go, my lambs, untended homeward fare;
My thoughts are all now due to other care.
While bright the dewy grass with moon-beams shone,
And I stood hurdling in my kids alone,
How often have I said (but thou hadst found
Ere then thy dark cold lodgment under ground)
Now Damon sings, or springes sets for hares,
Or wicker-work for various use prepares!
How oft, indulging fancy, have I plann'd
New scenes of pleasure, that I hoped at hand,
Called thee abroad as I was wont, and cried—
'What hoa! my friend—come lay thy task aside,
Haste, let us forth together, and beguile
The heat, beneath you whisp'ring shades awhile,
Or on the margin stray of Colne's clear flood,
Or where Cassibelan's grey turrets stood!
There thou shalt cull me simples, and shalt teach
Thy friend the name, and healing pow'rs of each,
From the tall blue-bell to the dwarfish weed,
What the dry land, and what the marshes breed;
For all their kinds alike to thee are known,
And the whole heart of Galen is thy own.
Ah, perish Galen's art, and with'r'd be
The useless herbs, that gave not health to thee!
Twelve evenings since, as in poetic dream
I meditating sat some statelier theme,
The reeds no sooner touch'd my lip, though new,
And unessay'd before, than wide they flew,
Bursting their waxen bands nor could sustain
The deep-toned music of the solemn strain:
And I am vain perhaps, but I will tell
How proud a theme I choose—ye groves, farewell
"Go, go, my lambs, untended homeward fare;
My thoughts are all now due to other care.
Of Brutus, Dardan chief, my song shall be,

How with his barks he plough'd the British sea,
First from Rutupia's tow'ring headland seen,
And of his consort's reign, fair Imogen;
Of Brennus and Belinus, brothers bold,
And of Arviragus, and how of old
Our hardy sires th' Armorican controll'd,
And of the wife of Gorloïs, who, surprised
By Uther, in her husband's from disguised,
(Such was the force of Merlin's art) became
Pregnant with Arthur of heroic fame.
These themes I now revolve—and oh—if Fate
Proportion to these themes my lenthen'd date,
Adieu my shepherd's reed—yon pine-tree bough
Shall be thy future home, there dangle thou
Forgotten and disused, unless ere long
Thou change thy Latian for a British song;
A British?—even so—the pow'rs of man
Are bounded; little is the most he can;
And it shall well suffice me, and shall be
Fame, and proud recompense enough for me,
If Usa, golden-hair'd my verse may learn,
If Alain bending o'er his crystal urn,
Swift whirling Abra, Trent's o'ershadow'd stream,
Thames, lovelier far than all in my esteem,
Tamar's ore-tinctured flood, and, after these,
The wave-worn shores of utmost Orcades.
"Go, go, my lambs, untended homeward fare;
My thoughts are all now due to other care.
All this I kept in leaves of laurel-rind
Enfolded safe, and for thy view design'd,
This—and a gift from Manso's hand beside,
(Manso, not least his native city's pride)
Two cups, that radiant as their giver shone,
Adorn'd by sculpture with a double zone.
The spring was graven there; here slowly wind
The Red-sea shores with groves of spices lined;
Her plumes of various hues amid the boughs
The sacred solitary Phœnix shows,
And watchful of the dawn reverts her head,
To see Aurora leave her wat'ry bed
"In other part th'expansive vault above,
And there too, even there, the god of love:
With quiver arm'd he mounts, his torch displays
A vivid light, his gem-tipt arrows blaze,
Around his bright and fiery eyes he rolls,
Nor aims at vulgar minds, or little souls,
Nor deigns one look below, but aiming high
Sends every arrow to the lofty sky;
Hence forms divine, and minds immortal, learn

The pow'r of Cupid, and enamour'd burn.
"Thou also, Damon, (neither need I fear
That hope delusive), thou art also there;
For whither should simplicity like thine
Retire? where else such spotless virtue shine?
Thou dwell'st not (thought profane) in shades below,
Nor tears suit thee—cease then my tears to flow;
Away with grief! on Damon ill bestow'd!
Who, pure himself, has found a pure abode,
Has pass'd the show'ry arch, henceforth resides
With saints and heroes, and from flowing tides
Quaffs copious immortality, and joy,
With hallow'd lips:—Oh! blest without alloy,
And now enrich'd, with all that faith can claim,
Look down, entreated by whatever name,
If Damon please thee most (that rural sound
Shall oft with echoes fill the groves around),
Or if Diodatus, by which alone
In those ethereal mansions thou art known.
Thy blush was maiden, and thy youth the taste
Of wedded bliss knew never, pure and chaste,
The honors, therefore, by divine decree
The lot of virgin worth, are given to thee;
Thy brows encircled with a radiant band,
And the green palm branch waving in thy hand,
Thou in immortal nuptials shalt rejoice,
And join with seraphs thy according voice,
Where rapture reigns, and the ecstatic lyre
Guides the blest orgies of the blazing quire."

AN ODE

ADDRESSED TO MR. JOHN ROUSE,

LIBRARIAN OF THE UNIVERSITY OF OXFORD

On a lost Volume of my Poems, which he desired me to replace, that he might add them to my other Works deposited in the Library

---

This ode is rendered without rhyme, that it might more adequately represent the original, which, as Milton himself informs us, is of no certain measure. It may possibly for this reason disappoint the reader, though it cost the writer more labour than the translation of any other piece in the whole collection.

STROPHE.

My two-fold book! single in show
But double in contents,
Neat but not curiously adorn'd,
Which in his early youth,
A poet gave, no lofty one in truth,
Although an earnest wooer of the Muse—
Say while in cool Ausonian shades,
Or British wilds he roam'd,
Striking by turns his native lyre,
By turns the Daunian lute,
And stepp'd almost in air,—

ANTISTROPHE.

Say, little book, what furtive hand
Thee from thy fellow-books convey'd,
What time at the repeated suit
Of my most learned friend,
I sent thee forth an honor'd traveller

From our great city to the source of Thames,
Cœrulean sire!
Where rise the fountains, and the raptures ring,
Of the Aonian choir,
Durable as yonder spheres,
And though the endless lapse of years
Secured to be admired!

STROPHE II.

Now what god, or demigod,
For Britain's ancient genius moved
(If our afflicted land
Have expiated at length the guilty sloth
Of her degenerate sons)
Shall terminate our impious feuds,
And discipline, with hallowed voice recall?
Recall the Muses too,
Driven from their ancient seats,
In Albion, and well nigh from Albion's shore,
And with keen Phœbean shafts
Piercing th' unseemly birds,
Whose talons menace us,
Shall drive the harpy race from Helicon afar?

ANTISTROPHE

But thou, my book, though thou hast stray'd,
Whether by treach'ry lost,
Or indolent neglect, thy bearer's fault,
From all thy kindred books,
To some dark cell, or cave forlorn,
Where thou endur'st, perhaps,
The chafing of some hard untutor'd hand,
Be comforted—
For lo, again the splendid hope appears
That thou may'st yet escape
The gulfs of Lethe, and on oary wings
Mount to the everlasting courts of Jove!

STROPHE III.

Since Rouse desires thee, and complains,
That, though by promise his,
Thou yet appear'st not in thy place
Among the literary noble stores,
Given to his care,
But, absent, leav'st his numbers incomplete,
He, therefore, guardian vigilant

Of that unperishing wealth,
Calls thee to the interior shrine, his charge,
Where he intends a richer treasure far
Than Iön kept (Iön, Erectheus' son,
Illustrious, of the fair Creüsa born)
In the resplendent temple of his god,
Tripods of gold, and Delphic gifts divine.

ANTISTROPHE.

Haste, then, to the pleasant groves,
The Muses' fav'rite haunt;
Resume thy station in Apollo's dome.
Dearer to him
Than Delos, or the fork'd Parnassian hill!
Exulting go,
Since now a splendid lot is also thine,
And thou art sought by my propitious friend;
For there thou shalt be read
With authors of exalted note,
The ancient glorious lights of Greece and Rome.

EPODE.

Ye then, my works, no longer vain,
And worthless deem'd by me!
Whate'er this steril genius has produced
Expect, at last, the rage of envy spent,
An unmolested happy home,
Gift of kind Hermes, and my watchful friend,
Where never flippant tongue profane
Shall entrance find,
And whence the coarse unletter'd multitude
Shall babble far remote.
Perhaps some future distant age,
Less tinged with prejudice, and better taught,
Shall furnish minds of pow'r
To judge more equally.
Then, malice silenced in the tomb,
Cooler heads and sounder hearts,
Thanks to Rouse, if aught of praise
I merit, shall with candour weigh the claim.

TRANSLATIONS

OF

THE ITALIAN POEMS.

SONNET.

Fair lady! whose harmonious name the Rhine,
Through all his grassy vale, delights to hear,
Base where indeed the wretch who could forbear
To love a spirit elegant as thine,
That manifests a sweetness all divine,
Nor knows a thousand winning acts to spare,
And graces, which Love's bow and arrows are,
Temp'ring thy virtues to a softer shine.
When gracefully thou speak'st, or singest gay,
Such strains, as might the senseless forest move,
Ah then—turn each his eyes, and ears, away,
Who feels himself unworthy of thy love!
Grace can alone preserve him, ere the dart
Of fond desire yet reach his inmost heart.

SONNET.

As on a hill-top rude, when closing day
Imbrowns the scene, some past'ral maiden fair
Waters a lovely foreign plant with care,
Borne from its native genial air away,
That scarcely can a tender bud display;
So, on my tongue these accents, new and rare,
Are flow'rs exotic, which Love waters there,
While thus, O sweetly scornful, I essay
Thy praise, in verse to British ears unknown.
And Thames exchanged for Arno's fair domain,
So Love as will'd, and ofttimes Love has shown,
That what he wills, he never wills in vain:
Oh that his hard and steril breast might be
To him, who plants from heav'n, a soil as free!

CANZONE.

They mock my toil, the nymphs and am'rous swains,
And whence this fond attempt to write, they cry,
Love songs in language that thou little know'st?
How dar'st thou risk to sing these foreign strains?
Say truly. Find'st not oft thy purpose cross'd,
And that thy fairest flowers here fade and die?
Then with pretence of admiration high—
Thee other shores expect, and other tides;
Rivers, on whose grassy sides
Her deathless laurel-leaf, with which to bind
Thy flowing locks, already Fame provides;
Why then this burthen, better far declined?

Speak, Muse! for me.—The fair one said, who guides
My willing heart, and all my fancy's flights,
"This is the language in which love delights."

SONNET.

Lady! it cannot be but that thine eyes
Must be my sun, such radiance they display,
And strike me e'en as Phœbus him, whose way
Through horrid Libya's sandy desert lies.
Meantime, on that side steamy vapours rise
Where most I suffer. Of what kind are they,
New as to me they are, I cannot say,
But deem them, in the lover's language—sighs.
Some, though with pain, my bosom close conceals,
Which, if in part escaping thence, they tend
To soften time, thy coldness soon congeals.
While others to my tearful eyes ascend,
Whence my sad nights in show'rs are ever drown'd,
Till my Aurora comes, her brow with roses bound.

POEMS,

TRANSLATED FROM THE FRENCH OF MADAME DE LA MOTHE GUION.

THE NATIVITY.

'Tis folly all—let me no more be told
Of Parian porticos, and roofs of gold;
Delighted views of Nature, dress'd by Art,
Enchant no longer this indiff'rent heart;
The Lord of all things, in his humble birth,
Makes mean the proud magnificence of Earth:
The straw, the manger, and the mould'ring wall
Eclipse its lustre; and I scorn it all.
Canals, and fountains, and delicious vales,
Green slopes and plains, whose plenty never fails;
Deep-rooted groves, whose heads sublimely rise,
Earth-born, and yet ambitious of the skies;
The abundant foliage of whose gloomy shades,
Vainly the sun, in all its pow'r invades;
Where warbled airs of sprightly birds resound,
Whose verdure lives while Winter scowls around,
Rocks, lofty mountains, caverns dark and deep,
And torrents raving down the rugged steep,
Smooth downs, whose fragrant herbs the spirits cheer;
Meads crown'd with flow'rs; streams musical and [clear,
Whose silver waters, and whose murmurs, join
Their artless charms, to make the scene divine;
The fruitful vineyard, and the furrow'd plain,
That seems a rolling sea of golden grain:
All, all have lost the charms they once possess'd;
An infant God reigns sov'reign in my breast;
From Bethl'em's bosom I no more will rove;
There dwells the Saviour, and there rests my love.
Ye mightier rivers, that, with sounding force,
Urge down the valleys your impetuous course! [heads,
Winds, clouds, and lightnings! and ye waves, whose
Curl'd into monstrous forms, the seaman dreads!

Horrid abyss, where all experience fails,
Spread with the wreck of planks and shatter'd sails;
On whose broad back grim Death triumphant rides,
While havoc floats on all thy swelling tides,
Thy shores a scene of ruin, strew'd around
With vessels bulged, and bodies of the drown'd!
Ye fish, that sport beneath the boundless waves,
And rest, secure from man, in rocky caves;
Swift-darting sharks, and whales of hideous size,
Whom all th'aquatic world with terror eyes!
Had I but faith immovable and true,
I might defy the fiercest storm, like you;
The world, a more disturb'd and boist'rous sea,
When Jesus shows a smile, affrights not me;
He hides me, and in vain the billows roar,
Break harmless at my feet, and leave the shore.
Thou azure vault, where, through the gloom of night
Thick sown, we see such countless worlds of light!
Thou Moon, whose car, encompassing the skies,
Restores lost Nature to our wond'ring eyes;
Again retiring, when the brighter Sun
Begins the course he seems in haste to run!
Behold *him* where he shines! His rapid rays,
Themselves unmeasured, measure all our days;
Nothing impedes the race he would pursue,
Nothing escapes his penetrating view,
A thousand lands confess his quick'ning heat,
And all he cheers are fruitful, fair, and sweet.
Far from enjoying what these scenes disclose,
I feel the thorn, alas! but miss the rose;
Too well I know this aching heart requires
More solid good to fill its vast desires;
In vain they represent his matchless might,
Who call'd them out of deep primæval night
Their form and beauty but augment my woe:
I seek the giver of those charms and show:
Nor, Him beside, throughout the world he made
Lives there, in whom I trust for cure or aid.
Infinite God, thou great unrivall'd ONE?
Whose glory makes a blot of yonder sun;
Compared with thine, how dim his beauty seems,
How quench'd the radiance of his golden beams!
Thou art my bliss, the light by which I move;
In thee alone dwells all that I can love;
All darkness flies when thou art pleased t' appear,
A sudden spring renews the fading year;
Where'er I turn, I see thy pow'r and grace
The watchful gaurdians of our heedless race;
Thy various creatures in one strain agree,

All, in all times and places, speak of thee;
Ev'n I, with trembling heart and stamm'ring tongue,
Attempt thy praise, and join the gen'ral song.
Almighty Former of this wondrous plan,
Faintly reflected in thine image, Man—
Holy and just—the Greatness of whose name
Fills and supports this universal frame,
Diffused throughout th' infinitude of space;
Who art thyself thine own vast dwelling place;
Soul of our soul, whom yet no sense of ours
Discerns, eluding our most active pow'rs;
Encircling shades attend thine awful throne,
That veil thy face, and keep thee still unknown;
Unknown, though dwelling in our inmost part,
Lord of the thoughts, and Sov'reign of the heart!
Repeat the charming truth, that never tires,
No God is like the God my soul desires;
He at whose voice Heav'n trembles, even He,
Great as he is, knows how to stoop to me—
Lo! there he lies—that smiling infant said,
"Heav'n, Earth, and Sea, exist!"—and they obey'd.
E'en He, whose being swells beyond the skies,
Is born of woman, lives, and mourns, and dies;
Eternal and Immortal, seems to cast
That glory from his brow, and breathes his last.
Trivial and vain the works that man has wrought,
How do they shrink, and vanish at the thought!
Sweet Solitude, and scene of my repose!
This rustic sight assuages all my woes—
That crib contains the Lord, whom I adore;
And Earth's a shade, that I pursue no more.
He is my firm support, my rock, my tow'r,
I dwell secure beneath his shelt'ring power,
And hold this mean retreat for ever dear,
For all I love, my soul's delight, is here.
I see th' Almighty swathed in infant bands,
Tied helpless down the Thunder-bearer's hands!
And, in this shed, that mystery discern,
Which faith and love, and they alone, can learn.
Ye tempests, spare the slumbers of your Lord!
Ye zephyrs, all your whisper'd sweets afford!
Confess the God, that guides the rolling year:
Heav'n to him homage; and thou, Earth, revere!
Ye shepherds, monarchs, sages, hither bring
Your hearts an off'ring, and adore your King!
Pure be those hearts, and rich in faith and love;
Join, in his praise, th' harmonious world above;
To Beth'lem haste, rejoice in his repose,
And praise him there for all that he bestows!

Man, busy Man, alas! can ill afford
T' obey the summons, and attend the Lord;
Perverted Reason revels and runs wild,
By glitt'ring shows of pomp and wealth beguiled;
And, blind to genuine excellence and grace,
Finds not her author in so mean a place.
Ye unbelieving! learn a wiser part,
Distrust your erring sense, and search your heart;
There, soon ye shall perceive a kindling flame
Glow for that Infant God, from whom it came;
Resist not, quench not, that divine desire,
Melt all your adamant in heav'nly fire!
Not so will I requite thee, gentle Love!
Yielding and soft this heart shall ever prove:
And every heart beneath thy power should fall,
Glad to submit, could mine contain them all.
But I am poor, oblation I have none,
None for a Saviour, but Himself alone:
Whate'er I render thee, from thee it came;
And, if I give my body to the flame,
My patience, love, and energy divine
Of heart, and soul, and spirit, all are thine.
Ah, vain attempt, t' expunge the mighty score!
The more I pay, I owe thee still the more.
Upon my meanness, poverty, and guilt,
The trophy of thy glory shall be built;
My self-disdain shall be th' unshaken base,
And my deformity its fairest grace;
For destitute of good, and rich in ill,
Must be my state and my description still.
And do I grieve at such an humbling lot?
Nay, but I cherish and enjoy the thought—
Vain pageantry and pomp of Earth, adieu!
I have no wish, no memory for you;
The more I feel my mis'ry, I adore
The sacred Inmate of my soul the more;
Rich in his love, I feel my noblest pride
Spring from the sense of having nought beside.
In thee I find wealth, comfort, virtue, might;
My wand'rings prove thy wisdom infinite;
All that I have, I give thee; and then see
All contrarieties unite in thee;
For thou hast join'd them, taking up our woe,
And pouring out thy bliss on worms below,
By filling with thy grace and love divine
A gulf of evil in this heart of mine.
This is indeed to bid the valleys rise,
And the hills sink—'tis matching Earth and Skies!
I feel my weakness, thank thee, and deplore

An aching heart, that throbs to thank thee more;
The more I love thee, I the more approve
A soul so lifeless, and so slow to love;
Till, on a deluge of thy mercy toss'd,
I plunge into that sea, and there am lost.

GOD NEITHER KNOWN NOR LOVED BY THE WORLD.

Ye Linnets, let us try, beneath this grove,
  Which shall be loudest in our Maker's praise!
In quest of some forlorn retreat I rove,
  For all the world is blind, and wanders from his ways.

That God alone should prop the sinking soul,
  Fills them with rage against his empire now;
I traverse Earth in vain from pole to pole,
  To seek one simple heart, set free from all below.

They speak of love, yet little feel its sway,
  While in their bosoms many an idol lurks:
Their base desires, well satisfied, obey,
  Leave the Creator's hand, and lean upon his works.

'Tis therefore I can dwell with man no more;
  Your fellowship, ye warblers! suits me best;
Pure love has lost its prize, though prized of yore,
  Profaned by modern tongues, and slighted as a jest.

My God, who form'd you for his praise alone,
  Beholds his purpose well fulfilled in you;
Come, let us join the choir before his throne,
  Partaking in his praise with spirits just and true!

Yes, I will always love; and, as I ought,
  Tune to the praise of love my ceaseless voice;
Preferring Love too vast for human thought,
  In spite of erring men who cavil at my choice.

Why have I not a thousand thousand hearts,
  Lord of my soul! that they might all be thine?
If thou approve—the zeal thy smile imparts,
  How should it ever fail! Can such a fire decline?

Love, pure and holy, is a deathless fire;
Its object heav'nly, it must ever blaze:
Eternal love a God must needs inspire,
When once he wins the heart, and fits it for his praise

Self-love dismiss'd—'tis then we live indeed—
In her embrace, death, only death is found:
Come then, one noble effort, and succeed,
Cast off the chain of Self with which thy soul is bound!

Oh! I would cry, that all the world might hear,
Ye self-tormentors, love your God alone;
Let his unequall'd excellence be dear,
Dear to your inmost souls, and make him all your own!

They hear me not—alas! how fond to rove
In endless chase of Folly's specious lure!
'Tis here alone, beneath this shady grove,
I taste the sweets of Truth—here only am secure.

THE SWALLOW.

I am fond of the swallow—I learn from her flight,
Had I skill to improve it, a lesson of love:
How seldom on earth do we see her alight!
She dwells in the skies, she is ever above.

It is on the wing that she takes her repose,
Suspended and poised in the regions of air,
'Tis not in our fields that her sustenance grows,
It is wing'd like herself, 'tis ethereal fare.

She comes in the spring, all the summer she stays,
And, dreading the cold, still follows the sun—
So, true to our Love, we should covet his rays,
And the place where he shines not, immediately shun

Our light should be love, and our nourishment prayer,
It is dangerous food that we find upon earth;
The fruit of this world is besetwith a snare,
In itself it is hurtful, as vile in its birth

'T is rarely, if ever, she settles below,
  And only when building a nest for her young:
Were it not for her brood, she would never bestow
  A thought upon anything filthy as dung.

Let us leave it ourselves, ('tis a mortal abode),
  To bask ev'ry moment in infinite love;
Let us fly the dark winter, and follow the road,
  That leads to the day-spring appearing above.

THE

TRIUMPH OF HEAVENLY LOVE DESIRED.

Ah! reign, whatever man is found,
  My Spouse, beloved and divine!
Then I am rich, and I abound,
  When ev'ry human heart is thine.

A thousand sorrows pierce my soul,
  To think that all are not thine own:
Ah! be adored from pole to pole;
  Where is thy zeal? arise; be known!

All hearts are cold, in ev'ry place,
  Yet earthly good with warmth pursue;
Dissolve them with a flash of grace,
  Thaw these of ice, and give us new!

A FIGURATIVE DESCRIPTION OF

THE PROCEDURE OF DIVINE LOVE.

'Twas my purpose, on a day,
To embark, and sail away:
As I climbed the vessel's side,
Love was sporting in the tide;
"Come," he said,—"ascend—make haste,
Launch into the boundless waste."

Many mariners were there,
Having each his sep'rate care;
They that row'd us, held their eyes
Fix'd upon the starry skies;
Others steer'd, or turn'd the sails
To receive the shifting gales.

Love, with pow'r divine supplied,
Suddenly my courage tried;
In a moment it was night,
Ship and skies were out of sight;
On the briny wave I lay,
Floating rushes all my stay.

Did I with resentment burn
At this unexpected turn?
Did I wish myself on shore,
Never to forsake it more?
No—"My soul," I cried, "be still;
If I must be lost, I will."

Next, he hasten'd to convey
Both my frail supports away;
Seiz'd my rushes; bade the waves
Yawn into a thousand graves:
Down I went, and sunk as lead,
Ocean closing o'er my head.

Still, however, life was safe:
And I saw him turn and laugh;
"Friend," he cried, "adieu! lie low,
While the wintry storms shall blow;
When the spring has calm'd the main,
You shall rise and float again."

Soon I saw him, with dismay,
Spread his plumes and soar away;
Now I mark his rapid flight;
Now he leaves my aching sight;
He is gone whom I adore,
'Tis in vain to seek him more.

How I trembled then and fear'd,
When my love had disappear'd!
"Wilt thou leave me thus," I cried,
"Whelm'd beneath the rolling tide?"

Vain attempt to reach his ear!
Love was gone, and would not hear.

Ah! return, and love me still;
See me subject to thy will;
Frown with wrath, or smile with grace,
Only let me see thy face!
Evil I have none to fear,
All is good, if thou art near.

Yet he leaves me—cruel fate!
Leaves me in my lost estate—
Have I sinn'd? O say wherein;
Tell me, and forgive my sin!
King, and Lord, whom I adore,
Shall I see thy face no more?

Be not angry; I resign,
Henceforth, all my will to thine;
I consent that thou depart,
Though thine absence breaks my heart;
Go then, and for ever too;
All is right that thou wilt do.

This was just what Love intended,
He was now no more offended;
Soon as I became a child,
Love returned to me and smil'd:
Never strife shall more betide
'Twixt the Bridegroom and his Bride.

A CHILD OF GOD LONGING TO SEE HIM BELOVED

There's not an Echo round me,
  But I am glad should learn,
How pure a fire has found me,—
  The love with which I burn.
For none attends with pleasure,
  To what I would reveal;
They slight me out of measure,
  And laugh at all I feel.

The rocks receive less proudly
  The story of my flame:
When I approach, they loudly
  Reverberate his name.
I speak to them of sadness,
  And comforts at a stand;
They bid me look for gladness,
  And better days at hand.

Far from all habitation,
  I heard a happy sound;
Big with the consolation,
  That I have often found,
I said, "my lot is sorrow,
  My grief has no alloy;"
The rocks replied—"to-morrow,
  To-morrow brings thee joy."

These sweet and secret tidings,
  What bliss it is to hear!
For, spite of all my chiding,
  My weakness and my fear,
No sooner I receive them,
  Than I forget my pain,
And happy to believe them,
  I love as much again.

I fly to scenes romantic,
  Where never men resort;
For in an age so frantic,
  Impiety is sport.
For riot and confusion,
  They barter things above;
Condemning, as delusion,
  The joy of perfect love.

In this sequester'd corner,
  None hears what I express;
Deliver'd from the scorner,
  What peace do I possess!
Beneath the boughs reclining,
  Or roving o'er the wild,
I live, as undesigning,
  And harmless as a child.

No troubles here surprise me,
  I innocently play,

While Providence supplies me,
  And guards me all the day:
My dear and kind Defender
  Preserves me safely here,
From men of pomp and splendour,
  Who fill a child with fear.

ASPIRATION OF THE SOUL AFTER GOD.

My Spouse! in whose presence I live,
  Sole object of all my desires,
Who know'st what a flame I conceive,
  And canst easily double its fires;
How pleasant is all that I meet!
  From fear of adversity free,
I find even sorrow made sweet;
  Because 'tis assign'd me by Thee.

Transported I see thee display
  Thy riches and glory divine;
I have only my life to repay,
  Take what I would gladly resign.
Thy will is the treasure I seek,
  For thou art as faithful as strong;
There let me, obedient and meek,
  Repose myself all the day long.

My spirit and faculties fail;
  Oh finish what love has begun!
Destroy what is sinful and frail,
  And dwell in the soul thou hast won!
Dear theme of my wonder and praise,
  I cry, who is worthy as Thou!
I can only be silent and gaze;
  'Tis all that is left to me now.

Oh glory, in which I am lost,
  Too deep for the plummet of thought;
On an ocean of deity toss'd,
  I am swallow'd, I sink into nought:
Yet, lost and absorb'd as I seem,
  I chaunt to the praise of my King;
And though overwhelm'd by the theme,
  Am happy whenever I sing.

GRATITUDE AND LOVE TO GOD.

All are indebted much to Thee,
  But I far more than all,
From many a deadly snare set free,
  And raised from many a fall.
Overwhelm me, from above,
Daily with thy boundless Love.

What bonds of Gratitude I feel,
  No language can declare;
Beneath th'oppressive weight I reel,
  'Tis more than I can bear:
When shall I that blessing prove,
To return thee Love, for Love?

Spirit of Charity, dispense
  Thy grace to ev'ry heart;
Expel all other Spirits thence,
  Drive self from ev'ry part;
Charity divine, draw nigh,
Break the chains in which we lie!

All selfish souls, whate'er they feign,
  Have still a slavish lot;
They boast of liberty in vain,
  Of Love, and feel it not.
He whose bosom glows with Thee,
He, and he alone, is free.

Oh blessedness, all bliss above,
  When *thy* pure fires prevail;
Love only teaches what is Love;
  All other lessons fail;
We learn its name, but not its pow'rs,
Experience only makes it ours.

HAPPY SOLITUDE—UNHAPPY MEN.

My heart is easy, and my burden light:
I smile, though sad, when thou art in my sight;
The more my woes in secret I deplore,
I taste thy goodness, and I love thee more.

There, while a solemn stillness reigns around,
Faith, Love, and Hope, within my soul abound!
And, while the world suppose me lost in care,
The joys of angels, unperceived, I share.

Thy creatures wrong thee, O thou sov'reign Good!
Thou art not loved, because not understood;
This grieves me most, that vain pursuits beguile
Ungrateful men, regardless of thy smile.

Frail beauty, and false honor, are adored;
While thee they scorn, and trifle with thy word;
Pass, unconcern'd, a Saviour's sorrows by;
And hunt their ruin with a zeal to die.

LIVING WATER.

The fountain in its source,
  No drought of summer fears:
The farther it pursues its course,
  The nobler it appears.

But shallow cisterns yield
  A scanty, short supply;
The morning sees them amply fill'd,
  At ev'ning they are dry.

TRUTH AND DIVINE LOVE REJECTED BY THE WORLD

O Love, of pure and heav'nly birth !
O simple Truth, scarce known on earth !
Whom men resist with stubborn will;
And, more perverse and daring still,
Smother and quench with reas'nings vain,
While Error and deception reign.

Whence comes it, that, your pow'r the same
As His on high, from whence you came,
Ye rarely find a list'ning ear,
Or heart that makes you welcome here ?
Because you bring reproach and pain,
Where'er ye visit, in your train.

The world is proud, and cannot bear
The scorn and calumny ye share;
The praise of men the mark *they* mean,
They fly the place where *ye* are seen;
Pure Love, with scandal in the rear,
Suits not the vain: it costs too dear.

Then, let the price be what it may,
Though poor, I am prepared to pay;
Come shame, come sorrow; spite of tears,
Weakness, and heart-oppressing fears;
One soul, at least, shall not repine,
To give *you* room; come, reign in mine !

DIVINE JUSTICE AMIABLE.

Thou hast no lightnings, O thou Just!
Or I their force should know;
And, if thou strike me into dust,
My soul approves the blow.

The heart, that values less its ease,
Than it adores thy ways,
In thine avenging anger sees
A subject of its praise.

Pleased I could lie, conceal'd and lost,
  In shades of central night;
Not to avoid thy wrath, thou know'st,
  But lest I grieve thy sight.

Smite me, O thou whom I provoke!
  And I will love thee still;
The well deserved, and righteous stroke
  Shall please me, though it kill.

Am I not worthy to sustain
  The worst thou canst devise:
And dare I seek thy throne again,
  And meet thy sacred eyes?

Far from afflicting, thou art kind;
  And in my saddest hours,
An unction of thy grace I find
  Pervading all my pow'rs.

Alas! thou spar'st me yet again;
  And when thy wrath should move,
Too gentle to endure my pain,
  Thou sooth'st me with thy love.

I have no punishment to fear:
  But ah! that smile from thee,
Imparts a pang far more severe,
  Than woe itself would be.

THE SOUL THAT LOVES GOD FINDS HIM EVERY WHERE.

Oh thou, by long experience tried,
Near whom no grief can long abide:
My love! how full of sweet content
I pass my years of banishment!

All scenes alike engaging prove,
To souls impress'd with sacred love!
Where'er they dwell, they dwell in thee:
In heav'n, in earth or on the sea.

To me remains nor place nor time;
My country is in ev'ry clime;
I can be calm and free from care
On any shore, since God is there

While place we seek, or place we shun,
The soul finds happiness in none;
But with a God to guide our way,
'Tis equal joy to go or stay.

Could I be cast where thou art not,
That were indeed a dreadful lot:
But regions none remote I call,
Secure of finding God in all.

My country, Lord, art thou alone:
Nor other can I claim or own;
The point where all my wishes meet:
My Law, my Love; life's only sweet!

I hold my nothing here below;
Appoint my journey, and I go;
Though pierced by scorn, oppress'd by pride,
I feel thee good—feel nought beside.

No frowns of men can hurtful prove
To souls on fire with heav'nly love;
Though men and devils both condemn,
No gloomy days arise from them.

Ah then! to this embrace repair;
My soul, thou art no stranger there;
There love divine shall be thy guard,
And peace and safety thy reward.

THE TESTIMONY OF DIVINE ADOPTION.

How happy are the new-born race,
Partakers of adopting grace:
  How pure the bliss they share!
Hid from the world and all its eyes,
Within their heart the blessing lies,
  And conscience feels it there.

The moment we believe, 'tis ours;
And if love with all our pow'rs
The God from whom it came,
And if we serve with hearts sincere,
'Tis still discernible and clear.
An undisputed claim.

But ah! if foul and wilful sin
Stain and dishonor us within,
Farewell the joy we knew;
Again the slaves of Nature's sway,
In lab'rinths of our own we stray,
Without a guide or clue.

The chaste and pure who fear to grieve
The gracious Spirit they receive,
His work distinctly trace;
And, strong in undissembling love,
Boldly assert and clearly prove,
Their hearts his dwelling-place.

Oh messenger of dear delight,
Whose voice dispels the deepest night,
Sweet peace-proclaiming Dove!
With the at hand to soothe our pains
No wish unsatisfied remains,
No task, but that of love.

'Tis love unites what sin divides;
The centre where all bliss resides;
To which the soul once brought,
Reclining on the first great Cause,
From his abounding sweetness draws
Peace passing human thought.

Sorrow foregoes its nature there,
And life assumes a tranquil air,
Divested of its woes;
There sov'reign goodness soothes the breast,
Till then incapable of rest,
In sacred sure repose.

DIVINE LOVE ENDURES NO RIVAL.

Love is the Lord whom I obey,
Whose will transported I perform;
The centre of my rest, my stay,
Love's all in all to me, myself a worm.

For uncreated charms I burn,
Oppress'd by slavish fear no more:
For one, in whom I may discern,
Ev'n when he frowns, a sweetness I adore.

He little loves Him, who complains,
And finds him rig'rous and severe;
His heart is sordid, and he feigns,
Though loud in boasting of a soul sincere.

Love causes grief, but 'tis to move
And stimulate the slumb'ring mind;
And he has never tasted Love,
Who shuns a pang so graciously design'd.

Sweet is the cross, above all sweets,
To souls enamour'd with thy smiles!
The keenest woe life ever meets,
Love strips of all its terrors, and beguiles.

'Tis just, that God should not be dear,
Where self engrosses all the thought,
And groans and murmurs make it clear,
Whatever else is loved, the Lord is not

The love of Thee flows just as much
As that of ebbing self subsides;
Our hearts—their scantiness is such—
Bear not the conflict of two rival tides.

Both cannot govern in one soul;
Then let self-love be dispossess'd;
The love of God deserves the whole,
And will not dwell with so despised a guest.

SELF-DIFFIDENCE.

Source of love, and light of day,
Tear me from myself away!
Ev'ry view and thought of mine,
Cast into the mould of thine
Teach, O teach this faithless heart,
A consistent constant part;
Or, if it must live to grow
More rebellious, break it now!

Is it thus that I requite
Grace and goodness infinite?
Ev'ry trace of ev'ry boon
Cancell'd and erased so soon!
Can I grieve thee, whom I love;
Thee, in whom I live and move?
If my sorrow touch thee still,
Save me from so great an ill!

Oh! th' oppressive, irksome weight,
Felt in an uncertain state;
Comfort, peace, and rest, adieu,
Should I prove at last untrue!
Still I choose thee, follow still
Ev'ry notice of thy will.
But, unstable, strangely weak,
Still let slip the good I seek.

Self-confiding wretch, I thought,
I could serve thee as I ought,
Win thee, and deserve to feel
All the love thou canst reveal!
Trusting self, a bruised reed,
Is to be deceived indeed:
Save me from this harm and loss,
Lest my gold turn all to dross.

Self is earthly—Faith alone
Makes an unseen world our own;
Faith relinquish'd, how we roam,
Feel our way, and leave our home!
Spurious gems our hopes entice,
While we scorn the pearl of price;
And, preferring servants' pay,
Cast the children's bread away.

THE ACQUIESCENCE OF PURE LOVE.

Love! if thy destined sacrifice am I,
Come, slay thy victim, and prepare thy fires;
Plunged in thy depths of mercy, let me die
The death, which ev'ry soul that lives desires!

I watch my hours, and see them fleet away;
The time is long that I have languished here;
Yet all my thoughts thy purposes obey,
With no reluctance, cheerful and sincere.

To me 'tis equal, whether Love ordain
My life or death, appoint me pain or ease;
My soul perceives no real ill in pain;
In ease or health, no real good she sees.

One good she covets, and that good alone;
To choose thy will, from selfish bias free;
And to prefer a cottage to a throne,
And grief to comfort, if it pleases Thee.

That we should bear the cross, is thy command;
Die to the world, and live to self no more;
Suffer, unmoved, beneath the rudest hand,
As pleased when shipwreck'd, as when safe on shore.

REPOSE IN GOD.

Blest! who, far from all mankind,
This world's shadows left behind,
Hears from heav'n a gentle strain
Whisp'ring love, and loves again.

Blest! who, free from self-esteem,
Dives into the Great Supreme,
All desires beside discards,
Joys inferior none regards.

Blest! who in thy bosom seeks
Rest that nothing earthly breaks,
Dead to self and worldly things,
Lost in thee, thou King of Kings!

Ye that know my seeret fire,
Softly speak and soon retire;
Favor my divine repose,
Spare the sleep a God bestows.

GLORY TO GOD ALONE.

Oh loved! but not enough—though dearer far
Than self and its most loved enjoyments are;
None duly loves thee, but who, nobly free
From sensual objects, finds his all in thee.

Glory of God! though stranger here below,
Whom man nor knows, nor feels a wish to know;
Our Faith and Reason are both shock'd to find
Man in the post of honor—Thee behind.

Reason exclaims—"Let ev'ry creature fall,
Ashamed, abased, before the Lord of all;"
And Faith, o'erwhelm'd with such a dazzling blaze,
Feebly describes the beauty she surveys.

Yet man, dim-sighted man, and rash as blind,
Deaf to the dictates of his better mind,
In frantic competition dares the skies,
And claims precedence of the Only-wise.

Oh lost in vanity, till once self-known!
Nothing is great, or good, but God alone;
When thou shalt stand before his awful face,
Then, at the last, thy pride shall know His place.

Glorious, Almighty, First, and without end!
When wilt thou melt the mountains, and descend?
When will thou shoot abroad thy conq'ring rays,
And teach these atoms, thou hast made, thy praise?

Thy Glory is the sweetest heav'n I feel;
And, if I seek it with too fierce a zeal,
Thy love, triumphant o'er a selfish will,
Taught me the passion, and inspires it still.

My reason, all my faculties, unite,
To make thy Glory their supreme delight;
Forbid it, Fountain of my brighter days,
That I should rob thee, and usurp thy praise!

My soul! rest happy in thy low estate,
Nor hope, nor wish, to be esteem'd or great;
To take th'impression of a will divine,
Be that thy glory, and those riches thine.

Confess Him righteous in his just decrees,
Love what he loves, and let his pleasure please;
Die daily; from the touch of sin recede;
Then thou hast crown'd him, and he reigns indeed.

SELF-LOVE AND TRUTH INCOMPATIBLE.

From thorny wilds a monster came,
That fill'd my soul with fear and shame;
The birds, forgetful of their mirth,
Droop'd at the sight, and fell to earth;
When thus a sage address'd mine ear,
Himself unconscious of a fear:

"Whence all this terror and surprise,
Distracted looks, and streaming eyes?
Far from the world and its affairs,
The joy it boasts, the pain it shares,
Surrender, without guile or art,
To God, an undivided heart;
The savage form, so fear'd before,
Shall scare your trembling soul no more;
For, loathsome as the sight may be,
'Tis but the *Love of self* you see.
Fix all your love on God alone,
Choose but His will, and hate your own;
No fear shall in your path be found,
The dreary waste shall bloom around,
And you, through all your happy days,
Shall bless his name, and sing his praise."

Oh lovely solitude, how sweet
The silence of this calm retreat!
Here Truth, the fair whom I pursue,
Gives all her beauty to my view;
The simple, unadorn'd display,
Charms ev'ry pain and fear away.
O Truth, whom millions proudly slight;
O Truth, my treasure and delight;
Accept this tribute to thy name,
And this poor heart, from which it came!

THE LOVE OF GOD, THE END OF LIFE.

Since life in sorrow must be spent,
So be it—I am well content,
And meekly wait my last remove,
Seeking only growth in Love.

No bliss I seek, but to fulfil
In life, in death, thy lovely will;
No succours in my woes I want,
Save what thou art pleased to grant

Our days are number'd, let us spare
Our anxious hearts a needless care:
'Tis thine to number out our days;
Ours to give them to thy praise.

Love is our only bus'ness here,
Love, simple, constant, and sincere;
O blessed days, thy servant see!
Spent, O Lord! in pleasing Thee.

LOVE FAITHFUL IN THE ABSENCE OF THE BELOVED.

In vain ye woo me to your harmless joys,
Ye pleasant bow'rs, remote from strife or noise;
Your shades, the witnesses of many a vow,
Breathed forth in happier days, are irksome now;
Denied that smile, 't was once my heav'n to see,
Such scenes, such pleasures, are all past with me.

In vain he leaves me, I shall love him still;
And, though I mourn, not murmur at his will;
I have no cause—an object all divine
Might well grow weary of a soul like mine:
Yet pity me, great God! forlorn, alone,
Heartless and hopeless, Life and Love all gone.

LOVE PURE AND FERVENT.

Jealous, and with love o'erflowing,
  God demands a fervent heart;
Grace and bounty still bestowing,
  Calls us to a grateful part.

Oh, then, with supreme affection,
  His paternal Will regard!
If it costs us some dejection,
  Ev'ry sigh has its reward.

Perfect Love has pow'r to soften
  Cares that might our peace destroy,
Nay, does more—transforms them often,
  Changing sorrow into joy.

Sov'reign Love appoints the measure,
  And the number of our pains;
And is pleased when we find pleasure
  In the trials he ordains.

THE ENTIRE SURRENDER.

Peace has unveil'd her smiling face,
And wooes thy soul to her embrace;
Enjoy'd with ease, if thou refrain
From earthly love, else sought in vain;
She dwells with all who Truth prefer,
But seeks not them who seek not her.

Yield to the Lord, with simple heart,
All that thou hast, and all thou art;
Renounce all strength but strength divine;
And peace shall be for ever thine:
Behold the path which I have trod,
My path, till I go home to God.

THE PERFECT SACRIFICE.

I place an off'ring at thy shrine,
  From taint and blemish clear,
Simple and pure in its design,
  Of all that I hold dear.

I yield thee back thy gifts again,
  Thy gifts which most I prize;
Desirous only to retain
  The notice of thine eyes.

But if, by thine adored decree,
  That blessing is denied;
Resign'd, and unreluctant, see
  My ev'ry wish subside.

Thy will in all things I approve,
  Exalted or cast down!
Thy will in ev'ry state I love,
  And even in thy frown.

GOD HIDES HIS PEOPLE.

To lay the soul that loves him low,
  Becomes the Only-wise;
To hide, beneath a veil of woe,
  The children of the skies.

Man, though a worm, would yet be great,
  Though feeble, would seem strong;
Assumes an independent state,
  By sacrilege and wrong.

Strange the reverse, which, once abused,
  The haughty creature proves!
He feels his soul a barren waste,
  Nor dares affirm, he loves.

Scorn'd by the thoughtless and the vain,
  To God he presses near;
Superior to the world's disdain,
  And happy in its sneer.

Oh welcome, in his heart he says,
  Humility and shame!
Farewell the wish for human praise,
  The music of a name!

But will not scandal mar the good
  That I might else perform?
And can God work it, if he would,
  By so despised a worm?

Ah, vainly anxious!—leave the Lord
  To rule thee, and dispose;
Sweet is the mandate of his word,
  And gracious all he does.

He draws from human littleness
  His grandeur and renown;
And gen'rous hearts with joy confess
  The triumph all his own.

Down then with self-exalting thoughts;
Thy faith and hope employ,
To welcome all that he allots,
And suffer shame with joy.

No longer, then, thou wilt encroach
On his eternal right;
And he shall smile at thy approach,
And make thee his delight.

THE SECRETS OF DIVINE LOVE ARE TO BE KEPT.

Sun! stay thy course, this moment stay—
Suspend th' o'erflowing tide of day,
Divulge not such a love as mine,
Ah! hide the mystery divine.
Lest man, who deems my glory shame,
Should learn the secret of my flame.

O night! propitious to my views,
Thy sable awning wide diffuse;
Conceal alike my joy and pain,
Nor draw thy curtain back again,
Though morning, by the tears she shows,
Seems to participate my woes.

Ye stars! whose faint and feeble fires
Express my lanquishing desires,
Whose slender beams pervade the skies
As silent as my secret sighs,
Those emanations of a soul,
That darts her fires beyond the Pole;

Your rays, that scarce assist the sight,
That pierce, but not displace the night,
That shine indeed, but nothing show
Of all those various scenes below,
Bring no disturbance, rather prove
Incentives to a sacred Love.

Thou Moon! whose never-failing course
Bespeaks a providential force,
Go, tell the tidings of my flame
To him who calls the stars by name;
Whose absence kills, whose presence cheers,
Who blots, or brightens, all my years.

While, in the blue abyss of space,
Thine orb performs its rapid race;
Still whisper in his list'ning ears
The language of my sighs and tears;
Tell him, I seek him, far below,
Lost in a wilderness of woe.

Ye thought-composing, silent hours,
Diffusing peace o'er all my pow'rs!
Friends of the pensive! who conceal,
In darkest shades, the flames I feel;
To you I trust, and safely may,
The love that wastes my strength away.

In sylvan scenes, and caverns rude,
I taste the sweets of solitude;
Retired indeed, but not alone,
I share them with a Spouse unknown,
Who hides me here, from envious eyes,
From all intrusion and surprise.

Imbow'ring shades, and dens profound!
Where echo rolls the voice around;
Mountains! whose elevated heads
A moist and misty veil o'erspreads;
Disclose a solitary Bride
To him I love—to none beside.

Ye rills! that, murm'ring all the way
Among the polish'd pebbles stray;
Creep silently along the ground,
Lest, drawn by that harmonious sound,
Some wand'rer, whom I would not meet,
Should stumble on my loved retreat.

Enamell'd meads, and hillocks green,
And streams, that water all the scene!
Ye torrents, loud in distant ears!
Ye fountains, that receive my tears!
Ah! still conceal, with caution due,
A charge, I trust with none but you.

If, when my pain and grief increase,
I seem t' enjoy the sweetest peace,
It is because I find so fair
The charming object of my care,
That I can sport and pleasure make
Of torment suffer'd for his sake.

Ye meads and groves, unconscious things!
Ye know not whence my pleasure springs;
Ye know not, and he cannot know,
The scource from which my sorrows flow;
The dear sole Cause of all I feel,—
He knows, and understands them well.

Ye deserts! where the wild beast roves,
Scenes sacred to my hours of love;
Ye forests! in whose shades I stray,
Benighted under burning day;
Ah! whisper not how blest am I,
Nor while I live nor when I die.

Ye lambs! who sport beneath these shades,
And bound along the mossy glades;
Be taught a salutary fear,
And cease to bleat when I am near:
The wolf may hear your harmless cry,
Whom ye should dread as much as I.

How calm, amid these scenes, my mind!
How perfect is the peace I find!
Oh hush! be still my ev'ry part,
My tongue, my pulse, my beating heart!
That love, aspiring to its cause,
May suffer not a moment's pause.

Ye swift-finn'd nations, that abide
In seas as fathomless as wide;
And, unsuspicious of a snare,
Pursue at large your pleasures there:
Poor sportive fools! how soon does man
Your heedless ignorance trepan!

Away! dive deep into the brine,
Where never yet sunk plummet line;
Trust me, the vast leviathan
Is merciful, compared with man;
Avoid his arts, forsake the beach,
And never play within his reach.

My soul her bondage ill endures:
I pant for liberty like yours;
I long for that immense profound,
That knows no bottom, and no bound;
Lost in infinity to prove
Th' Incomprehensible of Love.

Ye birds! that lessen as ye fly,
And vanish in the distant sky;
To whom yon airy waste belongs,
Resounding with your cheerful songs;
Haste to escape from human sight;
Fear less the vulture and the kite.

How blest, and how secure am I,
When, quitting earth, I soar on high:
When lost, like you I disappear,
And float in a sublimer sphere!
Whence falling, within human view,
I am ensnared, and caught like you.

Omniscient God, whose notice deigns
To try the heart and search the reins,
Compassionate the num'rous woes,
I dare not, e'en to thee disclose;
Oh save me from the cruel hands
Of men who fear not thy commands!

Love, all-subduing and divine,
Care for a creature truly thine;
Reign in a heart, disposed to own
No sov'reign, but thyself alone;
Cherish a Bride, who cannot rove,
Nor quit thee for a meaner Love!

THE VICISSITUDES EXPERIENCED IN THE CHRISTIAN LIFE.

I suffer fruitless anguish day by day,
Each moment, as it passes, marks my pain;
Scarce knowing whither, doubtfully I stray,
And see no end of all that I sustain.

The more I strive, the more I am withstood;
Anxiety increasing ev'ry hour,
My spirit finds no rest, performs no good,
And nought remains of all my former pow'r.

My peace of heart is fled, I know not where;
My happy hours, like shadows, pass'd away;
Their sweet remembrance doubles all my care,
Night darker seems, succeeding such a day.

Dear faded joys, and impotent regret,
What profit is there in incessant tears?
O thou, whom, once beheld, we ne'er forget,
Reveal thy love, and banish all my fears!

Alas!—he flies me—treats me as his foe,
Views not my sorrows, hears not when I plead;
Woe such as mine, despised, neglected woe,
Unless it shortens life, is vain indeed.

Pierced with a thousand wounds, I yet survive;
My pangs are keen, but no complaint transpires;
And, while in terror of thy wrath I live,
Hell seems to lose its less tremendous fires.

Has hell a pain I would not gladly bear,
So thy severe displeasure might subside?
Hopeless of ease, I seem already there,
My life extinguish'd, and yet death denied.

Is this the joy so promised—this the love,
Th' unchanging love, so sworn in better days?
Ah! dang'rous glorious! shown me, but to prove
How lovely thou, and I how rash to gaze.

Why did I see them? had I still remain'd
  Untaught, still ignorant how fair thou art,
My humbler wishes I had soon obtain'd,
  Nor known the torments of a doubting heart.

Deprived of all, yet feeling no desires,
  Whence then, I cry, the pangs that I sustain?
Dubious and uninform'd, my soul inquires,
  Ought she to cherish, or shake off her pain.

Suff'ring, I suffer not—sincerely love,
  Yet feel no touch of that enliv'ning flame;
As chance inclines me, unconcern'd I move,
  All times, and all events, to me the same.

I search my heart, and not a wish is there,
  But burns with zeal that hated self may fall;
Such is the sad disquietude I share,
  A sea of doubts, and self the source of all.

I ask not life, nor do I wish to die;
  And, if thine hand accomplish not my cure,
I would not purchase with a single sigh,
  A free discharge from all that I endure.

I groan in chains, yet want not a release:
  Am sick, and know not the distemper'd part;
Am just as void of purpose, as of peace;
  Have neither pain, nor fear, nor hope, nor heart.

My claim to life, though sought with earnest care,
  No light within me, or without me, shows;
Once I had faith; but now, in self-despair
  Find my chief cordial, and my best repose.

My soul is a forgotten thing; she sinks,
  Sinks and is lost, without a wish to rise;
Feels an indiff'rence she abhors, and thinks
  Her name erased for ever from the skies.

Language affords not my distress a name,—
  Yet is it real, and no sickly dream;
'Tis Love inflicts it; though to feel that flame,
  Is all I know of happiness supreme.

When Love departs, a chaos wide and vast,
  And dark as hell, is open'd in the soul;

When Love returns, the gloomy scene is past,
No tempests shake her, and no fears control.

Then tell me, why these ages of delay?
Oh Love, all-excellent, once more appear;
Disperse the shades, and snatch me into day,
From this abyss of night, these floods of fear!

No—Love is angry, will not now endure
A sigh of mine, or suffer a complaint;
He smites me, wounds me, and withholds the cure!
Exhausts my pow'rs, and leaves me sick and faint.

He wounds, and hides the hand that gave the blow;
He flies, he re-appears, and wounds again—
Was ever heart that loved thee treated so?
Yet I adore thee, though it seem in vain.

And wilt thou leave me, whom, when lost and blind;
Thou didst distinguish, and vouchsafe to choose,
Before thy laws were written in my mind,
While yet the world had all my thoughts and views?

Now leave me? when, enamour'd of thy laws,
I make thy glory my supreme delight;
Now blot me from thy register, and cause
A faithful soul to perish from thy sight?

What can have caused the change which I deplore!
Is it to prove me, if my heart be true!
Permit me then, while prostrate I adore,
To draw, and place its picture in thy view.

'Tis thine without reserve, most simply thine:
So given to thee, that it is not my own;
A willing captive of thy grace divine;
And loves, and seeks thee, for thyself alone.

Pain cannot move it, danger cannot scare;
Pleasure and wealth, in its esteem, are dust;
It loves thee e'en when least inclined to spare
Its tend'rest feelings, and avows thee just.

'Tis all thine own; my spirit is so too,
An undivided off'ring at thy shrine!
It seeks thy glory with no double view,
Thy glory, with no secret bent to mine

Love, holy Love! and art thou not severe,
  To slight me, thus devoted, and thus fix'd!
Mine is an everlasting ardour, clear
  From all self-bias, gen'rous and unmix'd.

But I am silent, seeing what I see—
  And fear, with cause, that I am self-deceived:
Not e'en my faith is from suspicion free,
  And, that I love, seems not to be believed.

Live thou, and reign, for ever, glorious Lord!
  My last, least off'ring, I present thee now—
Renounce me, leave me, and be still adored;
  Slay me, my God, and I applaud the blow.

WATCHING UNTO GOD IN THE NIGHT SEASON

Sleep at last has fled these eyes,
  Nor do I regret his flight,
More alert my spirits rise,
  And my heart is free and light.

Nature silent all around,
  Not a single witness near;
God as soon as sought is found;
  And the flame of love burns clear.

Interruption, all day long,
  Checks the current of my joys;
Creatures press me with a throng,
  And perplex me with their noise.

Undisturb'd I muse all night,
  On the first Eternal Fair;
Nothing there obstructs delight,
  Love is renovated there.

Life with its perpetual stir,
  Proves a foe to Love and me
Fresh entanglements occur—
  Comes the night, and sets me free

Never more, sweet sleep, suspend
  My enjoyments, always new;
Leave me to possess my Friend;
  Other eyes and hearts subdue.

Hush the world that I may wake
  To the taste of pure delights;
Oh the pleasure I partake—
  God, the partner of my night!

David, for the self-same cause,
  Night preferr'd to busy day;
Hearts, whom heav'nly beauty draws,
  Wish the glaring sun away.

Sleep, self-lovers, is for you—
  Souls that love *celestial* know,
Fairer scenes by night can view,
  Than the sun could ever show.

ON THE SAME.

Season of my purest pleasure,
  Sealer of observing eyes!
When, in larger, freer measure,
  I can commune with the skies;
While, beneath thy shade extended,
  Weary man forgets his woes;
I, my daily trouble ended,
  Find, in watching, my repose.

Silence all around prevailing,
  Nature hush'd in slumber sweet,
No rude noise mine ears assailing,
  Now my God and I can meet:
Universal nature slumbers,
  And my soul partakes the calm,
Breathes her ardour out in numbers,
  Plaintive song or lofty psalm.

Now my passion, pure and holy,
  Shines and burns, without restraint!
Which the day's fatigue and folly
  Cause to lanquish dim and faint:
Charming hours of relaxation!
  How I dread th' ascending sun!
Surely, idle conversation
  Is an evil match'd by none.

Worldly prate and babble hurt me;
  Unintelligible prove;
Neither teach me nor divert me;
  I have ears for none but love.
Me, they rude esteem, and foolish,
  Hearing my absurd replies;
I have neither art's fine polish,
  Nor the knowledge of the wise.

Simple souls and unpolluted,
  By conversing with the Great,
Have a mind and taste, ill suited
  To their dignity and state;
All their talking, reading, writing,
  Are but talents misapplied;
Infant's prattle I delight in,
  Nothing human choose beside.

'Tis the secret fear of sinning
  Checks my tongue, or I should say,
When I see the night beginning,
  I am glad of parting day;
Love, this gentle admonition
  Whispers soft within my breast?
"Choice befits not thy condition
  "Acquiescence suits thee best."

Henceforth, the repose and pleasure
  Night affords me, I resign:
And thy will shall be the measure,
  Wisdom infinite! of mine:
Wishing is but inclination
  Quarrelling with thy decrees;
Wayward nature finds th' occasion—
  'Tis her folly and disease.

Night, with its sublime enjoyments,
  Now no longer will I choose;
Nor the day with its employments,

Irksome as they seem, refuse;
Lessons of a God's inspiring,
Neither time nor place impedes;
From our wishing and desiring,
Our unhappiness proceeds.

ON THE SAME.

Night! how I love thy silent shades,
My spirits they compose;
The bliss of heav'n my soul pervades,
In spite of all my woes.

While sleep instils her poppy dews
In ev'ry slumb'ring eye,
I watch to meditate and muse,
In blest tranquillity.

And when I feel a God immense
Familiarly impart,
With ev'ry proof he can dispense,
His favor to my heart.

My native meanness I lament,
Though most divinely fill'd
With all th' ineffable content,
That Deity can yield.

His purpose and his course he keeps;
Treads all my reas'nings down;
Commands me out of nature's deeps,
And hides me in his own.

When in the dust, its proper place,
Our pride of heart we lay,
'Tis then, a deluge of his grace
Bears all our sins away.

Thou, whom I serve, and whose I am,
Whose influence from on high
Refines, and still refines my flame,
And makes my fetters fly.

How wretched is the creature's state,
Who thwarts thy gracious pow'r;
Crush'd under sin's enormous weight,
Increasing ev'ry hour!

The night, when pass'd entire with thee
  How luminous and clear!
Then sleep has no delights for me,
  Lest *Thou* shouldst disappear.

My Saviour! occupy me still
  In this secure recess;
Let Reason slumber if she will,
  My joy shall not be less:

Let Reason slumber out the night;
  But if *Thou* deign to make
My soul th'abode of truth and light,
  Ah, keep my heart awake!

THE JOY OF THE CROSS.

Long plunged in sorrow, I resign
My soul to that dear hand of thine,
  Without reserve or fear;
That hand shall wipe my streaming eyes,
Or into smiles of glad surprise
  Transform the falling tear.

My sole possession is thy love;
In earth beneath, or heav'n above,
  I have no other store;
And, though with fervent suit I pray,
And importune thee night and day,
  I ask thee nothing more.

My rapid hours pursue the course
Prescribed them by love's sweetest force!
  And I, thy sov'reign Will,
Without a wish t'escape my doom;
Though still a suff'rer from the womb,
  And doom'd to suffer still.

By thy command, where'er I stray,
Sorrow attends me all my way,
  A never-failing friend;
And if my suff'rings may augment
Thy praise, behold me well content—
  Let sorrow still attend?

It costs me no regret, that she,
Who follow'd Christ, should follow me.
And though, where'er she goes,
Thorns spring spontaneous at her feet,
I love her, and extract a sweet
From all my bitter woes.

Adieu! ye vain delights of earth;
Insipid sports, and childish mirth,
I taste no sweets in you;
Unknown delights are in the Cross,
All joy beside, to me is dross;
And Jesus thought so too.

The Cross! Oh ravishment and bliss—
How grateful e'en its anguish is;
Its bitterness, how sweet!
There ev'ry sense, and all the mind
In all her faculties refined,
Tastes happiness complete.

Souls once enabled to disdain
Base sublunary joys, maintain
Their dignity secure;
The fever of desire is pass'd,
And Love has all its genuine taste,
Is delicate and pure.

Self-love no grace in sorrow sees,
Consults her own peculiar ease;
'Tis all the bliss she knows;
But nobler aims *true* Love employ;
In self-denial is her joy,
In suff'ring, her repose.

Sorrow, and Love, go side by side;
Nor height, nor depth, can e'er divide
Their heav'n-appointed bands;
Those dear associates still are one,
Nor, till the race of life is run,
Disjoin their wedded hands.

Jesus, avenger of our fall,
Thou faithful lover above all,
The cross has ever borne!
Oh tell me,—life is in thy voice—
How much afflictions were thy choice,
And sloth and ease thy scorn!

Thy choice and mine shall be the same
Inspirer of that holy flame,
  Which must for ever blaze!
To take the cross and follow thee,
Where love and duty lead, shall be
  My portion and my praise.

JOY IN MARTYRDOM.

Sweet tenants of this grove!
  Who sing, without design,
A song of artless love,
  In unison with mine:
These echoing shades return
  Full many a note of ours,
That wise ones cannot learn,
  With all their boasted pow'rs.

O thou! whose sacred charms
  These hearts so seldom love,
Although thy beauty warms
  And blesses all above;
How slow are human things
  To choose their happiest lot!
All-glorious King of kings,
  Say, why we love thee not?

This heart, that cannot rest,
  Shall thine for ever prove;
Though bleeding and distress'd,
  Yet joyful in thy love:
'Tis happy, though it breaks
  Beneath thy chast'ning hand;
And speechless, yet it speaks
  What thou canst understand.

SIMPLE TRUST.

Still, still, without ceasing,
I feel it increasing,
This fervour of holy desire;
And often exclaim,
Let me die in the flame
Of a love that can never expire!

Had I words to explain
What *she* must sustain,
Who dies to the world and its ways
How joy and affright,
Distress and delight,
Alternately chequer her days;

Thou, sweetly severe!
I would make thee appear,
In all thou art pleased to award,
Not more in the sweet,
Than the bitter I meet,
My tender and merciful Lord.

This faith in the dark,
Pursuing its mark
Through many sharp trials of love,
Is the sorrowful waste,
That is to be pass'd
In the way to the Canaan above.

THE NECESSITY OF SELF-ABASEMENT.

Source of Love, my brighter Sun,
Thou alone my comfort art;
See, my race is almost run;
Hast thou left this trembling heart?

In my youth, thy charming eyes
Drew me from the ways of men;
Then I drank unmingled joys;
Frown of thine saw never *then*.

Spouse of Christ was then my name;
  And devoted all to thee,
Strangely jealous I became—
  Jealous of this self in me.

Thee to love, and none beside,
  Was my darling, sole employ;
While alternately I died,
  Now of grief, and now of joy.

Through the dark and silent night,
  On thy radiant smiles I dwelt:
And to see the dawning light,
  Was the keenest pain I felt.

Thou my greatest teacher wert!
  And thine eye, so close applied,
While it watch'd thy pupil's heart,
  Seem'd to look at none beside.

Conscious of no evil drift,
  This, I cried, is Love indeed—
'Tis the Giver, not the gift,
  Whence the joys I feel proceed.

But soon humbled, and laid low,
  Stript of all thou hast conferr'd,
Nothing left but sin and woe,
  I perceived how I had err'd.

Oh, the vain conceit of man,
  Dreaming of a good his own,
Arrogating all he can,
  Though the Lord is good alone!

He, the graces Thou hast wrought,
  Makes subservient to his pride;
Ignorant that one such thought
  Passes all his sin beside.

Such his folly—proved, at last,
  By the loss of that repose
Self-complacence cannot taste,
  Only Love divine bestows.

'Tis by this reproof severe,
  And by this reproof alone,
His defects at last appear,
  Man is to himself made known.

Learn, all Earth! that feeble Man,
Sprung from this terrestial clod,
Nothing is, and nothing can;
Life, and pow'r, are all in God.

LOVE INCREASED BY SUFFERING.

"I love the Lord," is still the strain
This heart delights to sing;
But I reply—your thoughts are vain,
Perhaps 'tis no such thing.

Before the pow'r of Love divine,
Creation fades away!
Till only God is seen to shine
In all that we survey.

In gulfs of awful night we find
The God of our desires;
'Tis there he stamps the yielding mind,
And doubles all its fires.

Flames of encircling love invest,
And pierce it sweetly through;
'Tis fill'd with sacred joy, yet press'd
With sacred sorrow too.

Ah Love! my heart is in the right—
Amidst a thousand woes.
To thee, 'tis ever new delight,
And all its peace, it owes.

Fresh causes of distress occur,
Where'er I look or move;
The comforts, I to all prefer,
Are solitude and love.

Nor exile I, nor prison fear;
Love makes my courage great;
I find a Saviour ev'ry where,
His grace in ev'ry state.

Nor castle walls, nor dungeons deep,
Exclude his quick'ning beams;
There I can sit, and sing, and weep,
And dwell on heav'nly themes.

There, sorrow, for his sake, is found
  A joy beyond compare;
There, no presumptuous thoughts abound
  No pride can enter there.

A saviour doubles all my joys,
  And sweetens all my pains,
His strength in my defence employs,
  Consoles me and sustains.

I fear no ill, resent no wrong:
  Nor feel a passion move,
When malice whets her sland'rous tongue;
  Such patience is in Love.

SCENES FAVORABLE TO MEDITATION.

Wilds horrid and dark with o'ershadowing trees,
  Rocks that ivy and briers enfold,
Scenes nature with dread and astonishment sees,
  But I with a pleasure untold.

Though awfully silent, and shaggy, and rude,
  I am charm'd with the peace ye afford,
Your shades are a temple where none will intrude,
  The abode of my Lover and Lord.

I am sick of thy splendor, O fountain of day,
  And here I am hid from its beams,
Here safely contemplate a brighter display
  Of the noblest and holiest of themes.

Ye forests, that yield me my sweetest repose,
  Where stillness and solitude reign,
To you I securely and boldly disclose
  The dear anguish of which I complain.

Here, sweetly forgetting and wholly forgot
  By the world and its turbulent throng,
The birds and the streams lend me many a note
  That aids meditation and song.

Here, wand'ring in scenes that are sacred to night,
  Love wears me and wastes me away,
And often the sun has spent much of his light,
  Ere yet I perceive it is day.

While a mantle of darkness envelopes the sphere,
  My sorrows are sadly rehearsed,
To me the dark hours are all equally dear,
  And the last is as sweet as the first.

Here I and the beasts of the deserts agree,
  Mankind are the wolves that I fear,
They grudge me my natural right to be free,
  But nobody questions it here.

Though little is found in this dreary abode
  That appetite wishes to find,
My spirit is sooth'd by the presence of God,
  And appetite wholly resign'd.

Ye desolate scenes, to your solitude led,
  My life I in praises employ,
And scarce know the source of the tears that I shed,
  Proceed they from sorrow or joy.

There's nothing I seem to have skill to discern
  I feel out my way in the dark,
Love reigns in my bosom, I constantly burn,
  Yet hardly distinguish the spark.

I live, yet I seem to myself to be dead,
  Such a riddle is not to be found,
I am nourish'd without knowing how I am fed,
  I have nothing, and yet I abound.

Oh Love! who in darkness art pleased to abide,
  Though dimly, yet surely I see,
That these contrarieties only reside
  In the soul that is chosen of thee.

Ah send me not back to the race of mankind,
  Perversely by folly beguiled,
For where in the crowds I have left, shall I find
  The spirit and heart of a child.

Here let me, though fix'd in a desert, be free;
  A little one whom they despise,
Though lost to the world, if in union with thee,
  Shall be holy, and happy, and wise.

MINOR POEMS.

VERSES WRITTEN AT BATH, ON FINDING THE HEEL OF A SHOE.

Fortune! I thank thee: gentle goddess! thanks!
Not that my muse, though bashful, shall deny
She would have thank'd thee rather hadst thou cast
A treasure in her way; for neither meed
Of early breakfast, to dispel the fumes,
And bowel-racking pains of emptiness,
Nor noontide feast, nor evening's cool repast,
Hopes she from this—presumptuous, though, perhaps
The cobbler, leather-carving artist! might.
Nathless she thanks thee, and accepts thy boon,
Whatever; not as erst the fabled cock,
Vain-glorious fool! unknowing what he found,
Spurn'd the rich gem thou gavest him. Wherefore, ah
Why not on me that favor, (worthier sure!)
Conferr'dst thou, goddess! Thou art blind, thou sayst:
Enough!—thy blindness shall excuse the deed.
Nor does my muse no benefit exhale
From this thy scant indulgence!—even here
Hints worthy sage philosophy are found;
Illustrious hints, to moralize my song!
This ponderous heel of perforated hide
Compact, with pegs indented, many a row,
Haply (for such its massy form bespeaks)
The weighty tread of some rude peasant clown
Upbore; on this supported oft, he stretch'd,
With uncouth strides, along the furrow'd glebe
Flattening the stubborn clod, till cruel time
(What will not cruel time) on a wry step
Severed the strict cohesion; when, alas!
He, who could erst, with even, equal pace,
Pursue his destined way with symmetry,
And some proportion form'd, now on one side,
Curtail'd and maim'd, the sport of vagrant boys,
Cursing his frail supporter, treacherous prop,
With toilsome steps, and difficult, moves on:

Thus fares it oft with other than the feet
Of humble villager—the statesman thus,
Up the steep road where proud ambition leads,
Aspiring, first, uninterrupted winds
His prosperous way; nor fears miscarriage foul,
While policy prevails, and friends prove true:
But that support soon failing, by him left,
On whom he most depended, basely left,
Betray'd, deserted; from his airy height
Headlong he falls; and through the rest of life
Drags the dull load of disappointment on.

AN ODE,

ON READING RICHARDSON'S HISTORY OF SIR CHARLES GRANDISON.

Say, ye apostate and profane
Wretches, who blush not to disdain
Allegiance to your God,—
Did e'er your idly wasted love
Of virtue for her sake remove,
And lift you from the crowd?

Would you the race of glory run;
Know, the devout and they alone,
Are equal to the task:
The labours of the illustrious course
Far other than the unaided force
Of human vigor ask.

To arm against reputed ill,
The patient heart too brave to feel
The tortures of despair:
Nor safer yet high-crested pride,
When wealth flows in with ev'ry tide
To gain admittance there.

To rescue from the tyrant's sword
The oppress'd;—unseen and unimplored,
To cheer the face of woe;
From lawless insult to defend
An orphan's right—a fallen friend,
And a forgiven foe;

These, these distinguish from the crowd,
And these alone, the great and good,
The guardians of mankind;
Whose bosoms with these virtues heave,
O, with what matchless speed they leave
The multitude behind!

Then ask ye, from what cause on earth
Virtues like these derive their birth:
Derived from Heaven alone;
Full on that favour'd breast they shine,
Where faith and resignation join
To call the blessing down.

Such is that heart:—but while the muse
Thy theme, O Richardson, pursues,
Her feeble spirits faint:
She cannot reach, and would not wrong,
That subject for an angel's song,
The hero, and the saint!

AN EPISTLE TO ROBERT LLOYD, ESQ.

'Tis not that I design to rob
Thee of thy birthright, gentle Bob,
For thou art born sole heir, and single,
Of dear Mat Prior's easy jingle;
Not that I mean, while thus I knit
My threadbare sentiments together,
To show my genius or my wit,
When God and you know I have neither;
Or such as might be better shown
By letting poetry alone.
'Tis not with either of these views
That I presumed to address the muse;
But to divert a fierce banditti,
(Sworn foes to every thing that's witty!)
That, with a black, infernal train,
Make cruel inroads in my brain,
And daily threaten to drive thence
My little garrison of sense;
The fierce banditti which I mean
Are gloomy thoughts, led on by spleen.
Then there's another reason yet,
Which is, that I may fairly quit

The debt, which justly became due
The moment when I heard from you:
And you might grumble, crony mine,
If paid in any other coin;
Since twenty sheets of lead, God knows,
(I would say twenty sheets of prose)
Can ne'er be deem'd worth half so much
As one of gold, and your's was such.
Thus, the preliminaries settled,
I fairly find myself pitchkettled,
And cannot see, though few see better,
How I shall hammer out a letter.
First, for a thought—since all agree—
A thought—I have it—let me see—
'Tis gone again—plague on't! I thought
I had it—but I have it not.
Dame Gurton thus, and Hodge her son,
That useful thing, her needle, gone!
Rake well the cinders, sweep the floor,
And sift the dust behind the door;
While eager Hodge beholds the prize
In old grimalkin's glaring eyes;
And gammer finds it on her knees
In every shining straw she sees.
This simile were apt enough;
But I've another, critic proof,
The virtuoso thus, at noon,
Broiling beneath a July sun,
The gilded butterfly pursues,
O'er hedge and ditch, through gaps and mews:
And, after many a vain essay,
To captivate the tempting prey,
Gives him at length the lucky pat,
And has him safe beneath his hat:
Then lifts it gently from the ground;
But ah! 'tis lost as soon as found;
Culprit his liberty regains,
Flits out of sight, and mocks his pains.
The sense was dark; 'twas therefore fit
With simile to illustrate it;
But as too much obscures the sight,
As often as too little light,
We have our similes cut short,
For matters of more grave import.
That Matthew's numbers run with ease,
Each man of common sense agrees!
All men of common sense allow
That Robert's lines are easy too:
Where then the preference shall we place,

Or how do justice in this case ?
Matthew (says Fame) with endless pains
Smooth'd and refined the meanest strains;
Nor suffer'd one ill chosen rhyme
To escape him at the idlest time;
And thus o'er all a lustre cast,
That, while the language lives, shall last.
An't please your ladyship (quoth I),
For 'tis my business to reply;
Sure so much labour, so much toil,
Bespeak at least a stubborn soil:
Theirs be the laurel-wreath decreed,
Who both write well, and write full speed;
Who throw their Helicon about
As freely as a conduit spout!
Friend Robert, thus like chien scavant,
Lets fall a poem en passant,
Nor needs his geniune ore refine!
'Tis ready polish'd from the mine.

A TALE FOUNDED ON A FACT,

WHICH HAPPENED IN JANUARY, 1799.

Where Humber pours his rich commercial stream,
There dwelt a wretch, who breath'd but to blaspheme;
In subterraneous caves his life he led,
Black as the mine in which he wrought for bread.
When on a day, emerging from the deep,
A sabbath-day, (such sabbaths, thousands keep!,
The wages of his weekly toil he bore
To buy a cock—whose blood might win him more;
As if the noblest of the feather'd kind
Were but for battle and for death design'd;
As if the consecrated hours were meant
For sport, to minds on cruelty intent;
It chanced (such chances Providence obey)
He met a fellow-labourer on the way,
Whose heart the same desires had once inflamed
But now the savage temper was reclaim'd,
Persuasion on his lips had taken place;
For all plead well who plead the cause of grace.
His iron heart with scripture he assail'd,
Woo'd him to hear a sermon, and prevail'd.
His faithful bow the mighty preacher drew,
Swift as the light'ning-glimpse the arrow flew.

He wept; he trembled; cast his eyes around,
To find a worse than he; but none he found.
He felt his sins, and wonder'd he should feel.
Grace made the wound, and grace alone could heal.
 Now farewell oaths, and blasphemies, and lies!
He quits the sinner's for the martyr's prize.
That holy day was wash'd with many a tear,
Gilded with hope, yet shaded too by fear.
The next, his swarthy brethren of the mine
Learn'd, by his alter'd speech, the change divine!
Laugh'd when they should have wept, and swore the day
Was nigh when he would swear as fast as they.
'No,' said the penitent, 'such words shall share
This breath no more; devoted now to prayer.
O! if Thou seest (thine eye the future sees)
That I shall yet again blaspheme, like these;
Now strike me to the ground on which I kneel,
Ere yet this heart relapses into steel:
Now take me to that Heav'n I once defied,
Thy presence, thy embrace!'—He spoke, and died!

TO THE REV. MR. NEWTON, ON HIS RETURN FROM RAMSGATE.

That ocean you have late survey'd,
 Those rocks I too have seen,
But I afflicted and dismay'd,
 You tranquil and serene.

You from the flood-controlling steep
 Saw stretch'd before your view,
With conscious joy, the threatening deep,
 No longer such too you.

To me the waves, that ceaseless broke
 Upon the dangerous coast,
Hoarsely and ominously spoke
 Of all my treasure lost.

Your sea of troubles you have past,
 And found the peaceful shore;
I, tempest-toss'd, and wreck'd at last,
 Come home to port no more.

Oct. 1780.

LOVE ABUSED.

What is there in the vale of life
Half so delightful as a wife,
When friendship, love, and peace combine
To stamp the marriage-bond divine?
The stream of pure and genuine love
Derives its current from above;
And Earth a second Eden shows,
Where'er the healing water flows:
But ah, if from the dykes and drains
Of sensual nature's feverish veins,
Lust, like a lawless, headstrong flood,
Impregnated with ooze and mud,
Descending fast on every side,
Once mingles with the sacred tide,
Farewell the soul-enlivening scene!
The banks that wore a smiling green,
With rank defilement overspread,
Bewail their flowery beauties dead.
The stream polluted, dark, and dull,
Diffused into a Stygian pool,
Through life's last melancholy years
Is fed with ever-flowing tears:
Complaints supply the zeyphyr's part,
And sighs that heave a breaking heart.

THE COLUBRIAD.

Close by the threshold of a door nail'd fast
Three kittens sat; each kitten look'd aghast.
I, passing swift and inattentive by,
At the three kittens cast a careless eye;
Not much concern'd to know what they did there;
Not deeming kittens worth a poet's care.
But presently a loud and furious hiss
Caused me to stop, and to exclaim, 'What's this?'
When lo! upon the threshold met my view,
With head erect, and eyes of fiery hue,
A viper, long as Count de Grasse's queue.
Forth from his head his forked tongue he throws,
Darting it full against a kitten's nose;

Who having never seen, in field or house,
The like, sat still and silent as a mouse;
Only projecting, with attention due,
Her whisker'd face, she ask'd him, 'Who are you?
On to the hall went I, with pace not slow,
But swift as lightning, for a long Dutch hoe:
With which well-arm'd I hasten'd to the spot,
To find the viper, but I found him not,
And turning up the leaves and shrubs around,
Found only that he was not to be found.
But still the kittens, sitting as before,
Sat watching close the bottom of the door.
'I hope,' said I, 'the villain I would kill
Has slipped between the door and the door-sill;
And if I make dispatch, and follow hard,
No doubt but I shall find him in the yard:'
For long ere now it should have been rehearsed,
'T was in the garden that I found him first.
E'en there I found him, there the full-grown cat
His head, with velvet paw, did gently pat;
As curious as the kittens erst had been
To learn what this phenomenon might mean.
Fill'd with heroic ardour at the sight,
And fearing every moment he would bite,
And rob our household of our only cat
That was of age to combat with a rat;
With outstretch'd hoe I slew him at the door,
And taught him NEVER TO COME THERE NO MORE

1782.

VERSES SELECTED FROM AN OCCASIONAL POEM ENTITLED VALEDICTION.

Oh Friendship! cordial of the human breast!
So little felt, so fervently profess'd!
Thy blossoms deck our unsuspecting years;
The promise of delicious fruit appears:
We hug the hopes of constancy and truth,
Such is the folly of our dreaming youth;
But soon, alas! detect the rash mistake
That sanguine inexperience loves to make;
And view with tears the expected harvest lost,
Decay'd by time, or wither'd by a frost.
Whoever undertakes a friend's great part
Should be renew'd in nature, pure in heart,
Prepar'd for martyrdom, and strong to prove

A thousand ways the force of genuine love.
He may be call'd to give up health and gain,
To exchange content for trouble, ease for pain,
To echo sigh for sigh, and groan for groan,
And wet his cheeks with sorrows not his own.
The heart of man, for such a task too frail,
When most relied on is most sure to fail;
And, summon'd to partake its fellow's woe,
Starts from its office like a broken bow.
  Votaries of business and of pleasure prove
Faithless alike in friendship and in love.
Retir'd from all the circles of the gay,
And all the crowds that bustle life away,
To scenes where competition, envy, strife,
Beget no thunder-clouds to trouble life,
Let me, the charge of some good angel, find
One who has known, and has escaped mankind;
Polite, yet virtuous, who has brought away
The manners, not the morals, of the day:
With him, perhaps with her (for men have known
No firmer friendships than the fair have shown),
Let me enjoy, in some unthought-of spot,
All former friends forgiven, and forgot,
Down to the close of life's fast-fading scene,
Union of hearts without a flaw between.
'Tis grace, 'tis bounty, and it calls for praise,
If God give health, that sunshine of our days!
And if he add, a blessing shared by few,
Content of heart, more praises still are due—
But if he grant a friend, that boon possess'd
Indeed is treasure, and crowns all the rest;
And giving one, whose heart is in the skies,
Born from above and made divinely wise,
He gives, what bankrupt nature never can,
Whose noblest coin is light and brittle man,
Gold, purer far than Ophir ever knew,
A soul, an image of himself, and therefore true.

Nov. 1783.

LINES COMPOSED FOR A MEMORIAL OF ASHLEY COWPER ESQ.

IMMEDIATELY AFTER HIS DEATH, BY HIS NEPHEW WILLIAM OF WESTON.

Farewell! endued with all that could engage
All hearts to love thee, both in youth and age!
In prime of life, for sprightliness enroll'd
Among the gay, yet virtuous as the old;

In life's last stage, (O blessings rarely found!)
Pleasant as youth with all its blossoms crown'd;
Through every period of this changeful state
Unchanged thyself—wise, good, affectionate!

Marble may flatter, and lest this should seem
O'ercharged with praises on so dear a theme,
Although thy worth be more than half supprest,
Love shall be satisfied, and veil the rest.

June, 1788.

ON THE QUEEN'S VISIT TO LONDON,

THE NIGHT OF THE SEVENTEENTH OF MARCH, 1789.

When, long sequester'd from his throne,
George took his seat again,
By right of worth, not blood alone,
Entitled here to reign.

Then loyalty, with all his lamps
New trimm'd, a gallant show!
Chasing the darkness and the damps,
Set London in a glow.

'Twas hard to tell, of streets or squares,
Which form'd the chief display,
These most resembling cluster'd stars,
Those the long milky way.

Bright shone the roofs, the domes, the spires,
And rockets flew, self-driven,
To hang their momentary fires
Amid the vault of heaven.

So fire with water to compare,
The ocean serves, on high
Up-spouted by a whale in air,
To express unwieldy joy.

Had all the pageants of the world
In one procession join'd,
And all the banners been unfurl'd
That heralds e'er design'd,

For no such sight had England's Queen
Forsaken her retreat,
Where George, recover'd, made a scene
Sweet always, doubly sweet.

Yet glad she came that night to prove,
A witness undescried,
How much the object of her love
Was lov'd by all beside.

Darkness the skies had mantled o'er
In aid of her design——
Darkness, O Queen! ne'er call'd before
To veil a deed of thine!

On borrow'd wheels away she flies,
Resolv'd to be unknown,
And gratify no curious eyes
That night except her own.

Arrived, a night like noon she sees,
And hears the million hum;
As all by instinct, like the bees,
Had known their sovereign come

Pleased she beheld aloft pourtray'd,
On many a splendid wall,
Emblems of health and heavenly aid,
And George the theme of all.

Unlike the enigmatic line,
So difficult to spell,
Which shook Belshazzar at his wine
The night his city fell.

Soon wat'ry grew her eyes and dim,
But with a joyful tear,
None else, except in prayer for him,
George ever drew from her.

It was a scene in every part
Like those in fable feign'd,
And seem'd by some magician's art
Created and sustain'd.

But other magic there, she knew,
Had been exerted none,
To raise such wonders in her view,
Save love of George alone.

That cordial thought her spirit cheer'd,
And through the cumb'rous throng
Not else unworthy to be fear'd,
Convey'd her calm along.

So, ancient poets say, serene
The sea-maid rides the waves,
And fearless of the billowy scene
Her peaceful bosom laves.

With more than astronomic eyes
She view'd the sparkling show;
One Georgian star adorns the skies,
She myriads found below.

Yet let the glories of a night
Like that, once seen, suffice,
Heav'n grant us no such future sight
Such previous woe the price!

TO MRS. THROCKMORTON,

ON HER BEAUTIFUL TRANSCRIPT OF HORACE'S ODE, 'AD LIBRUM SUUM.'

Maria, could Horace have guess'd
What honor awaited his ode
To his own little volume address'd,
The honor which you have bestow'd;

Who have traced it in characters here,
  So elegant, even, and neat,
He had laughed at the critical sneer
  Which he seems to have trembled to meet.

And sneer, if you please, he had said,
  A nymph shall hereafter arise
Who shall give me, when you all are dead,
  The glory your malice denies;
Shall dignity give to my lay,
  Although but a mere bagatelle;
And even a poet shall say,
  Nothing ever was written so well.

TO THE IMMORTAL MEMORY OF THE HALIBUT ON WHICH I DINED THIS DAY, MONDAY, APRIL 26, 1784.

Where hast thou floated, in what seas pursued
Thy pastime? when wast thou an egg new spawn'd,
Lost in the immensity of ocean's waste?
Roar as they might, the overbearing winds
That rock'd the deep, thy cradle, thou wast safe—
And in thy minikin and embryo state,
Attach'd to the firm leaf of some salt weed,
Didst outlive tempests, such as wrung and rack'd
The joints of many a stout and gallant bark,
And whelm'd them in the unexplored abyss.
Indebted to no magnet and no chart,
Nor under guidance of the polar fire,
Thou wast a voyager on many coasts,
Grazing at large in meadows submarine,
Where flat Batavia just emerging peeps
Above the brine—where Caledonia's rocks
Beat back the surge—and where Hibernia shoots
Her wondrous causeway far into the main.
—Wherever thou hast fed, thou little thought's,
And I not more, that I should feed on thee.
Peace, therefore, and good health, and much good fish,
To him who sent thee! and success, as oft
As it descends into the billowy gulf,
To the same drag that caught thee!—Fare thee well!
Thy lot thy brethren of the slimy fin
Would envy, could they know that thou wast doom'd
To feed a bard, and to be praised in verse.

INSCRIPTION FOR A STONE

ERECTED AT THE SOWING OF A GROVE OF OAKS AT CHILLINGTON, THE SEAT OF T. GIFFARD, ESQ., 1790

Other stones the era tell
When some feeble mortal fell;
I stand here to date the birth
Of these hardy sons of earth.
Which shall longest brave the sky,
Storm and frost—these oaks or I?
Pass an age or two away,
I must moulder and decay,
But the years that crumble me
Shall invigorate the tree,
Spread its branch, dilate its size,
Lift its summit to the skies.
Cherish honor, virtue, truth,
So shalt thou prolong thy youth:
Wanting these, however fast
Man be fix'd, and form'd to last,
He is lifeless even now,
Stone at heart, and cannot grow.

IN MEMORY OF

THE LATE JOHN THORNTON, ESQ.

Poets attempt the noblest task they can,
Praising the Author of all good in man,
And, next, commemorating worthies lost,
The dead in whom that good abounded most.
Thee, therefore, of commercial fame, but more
Famed for thy probity from shore to shore,
Thee, Thornton! worthy in some page to shine
As honest and more eloquent than mine,
I mourn; or, since thrice happy thou must be,
The world no longer thy abode, not thee.
Thee to deplore were grief misspent indeed;
It were to weep that goodness has its meed,
That there is bliss prepared in yonder sky,
And glory for the virtuous when they die.

What pleasure can the miser's fondled hoard,
Or spendthrift's prodigal excess afford,
Sweet as the privilege of healing woe
By virtue suffer'd combating below;
That privilege was thine: Heaven gave thee means
To illumine with delight the saddest scenes,
Till thy appearance chased the gloom, forlorn
As midnight, and despairing of a morn.
Thou hast an industry in doing good,
Restless as his who toils and sweats for food;
Avarice in thee was the desire of wealth
By rust unperishable or by stealth,
And if the genuine worth of gold depend
On application to its noblest end,
Thine had a value in the scales of Heaven
Surpassing all that mine or mint had given.
And though God made thee of a nature prone
To distribution boundless of thy own,
And still by motives of religious force
Impell'd thee more to that heroic course,
Yet was thy liberality discreet,
Nice in his choice, and of a temper'd heat;
And though in act unwearied, secret still,
As in some solitude the summer rill
Refreshes, where it winds, the faded green,
And cheers the drooping flowers, unheard, unseen.
Such was thy charity; no sudden start,
After long sleep, of passion in the heart,
But stedfast principle, and, in its kind,
Of close relation to the Eternal Mind,
Traced easily to its true source above,
To him whose works bespeak his nature, love.
Thy bounties all were Christian, and I make
This record of thee for the Gospel's sake;
That the incredulous themselves may see
Its use and power exemplified in thee.

THE FOUR AGES.

(A BRIEF FRAGMENT OF AN EXTENSIVE PROJECTED POEM.)

"I could be well content, allow'd the use
Of past experience, and the wisdom glean'd
From worn-out follies, now acknowledged such,
To recommence life's trial, in the hope
Of fewer errors, on a second proof!"
Thus, while grey evening lull'd the wind, and call'd
Fresh odours from the shrubbery at my side,
Taking my lonely winding walk, I mus'd,
And held accustom'd conference with my heart;
When from within it thus a voice replied:
"Couldst thou in truth? and art thou taught at length
This wisdom, and but this, from all the past?
Is not the pardon of thy long arrear,
Time wasted, violated laws, abuse
Of talents, judgment, mercies, better far
Than opportunity, vouchsafed to err
With less excuse, and haply, worse effect?"
I heard, and acquiesced: then to and fro
Oft pacing, as the mariner his deck,
My gravelly bounds, from self to human-kind
I pass'd, and next consider'd—what is man?
Knows he his origin? can he ascend
By reminiscence to his earliest date?
Slept he in Adam? And in those from him
Through numerous generations, till he found
At length his destined moment to be born?
Or was he not, till fashioned in the womb?
Deep mysteries both! which schoolmen must have toil'd
To unriddle, and have left them mysteries still.
It is an evil incident to man,
And of the worst, that unexplored he leaves
Truths useful and attainable with ease,
To search forbidden deeps, where mystery lies
Not to be solved, and useless if it might.
Mysteries are food for angels; they digest
With ease, and find them nutriment; but man,
While yet he dwells below, must stoop to glean
His manna from the ground, or starve and die.

EPITAPH ON A HARE.

Here lies, whom hound did ne'er pursue,
Nor swifter greyhound follow,
Whose foot ne'er tainted morning dew,
Nor ear heard hunstsman's hallo'.

Old Tiney, surliest of his kind,
Who, nurs'd with tender care,
And to domestic bounds confin'd,
Was still a wild Jack-hare.

Though duly from my hend he took
His pittance ev'ry night,
He did it with a jealous look,
And, when he could, would bite.

His diet was of wheaten bread,
And milk, and oats, and straw;
Thistles, or lettuces instead,
With sand to scour his maw.

On twigs of hawthorn he regal'd,
On pippins' russet peel,
And, when his juicy salads fail'd,
Slic'd crrrot pleas'd him well.

A turkey carpet was his lawn,
Whereon he lov'd to bound,
To skip and gambol like a fawn,
And swing his rump around.

His frisking was at ev'ning hours,
For then he lost his fear,
But most before approaching show'rs,
Or when a storm drew near.

Eight years and five round-rolling moons
He thus saw steal away,
Dozing out all his idle noons,
And ev'ry night at play.

I kept him for his humour's sake,
  For he would oft beguile
My heart of thoughts, that made it ache,
  And force me to a smile.

But, now beneath his walnut shade
  He finds his long last home,
And waits, in snug concealment laid,
  Till gentler Puss shall come.

He, still more aged, feels the shocks,
  From which no care can save,
And, partner once of Tiney's box,
  Must soon partake his grave.

EPITAPHIUM ALTERUM.

Hic etiam jacet,
Qui totum novennium vixit,
Puss.
Siste paulisper,
Qui præteriturus es,
Et tecum sic reputa—
Hunc neque canis venacitus,
Nec plumbum missile,
Nec laqueus,
Nec imbres nimii,
Confecere:
Tamen mortuus est—
Et moriar ego.

The following Account of the Treatment of his Hares was inserted by Mr. Cowper in the Gentleman's Magazine, whence it is transcribed.

In the year 1774, being much indisposed both in mind and body, incapable of diverting myself either with company or books, and yet in a condition that made some diversion necessary, I was glad of anything that would engage my attention without fatiguing it. The children of a neighbour of mine had a leveret given them for a plaything; it was at that time about three months old. Understanding better how to tease the poor creature than to feed it, and soon becoming weary of their charge, they readily consented that their father, who saw it pining and growing leaner every day, should offer it to my acceptance. I was willing enough to take the prisoner under my protection, perceiving that, in the management of such an animal, and in the attempt to tame it, I should find just that sort of employment which my case required. It was soon known among the neighbours that I was pleased with the present: and the consequence was, that in a short time I had as many leverets offered to me as would have stocked a paddock. I undertook the care of three, which it is necessary that I should here distinguish by the names I gave them—Puss, Tiney, and Bess. Notwithstanding the two feminine appellatives, I must inform you that they were all males. Immediately commencing carpenter, I built them houses to sleep in; each had a separate apartment, so contrived, that their ordure would pass through the bottom of it; an earthen pan placed under each received whatsoever fell, which being duly emptied and washed, they were thus kept perfectly sweet and clean. In the day-time they had the range of a hall, and at night retired each to his own bed, never intruding into that of another.

Puss grew presently familiar, would leap into my lap, raise himself upon his hinder feet, and bite the hair from my temples. He would suffer me to take him up, and to carry him about in my arms, and has more than once fallen fast asleep upon my knee. He was ill three days, during which time I nursed him, kept him apart from his fellows, that they might not molest him (for, like many other wild animals, they persecute one of their own species that is sick), and by constant care, and trying him with a variety of herbs, restored him to perfect health. No creature could be more grateful than my patient after his recovery; a sentiment which he most significantly expressed by licking my hand, first the back of it, then the palm, then every finger separately, then between all the fingers, as if anxious to leave no part of it unsaluted; a ceremony which he never performed but once again upon a similar occasion. Finding him extremely tractable, I made it my custom to carry him always after breakfast into the garden, where he hid himself generally under the leaves of a cucumber vine, sleeping or chewing the cud till evening; in the leaves also of that vine he found a favorite repast. I had not long habituated him to this taste of liberty, before he began to be impatient for the return of the time when he might enjoy it. He would invite me to the garden by drumming upon my knee, and by a look of such expression, as it was not possible to misinterpret. If this rhetoric did not immediately succeed, he would take the skirt of my coat between his teeth, and pull at it with all his force. Thus Puss might be said to be perfectly tamed, the shyness of his nature was done away, and on the whole it was visible by many symptoms, which I have not room to enumerate, that he was happier in human society, than when shut up with his natural companions.

Not so Tiney: upon him the kindest treatment had not the least effect. He too was sick, and in his sickness had an equal share of my attention; but if, after his recovery, I took the liberty to stroke him, he would grunt, strike with his fore feet, spring forward, and bite. He was however very entertaining in his way; even his surliness was matter of mirth; and in his play he preserved such an air of gravity, and performed his feats with such a solemnity of manner, that in him too I had an agreeable companion.

Bess, who died soon after he was full grown, and whose death was occasioned by his being turned into his box, which had been washed, while it was yet damp, was a hare of great humour and drollery. Puss was tamed by gentle usage; Tiney was not to be tamed at all; and Bess had a courage and confidence that made him tame from the beginning. I always admitted them into the parlor after supper, when, the carpet affording their feet a firm hold, they would frisk, and bound, and play a thousand gambols, in which Bess, being remarkably strong and fearless, was always superior to the rest, and proved himself the Vestris of the party. One evening the cat, being in the room, had the hardiness to pat Bess upon the cheek, an indignity which he resented by drumming upon her back with such violence, that the cat was happy to escape from under his paws, and hide herself.

I describe these animals as having each a character of his own. Such they were in fact, and their countenances were so expressive of that character, that, when I looked only on the face of either, I immediately knew which it was. It is said that a shepherd, however numerous his flock, soon becomes so familiar with their features, that he can, by that indication only, distinguish each from all the rest; and yet, to a common observer, the difference is hardly perceptible. I doubt not that the same discrimination in the cast of countenances would be discoverable in hares, and am persuaded that among a thousand of them no two could be found exactly similar: a circumstance little suspected by those who have not had opportunity to observe it. These creatures have a singular sagacity in discovering the minutest alteration that is made in the place to which they are accustomed, and instantly apply their nose to the examination of a new object. A small hole being burnt in the carpet, it was mended with a patch, and that patch in a moment underwent the strictest scrutiny. They seem too to be very much directed by the smell in the choice of their favourites: to some persons, though they saw them daily, they could never be reconciled, and would even scream when they attempted to touch them; but a miller coming in engaged their affections at once; his powdered coat had charms that were irresistible. It is no wonder that my intimate acquaintance with these specimens of the kind has taught me to hold the sportsman's amusement in abhorrence; he little knows what amiable creatures he persecutes, of what gratitude they are capable, how cheerful they are in their spirits, what enjoyment they have of life, and that, impressed as they seem with a peculiar dread of man, it is only because man gives them a peculiar cause for it.

That I may not be tedious, I will just give a short summary of those articles of diet that suit them best.

I take it to be a general opinion that they graze, but it is an erroneous one, at least grass is not their staple; they seem rather to use it medicinally, soon quitting it for leaves of almost any kind. Sowthistle, dandelion, and lettuce, are their favourite vegetables, especially the last. I discovered by accident, that fine white sand is in great estimation with them; I suppose as a digestive. It happened that I was cleaning a a bird-cage while the hares were with me: I placed a pot filled with such sand upon the floor, which being at once directed to by a strong instinct, they devoured voraciously; since that time I have generally taken care to see them well supplied with it. They accouut green corn a delicacy, both blade and stalk, but the ear they seldom eat; straw of any kind, especially wheat straw, is another of their dainties; they will feed greedily upon oats, but if furnished with clean straw never want them: it serves them also for a bed, and if shaken up daily, will be kept sweet and dry for a considerable time. They do not indeed require aromatic herbs, but will eat a small quantity of them with great relish, and are particularly fond of the plant called musk; they seem to resemble sheep in this, that, if their pasture be too succulent, they are very subject to the rot; to prevent which, I always made bread their principal nourishment, and filling a pan with it cut into small squares, placed it every evening in their chambers, for they feed only at evening and in the night: during the winter, when vegetables were not to be got, I mingled this mess of bread with shreds of carrot, adding to it the rind of apples cut extremely thin; for, though they are fond of the paring, the apple itself disgusts them. These however not being a sufficient substitute for the juice of summer herbs, they must, at this time be supplied with water; but so placed, that they cannot overset it into their beds. I must not omit, that occasionally they are much pleased with twigs of hawthorn, and of the common brier, eating even the very wood when it is of considerable thickness.

Bess, I have said, died young; Tiney lived to be nine years old, and died at last, I have reason to think, of some hurt in his loins by a fall; Puss is still living, and has just completed his tenth year, discovering no signs of decay, nor even of age, except that he is grown more discreet and less frolicsome than he was. I cannot conclude without observing, that I have lately introduced a dog to his acquaintance, a spaniel that had never seen a hare, to a hare that had never seen a spaniel. I did it with great caution, but there was no real need of it. Puss discovered no token of fear, nor Marquis the least symptoms of hostility. There is therefore, it should seem, no natural antipathy between dog and hare, but the pursuit of the one occasions the flight of the other, and the dog pursues because he is trained to it; they eat bread at the same time out of the same hand, and are in all respects sociable and friendly.

I should not do complete justice to my subject, did I not add, that they have no ill scent belonging to them, that they are indefatigably nice in keeping themselves clean, for which purpose nature has furnished them with a brush under each foot, and that they are never infested by any vermin.

May 28, 1784.

Memorandum found among Mr. Cowper's papers.

Tuesday, March 9, 1786.

This day died poor Puss, aged eleven years eleven months. He died between twelve and one at noon, of mere old age, and apparently without pain.

THE END.

www.ingramcontent.com/pod-product-compliance
Lightning Source LLC
LaVergne TN
LVHW021319110826
845150LV00003B/618

* 9 7 8 1 4 2 5 5 5 6 9 7 6 *